COGNITION AND INSTRUCTION

COGNITION AND INSTRUCTION

EDITED BY

DAVID KLAHR
Carnegie-Mellon University

LAWRENCE ERLBAUM ASSOCIATES, PUBLISHERS

1976   Hillsdale, New Jersey

DISTRIBUTED BY THE HALSTED PRESS DIVISION OF

JOHN WILEY & SONS

New York   Toronto   London   Sydney

Lawrence Erlbaum Associates, Inc., Publishers
62 Maria Drive
Hillsdale, New Jersey 07642

Distributed solely by Halsted Press Division
John Wiley & Sons, Inc., New York

This work relates to the Department of the Navy Contract N00014-73-C-0405 issued by
the Office of Naval Research under Contract Authority No. NR 154-363. However, the
content does not necessarily reflect the position or policy of the Department of the Navy
or the Government and no official endorsement should be inferred.

The United States Government has a royalty-free, nonexclusive and irrevocable license
throughout the world for Government purposes to publish, translate, reproduce, deliver,
perform, dispose of, and to authorize others so to do, all or any portion of this work.

Library of Congress Cataloging in Publication Data

Main entry under title:

Cognition and instruction.

    Includes indexes.
    1. Learning, Psychology of.   2. Cognition.
I. Klahr, David. [DNLM: 1. Cognition.   2. Teaching.
BF311 C674]
LB1051.C3417   370.15'2   75-42102
ISBN 0-470-15226-5

Printed in the United States of America

To

A.R.K. and L.K.K.
Who turned me toward
thinking and learning

Contents

PART III: FUNDAMENTAL PROCESSES IN COMPREHENDING AND UNDERSTANDING INSTRUCTIONS

PART IV: GENERAL COMMENTS

Preface

What contributions can current research in cognitive psychology make to the solution of problems in instructional design? This volume presents responses to this question from some of the best workers in an emerging field that I have labeled "Cognition and Instruction": people concerned with the investigation of the cognitive processes involved in instructional situations. The focus of this volume was presaged by comments made in a previous volume on cognitive psychology (Forehand, 1974):

> In what seems remarkably few years, information-processing psychology has come to dominate the experimental study of complex human behavior. That rapid success encourages me to speculate that within a comparably short time the approach will have as much of an impact on psychology in the field as it has had on psychology in the laboratory. In particular, its potential for illuminating recalcitrant problems in education seems evident [p. 159].

The chapters in this volume indicate the extent to which this potential has already begun to be realized.

The book is divided into four parts. The first three parts include sets of research contributions followed by discussions, and the fourth part contains three chapters that offer critiques, syntheses, and evaluations of various aspects of the preceeding papers.

The chapters in Part I represent different strategies for instructional research. In the first chapter, Carroll, raising some of the issues facing psycholinguistic theory, asks whether we yet know enough to intentionally teach language skills according to a systematic instructional theory. He summarizes three lines of theoretical development—naive, behavioral, and cognitive—that bear upon the issue, and finally suggests that an information-processing view of the cognitive processes underlying language behavior may ultimately provide the basis for a theory of language instruction. In Chapter 2, Calfee presents a research strategy that focuses upon the interpretation of the empirical results obtained in both the laboratory and in instructional settings. He points out the potential pitfalls awaiting the instructional evaluator who has not carefully considered all possible sources of interdependency in the cognitive models. The statistical analyses proposed by Calfee may be useful to those faced with the task of identifying the extent and the pattern of the effects of instruction.

Resnick focuses upon the area of early mathematics instruction, and she reviews and evaluates the precursors of current procedures in task analysis. Her contribution traces the development of a strategy in instructional research that utilizes information-processing models of cognition to meet the practical demands of creating effective instructional procedures.

Atkinson provides a glimpse of the latest products of his extensive research program, which is aimed at developing what he calls "adaptive instructional systems." His research strategy is based upon the view that "an all-inclusive theory of learning is not a prerequisite for the development of optimal procedures."

Part I concludes with discussions by Gregg and Olson, and their comments further emphasise the variety of strategic approaches to research on instruction. Gregg argues for the importance of understanding and representing the learner's strategies in instructional situations, whereas Olson raises the issue of the ultimate social utility of what we decide to teach to children.

The chapters in Part II focus upon process and structure in learning. The emphasis is upon the precise, explicit, and detailed representation of what is learned, how it is utilized, and how it is modified. In Chapter 7, Greeno demonstrates what such an extensive representation might look like. He provides an elaborate statement of the cognitive objectives for three different areas: elementary arithmetic, high-school geometry, and college-level psychophysics. Knowledge in each area is represented by a different collection of building blocks taken from current information-processing theories.

One of the central issues in instructional research is how new knowledge is acquired. Hyman, in Chapter 8, describes a paradigm for exploring the ways in which memory is restructured when new information is discrepant from pre-existent stereotypes. Hyman uses a paradigm borrowed from social psychological studies of impression formation, and shows that it has implications for the more general issue of information acquisition.

In Chapter 9, Norman, Gentner, and Stevens utilize tools—some of them already described by Greeno—to define the general notion of "schema." The analysis by Norman, Gentner, and Stevens is extremely fine grained; they develop detailed representations for an increasingly rich understanding of such basic concepts as "give" and "buy." They argue that such representations make it possible to be quite precise about how instruction should proceed.

Shaw and Wilson, in Chapter 10, address the issues of process and structure from a more abstract—almost philosophical—position, but they also provide concrete examples from Shaw's work on perception. The central issues concern the ability to understand an entire concept from experience with just a subset of its instances. Such an ability, Shaw and Wilson argue, lies at the heart of an understanding of invariance.

The discussions by Farnham-Diggory (Chapter 11) and by Hayes (Chapter 12) offer stimulating critiques of the positions presented in Part II. Citing an alarmingly modern instructional program devised over half a century ago, Farnham-Diggory asks first "What's new?" and then "Is it better?" Hayes suggests some ways that one can begin to train students directly in cognitive skills. He focuses upon a recurring theme in the chapters of Part II: "What does the student know about his own cognitive processes?"

An essential but neglected element in instructional research is the role of instructions per se, and the contributions to Part III focus upon the processes that underlie the comprehension of verbal instructions. Just and Carpenter take the sentence as their unit of analysis. Using a sophisticated and explicit model of sentence processing, they are able to account for an impressive variety of empirical results. Then they suggest ways in which larger units, such as those used in reading comprehension tests, could be analyzed similarly. Simon and Hayes take a larger unit of analysis—the entire instruction set. They report on the development of an information-processing model aimed at explaining the processes that underly the understanding of instructions for complex puzzles. Then, using the unambiguous components of their model as points of reference, they sketch the broader implications that a theory of understanding could have for instructional research and practice.

In the discussions in Part III, Collins (Chapter 15) and Shaw (Chapter 16) suggest areas for extension of the models of comprehension described earlier. Collins asks about the nature of the comparison process—a basic unitary process in the Just and Carpenter model—and speculates that it might itself be composed of even more elementary subprocesses. Another issue raised by Collins is the role played by the broader knowledge base in which the comprehension processes for sentences or task instructions operate.

Shaw's comments range somewhat farther afield, touching on the papers in Part II as well as those in Part III. He outlines programs in two diverse areas—art instruction and treatment of aphasia—that derive from a theory of comprehension that draws upon elements of the models presented in many of the previous chapters.

The three chapters in the fourth and final section represent responses to many of the issues raised in previous chapters. Glaser (Chapter 17) addresses the issue of how we can take the results of scientific research and apply them to practical problems. He argues for the development of a linking science—a science of instructional design—that would transform our knowledge of cognitive processes into instructional procedures while at the same time providing tests and challenges for the existing theories. Cazden (Chapter 18) raises some very practical questions based upon her varied experience as both a classroom teacher and a research psychologist. One example of the kind of issue that is central to a theory of instruction but still inadequately handled by our current theories is Cazden's question: "What is the value of practice?" Finally, Klahr (Chapter 19) sketches some of the issues that would need to be resolved before one could construct a model of a learner.

ACKNOWLEDGMENTS

The contributions to this volume are based on some of the presentations given at the Tenth Annual Carnegie Symposium on Cognition, during the first week in June, 1974, in Vail, Colorado. The Symposium was supported by a contract jointly funded by the Personnel and Training Research Programs, Division of Psychological Sciences of the Office of Naval Research, and the Advanced Research Projects Agency of the Department of Defense. It was held under the auspices of the Department of Psychology at Carnegie-Mellon University.

Several people who do not have chapters in this volume nevertheless have had an influence on its contents. These people presented workshops at the Symposium: informal descriptions of on-going instructional explorations. The workshops were distributed through the week of the Symposium in order to provide some concrete instances of interesting instructional problems. The workshop leaders were not requested to prepare formal papers; thus, the workshops are not included in this volume. There seemed to be no adequate way to convey the content of the workshops and the discussion they generated, although much of the intellectual excitement during the Symposium came from these sources.

The workshops included:

1. "The adaptation of instruction to individual differences: an information-processing approach," by J. G. Wallace, University of Southampton.
2. "On some cognitive processes presumed to be operating in computer assisted instruction," by Dexter Fletcher, University of Illinois.
3. "Intuitive and formal modes of representing music," by Jean Bamberger, Massachusetts Institute of Technology.
4. "Teaching problem solving," by J. R. Hayes, Carnegie-Mellon University.
5. "Teaching formal operations," by Robert Siegler, Carnegie-Mellon University.

I would like to thank each of these participants for enriching the Symposium with their informal presentations.

In organizing the Tenth Symposium and in editing this volume, I was assisted in diverse ways by several of my colleagues at CMU. Careful and critical readings of early drafts of various chapters were ably done by John S. Carroll, J. R.

Hayes, William Leaf, and especially Jola A. Jakimik. Bibliographic assistance came from Elaine Shelton, and Marlene Naughton did the lioness' share of the secretarial work for both the Symposium and the book itself. Symposium planning, execution, and follow-up were masterfully managed by Marcia Goldstein, assisted by Marshall Atlas, Michelene Chi, and Kenneth Kotovsky. I would like to thank all of these people for assisting a neophyte editor and symposium organizer. I would also like to acknowledge the constructive approach to contract supervision that was evidenced by Dr. Joseph L. Young, Assistant Director of the Personnel and Training Research Programs, Office of Naval Research. He played a key role in the initial conception of the Symposium topic and provided unobtrusive encouragement throughout the whole enterprise.

Finally, I gladly thank my wife Pat for her advice, encouragement, and wisdom, and for the assumption of responsibilities that this book at times caused me to neglect.

DAVID KLAHR
Pittsburgh, Pennsylvania

COGNITION AND INSTRUCTION

Part I

STRATEGIES FOR INSTRUCTIONAL RESEARCH

It is often thought and said that what we most need in education is wisdom and broad understanding of the issues that confront us. Not at all, I say. What we need are deeply structured theories in education that drastically reduce, if not eliminate, the need for wisdom. I do not want wise men to design or build the airplane I fly in, but rather technical men who understand the theory of aerodynamics and the structural properties of metal ... And so it is with education ... I want to see a new generation of trained theorists and an equally competent band of experimentalists to surround them, and I look for a day when they will show that the theories I now cherish were merely humble way stations on the road to the theoretical palaces they have constructed [Suppes, 1974].

1
Promoting Language Skills: The Role of Instruction

John B. Carroll

Educational Testing Service[1]

Can language skills be taught? The answer to this question depends upon how we define "language skills" and what we mean by "teaching." There appears to be a fundamental divergence—usually between behavioral scientists on the one hand and educators on the other—as to what these terms mean.

In the context of behavioral science, *instruction* is often taken to mean definite, specifiable "behavioral" objectives, highly-controlled instructional settings and materials, and definite procedures for observing and measuring learning outcomes. But in the minds of educators, it is generally the case that:

> 'Instruction' is a word within the system (education) that has no operational definition. It refers to many different ways in which the relationships among students, teachers, learning materials may be structured. Discursive situations, at all levels of instruction, tend to be seen as effective. They, and other types of structured situations, are being defended against displacement by instruction geared only to operationalized episodes [Dickinson, 1971, p. 112].

Even McKeachie (1974), a behavioral scientist, is inclined to express his unhappiness with the term "instructional psychology," "for 'instruction' carries a connotation of teacher direction or building that is less pleasing ... than the emphasis on the student implied in 'learning' [p. 162] ."

Dispute over the meaning of "instruction" and "teaching" is found also among educational philosophers. It is commonly agreed that teaching is any activity that is designed to result in learning on the part of the individual being taught, but there is debate as to whether such an activity should be called teaching when there is no *intent* on the part of the teacher to teach, or when it is not *successful* in producing its intended outcome (Scheffler, 1960).

[1] Currently, Department of Psychology, University of North Carolina at Chapel Hill.

3

Consider the claim that the child learns his native language without being "taught," simply by "exposure" to adult models. To support such a claim, one would have to have in mind how he distinguishes between teaching and non-teaching, and how he means to define "exposure." On the other hand, it is commonly accepted that one can "teach" vocabulary knowledge, or a foreign language.

If we are to study rationally the problems of teaching language skills, we must embrace such concepts as "creativity in language" within a scientific, deterministic framework. If there is such a thing as a natively predetermined "language acquisition device" (McNeill, 1970) that accounts for the acquisition of language skills, we must describe it scientifically. If the system of language is "internalized" by language learners, the resultant internalized states must be open to scientific study by appropriate observation of the "behavior" (broadly defined) that occurs under specifiable conditions. Some of these "specifiable conditions" will fall under the concept of "instruction," but I assume that they will cover not only the kinds of deliberate, formal operations that a teacher performs in the classroom, but also the informal, largely nondeliberate actions of people interacting with each other through language and other means, for example, the interactions of a mother and her child, or the interactions of one student with another in a "discursive" situation. Whether these actions are taken with an "intent" to teach or produce learning, and whether these actions are "successful" in producing learning, are questions that are not of central interest. It does not much matter whether or not we say that the child learns his language "without being taught." What matters is what external influences, that we might be able to have under our option or control, there are upon the child's learning. There are many kinds of "language skills": speaking, listening, reading, handwriting, spelling, and written composition are the native-language skills that are given most attention in the schools, but we might also want to discuss what are often called "communication skills," including nonverbal communication skills. In all these skills, there is a developmental dimension as the individual moves from infancy to adulthood. In a previous publication (Carroll, 1971b) I have reviewed the literature on the development of these native-language skills beyond the early years. In addition, we may want to consider the problems of teaching a second or a foreign language, or of teaching a "standard" form of a language when the learner's native tongue is a "nonstandard" form of that language. I have reviewed research on many aspects of these matters in a number of publications (Carroll, 1963, 1966, 1968a, 1971a), and I do not intend to recapitulate these reviews here. Instead, I propose to focus attention on the *models of the language learner* that seem to be implicitly assumed by teachers, writers of instructional materials, and others in education, as well as such models as are offered by psychologists, psycholinguists, and linguists. We must see in what respects these models are inadequate or conflict with one another. We must also attend to what role these models assume for "instruction"—defined broadly as any external influences on the development of language skills, as represented both by formal teaching actions and by more informal social interactions.

NOTIONS OF SKILL, COMPETENCE, AND PERFORMANCE

If we are to begin promoting language skills, we need a notion of what these skills consist of. Indeed, it would be to our advantage if we had available a complete theory of how people acquire and use language skills—both productive and receptive skills, and both skills with the spoken language and skills with the written forms of language.

One prerequisite for the development of such a theory is consideration of the relation between a language system, as described by linguists, and the activities and behaviors that involve its use. In recent years, this problem has been discussed in terms of the distinction, most trenchantly formulated by Chomsky (1965), between "competence" and "performance." The distinction has been debated almost ad nauseam (Bever, 1970; Fillenbaum, 1971; Fodor & Garrett, 1966; Hayes, 1970) and it would be a distraction to fully discuss the matter here, but since I have a particular viewpoint, I need to state my position with some semblance of justification. I believe that all Chomsky literally meant to refer to was, on the one hand, *what is learned* (competence), and on the other, the *behavior that manifests that learning* (performance), including both receptive and productive language behaviors. The notion of competence is entirely neutral as to what type of grammatical model should describe competence. Chomsky offered generative grammars as theories of competence, but linguists (and others) are free to select other kinds of grammar to describe competence. Further, the notion of performance is neutral as to what theory or model of performance *mechanisms* one might adopt; a model of performance mechanisms might be derived from behavioristic principles, from cognitive psychology, or from any other psychological system. Much of the discussion about competence and performance, however, has been concerned with the extent to which a model of performance must "incorporate" a competence model, and if so, whether the competence model (i.e., the type of grammar chosen) determines the form of the performance model. In my opinion the determination is in the opposite direction: the form chosen for the performance model will tend to dictate the form of the competence model and therefore the form of the grammar. This is the case because the mechanisms or processes that a performance model assumes are not indifferent to their content, i.e., to the elements upon which they operate.

There are perhaps many *possible* ways to write grammars for verbal output, but the type of grammar that makes psychological sense is determined by the kinds of mechanisms that are assumed in the performance model. There are various alleged demonstrations (e.g., Bever, Fodor, & Garrett, 1968) that a transformational grammar cannot be handled by an associationistic, "stimulus–response" theory. This is usually interpreted to mean that a behavioristic account of language behavior is unacceptable—so great is the faith in transformational grammar. Suppose, however, that *no* mechanism can be found to handle such a grammar. (In fact, I am not aware that anyone has formulated such a mechanism.) This would present a problem of the psychological acceptability of transformational grammar for any performance model.

My conclusion is that the designer of a performance model can afford to be indifferent concerning what type of grammatical theory the linguist may want to choose to satisfy his or her own criteria. As a psychologist, my criteria lie within the realm of psychology. Thus, the kind of grammar I choose must satisfy the basic psychological criterion that it must be plausible from the standpoint of being capable of being handled by known or discoverable psychological processes. In effect, this means that a grammar for a given language system must be included within the performance model for that language; the distinction between competence and performance remains as before—competence refers to what is learned, performance refers to a behavior manifesting that learning.

This point of view is actually not as heretical as it may seem. Labov (1971, p. 452) says: "There seems to be general agreement that a valid theory of language must eventually be based on rules that speakers actually use." Bever (1970, p. 345) tells his readers that if they will "accept the possibility that ongoing speech behavior does not utilize a linguistic grammar," they will not be surprised "that the mechanisms inherent to ongoing speech behavior do not manifest transformations or any operations directly based on them."

A point of view that seems much closer to mine is that of Schlesinger (1971), who writes:

> There is no place for intentions in a grammar, but any theory of performance which fails to take intentions into account must be considered inadequate. The model of a human speaker must, of course, contain rules that determine the grammatical structure of the output. These rules, however, must be assumed to operate on an input which represents the speaker's intentions [p. 64].

I would identify these rules as a grammar incorporated into a performance grammar—in Schlesinger's terms, they would be "realization rules" for converting "I markers" (input or intention markers) into utterances. There is a certain similarity here to Bever's (1970, p. 286) notion that "talking involves actively mapping internal structures onto external sequences, and understanding others involves mapping external sequences onto internal structures"—that is, if we identify internal structures with Schlesinger's I markers. Much of Bever's paper is concerned with trying to identify "heuristics" or "cognitive strategies" whereby the hearer finds out how "external sequences" (i.e., strings of speech) are to be mapped into internal structures. While it is debatable whether he has identified the heuristics that language users actually employ, the enterprise seems to be in the right direction.

To emphasize the claim that the grammar must be incorporated in, and determined by, the performance model, I have called the grammar that I have developed for a small subset of English sentences a "performance grammar" (Carroll, 1974a). This performance grammar thus far centers attention on language *production;* it is my belief that the problem of production must be dealt with before problems of reception and comprehension can properly be investigated. This is because the hearer's problem is to determine the I marker of the speaker; it seems reasonable to suppose that to the extent that speaker and hearer share the same language system, the hearer would rely to a large extent on the same "realization rules" for converting I markers into speech that the speaker does. The performance grammar is conceived of as having two components: the intentive component, and the code component. The intentive component specifies the elements, variables, and structures found in I markers, and the code component contains the "realization" rules for converting the contents of I markers into grammatically acceptable speech. The rules in the code component can be stated as "production systems" in Newell's (1973) sense, i.e., they can be stated in the form of one or more condition–action pairs. This type of grammar, incidentally, is exemplified also by Halliday's systemic grammar (Hudson, 1971; Muir, 1972), which Morton (1968) calls a "Category B" grammar that describes how language behavior can be produced outside the rules of grammars of a more linguistic character. Like my performance grammar, Halliday's systemic grammar emphasizes the choices open to the speaker as he speaks, but I would feel that the "intentive" component of Halliday's grammar is as yet only a latent structure; i.e., the conditions for the choices are not made explicit, whereas they would have to be in a complete performance grammar.

Discussions of "competence" in linguistics have laid little emphasis on whether the competence may vary from one speaker to another, or whether competence can be quantified. Muscat-Tabakowska (1969) has presented an interesting discussion of these as issues they apply in foreign-language teaching; her remarks are applicable also to the competence of native speakers. She narrows the definition of competence to mean "the actual knowledge of the underlying system of rules *at a given time,*" from which she concludes that (1) "competence . . . can be learned, and probably can also be taught; (2) competence is relative, for it can be bigger or smaller, both in different speakers at the same time and in the same speakers at different times; and (3) competence is measurable, in that it is possible to infer the *amount* of competence from the observable data (from performance) . . . [Muscat-Tabakowska, 1969, pp. 42–43] ."

Elsewhere (Carroll, 1968b) I have set forth a series of propositions about competence and performance in their application to problems of testing competence in a foreign language, but they are equally applicable to similar problems in a speaker's native language. Among these are:

Competence in a language consists of a series of interrelated habits (acquired stimulus–response mechanisms) which can be described in terms of stated 'rules' [p. 47].

The actual manifestation of linguistic competence . . . in behavior may be called linguistic performance, and is affected by a large number of nonlinguistic variables [p. 50].

I further asserted that:

There are individual differences, both in competence and performance variables, that may be a function of either constitutional or experiential variables [p. 51].

I pointed out that individual differences in competence might be found in different domains, such as phonology, morphology, lexicon, and grammar, and that individual differences in performance could be observed in such matters as speed of response, diversity of response, complexity of information processing, and awareness of competence.

Such an analysis of linguistic competences and performances suggests that it is quite possible that a diversity of detailed psychological models may need to be incorporated in a complete performance model. For example, the psychological model used to study the acquisition of a lexical item *as a linguistic form* may be different from the one used to study the *meaning* of that linguistic form, and a still different model may be required to account for the acquisition of the grammatical category and distributional characteristics of the form. Further, models for the acquisition of phonological items, or of grammatical rules, may be radically different from any of the models required in connection with lexical forms. We may already be able to apply certain standard paradigms (Melton, 1964) to several of these cases: for example, acquisition of lexical meanings may be a case of associationistic learning, or a case of concept learning; and acquisition of phonological competence may have elements of perceptual learning and of psychomotor learning. Where our standard paradigms seem to fail most is in explaining the acquisition of grammatical rules. It is still unclear what the source of the difficulty may be: is it that appropriate psychological models have not even been discovered, let alone refined, or is it that we have not discovered the way in which grammatical rules should be formulated so as to lend themselves to the application of psychological models? I suspect there are difficulties on both of these counts.

NAIVE, BEHAVIORISTIC, AND COGNITIVE THEORIES OF LANGUAGE LEARNING

What happens when people (or other organisms) acquire language skills? What models of the language learning process seem to be assumed by their teachers, or by people who prepare instructional materials?

That people do learn language, even when taught by teachers (e.g., mothers) uninformed about any systematic scientific principles of learning, is evident. Whether people learn any better when they are taught according to some systematic theory of instruction is not so evident. Even if the teacher, or the preparer of instructional materials, can be assumed to have been influenced by some doctrine about learning and teaching, it is hard to tell, from an instance of his or her teaching, whether he or she is actually being guided by that doctrine, unless he or she explicitly tells us so.

I will discuss three "theories" of language learning and teaching. I assume, first, that a "naive" or "common sense" theory of learning exists, that in fact it has existed for centuries, and that this "naive" theory underlies the instructional procedures used by most people engaged in promoting language skills—whether they be mothers teaching their children to speak or formally certified teachers of English or foreign languages. I do not employ the term "naive" in a pejorative sense, but rather to refer to the kind of "common-sense psychology," described by Heider (1958, pp. 5–7), as summarizing the common wisdom that people have about their behavior and motives. Of course, a naive theory of learning may in many respects be inaccurate, wrong, or wrongly applied. Nevertheless, it cannot be all wrong, since it has been part of the underlying foundation of teaching and learning over the centuries, that is, the kind of teaching that has been at least partly successful.

Second, I will describe how "behavior theory" has singled out for analysis and reinterpretation certain features of the naive theory. By "behavior theory," I mean one comparable to Skinner's (1953, 1957) with its emphasis on operant conditioning.

Third, I will indicate some limitations of Skinnerian behavior theory and point out how cognitive theory provides a refinement of naive theory (and a reinterpretation of behavior theory). The discussion will then lead to the implications of cognitive theory for instructional procedures in promoting language skills.

Assumptions of Naive Learning Theory

If we examine typical instructional materials, observe instructional episodes, or talk with teachers, we can infer that naive learning theory is based on eight principal implicit assumptions:

1. Learning occurs best when it is "motivated." Ideally, maximum learning occurs when the individual "wants to learn." Helen Keller (1936, pp. 23–24) recalls that after arriving at an understanding that "everything has a name" through being shown how the word *water* is finger spelled, she "left the well house eager to learn." Most textbooks are written on the assumption that they will be used by "motivated" students; some of them attempt, however, to stimulate motivation and interest. Naive theory further assumes that if an individual does not want to learn, he can nevertheless be made to learn by drawing his attention to the consequences of *not* learning. The critical role of motivation is assumed to be in every case to direct and focus the individual's attention on what is to be learned.

2. Thus, *a critical variable in learning is attention,* i.e., a state of the learner whereby he becomes consciously aware of the material to be learned and examines it according to whatever means are necessary. When the matter is complex, this may require diligent study, but even in simple cases, some degree of "attention" is required. We have a report (McNeill, 1970, p. 106) of a mother trying to "correct" her child's tendency of saying "Nobody don't like me." After a series of unsuccessful attempts, she says: "Now listen carefully: say 'nobody likes me.' " In the child's response, "Oh! Nobody don't likes me," it is evident that the child does in fact pay greater attention to the stimulus than before, even though the response is not quite what the mother hoped for. A series of steps recommended by Fitzgerald (1951) for learning to spell a word include admonitions to "look at the word . . . pronounce it . . . see the word . . . say it . . . make every letter carefully." In reporting how she learned the finger-spelling for *water,* Keller (1936) notes that "her whole attention was fixed" on the motion of her teacher's fingers.

A corollary of this proposition is the principle "one thing at a time." It is assumed that to maximize attention, attention should be directed at only one thing at a time. Divided attention and distractions retard learning. Thus, if the thing-to-be-learned is complex, its parts must be attended to separately. Fitzgerald (1951), in the prescriptions mentioned earlier, advises the student to "say the letters in order" and "make every letter carefully." Instructional materials generally attempt to focus the student's attention on particular aspects of what is to be learned.

Another corollary is that the learner controls the learning in that he can control his attention, and is generally aware of how much and how well he knows he has learned at a given point (the student, of course, be mistaken about his state of knowledge.).

3. *The result of learning is some change in internal state.* This can be either a change in state of knowledge about facts, rules, opinions, etc., ("knowledge *that* . . ."), or a change in state of knowledge about procedures and behaviors ("knowledge *how* to . . ."). Knowledge can come from a number of sources—experience, observations of place, events, and others' behavior, lectures and explanations, or even from mental discovery—"using one's head." Information may be stored as memories, although some memories can be forgotten. Memories about behaviors are stored as "habits." Knowledge can even include information about how to learn: Fitzgerald's prescriptions about learning to spell are of this nature. These assumptions about what is to be learned are illustrated in a "bulletin" suggested for use in a "better speech campaign" for speakers of nonstandard dialects at the secondary school level (Golden, 1960, p. 94). Golden assumes that in order for the nonstandard speaker to learn to avoid usages like *shouldn't ought, disremember,* and *irregardless,* he or she first needs to be told that they are "wastebasket" words even though there is "nothing really wrong" with their use in some situations. In his text on teaching English as

a second language, Dixson (1971, p. 2) gives rules for forming the negative of *to be:* "We form the negative of *to be* by placing *not* after the verb." A widely used textbook of Spanish (Bolinger *et al.,* 1960, p. 57) teaches the student the distinction between Spanish *ser* and *estar* by a lengthy discussion of the varying uses and meanings of these forms; that is, the student is assumed to need a store of information or knowledge about them in order to learn to use them according to Spanish norms.

4. *Practice and repetition contribute to the establishment and strengthening of memories.* Memories become clearer and firmer by repeated exposure to the subject to be learned. This is believed to be true both for memories of experiences and for memories of behaviors (i.e., habits). Retrieval of memories for experiences eventually becomes extremely facile after repeated exposure to the stimuli, and behavior repeatedly performed becomes extremely "automatic" when the conditions for that behavior are appropriate. Fitzgerald's (1951) prescriptions for the learning of spelling advise the student to spell a word several times, each time checking its correctness. Golden (1960) advises students:

"This shifting and perfecting of language pattern is not done easily or overnight. . . . As it takes continuous practice and many other factors to shift from being merely a chop-sticks player to being a good musician, so it takes practice and thought and desire and then more practice to shift into using the pattern that is universal, and to feel so much at home in the new pattern that we can truly 'make music' with it [p. 94].

Bloomfield's (1942) final admonition to the foreign language learner is "PRACTICE EVERYTHING UNTIL IT BECOMES SECOND NATURE [p. 16, capitalization in the original]."

5. *There are degrees of learning, and until perfect mastery is attained, responses must be checked for their "correctness."* "Feedback" has the primary function of giving the learner information which he can use to compare his or her response with what the response should be; whether it "rewards" or punishes the learner is of secondary concern. We have already cited Fitzgerald's advice to the learner to check the correctness of his efforts to spell a word each time he tries it.

6. *Rewards are administered by external agencies for the* act *of learning (and punishments for failures in learning); one does not reward or punish the actual behavior performed, but the learner himself.* Rewards and punishments are seen as constituting information to the learner regarding the consequences of learning or not learning; this is true whether the rewards and punishments are administered verbally or physically. Rewards (school grades, "A," "B," etc.) are also given to convey information to the learner concerning his overall progress in learning.

7. *Learning builds on prior knowledge and habits.* Teachers and textbook authors generally mean to take account of knowledge and habits already ac-

quired at a given point. If we look at random at almost any page of a textbook, we can usually infer what the textbook writer assumes the student knows or has learned up to that point.

8. *Learning is an active process;* "learning by doing" is a watchword among many educational writers. Textbook authors are aware of the need to have students be able to make active, uncued responses. For example, in the Spanish textbook cited earlier (Bolinger *et al.,* 1960, p. 28), it is pointed out that the students' books must be closed during the performance of a drill on person-number substitutions.

The above assumptions apply not only to language learning but in fact to most types of school learning, and to most other types of learning as well. The special difficulties in applying these assumptions to certain aspects of language learning (e.g., the child's learning of his native language, particularly its grammar) are only dimly perceived in naive theory, but a special theory, that of "imitation," is applied to explain language learning. Naive learning theory attaches importance to imitation as a learning process because behavior that is apparently imitative is frequently observed. Mothers try to get their children to imitate their language and are sometimes successful: Kobashigawa (1968) reports an episode in which a mother elicits a form by using a question intonation; the child tends to imitate not only the form but the intonation, and imitates a different intonation when the mother changes hers:

Mother:　That's a radio. . . . A radio? (with question intonation)
　Child:　[we-o] (with question intonation)
Mother:　Radio. (with falling intonation)
　Child:　[we-o] (with falling intonation)

McNeill (1970, p. 106) reports unpublished material from Roger Brown's research illustrating children's (usually shortened) imitations of adult sentences.

Behavioral Learning Theory

The behavior theory developed by Skinner (e.g., 1953) and his followers focuses on the properties of what are called operant responses and the conditions that are presumed to control their elicitation, learning, and extinction. The paradigm of classical conditioning is played down in this theory because it is thought to pertain mainly to responses of the autonomic nervous system, responses that are considered not to be of primary interest in educational settings. Discussions of classical conditioning rarely figure in writings about the application of behavior theory in instruction (Skinner, 1968).

The salient feature of behavior theory is its treatment of the relations among stimuli, overt responses, and reinforcements. In the strict form of behavior theory, mental events and covert responses are assumed to be of no scientific interest, and are therefore not considered. It is assumed that changes in probabilities of emission of overt responses are functionally related to the occurrence, at specifiable points of time, of "reinforcements"–stimuli tending to satisfy drives–, and, as the case may be, also to the occurrence of certain other stimuli ("discriminative stimuli") that may serve as cues for the emission of the overt responses. The overt responses thus come under the "control" of reinforcements and discriminative stimuli when the temporal relations and other conditions are as prescribed by the theory. The theory is also much concerned with the "topography" of the responses, i.e., with their differentiation, and with the manner in which rewards and also discriminative stimuli are differentiated.

It is useful to see how the assumptions of behavior theory compare with those of naive theory:

1. Behavior theory agrees that the learner must be motivated, but it sees the problem of motivation as one of identifying drives for which reinforcers can be specified. Many applications of behavior theory involve reinforcements for basic drives such as hunger and thirst, but according to the "Premack principle" (1959) any activity preferred by a learner can serve as a reinforcer for any less-preferred activity. Thus, in conducting "programmed instruction," getting through a program might be regarded as a reinforcer for the act of going through a program, on the assumption that the student would rather *not* be doing a program than doing it.

2. Any consideration of "attention" or conscious control of learning is not recognized in behavior theory. The principle of "one thing at a time," however, is utilized in behavior theory simply because of the necessity to establish precise temporal relations between particular responses and particular rewards.

3. The only thing that behavior theory recognizes as being learned is some overt response (or some integrated combination of responses), which occurs under appropriate circumstances or stimulus conditions. A strict form of behavior theory makes no assumptions about "information," "memories," "knowledge," or even "habits," although if a response is "reliably" established it is sometimes loosely referred to as a habitual response.

4. Matters having to do with the practice of responses and repeated exposures to stimuli are dealt with under the rubric of "schedules of reinforcement," i.e., with the specification of the temporal relations and repetitions of stimuli, responses, and reinforcing events. Some schedules are found more effective in producing learning than others. "Forgetting" of responses would be interpreted as extinction of those responses resulting from an ineffective schedule of reinforcement.

5. Feedback is considered to be a form of reinforcement; it applies to the learner's response, not to the learner.

6. Reward is obviously of central importance; like feedback, it applies to the learner's response and not to the learner. Positive reinforcements are believed to be more effective than negative ones; insofar as feedback regarding incorrect responses is aversive, the conditions for learning should be arranged so that the learner makes a minimum of errors.

7. In the theory, there is no such thing as prior knowledge; there are only behaviors and responses that have been learned previously. These previously learned responses are to be taken account of as "baseline" or "entry" behaviors which may in fact be prerequisite for further learning and for building integrated "response repertoires."

8. Since only overt responses are learned, learning is obviously "active." The prescriptions of naive theory about active learning are interpreted as referring to the necessity of "fading" irrelevant cues.

Despite a good deal of publicity and experimentation, it can hardly be said that behavior theory has become popular with all language teachers. However, the advent of a strict behavior theory was perhaps the precipitating factor in various investigators' attempts to teach some kind of language system to lower animals, specifically, chimpanzees.[2] Nevertheless, it is not clear that behavior theory was responsible for the successes of these investigators, such as they have been. The Gardners state that although they recognized the theoretical weaknesses of the behavioristic paradigm, they "never hesitated to apply those principles of reward theory that were relevant," but they cite a number of other teaching techniques (guidance, observational learning) that were generally more effective than straightforward instrumental conditioning procedures (Gardner & Gardner, 1971). It is obvious that Rumbaugh and his associates and the Premacks were strongly influenced by behavior theory in their work with animals, using standard instrumental conditioning techniques at least in the earlier phases of their work. Nevertheless, the learning behavior of the animals had many features that could not have been expected or easily accounted for by behavior theory. For example, Lana (the chimpanzee taught by Rumbaugh and his associates) would every once in a while make a mistake while she was punching a sentence into the computer; all by herself she discovered a "correction procedure" for canceling the input of such a sentence when she "knew" she had made a mistake.

Behavior theory has inspired the generation of instructional theorists who developed "programmed instruction" (Glaser, 1965); it has also been a source of guidance in the development of "behavior modification" techniques for changing children's language behavior (Hart & Risley, 1974; Sapon, 1969). One very explicit use of behavior theory is that of Mear (1971) for establishing "receptive repertoires" in children learning French.

---

[2] Gardner and Gardner (1971) taught a version of American Sign Language, the sign language of the deaf, to a female chimpanzee named Washoe. The Premacks (Premack, 1971; Premack & Premack, 1972) taught a chimpanzee named Sarah to use a "language" in which pieces of plastic of different colors and shapes were used to communicate simple ideas about eating, foods, etc. Rumbaugh, Gill, Brown, von Glasersfeld, Pisani, Warner, and Bell (1973) taught a chimpanzee named Lana to use a language in which sentences were composed of visual symbols ("lexigrams"); a computer was used to control the displays of these lexigrams, which could be produced either by the experimenter or by Lana, by the punching of buttons in the proper sequence.

Thus, behavior theory has been highly successful in many ways. By concentrating on directly observable events, it has achieved a kind of scientific respectability that was not achieved by previous learning theories, certainly not by any kind of naive theory. More importantly for our present purposes, it has served as a filtering device for sorting out critical elements and problems in learning theory. But in this respect it has revealed its weaknesses. There is a lingering appearance of circularity in a theory of reinforcement that seems to define reinforcers in terms of drives and drives in terms of reinforcers, but there are other matters to worry about. The major gaps in the theory are its inability to deal with covert events that are undoubtedly relevant in learning and its failure to recognize that reinforcers have their effect not on responses as such but on the covert events that antecede and trigger overt responses. It has no satisfactory theory of knowledge and information processing, nor of the parameters of memory structures that would presumably underlie the surface "laws" of reinforcement schedules. From a practical viewpoint, it has only a limited theory of the manner in which responses get emitted, so that the practitioner is often hard put to identify or elicit responses that can serve as a basis for further learning. The Gardners might have had to wait for an eternity before observing responses that could serve as the basis for communicative "mands," if they had not in the meantime discovered that guidance or "molding" (Fouts, 1972) could shape such responses.[3] From the reports published thus far, there is apparently no means of knowing how much "guidance" the Premacks had to give their chimpanzee Sarah in order to get her to make the responses she did.

Two fundamental questions about behavior learning theory are: (*a*) does learning truly take place on the basis of *solely* the variables indicated by the theory?, and (*b*) when language responses are acquired or modified by behavior modification techniques, is this learning of the same character, resulting in the same kind of competence, as occurs in normal language learning? I believe that the answers to both these questions are in the negative. The bulk of the evidence as to what goes on in the so-called "verbal conditioning" paradigm is that a change of behavior occurs only when subjects are consciously aware of, and pleasantly disposed towards, the arranged contingencies (e.g., Sallows, Dawes, & Lichtenstein, 1971). Weiss and Born (1967) doubt that "speech training" conducted according to behavior modification theory results in true language acquisition.

Cognitive Learning Theory

I am not aware that any reasonably adequate cognitive theory of learning has yet been developed. I would entertain the hypothesis, however, that such a theory

---

[3] A mand, according to Skinner's (1957) account, is a verbal response that, though initially occurring with no such function, has been conditioned to communicate some desire or motive ("de*mand*" "com*mand*") on the part of the learner.

would provide a much improved basis for interpreting language learning phenomena and for suggesting measures for promoting language skills. By "cognitive theory" I mean a theory that would embrace covert events such as expectancies, plans, sets, images, memory storage and retrieval, conscious control, and complex information processing. I assume that contemporary experimental technology (as represented for example by reaction time studies, computer simulations of behavior, etc.) has means for elevating these concepts to scientific respectability.

Let us see how a cognitive theory might deal with the major points of what I have called a naive learning theory, and incidentally how it would reinterpret the kinds of observations and procedures that result from investigations based on behavior theory.

1. The concept of "motivation" would be translated into terms of various kinds of internal events. Some of these would be associated with basic drives, that is, covert responses to changes in physiological states; others, however, might be labeled as conscious goals, plans of action to achieve those goals, and expectancies concerning future events, often in cognitive response to particular situational requirements. "Motivation to learn" would be interpreted as an expectancy of some future state of knowledge or ability that would result from performance of a learning task, for example, the ability to communicate in a foreign language. Certain kinds of motivational states (*intentions*) would have a peculiar importance in learning language. A communicative act involves the transmission of certain aspects of the speaker's intentions to the cognitive information store of the hearer. There is at least inferential evidence for the involvement of "intentions" in the communicative acts of the chimpanzees who have been studied by the Gardners and by Rumbaugh and his colleagues. Washoe communicated her desires for more tickling, more banana, etc. by using the sign for *more* (Gardner & Gardner, 1969, p. 669). Lana (Rumbaugh et al., 1973) communicated her desires (intentions) for juice, the presence of her keeper, or even background music by various button-pushings. (Apparently the Premacks' Sarah was never given the opportunity to communicate her desires.). Mear's (1971) first-grade students learned to apprehend the intentions of their teacher from her French vocal responses.

2. In contrast to behavior theory, but in agreement with naive theory, cognitive theory would acknowledge the importance of attention in learning. Neisser (1967, pp. 292 ff.) writes of the usefulness of assuming an "executive process" in an information-processing theory that controls the flow of information by addressing particular sensory registers or memory stores. Cognitive theory would assume that attention is important at *some* point in the learning process, even though its role might diminish after processes become automatized. Cognitive theory would agree with naive theory in asserting that "motivation" (as described above) enhances attention. Expectation of reward, for example, might

do this; problem difficulty would also do so. Rumbaugh et al. (1973) used expectation of reward to direct Lana's attention to the separate parts of visual messages. In learning the conditional relationship, Sarah is reported by the Premacks (1972) to have been led to "pay closer attention to the sentences," apparently because of difficulty experienced with the problem.

3. Cognitive theory would for the most part agree with naive theory in asserting that *information* is what is learned, and would object to behavior theory's postulation that it is the *responses* that are learned. According to cognitive theory, learning to *make* particular responses is an internal process, as is also a decision to emit them on a particular occasion and under particular conditions. Cognitive theory would provide for the automatization of response emission by assuming that information transfer processes can become extremely rapid and that cognitive sets are not necessarily always directly under the control of the executive. (In fact, an important feature of cognitive theory is its emphasis on the extreme rapidity of most cognitive processes.) Cognitive theory would further agree with naive theory in assuming that information can come from a great variety of sources—through any sensory modality, but it would lay stress on how this information is evaluated and possibly transformed by the central processor. It would also be concerned with situational contexts in which different kinds of information are arriving simultaneously and are evaluated in terms of each other. Learning the meanings of signs would be a special case of such processing, resulting (under suitable conditions) in some kind of awareness that "X means Y." In fact, the very concept of naming would be a special algorithm used in processing many types of information. Note that Sarah (Premack & Premack, 1972) was able to learn a sign for this concept, in a sense, a second-order, "metalinguistic" concept. (One may speculate, therefore, that the Gardners' Washoe acquired this concept and could easily have learned a sign for it if the proper contingencies had been arranged.)

4. In cognitive theory, the effects of practice and repetition would be handled through reference to the parameters of various memory systems and to the cognitive states occurring during practice and repetition. It would be an interesting exercise to reexamine the extensive literature on the subject from this point of view. In this way it might be possible to search for explanations of the fact that practice and repetition are not universally effective in promoting learning. It could be hoped that cognitive theory would extensively refine the assertions of naive learning theory.

5. Feedback and correction, in cognitive theory, would be regarded as merely one kind of information contributing to learning—though frequently an important kind of information.

6. Rewards and reinforcers (including aversive stimuli and their withdrawal) would merely constitute another kind of information utilized in producing learning, but rewards would be neither universally necessary nor sufficient. Their relevance is minimal, for example, in observational and incidental learning.

7. Previously acquired knowledge, stored in something other than short-term memory, would be regarded as important in learning to the extent that a particular learning process required use of that prior knowledge.

8. "Active learning" might be important, in cognitive theory, to insure that knowledge or other kinds of learning are truly in long-term memory and not dependent on irrelevant cues from short-term memory.

In addition to all these points, cognitive learning theory would lay stress on the organism's interpretation and further processing of the information available to it at given points during an instructional or problem-solving episode. Particular sequences and arrangements of stimuli in the instructional setting would evoke different mental processes, some being more conducive to learning than others. The Premacks (1972) seemed to be keenly aware of this in their speculations regarding what instructional sequences might be most productive of learning in Sarah. In teaching language concepts, it seemed to be most useful to present two positive instances and two negative instances. One may hypothesize that such an arrangement provided Sarah with precisely the information that was both necessary and sufficient to define the concept. The common features in the positive instances were perceived as defining the concept only when they were seen as contrasting with the common features in the negative instances. The way in which information to be processed must be adequately presented is also illustrated in the teaching of the *if–then* conditional sign. Before teaching this sign, it was necessary to establish a referent for it, namely a set of situations in which a contingency was present. The Premacks' teaching of the conditional sign to Sarah is almost precisely parallel to the manner in which Bereiter (Bereiter & Engelmann, 1966) taught the meaning of *if* to disadvantaged children. He did this by setting up on the blackboard several situations demonstrating a contingency: If a a square is red, it is little; if a square is green, it is big; etc. From this it was easy to move to teaching the meaning of the word.

CAN LANGUAGE SKILLS BE PROMOTED?— ANSWERS FROM COGNITIVE THEORY

If it has been possible to develop a "behavioral technology" based for the most part on reinforcement theory, it may also be possible to formulate a cognitive learning technology, with a much broader base in information-processing theory, that would be more generally applicable, more efficacious, and, perhaps, more "humane" than behavioral technology. Such a technology would, I believe, be a better guide to the promotion of language skills.

It has become fashionable, in recent years, to speak of language *acquisition* rather than language *learning,* at least in reference to child language. Apparently, this weasel word is used to dodge the question of whether language is actually "learned." Indeed, it has been suggested that it is "acquired" through some sort of "language acquisition device" (LAD) that is innately specific to the human species (Lenneberg, 1967; McNeill, 1970). The hypotheses of a language acquisition device and of species specificity are becoming more suspect in view of the recent findings with Washoe, Lana, and Sarah. I forego discussion of whether these animals attained systems with all the essential properties of human language, partly because the data are not all in (for discussion of this point, see Bronowski & Bellugi, 1970; McNeill, 1974). We have little information as to the full range of Washoe's *comprehension* of American Sign Language, and at this writing studies with Lana and Sarah (or their friends) are still in progress. On the basis of my analysis of instructional episodes with these animals, I suggest that it should be possible to teach chimpanzees languages more closely related to the human language than those thus far taught. For example, Washoe could have been taught a sign for the concept *name-of,* for Sarah learned this concept quite readily. Sarah, in turn, could possibly have been taught a language system with a complexity approaching that of natural language—rather than the relatively "telegraphic" syntax that was taught.

If language systems can be taught to primates, it would seem that they could certainly be taught to human children, but ordinarily one does not think of any need to teach a child his native language, since he seems to learn it by himself or herself. Of course there are some children who for one reason or another (deafness, autism, etc.) do not "acquire" language in the normal manner and who present serious learning problems. Possibly a cognitive learning technology could contribute towards the solution of such problems, even more than behavioral technology has already contributed. Even in the case of "normal" children, there are variations in rate of language development; we know very little about the causes of such variations. To the extent that such variation might be genetically determined, there is little that the cognitive learning technologist can do about them. To the extent that they might have environmental antecedents (as they very likely do), the cognitivist might suggest procedures by which retarded development could be remedied. The essential need at this time is to start applying cognitive learning theory more seriously in research on child language *learning* (and I use that word advisedly), not only to explore possible applications but also to refine the theory itself. Similarly, cognitive learning theory could inspire research on second-language learning (Carroll, 1974b).

Several lines of theoretical and empirical investigation may be suggested. A further analysis of the experiments with animals would clarify cognitive language learning theory because these experiments involve organisms that do not ordinarily possess anything like human language: since they cannot be said to possess a language acquisition device like that of human beings, the special procedures that have been used to teach animals language must exemplify arrangements that cause learning rather than a fulfillment of maturational possibilities.

There is also great need and opportunity to reanalyze and reinterpret, from a cognitive learning standpoint, findings from studies of child language acquisition. The research strategy should be to see how much the role of a language acquisition device can be delimited and how much the role of learning can be amplified.

Take, for example, the concept of imitation, the status of which has had an interesting history in the study of child language learning. Enshrined as an important concept in naive learning theory, and interpreted in terms of "echoic operants" in behavior theory, the concept has generally been downgraded in importance by specialists in child language study. Ervin-Tripp (1964) at one point says, " . . . there is not a shred of evidence supporting a view that progress toward adult norms of grammar arises merely from practice in overt imitation of adult sentences [p. 172]." Yet Ervin-Tripp and others (Slobin, 1968) have used imitation tasks extensively to study grammatical development. The problem is partly semantic: on the one hand, "imitation" can refer to an alleged learning process; on the other, it can refer to an observed behavior. But the problem lies also in a confusion about what is imitated. It seems almost certain that children imitate, or try to imitate, elements such as intonation patterns or single words. They can also imitate longer segments, or parts of these segments, but only within memory limitations and the competence they have already achieved. If the concept or process of imitation is to be used in explaining or promoting language acquisition, it must be considered as only one process among possibly many others. Bloom, Hood, and Lightbown (1974) suggest: "One might explain imitation as a form of encoding that continues the processing of information that is necessary for the representation of linguistic schemas (both semantic and syntactic) in cognitive memory [p. 418]."

A further analysis of imitation in terms of cognitive theory might deal with the manner in which sensory information from the person or utterance being imitated is transformed into memory templates and, conversely, how memory templates for phonetic material are manifested in motor performance (Posner & Keele, 1973, pp. 824–825). Temporal parameters may be important in imitation. The Gardners (1971) speculated that some of Washoe's learning resulted from what they called *delayed imitation;* that is, Washoe's imitations of signs sometimes did not occur until long after the original observations. A process of delayed imitation might account for the observation that children sometimes come out with a new word or grammatical structure "overnight," long after original exposure to models.

Britton (1970) remarks that "It would seem to be nearer the truth to say that [children] imitate people's *method of going about saying things* than that they imitate the things said [p. 42]." Such an imitative process would account for improvisations like "I'm spoonfulling it in" or "I'm jumper than you are," all based on the imitation of speech patterns that the child observes.

If we regard language production as a process of converting intentions into speech, it often presents features of problem solving: the child uses whatever methods he may have acquired that seem reasonable in this kind of problem solving. Promoting language skills might entail teaching children useful methods for expressing their intentions.

SOME BRIEF BUT DIFFICULT PRESCRIPTIONS

The instructional prescriptions I have to offer will sound rather similar to those of the behavioral technologists, but I hope the reader will appreciate the subtle but essential difference in theoretical outlook.

Like the behavioral technologists, I recommend careful analysis of what is to be learned—usually, analysis into rather small units, but also analysis in terms of whatever larger structures may seem relevant. The analysis, however, is to be made in terms of *information,* and only secondarily in terms of overt responses to be made on the basis of that information. In the case of language skills, the analysis of information to be learned will have much to say about the stimulus conditions that correspond to meanings and communicative intentions, and the linguistic constraints whereby those meanings and communicative intentions are manifested in overt behavior in a particular language system.

In the preparation of instructional materials and procedures, careful attention is to be paid to the manner in which the relevant information is presented to the learner. Account must be taken of what prior information can reliably be presumed to be available to the learner at any given point. There must be great concern with exactly what new information is presented from moment to moment in the instruction, with reference to what processing of that information is likely to be performed by the learner. This information processing should be of a nature desired by the instructor.

In the actual process of teaching, the learner should be prepared for what he is learning by evoking appropriate sets and expectancies that will direct and focus his or her attention on particular units of information. Information about the manner in which new information fits in with the overall structure of what is to be learned, and its relevance to more general goals of the learner, would be incorporated in the learning situation. Instead of speaking of reinforcement, we should speak of the role that certain types of information can serve in directing the cognitive processes of the learner [support for this type of prescription can be found, for example, in recent papers by Bindra (1974) and Boneau (1974)].

The planning of instructional sequences over stretches of time requires consideration of the "cognitive history" of new information in terms of its probable course through various memory systems. Although as yet we know little about the properties of memory systems, an ideal cognitive history of any element of information to be learned might be something like this: In a first phase, presentations would concentrate on obtaining increased clarity and definition of the learner's perceptions of stimulus materials, leading to a point when the thing-to-be-learned receives the greatest possible attention from an "executive" element. In a second phase, the information is processed through short-term memory and eventually into long-term memory, passing into a state where it no longer needs to be dealt with by an executive in the focus of attention; it becomes, however, more and more readily accessible from long-term memory and thus acquires a characteristic of automaticity.

Throughout this discussion, it is assumed that account will be taken of individual differences in learners. In a recent paper (Carroll, in press) I have suggested that individual differences in the performance of cognitive tasks are reflections of parameters of memory stores and of the production systems that control the flow of information in a total memory model.

I have discussed three types of theory that might apply to the promotion of language skills. Obviously, I favor cognitive learning theory. I fear, however, that my formulations will remain fanciful until they prove productive of improved instructional outcomes.

2
Sources of Dependency in Cognitive Processes

Robert C. Calfee

Stanford University

For some years I have worked at untangling and measuring independent cognitive skills in beginning reading (Calfee, in press). The goal of this work was threefold: (*a*) to create a theoretical model (or models) to describe the process by which the ability to read is acquired, (*b*) to use this model to develop a system of assessment instruments, each providing independent, unique sources of information to the classroom teacher and other individuals responsible for evaluation of a beginning reader, and (*c*) to establish the feasibility of independent instructional modules. Given solid evidence for independent stages in the acquisition of reading, then perhaps these can be handled instructionally as separate matters, contrary to the current practice of trying to handle everything at once.

Briefly, my previous efforts focussed on the development of "clean" tests, in which there was some assurance that ancillary task requirements (understanding instructions, familiarity with materials) were eliminated as differential sources of variability between children. Multiple regression served as an analytic tool for determining the independent contribution of various precursor tests for predicting criterion performance in reading achievement (Calfee, 1972; Calfee, Chapman, & Venezky, 1972).

More recently I have been thinking about the general question of what is meant by *independence* of cognitive processes, and the related question of how we might test various sources of independence. Sternberg (1969) was the first to point out the central importance of independence to information-processing models. His presentation was quite clear and has served as a basis for a great deal of fruitful research on cognition. However, I now realize that several different interpretations of independence have been intertwined in my thinking and, I suspect, in the thinking of other investigators as well.

In this chapter, I will first present a generalization of Sternberg's additive-factor paradigm for testing stage independence. Next, I will turn to the question of how to evaluate individual differences in an independent-process analysis, and will present a unified framework for testing different classes of hypotheses about the independence of cognitive processes. An illustration of these techniques will then be discussed. Finally, some implications of this work for test design will be pointed out.

This chapter deals with assessment of instruction, rather than with methods of instruction, and hence is most readily applicable to test design and interpretation of test data. But assessment is intimately interwoven with the development of substantive theories of instruction. A process-oriented assessment system should help us understand how a student thinks when he is learning something. This allows us to formulate reasonable hypotheses about the character of efficient instructional strategies, and to evaluate the effects of variation in instructional strategy.

STERNBERG'S ADDITIVE-FACTOR PARADIGM

It has been the fashion for the past several years among cognitive psychologists to represent theoretical ideas in the form of flow charts or block diagrams. Sternberg (1969) pointed out that, if this activity was to be taken seriously, it was necessary to demonstrate the functional independence of the processes represented by different blocks in the system. He presented a methodology for showing process independence for the case of a single additive measure, reaction time.

The first step in this paradigm is the analysis of the underlying cognitive operations required to perform a task. This provides a rudimentary information-processing model. The next step is to identify one or more factors uniquely associated with each operation. Then a procedure is developed in which it seems reasonable to suppose that the operations are carried out as a series of stages, one following the other. The total time to perform the task is the sum of the times taken by each stage.

For example, consider a task in which a subject is asked to read a list of words, and to memorize them so that he can recall them after a delay interval. The list is long, and during the delay interval the subject is distracted in some way, so the task requires more than short-term memory. The subject can study the list for as long as he wishes; the study time is the primary dependent measure.

The first step is to specify the mental operations required to perform the task. The model in Fig. 1 appears reasonable for this situation. The subject uses some time to read each word in the list and some more time adding the word to an organized semantic structure which aids later recall.

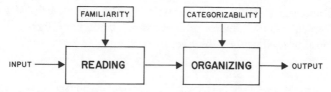

FIG. 1   Relation of factors to processes in "study" model.

The next step is to identify one or more factors that should have a unique effect on a given stage. In Fig. 1, one such factor is suggested for each stage. We then construct a factorial design around these variables; a subject is given word lists containing familiar or unfamiliar words which are either easy or difficult to categorize.

If the processes in Fig. 1 are sequentially independent, and if the assignment of factors to processes is appropriate, then a rigorous test of the model is possible: there should be no interaction between factors associated with different stages.

This conclusion is reached as follows. Assume it takes f seconds to read a list of familiar words, and u seconds to read a list of unfamiliar words, and that $f <$ u. Similarly, the time, e, to organize an easily categorizable list is assumed to be less than the time, d, for a list that is difficult to categorize. Then the independent-process hypothesis predicts that for each type of list specified by the design factors, study time should be the sum of the component times. The prediction is shown in Fig. 2 algebraically and graphically.

An observable feature of this prediction is that the data should trace out parallel functions. The effect of the categorizability factor should be the same at both levels of the familiarity factor. Any other result—any deviation from parallel functions—is evidence of an interaction, which would mean that the

FAMILIARITY

		FAMILIAR	UNFAMILIAR
	EASY	f + e	u + e
	DIFFICULT	f + d	u + d

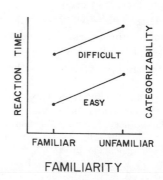

PREDICTED
REACTION TIMES

FAMILIARITY

FIG. 2   Algebraic and graphical predictions based on "study" model with two independent processes.

theoretical analysis is faulty at some point. In this event, general statements about the effects of either factor are impossible, since the effects of one factor vary from level to level of the other factor.

A GENERALIZATION OF THE ADDITIVE-FACTOR PARADIGM

A representative of a generalized process model is shown in Fig. 3. Processes A, B, and C are assumed to be cognitive operations underlying the performance of some task. To establish the independence of these processes,[1] it is necessary to associate with each process a *factor set* and a *measure set*. A factor set consists of one or more independent variables, variation in which is presumed to influence the corresponding process and that process only. A measure set consists of one or more dependent variables, each of which reflects the operation of the corresponding process and that process only. In other words, for a process model to serve any useful purpose theoretically or practically, we ought to be able to specify the input—output features of each process — what sorts of variables affect the processes, and how can its operation be measured? If every factor interacts with every other factor, and if we have no clear-cut way of measuring the underlying processes, so that every measure correlates with every other measure, we have gained little understanding no matter how elaborate our flow charts.

How is a model like that in Fig. 3 to be tested? It requires a multifactor experiment with multivariate measures, in which each subject is tested under a variety of combinations of factors from each of the factor sets, and a variety of measures taken under each combination to provide links to each component process.[2]

Throughout this chapter we consider only designs with two processes, two two-lever factors in each set, and a single measure for each process. This implies a 2^4 design, in which each subject is tested 16 times, once on each of the factorial combinations. Two measures are taken under each combination. Only main effects and two-way interactions are discussed since these suffice to test the model and to describe fully the operation of each process.

[1] The term, *process,* is used extensively and more or less uncritically throughout this paper, to refer to a mental operation of some kind. *Stage* has been avoided because of the possible confusion with developmental stages. Process independence is a property of a particular task for subjects of a given sort. There is no effort to deal with the question of whether "independent processes" might be structural in nature, the result of learning, or situation specific. Finally, process independence does not imply instructional independence, although as suggested earlier this is a possibility worth pursuing.

[2] The present proposal is intended only as a generalization of Sternberg's ideas, not a replacement. In particular, single-measure analysis remains an important technique for investigation of process independence. This includes additive measures like reaction time, but might be usefully extended to multiplication measures like proportions (Calfee, 1970).

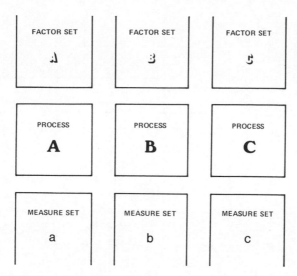

FIG. 3   A generalization of the independent-process model. Associated with each component process is a set of factors and a set of measures, each assumed to be uniquely linked to the process.

The details of the design are spelled out in Fig. 4. The sixteen cells are labeled according to the four factors, two in each factor set. Below the design are contrast coefficients for the computation of the *linear contrast* for that source. These will be discussed shortly. Below that the data are represented in a general way. The indices i to l serve as usual to denote levels of the factors A through B'. The m and n indices denote a particular measure (a or b corresponding to process A or B, respectively) and subject.

In Fig. 5 is the general linear factorial model for the design. Each observation is fully accounted for by this set of parameters. The methods of estimating the parameters is well known, and will not be dealt with here in any detail.

There are several ways to carry out an analysis of variance for the data set in Fig. 4 based on the model in Fig. 5. The most convenient method for present purposes is based on linear contrasts (Dayton, 1970, pp. 37–48, 78–81, 256–268). It is possible to express the magnitude of each source as a one-degree-of-freedom linear contrast on the data. For instance, the A source (the main effect of the A factor) is the difference between the A_1 and A_2 scores; the A' source is the difference between A_1' and A_2', and so on. These contrasts are represented by the corresponding sets of coefficients, c, in Fig. 4. In a factorial design, the two-way interaction between factors is the crossproduct of the two sets of coefficients. The coefficients for the AA' interaction source in Fig. 4 were generated in this fashion.

The contrast coefficients are used to calculate a set of orthogonal parameter estimates from each subject's raw data. The magnitude of source S for a given

FACTOR SET A: FACTOR A, FACTOR A'
FACTOR SET B: FACTOR B, FACTOR B'

CONTRAST COEFFICIENTS

	A₁								A₂							
	A'₁				A'₂				A'₁				A'₂			
	B₁		B₂		B₁		B₂		B₁		B₂		B₁		B₂	
	B'_1	B'_2	B'_1	B'_2	B'_1	B'_2	B'_1	B'_2	B'_1	B'_2	B'_1	B'_2	B'_1	B'_2	B'_1	B'_2
A	-1	-1	-1	-1	-1	-1	-1	-1	1	1	1	1	1	1	1	1
A'	-1	-1	-1	-1	1	1	1	1	-1	-1	-1	-1	1	1	1	1
AA'	1	1	1	1	-1	-1	-1	-1	-1	-1	-1	-1	1	1	1	1
BB'	1	-1	-1	1	1	-1	-1	1	1	-1	-1	1	1	-1	-1	1

SOURCE

S : $c_{S_{ijk\,lm}}$

Sources: A, A', AA', S, BB'

DATA

MEASURES, SUBJECT n

m, n: 1,1; 1,2; ... M,N

X_{ijklmn}

FIG. 4 Design of 2⁴ factorial experiment, contrast coefficients for illustrative sources, and data representation. S indicates a particular source in the analysis of variance model; i, j, k, and l are indices for factors A, A', B, and B', respectively; m is an index for the measure; and n is the subject index.

$$
\begin{aligned}
X_{ijkl,m,n} = \ &\mu_m \\
&+ \alpha_{i,m} + \alpha'_{j,m} + (\alpha\alpha')_{ij,m} \\[4pt]
&+ \beta_{k,m} + \beta'_{l,m} + (\beta\beta')_{kl,m} \\[4pt]
&+ (\alpha\beta)_{ii,m} + \ldots + (\alpha'\beta')_{jl,m} \\[10pt]
&+ \nu_{m,n} \\
&+ (\alpha\nu)_{i,m,n} + \ldots + (\alpha\alpha'\nu)_{ij,m,n} \\[4pt]
&+ (\beta\nu)_{k,m,n} + \ldots + (\beta\beta'\nu)_{kl,m,n} \\[4pt]
&+ (\alpha\beta\nu)_{ik,m,n} + \ldots (\alpha'\beta'\nu)_{jl,m,n} \\[10pt]
&+ \epsilon_{ijkl,m,n}
\end{aligned}
$$

Mean of measure m

Effects of factor set **A**
(by independence, negligible if $m = b$)

Effects of factor set **B**
(by independence, negligible if $m = a$)

Joint effects of **A** and **B**
(by independence, these should always be negligible)

General effect for subject n

Subject-treatment effects of **A**
(negligible if $m = b$)

Subject-treatment effects of **B**
(negligible if $m = a$)

Subject-treatment effects of **A** and **B**
(should always be negligible)

Residual error

FIG. 5   The general linear factorial model for the design in Fig. 4.

measure, m, and a particular subject, n, is computed from the contrast coefficients for that source and the set of observations on the given measure for that subject:

$$
C_{S,m,n} = \frac{\sum_{ijkl} c_{Sijkl,m} X_{ijkl,m,n}}{\sqrt{\sum_{ijkl} (c_{S,ijkl,m})^2}} .
$$

For 2^p designs like the one under discussion, the numerator of each contrast is a simple difference score; the denominator normalizes the expression so that regardless of the choice of coefficients the variance of the contrast is equal to the population variance under the null hypothesis.

There is a direct correspondence between the variance estimate of a source by means of a linear contrast and the parameters from the linear model (Fig. 5), the latter serving often to teach analysis of variance in statistics courses. The variance estimate for source S over subjects, $MS(S)$, is based on the average of the corresponding contrasts, $C_{S,m}, \cdot\cdot$. This average, squared and multiplied by the number of subjects, is equal to the $MS(S)$. If the null hypothesis holds for source S, then $MS(S)$ is an estimate of the population variance. The residual variance in the contrast scores for source S provides a second estimate of the population variance. The two variance estimates generate an F ratio to test the plausibility of the null hypothesis.

The point to emphasize here is that the linear contrast provides a convenient method for representing each independent parameter estimate in the general linear factorial model in Fig. 5. The procedure, in its essentials, is to compute each estimate in the form of a normalized difference score for each subject. The analysis of variance becomes, to all intents and purposes, an orthogonal collection of *t* tests on difference scores. This method is algebraically equivalent to a conventional repeated-measures analysis of variance. I am overlooking the use of multivariate analysis of variance as an alternative method of analysis, as well as questions about the dangers of relying on the acceptance of the null hypothesis as a way of supporting a substantive hypothesis. These are matters of some concern, but they have been discussed elsewhere and are not central to the problem.

Process Independence—On the Average

The major prediction of an independent-process model for data like that described in Fig. 4 is straightforward. The factor(s) associated with a given process can affect only the measure(s) associated with the process. No other sources of variance should be substantial. The details are indicated to the right of Fig. 5. Variation in Factor A or A' or the interaction AA' might be expected to substantially (and significantly) affect measure a; these sources should not have any noticeable effect on measure b. A similar state of affairs holds for factors B and B' with regard to measure b. Any interaction between the two factor sets is evidence against the independence of the processes, no matter which measure is affected.

A concrete example may be useful at this point. This study (after Floyd, 1972) is designed to investigate the processes by which young children read single words presented in isolation.

The model for this task is shown in Fig. 6. Two processes are proposed: decoding and semantic matching. Reading is conceived as an initial translation of the printed word into an auditory form, then a search in memory for a lexical

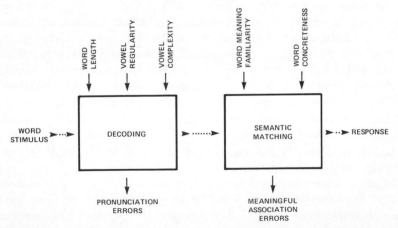

FIG. 6   Example of a two-process model for reading a word in isolation. (After Floyd, 1972.)

match. For each process, a factor set and a measure set are suggested. The stimulus words comprise factorial combinations of all the factors shown. The subject's task is to pronounce each word, and then to give an associate to the word. If the pronunciation is incorrect, the proper pronunciation is provided by the tester. Otherwise the measures would be dependent of necessity. If a child failed to pronounce a word correctly, then subsequent associations would necessarily be strange.

The predictions, assuming that decoding and semantic matching are independent processes, are as follows: pronunciation should be affected by orthographic factors, and word association should depend on semantic factors. The test is not a trivial one in this instance; for example, frequency is thought by many investigators to have substantial effects on "word recognition," which presumably includes the ability to pronounce a word.

To test these predictions, we compute for each source the appropriate linear contrast for every individual subject. The average of these contrasts provides a measure of the magnitude of this source over subjects. The residual variance between subjects in the contrast yields a measure of error variance for a test of statistical significance. The ratio

$$F = \frac{MS(\text{vowel complexity for pronunciation})}{MS(\text{subjects by vowel complexity for pronunciation})}$$

if statistically significant, would fit the hypothesis of process independence. The ratio

$$F = \frac{MS(\text{word familiarity for pronunciation})}{MS(\text{subjects by word familiarity for pronunciation})}$$

if significant, would be evidence against the hypothesis of process independence.

Process independence is evaluated here by the magnitude of the average effects due to a given source, compared to between-subject variability in the source. This procedure provides a reasonably workable approach for testing the general independence (or dependency) of the components of an information-processing model. If the empirical results fit the pattern predicted by the assignment of factors and measures to a postulated cognitive structure, we have a parsimonious and useful way of understanding how a subject performs the task.

Process Independence—Individual Differences

The preceding test of process independence involved comparison with an error variance estimate based on individual differences in subjects' performance on a particular contrast. While it is customary in research on cognition to treat individual differences as "error" (Hunt, Frost, & Lunneborg, 1973, and Carroll, 1976, are exceptions: also, cf. Sternberg, 1969, pp. 307–308), this is not an adequate treatment for educational research and practice.

Several distinctive sources of individual differences are represented in the general linear factorial model (Fig. 5). Half-way down the list are parameters, $v_{m,n}$ which measure subject n's general performance level for measure m, averaged over all factorial combinations. Below that are subject-factor parameters for factor set **A**, $(\alpha v)_{i,m,n}$, $(\alpha' v)_{j,m,n}$, etc., next are the corresponding parameters for factor set **B**, and finally the parameters for the interactions of these sets. As indicated in the figure, if the independent-process hypothesis is correct, only certain of these parameters should produce substantial variance estimates.

For instance, suppose that for certain subjects factor A had a large effect on measure b, contrary to the process independence hypothesis, whereas for other subjects this effect was negligible. Then MS(subjects by A for measure b) would be relatively large. MS(A for measure b), which represents the general effect of the A factor on measure b, might be nonsignificant when compared to MS(subjects by A for measure b). Acceptance of the null hypothesis might be taken as evidence in support of general process independence—an erroneous conclusion, at least for some subjects.

Large variation between subjects in the parameters for a given source may compromise the interpretation of the overall variance source. The most obvious danger is that an unduly large error variance estimate may obscure evidence contrary to the independent-process hypothesis. In this regard, comparison of variance components provides a useful supplement to significance tests in the examination of data.

Under certain conditions it is possible to test the hypothesis that a subject-factor variance estimate is larger than expected. The design must permit the estimation of a residual variance term; replication within subjects or pooling of high-order interactions often serves this purpose. The test compares each subject-factor source with the residual error variance. For example, if

$$F = \frac{MS(\text{subjects by vowel complexity for pronunciation})}{MS(\text{residual error})}$$

is a significant source of variance, this is compatible with the independence hypothesis. On the other hand, the finding that

$$F = \frac{MS(\text{subjects by word familiarity for pronunciation})}{MS(\text{residual error})}$$

is highly significant constitutes evidence contrary to the hypothesis. Such tests are quite sensitive because of the large number of degrees of freedom for each variance estimate.

Subject-factor sources may provide the strongest evidence for or against process independence. If MS(subjects by vowel complexity for pronunciation) is large, then MS(vowel complexity for pronunciation) will seem relatively small, and may be insignificant. Such a result does not mean that vowel complexity has no effect on the decoding process, but rather that the magnitude of that effect varies widely from subject to subject, in ways that are not controlled by the between-subject design. Similarly, *MS*(word familiarity by pronunciation) might be insignificant when tested against *MS*(subjects by word familiarity for pronunciation). But if the latter variance is large relative to *MS*(residual error), this is evidence contrary to process independence, just as surely as a large average effect is contrary evidence.

Modification of a Model

The preceding discussion of statistical "tests" may imply a destructive approach, in which a model is proposed and then all efforts are directed toward questioning its adequacy. In fact, the factor-process measure approach is self-correcting in the development of a model. Examination of a series of experiments provides positive information about the character of underlying processes, the specification of useful correspondences between factors and processes, and the description of factors and measures in a precise, unconfounded manner. The results of each experiment lead to "perfecting" modifications in the basic model, which can be subjected to further test.

Parameter Independence

To this point, independence has referred to the absence of interactions between factors associated with different processes. Closer examination of the question of individual differences reveals the existence of another type of independence, namely, the extent to which the parameters of the general linear factorial model are correlated. This property of a data set will be called *parameter independence.*[3]

The idea of looking at the between-subjects correlation between a pair of analysis-of-variance parameters is somewhat unconventional, but this appears to be a reasonable question to raise of a data set. Consider the linear contrasts $C_{A,a,n}$ and $C_{A',a,n}$—these are difference scores for the A and A' factors for measure a, calculated for each subject n. Imagine that these pairs of scores are arranged in a scattergram. The previous analyses have dealt with the marginal distributions, asking whether the marginal means are zero, and whether the variance around each marginal mean is comparable in magnitude to an estimate of the population variance.

The size of the correlation between $C_{A,a,n}$ and $C_{A',a,n}$, is therefore a new question, and statistically independent of the previous questions asked of the

---

[3] To the best of my knowledge, examination of the specifics of a variance–covariance matrix along the lines suggested below has not been suggested before. Test for homogeneity of the matrix is a crude effort at best. Multivariate analysis of variance is mainly concerned with appropriate statistical inference when the dependent variable is a vector.

data. A large correlation would mean that subjects who are strongly affected by variation in factor A are also strongly affected by factor A', and contrariwise. If the correlation is negligible, then the effects of the two factors are independent of each other, in the sense that the knowledge that a subject is strongly affected by variation in one factor says nothing about his or her reaction to another factor.

In the preceding example, the contrasts $C_{A,a,n}$ and $C_{A',a,n}$ estimate parameters for factors A and A' which linked to the same process. This analysis will be referred to as a test of *intraprocess parameter independence*. One can look at correlations with interaction contrasts as well as comparing main effect contrasts. For instance, the correlation between $C_{A,a,n}$ and $C_{AA',a,n}$ asks whether the size of the effects of variation due to factor A are correlated with the magnitude of differential effects of A at the two levels of A'. It should be stressed that the correlation between contrasts is not the same as the interaction between factors. Moreover, one may examine these correlations regardless of the outcome of the analyses of the marginal distributions.

It is also possible to examine the between-subject correlation of contrasts for sources from two different processes: $C_{A,a,n}$ and $C_{B,b,n}$, for example. It is consistent with the process-independence hypothesis that both of these sets of contrasts could be significant sources of variance, either on the average or as subject-factor interactions; factor A is linked with measure a, and factor B with measure b. The magnitude of the correlation between contrasts is a separate question, and has no bearing on process independence. If two such contrasts are highly correlated, it means that a subject who is strongly affected by a factor in one process is likely to be strongly affected by another factor linked to a second process, whereas a subject showing little effect of one factor would not be much affected by variation in the other factor. This will be called an analysis of *interprocess independence*.

General Parameter Independence

There are two other types of independence to be considered in examining individual differences. These are measured by the correlation (a) between general parameters, each based on the average for a given measure over factorial conditions for an individual subject, and (b) between general parameters and specific contrast parameters. If you refer to the general linear factorial model (Fig. 5), the first correlation is between the estimates of $v_{a,n}$ and $v_{b,n}$. This is the correlation between the average scores for different dependent variables, which is frequently calculated by researchers. I will refer to this as *independence of general parameters*.

The correlation between general and specific parameters has been examined less often. It consists of the comparison of terms like $v_{a,n}$ and $C_{A,a,n}$. Actually for two-level factors the correlation of $\nu_{a,n}$ and $\alpha_{l,n}$ is equivalent to the preceding correlation, and perhaps is a bit easier to grasp. The question raised here is whether subjects who do better on the average over all conditions also tend to be more strongly affected by factor variations. For example, the student who pronounces words quite well on the average is strongly affected by variation in vowel complexity, whereas the student whose pronunciation is generally poor does about the same whether the words contain simple or complex vowels. I will refer to this analysis as a test of the *independence of general and specific parameters*.

Sources of Dependency: An Overview

It should be emphasized that the different types of independence described above are statistically separate, and that the answer to one question does not directly determine answers to any other. That is, one can usefully inquire about each of the following substantive questions:

1. *Process independence, average over subjects:*
   Are any between-process sources of variance so large, on the average, that the hypothesis of process independence is untenable?
2. *Process independence, subject-factor interactions:*
   Are any between-process subject-factor interactions so large that the hypothesis of process independence is untenable?
3. *Intraprocess parameter independence:*
   Are effects of within-process factors correlated?
4. *Interprocess parameter independence:*
   Are effects of between-process factors correlated?
5. *General parameter independence:*
   Are total scores for different measures correlated?
6. *General–specific parameter independence:*
   Are the specific effects of process factors correlated with generalized performance as measured by total scores?

The answers to these different questions carry different implications. Questions (1) and (2) bear on the adequacy of a proposed information-processing model. Questions (3) and (4) have to do with the degree to which individual subjects are more or less generally labile in reaction to factor variation. Questions (5) and (6) deal with the relation of general performance and process-linked shifts in performance.

If process independence, (1) and (2), is supported by the data, this is evidence that assessment (and possibly instruction) may proceed by investigation of each process as a separable entity. For instance, suppose decoding and semantic matching operated as independent processes in a series of experiments. Then it might be reasonable to design assessment and instructional programs that focussed specifically on decoding skills, with minimal concern about the corresponding comprehension processes, and vice-versa.

If answers to Questions (3) through (6) reveal frequent and marked dependencies, this supports a *"G* factor" interpretation of individual differences in cognitive processes for the task. If strong correlations hold between measures in different tasks, there is little need for extensive assessment of an individual student. Administration of a few "subtests" will indicate the student's general level of performance, or his reaction to factor variation, or both. From this we can predict his performance under other conditions. On the other hand, if dependencies are negligible, the development of comprehensive assessment systems becomes a worthwhile endeavor.

AN EXPERIMENT ON LINE DRAWING

Here is an illustration of how to apply these techniques to a data set. The study was not designed to test an independent-process model, and it seems unlikely that the treatment factors are uniquely linked to underlying processes. But the within-subjects portion of the design raises interesting questions, and the data were readily available for the analysis.

The study was part of an investigation of impulsivity—reflectivity in young children (Kagan, Rosman, Day, Albert, & Phillips, 1964). Some children seem to attack a problem impulsively—more quickly and with a higher error rate. Others tend to work reflectively—more carefully and accurately. There is some evidence that impulsivity is correlated with poorer reading achievement. Our particular interest was in determining the extent to which speed and accuracy measures were affected by situational variables in a simple motor task.

The children were shown a paper with half a dozen items like the ones in Fig. 7, and told that their job was to draw a line from each rabbit along the "road" to the carrot without touching the lines. Time to complete all six items on a page was measured, as were the total number of line-touching errors. The

FIG. 7　Example of materials used in line-drawing task.

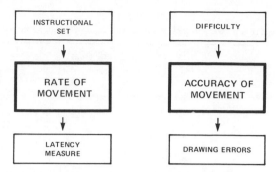

FIG. 8   Information-processing model for line-drawing experiment.

children, first-graders and kindergartners, were tested twice with three months or so between sessions.

The two within-subject factors of primary interest are related in Fig. 8 to a tentative processing model. One process determines rate of movement, and the second process determines accuracy. Latency and errors seem natural measures for these processes.

The *Set* factor describes the instructional conditions under which the child performed the task. The first two pages were always done with no set. The instructions emphasized neither speed nor accuracy: "Draw a line down each road from each bunny to his carrot. Try not to touch the sides of the road. If you do touch the side of the road, it's okay, keep going, but try not to touch the lines." On the next two pages, accuracy was stressed: "Be very, very careful not to touch the sides of the road." Finally on the last two pages, the child was asked to draw as fast as possible: "Get each bunny to his carrot as quickly as possible. Try not to touch the sides of the road, but if you do, it doesn't matter, the important thing is to complete the page as quickly as possible." Set and order are confounded in this design as a matter of practical necessity.

The *Difficulty* factor denotes whether each page had easy items (the lines connecting rabbit and carrot were 5/8 inch apart) or difficult items (the lines were 1/4 inch apart).

For purposes of analysis, the Set factor has been identified with the timing process, and the Difficulty factor with the movement process. This linkage is not really satisfactory, as noted earlier. Each factor seems likely to affect both processes as constituted. Nonetheless, let us see what the analysis tells us about the data.

Analysis of Process Independence

Univariate analyses of variance were carried out on the two measures for preliminary statistical evaluation; these are presented in Table 1. In Fig. 9 time and error scores are shown as a function of Grade, Set, and Difficulty. Grade,

TABLE 1
Analysis of Variance (selected sources) of Line-Drawing Experiment[a]

Source	Time (sec)		Errors	
	F	MS(E)	F	MS(E)
Grade/Age (G)	5.6*	–	13.2*	–
Ability (A)	<1	–	<1	–
G × A	~1	–	~1	–
N(GA)	–	1743.	–	45.9
Instructional set (I)				
No set versus accuracy + speed (I₁)	44.8**	247.9	21.5**	4.7
Accuracy versus speed (I₂)	113.2**	449.5	47.7**	9.6
Difficulty (D)	188.9**	416.6	76.0**	24.9
Session (S)	3.5	677.5	<1	12.6
I₁ × D	20.7**	108.7	22.1**	3.9
I₂ × D	64.0**	78.7	39.0**	5.2
I₁ × S	1.7	479.8	<1	3.0
I₂ × S	3.2	326.3	<1	2.5
D × S	3.7	275.6	<1	9.7
G × I₁	<1	247.9	9.1**	4.7
G × I₂	2.5	449.5	9.5**	9.6
G × D	<1	416.6	13.1**	24.9
G × I₁ × D	2.7	108.7	8.6**	3.9
G × I₂ × D	<1	78.7	5.9**	5.2
Residual	–	154.0	–	2.5

[a]df for all tests are 1 and 36.
*F(1, 36, .05) = 4.12.   **F(1, 36, .01) = 7.40.

the two Set contrasts and Difficulty are all significant sources of variance for both measures, as are certain interactions among these factors. Instructions to "be more accurate" slow the children down a little, without any noticeable decrease in errors. Instructions to "speed up" are obeyed by the children (and happily so), but with a marked increase in errors. Difficulty has a large effect on both time and errors. The children take much longer to connect the rabbit and carrot when the lines are close together, but they also make a greater number of errors under this condition. The interaction between the Set and Difficulty factors can be traced to the speed instructions. The effect of the Difficulty

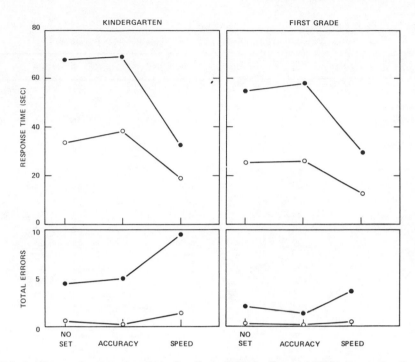

FIG. 9 Time and error scores as a function of Grade, Set, and Difficulty, averaged over sessions. Easy items are open circles. Hard items are filled circles. $N = 20$ in each group.

factor is greater for errors and smaller for response time under speed instructions compared to the other two instructional conditions. The kindergartners make more errors than first graders, especially in the difficult condition and under instructions stressing speed.

On the average, then, the students performed the line-drawing task fairly efficiently without explicit instructions about how to arrange the trade off between speed and accuracy. They worked about as slowly as they felt they could, and speeding up led to an increase in errors.

Certain of the subject-factor variance estimates are substantially (and significantly) larger than the residual variance based on the highest-order interaction. There are large individual differences in the time measure due to variation in accuracy vs. speed and difficulty, as well as variation from the first session to the second. Variation in difficulty is the largest source of individual difference in the error scores, followed by session and accuracy-speed.

The process model in Fig. 8 must be rejected on several grounds. Both measures are strongly affected by both factors, and the interaction between the two factors is significant. The large subject-factor variance in time due to variation in difficulty is also evidence contrary to the model.

These findings suggest that either (a) the two processes are so complexly related that little is gained by postulating separate processes, or (b) the factors

TABLE 2

Correlation Matrix of Time and Error Scores, Line-Drawing Experiment[a]

VARIABLE		1	2	3	4	5	6	7	8	9
Time ave both	1			95		84	−20	54	68	75
Errors ave both	2	−62		24	96		96		−33	
Time ave I	3	86	−65		−23	61	−23	46	74	80
Error ave I	4	−55	89	−66			85		−33	
Time ave II	5	82	−38	42	−24			53	39	47
Error ave II	6	−52	83	−45	48	−42			−31	
Time I Ns E	7	79	−69	82	−69	49	−49		34	42
D	8	49	−56	72	−60		−36	65		36
Acc E	9	82	−42	91	−43	45	−29	71	44	
D	10	88	−59	94	−58	51	−41	71	54	93
Spd E	11	34	−39	53	−38		−29	26	34	34
D	12	56	−62	73	−63		−43	52	53	50
Error I Ns E	13	−22	42	−25	51			−39	−43	
D	14	−33	59	−37	77		21	−45	−47	
Acc E	15	−26	32	−20	49	−24		−24	−20	
D	16	−36	70	−50	86		30	−43	−42	−33
Spd E	17	−44	67	−38	62	−36	52	−51	−37	−22
D	18	−59	84	−73	89	−23	52	−73	−56	−53
Time II Ns E	19	−66	38	39	−26	74	−40	69	28	35
D	20	74	−21	39		89		48		50
Acc E	21	20				56	−21		−21	
D	22	74	−41	41	−28	87	−43	40	20	40
Spd E	23	20	−23			55	−37	21		
D	24	−65	−57	39	−32	73	−71	34	23	28
Error II Ns E	25		35				60			
D	26	−37	72	−34	42	−27	86	−43	−29	−20
Acc E	27	−30	39	−31	39		28	−35	−29	
D	28	−49	69	−30	36	−53	88	−43		−23
Spd E	29	−32	56	−35	41		57		−45	
D	30	−54	80	−79	47	−42	95	−56	−39	−35

[a]First graders above diagonal, kindergarteners below diagonal. For clarity, decimals omitted, r's above .5 are in boldface, and r's below .2 are deleted. Variable name codes are Ave (average), I and II (first and second session), Ns (No set), Acc (accuracy), Spd (Speed), E (Easy), and D (Difficulty).

are poorly defined with reference to the two processes, (which seems probable), or (c) the measures are poor indicators of the underlying processes.

Analysis of Parameter Independence

We turn next to an examination of intercorrelations among the measures. Typically, an investigator might look at correlational data like that in Table 2, or some portion thereof. The 2 × 2 matrix in the upper lefthand corner is a likely

TABLE 2 (continued)

10	11	12	13	14	15	16	17	18	19	20	21	22
87	74	78			~				80	84	29	64
−20			69	82	~	89	85	88			48	
94	72	78		−26	~	−23	−20		64	68		41
−21			81	89	~	88	77	93			49	
53	58	58			~				87	90	54	87
		−21	52	69	~	82	86	77			42	
25	37	28	25		~	−20	−21	26	61	44	31	49
58	20	35	−34	−46	~	−28	−28		32	51		37
76	63	63			~				51	47	25	30
	75	77		−24	~				59	62		29
34		81		20	~				69	54	24	29
57	88				~			−26	56	60		30
−20				91	~	53	36	76			46	
−36		−27	44		~	68	51	77			48	
		−24		70	~	~	~	~	~	~	~	~
−46	−37	−48	36	63	35		90	72			38	
−32		−36	61	51	38	23		63			37	
−62	−52	−76	24	47	32	72	47			23	46	
31				−21			−41	−26		76	46	70
51							−31		69		36	67
	−23	−29		−20				27	26	30		47
51			−21	−26	−28		−26	−23	48	63	67	
	20		30		−23		−27	−20	42	28	48	50
40	31	36				−24	−33	−38	49	47	37	70
	−23			−21			30			20	−32	
−26	−35	−36				38	33	46	−37			−25
−24	−29	−36		47	71	23	25	38				−28
−33		−20	21	24		21	46	31	−53	−35	38	−51
−35	−28	−46		35	33		53	38				26
−45	−26	−42	23			29	47	55	−41	−22		42

(continued)

candidate. It gives the correlation between time and error scores averaged for each student over the entire repeated-measures design structure. The correlation is negative in both groups, negligible in the first-grade data but fairly sizable in the kindergarten data. It appears that there is a tendency for children to trade off speed and accuracy on this task; the faster a child draws, the more likely he is to make an error.

The 4 × 4 matrix just down the diagonal is another reasonable analysis. It shows the relation between time and errors calculated for each student from the average conditions in each session. Again there is evidence of an inverse relation

TABLE 2 (continued)

VARIABLE		23	24	25	26	27	28	29	30
Time ave both	1	36	51	−27	−24	~		−20	
Errors ave both	2		−26	51	94	~	86	80	84
Time ave I	3		44	−29	−32	~		−25	
Error ave I	4		−23	37	87	~	74	74	72
Time ave II	5	63	51			~			
Error ave II	6		−27	61	93	~	92	81	90
Time I Ns E	7	26		−25		~		−29	
D	8			−33	−49	~		−32	
Acc E	9		34			~			
D	10		48	−22	−24	~			
Spd E	11	41	61			~			
D	12	40	75	−27		~			−32
Error I Ns E	13				62	~	42	29	44
D	14			29	78	~	59	49	56
Acc E	15	~	~	~	~	~	~	~	~
D	16	21		46	84	~	75	91	58
Spd E	17	25		55	86	~	79	93	65
D	18		−34	25	72	~	65	59	76
Time II Ns E	19	48	39			~			
D	20	49	42	−21		~			
Acc E	21	33		44	49	~	39	25	30
D	22	46	29	−23		~	−22		
Spd E	23		64			~			−23
D	24	59		−27		~	−20		−34
Error II Ns E	25	−26	−33		57	~	51	57	48
D	26	−26	−54	47		~	82	79	73
Acc E	27	−31				~	~	~	~
D	28	−26	−57	53	74			73	81
Spd E	29	−43	−48	53	27	33	34		58
D	30	−32	−74	45	79	26	79	48	

between time and error scores. Performance is reasonably stable from one session to the next in first graders, and moderately so in the kindergartners.

The remainder of the matrix presents the entire repeated-measures design structure, perhaps the most defensible way of presenting the raw data. The correlations between time and error measures are blocked in to emphasize a particular property of these data. The several time measures tend to be relatively highly correlated, as do the error measures, compared to the inter-measure correlations. But the patterns are admittedly fuzzy. It is the sort of matrix that might be subjected to factor analysis in order to clarify the underlying structures.

However, raw scores are not the measures to examine, given the theoretical point of view elaborated previously. Each raw score is a combination of factor effects (cf. Fig. 5) which may be interrelated in more or less complex fashion. Let us see what the relations between the parameters of this data set look like.

To determine relations among the basic parameters, we will use linear contrasts computed from the raw scores for several of the sources from the analysis of variance (Table 1). The correlation matrix displayed in Table 3 shows the relations between certain contrasts along with two average scores, the average over all conditions (All) and the average over all No-Set conditions (No Set). Each of the entries in this table stands for a parameter from the general linear factorial hypotheses for this experiment. For instance, Time All (Variable 1) is the average response time over all the design variations for a given subject. This is equivalent to an estimate of $\nu_{\text{time},n}$ for subject n. Time A vs S (Variable 4) is the contrast in time scores between the accuracy and speed conditions, averaged over difficulty and sessions. This is related to the estimate of the parameter $\alpha_{A/S,\text{time},n}$ for the subject n.

Table 3 was obtained by computing these parameter estimates for each subject, and entering these values into a standard correlation program. Since a great deal of information is compressed in this table, it may be worthwhile to describe its organization in more detail. There was reason to believe that the kindergarten and first-grade data might show different patterns, and so separate analyses were conducted at each grade level. Kindergarten results are below and to the left of the main diagonal, first-grade above and to the right. Time and error scores are analyzed separately. Along the margins are the residual standard deviations for each source (this is the square root of the error mean square from the analysis of variance calculated separately for each grade), and the F ratio for the source (again based on separate analyses for each grade). The major elements of an analysis of variance can be reconstructed from these marginal entries, and the relative magnitude of various sources and of error terms can be seen.

The off-diagonal entries in Table 3 are, as noted earlier, Pearson correlations between the contrast scores. To give a concrete idea of what the relations in Table 3 mean, two scatterplots are presented in Fig. 10. The kindergarten and first-grade data have been combined in these plots.

The correlation matrix in Table 3 has a reasonably simple structure. Certain correlations are very large (positive or negative) and the rest tend to be relatively small. Except for the No-Set vs. Accuracy-Speed contrast, and the interaction of this contrast with Difficulty, the correlations within the time and error submatrices are high. With few exceptions, the correlations outside these submatrices are small.

This pattern, together with an examination of the scatterplots for the larger correlations (those in Fig. 10 are typical), shows that children who either work fast or make lots of errors are relatively unaffected by variation in the situational factors, Set and Difficulty. Moreover, students who are strongly affected by variation in one situational factor (Set) are strongly affected by variation in the other situational factor (Difficulty).

TABLE 3
Correlation Matrix of Parameter Eestimates Based on Subject Averages and Contrast Coefficients.[a]

	SD	F*	VARIABLE #	1	2	3	4	5	6	7	8	9	10	11	12	13	14	15	16
			SD	9.5	12.0	12.8	16.3	21.2	10.0	10.3	19.6	1.5	1.6	1.4	1.9	4.4	1.2	1.7	1.6
			F*	–	–	22.8	37.2	45.0	9.4	23.5	13.0	17.4	13.3	7.7	19.8	19.8	9.0	16.2	6.1
TIME—All	14.2	–	1		91	28	88	-86		-76	57		-22				26		
Ns	17.8	–	2	91		66	77	-82	-35	-74	47		-28	-36			49	22	21
Ns vs A/S	18.7	20.0	3	27	64			-34	-67	-32			-25	-49	-23		66	42	23
A vs S	26.2	31.3	4	79	68			-71		-76	58			-23			33		
E vs D	23.8	40.8	5	-88	-83	-29	-69		28	85	-61	33	45	40	-28	-33	-40		
N/As by E/D	10.8	18.5	6	-49	-66	-62	-51	49						46			-49		
A/S by E/S	7.7	26.8	7	-52	-45		-63	69	23		-48	23	38	47	26	-21	-51		
Session I vs II	34.4	2.3	8			-34			25	25		-30	-39	-29		27	39		-26

Table showing standard deviations, F-ratios, and an intercorrelation matrix (kindergartners below, first-graders above the diagonal). Columns are indexed 9–16; the two margin columns are the standard deviation and the F-ratio for each source.

Source	SD	F	#	9	10	11	12	13	14	15	16
ERROR—Ave	2.3	–	9			–31	26	56	–33	–51	–62
Ns	1.6	–	10	90		–23	30	42	–27	–39	–45
Ns vs A/S	2.7	20.0	11	–78	–43			–56	30	49	65
A vs S	3.9	25.3	12	–73	–50	81		–45		45	55
E vs D	6.2	34.2	13	–92	–78	79	57		34	49	59
N/As by E/D	2.6	18.5	14	63	35	–81	35	–51		–26	–44
A/S by E/D	2.7	23.2	15	40	–73	–59	–49	36	–26		–39
Session I vs II	5.1	2.2	16	20	–23	–21	–23	22		–28	

aData from line-drawing experiment. Kindergartners below and first-graders above diagonal, $N = 20$ in each group. Standard deviations and F-ratios for each source are in margins. For emphasis, r's greater than .5 are in boldface, those less than .2 are deleted in correlations for clarity. Codes are same as in Table 2.
*$F(1, 19, .01) = 8.1$.

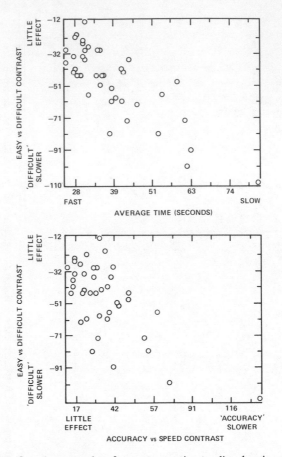

FIG. 10   Sample scatterplots for contrast estimates, line-drawing study.

A particularly interesting feature of these data is that the statements above apply independently to the two response measures. The correlation between time and error contrast scores is negligible, with a few exceptions to be discussed below. This result suggests that the process model in Fig. 9 might be reasonably adequate after all. The Set and Difficulty factors do not fulfill the requirements for testing an independent-process model—they were not selected to link uniquely to the proposed operations—but the model may be a useful approximation.

In any event, the purpose of this exercise is not to promote any substantive finding. It does seem noteworthy that the approach leads to a considerable simplification in the data on its maiden voyage. The data in Table 3 scarcely require further clarification. The basic structure is immediately apparent: time and error comprise two independent components, the constituent parameters of which are highly interrelated. It is obvious when a constituent drops out. For instance, the No-Set vs. Accuracy-Speed contrast in time scores is a substantial and significant source of variance, but unrelated to any other contrast. This contrast was chosen as the orthogonal complement to the Accuracy vs. Speed contrast, but it may not make psychological sense. One possibility is that the No-Set scores might serve better as a covariate. However, as can be seen in Table 3, these scores are highly correlated with the overall average, and the pattern of contrast relations with No-Set and All scores are practically identical. The matter remains unresolved at this point in the analysis.

The kindergarten sample also exhibits a noticeable departure from time-error independence. Average time is inversely correlated with average error (this was observed in Table 2), as well as with several error contrasts. The Easy vs. Difficult contrast for time measures is also correlated with the error rate. In the younger children, movement accuracy is more or less controlled depending on instructional set and difficulty. In the older children, the two systems are totally independent. This statement is more precise and informative than the conclusion from Table 2 that time and error scores were inversely correlated.

Analysis of the Line-Drawing Study: An Overview

Several features of the data are brought into focus by the variance–covariance analysis of specific linear contrasts that would be obscured in more conventional analyses. Let us review briefly the main implications of this analysis:

1. Process independence, based on the relations predicted in Fig. 8 for average factor effects, must be rejected. Factors linked to one process affect measures linked to other processes directly and through interaction.
2. Process independence, looking at subject–source interactions, is irrelevant given the preceding result. But subject–source interactions are large enough in at least one instance to suggest that independence can also be rejected by this test.
3. Intraprocess parameter independence is not testable in this design.
4. Interprocess parameter independence is supported by the low correlations between time and error contrasts. This suggests that time and errors tap separate processes which the design factors may be affecting in confounded fashion. Speed and accuracy are influenced in varying degrees from one student to another by variation in situational factors.
5. General parameter independence holds for the first-grade sample, but not the kindergarten sample.
6. General–specific parameter independence can be rejected in almost every instance. Average time and error scores are highly correlated with responsiveness to situational factors.

IMPLICATIONS FOR
EDUCATIONAL TEST PROCEDURES

Current test construction proceeds as if we place buckets under psychological processes and collect the output more or less directly from individual subtest measures (usually total correct responses). Control over variation in the input is modest at best, and nonexistent in most instances. This simple model has been extended by such methods as factor analysis, but it seems to have some inherent weaknesses. It does not provide a natural way for introducing process-oriented variables and contextual variables into the testing situation in an easy-to-measure fashion.

Factorial test designs seem to provide a simple but informative way to build a test around a process model. This approach is similar in spirit to the notion of facet tests discussed by Guttman (1965; Guttman & Schlesinger, 1967). Careful analysis of a task may turn up many factors of potential importance, but fractional factorial designs allow optimal arrangement of a factorial test structure so that a maximum amount of relevant information is obtained for a given number of test items (Kirk, 1968, Chapters 9, 10). The experimental control obtained in such designs provides great sensitivity with a reasonable constraint on test length.

Linear contrasts have come into common use in the experimental psychological literature, especially in the analysis of repeated-measures designs. Their use in test analysis as an alternative to subtest or factor scores holds considerable promise. To be sure, there are unsolved problems connected with item analysis and test reliability.

ADDENDUM

This volume has directed its attention to educational matters, and to the role of cognitive psychology in providing a better understanding of instructional processes. The preceding remarks on test procedures are directed toward educators. But for those readers whose interests are more directly related to cognitive psychology, I should point out again that the analysis of contrast scores has direct implications for tests of information-processing models. Since Sternberg's (1969) landmark paper on the use of factorial designs in evaluation of independent cognitive process models, repeated-measures designs have played a central role in research on cognition. The analysis of the variance–covariance structure of a set of contrasts described here is not covered by the standard methods of analysis now in use. These are new techniques. They ask new questions of data, questions which are critical to an understanding of individual differences in thought and action.

ACKNOWLEDGMENTS

Preparation of this chapter was supported by a grant from the Carnegie Corporation. I am grateful to Sol Pelavin and Rosedith Sitgreaves for their help and discussion with portions of this work, and to Linda Thompson, who conducted the line-drawing experiment.

As this chapter has evolved, I have become increasingly aware of the parallels between some of the concepts presented here and Cronbach's theory of generalizability (see Cronbach, Gleser, Nanda, & Rajaratnam, 1972).

3
Task Analysis in Instructional Design: Some Cases from Mathematics

Lauren B. Resnick

University of Pittsburgh
Learning Research and Development Center

This chapter takes as its general theme the actual and potential role of task analysis, particularly information-processing analysis, in instructional theory and instructional design. Some definitions are needed to make this opening statement sensible. The term "instruction" is used here in its most general sense to refer to any set of environmental conditions that are deliberately arranged to foster increases in competence. Instruction thus includes demonstrating, telling, and explaining, but it equally includes physical arrangements, structure of presented material, sequences of task demands, and responses to the learner's actions. A theory of instruction, therefore, must concern itself with the relationship between any modifications in the learning environment and resultant changes in competence. When the competence with which we are concerned is intellectual, development of a theory of instruction requires a means of describing states of intellectual competence, and ultimately of relating changes in these states to manipulations of the learning environment.

In developing a theory of instruction for intellectual or cognitive domains, task analysis plays a central role. I mean by task analysis the study of complex performances so as to reveal the psychological processes involved. These analyses translate "subject-matter" descriptions into psychological descriptions of behavior. They provide psychologically rich descriptions of intellectual competence and are thus a critical step in bringing the constructs of psychology to bear on instructional design.

Psychological analysis of complex tasks is not a totally new idea. Task analyses are performed, although not usually under that name, in virtually all psychological investigations of cognitive activity. Whenever performances are analyzed into components—for experimental, interpretive, or theoretical purposes—task analysis of some kind is involved. Although the study of complex cognitive tasks has never dominated empirical psychology, there have been significant occasions on which psychologists have turned their attention to such tasks. Not all have been instructional in intent, but several important attempts bear examination because they have substantially influenced instructional theory or practice, or because, considered with instructional questions in mind, they offer insight into the possible nature of a theory of instruction based on cognitive psychology.

Because task analysis is pervasive in psychological research, it is important to consider what kinds of analyses are particularly useful in instructional design. Several criteria can be used to evaluate the potential contribution to instruction of different approaches to the psychological analysis of tasks. Four such criteria seem particularly important:

Instructional relevance   Are the tasks analyzed ones we want to teach? That is, are the tasks studied because of their instructional or general social relevance, rather than because they are easy to study, have a history of past research that makes results easy to interpret, or are especially suited to elucidating a point of theory? The criterion of instructional relevance implies that most tasks analyzed will be complex relative to many of the laboratory tasks that experimental psychologists find useful when pursuing noninstructional questions.

Psychological formulation   Does the analysis yield descriptions of the task in terms of processes or basic units recognized by the psychological research community? Task analysis is a means of bringing complex tasks, which have generally resisted good experimental analysis, into contact with the concepts, methods, and theories of psychology. Thus, while the starting point for instructional task analysis is prescribed by social decisions—what is important to teach—the outcomes of such analysis, the terms used in breaking apart complex performances, must be determined by the state of theory and knowledge in psychology.

It is not always easy to fulfill both the instructional relevance and the psychological formulation criteria at once; instructional relevance is defined in different terms than those which psychological researchers use in building their theories. Nevertheless, it is important to try to analyze instructional tasks in terms that make contact with the current body of knowledge and constructs in psychology so that instructional practice can profit from scientific findings as they exist and as they develop.

Instructability   Because our concern here is with task analysis as an aid to instruction, an obvious question is whether the results of a particular analysis are useable in instructional practice. In other words, does the task analysis reveal elements of the task that lend themselves to instruction, i.e., that are "instructable?" It is the function of task analysis to examine complex performances and display in them a substructure that is teachable—either through direct instruction in the components, or by practice in tasks that call upon the same or related processes.

Recognition of stages of competence   Does the task analysis recognize a distinction between early forms of competence and later ones? Analyses for instructional purposes cannot *just* describe the expert's performance (although such description will almost always be a part of such analyses). They must also describe performance characteristics of novices and attempt to discover or point to key differences between novices and experts, suggesting thereby ways of arranging experiences that will help novices become experts. Instructional task analysis, in other words, should elucidate the relations between activity *during* learning and competence that *results from* learning. It should suggest ways of organizing knowledge to assist in acquisition, recognizing that this organization may differ from organizations that are most efficient for expert use of that knowledge.

In summary, four criteria can be applied in assessing the contributions of psychological task analyses to instruction: (1) instructional relevance; (2) psychological formulation; (3) instructability; and (4) recognition of stages of competence. In the course of this chapter, I shall examine several prominent approaches to the psychological analysis of complex tasks and consider their contributions to instruction in light of these criteria. I begin with some important past efforts to describe intellectual competence in psychological terms, and then turn to current information-processing approaches to task analysis. In order to make the domain of the chapter manageable, discussion is limited to analysis of mathematics tasks. The work discussed, however, is not intended to be exhaustive of task analysis efforts in mathematics. Rather, it is intended to highlight certain cases that have considerably influenced psychology or instruction, or both, and that form landmarks in whatever might today be written of a history and current status report on this branch of instructional psychology.

A SELECTIVE HISTORY OF TASK ANALYSIS

I will discuss first the work of three predecessors of modern information processing task analysis, in each case using work on mathematics as the substantive example. These are: (*a*) work in the associationist/behaviorist tradition (Thorndike, Gagné); (*b*) work of the Gestalt school (especially Max Wertheimer); and (*c*) the Piagetian task analyses. Both substantively and methodologically, the approaches of these groups to task analysis reflect differences in their theoretical positions, differences which in turn affect the kinds of contributions that each can make to instruction.

The Associationist/Behaviorist Tradition

Thorndike's analyses in terms of S–R bonds   In the early part of this century, experimental and educational psychology were closely allied. Many of the major psychologists of the period up to about 1930 were actively engaged in both laboratory research and applied research, some of it relevant to instructional practice. One of the foremost of these was Edward L. Thorndike. His work on *The Psychology of Arithmetic,* published in 1922, represents his attempt to translate the associationist theory of "laws of effect," which he himself was active in developing, into a set of prescriptions for teaching arithmetic. In the preface to the book, Thorndike states (1922) that there is now a "new point of view concerning the general process of learning. We now understand that learning is essentially the formation of connections or bonds between situations and responses, that the satisfyingness of the result is the force that forms them, and that habit rules in the realm of thought as truly and as fully as in the realm of action [p. v]." Based on this then widely agreed upon theory of psychological functioning, Thorndike proposed a pedagogy that has extensively influenced educational practice for many years.

Thorndike proposed the analysis of arithmetic tasks in terms of specific connections, or bonds, between sets of stimuli and responses, and the organiza- tion of instruction to maximize learning of both the individual bonds and the relations among them. His book began with a discussion of the general domains of arithmetic for which bonds must be formed—for example, the meanings of numbers, the nature of decimal notation, the ability to add, subtract, multiply, and divide, the ability to apply various concepts and operations in solving problems. Thorndike then spent some fifty pages discussing the types of bonds that give precise meaning to this broad definition of the domain of arithmetic. His analysis did not approach the level of individual stimulus–response pairs but remained on the more general level of connections between situations and sets of responses. Citing numerous examples, he argued that certain kinds of bonds taught in many of the standard textbooks of the day were misleading and should not be taught, while other helpful bonds were neglected in pedagogical practice. For example, verifying results of computations, learning addition and substrac- tion facts for fractions, and solving problems in equation form (even before algebra was added to the curriculum) were considered "desirable" bonds, where- as senseless drill in finding the lowest common denominator of fractions (when use of *any* common denominator would lead to solution of problems) and the posing of problems unrelated to real-life situations led to the formation of "wasteful and harmful" bonds that made arithmetic confusing and unpleasant. Discussion of appropriate and inappropriate forms of measurement of the bonds or elements of arithmetic knowledge were also included. Thus, the total effect of the book was to suggest the translation of a standard school subject into terms—collections of bonds—that suggested applications of known laws of learn- ing to the problems of instruction.

The laws of learning, and thus of pedagogy, were for Thorndike those dealing with such drill and practice as would strengthen the bonds. Questions such as amount of practice, under- and overlearning, and distribution of practice were considered. These are easily recognized as topics that have continued to occupy psychologists—although rarely directly in the context of school instruction—and that heavily though indirectly influence instructional practice. What is important about Thorndike's work, however, is that he developed a concern not only with the laws of learning in general, but also with the laws of learning as applied to a particular discipline, arithmetic. He left the laboratory to engage in applied research, but brought with him the theory, and to a large extent the methodology, of the experimental laboratory. He thus began a tradition of experimental work in instruction by psychologists. This tradition was interrupted for many years but is now being revived, as the chapters in this volume bear witness.

Gagné's hierarchies of learning sets   While Thorndike recognized the need for a theory of sequencing in his presentation of bonds identified as constituting the subject matter of arithmetic, he had no systematic theory of sequencing to propose. In the decades following Thorndike's work, mathematics educators and educational psychologists (e.g., Brownell & Stretch, 1931; Hydle & Clapp, 1927) studied, with varying degrees of care and precision, the relative difficulty of different kinds of mathematical problems. They thus empirically, if not theoretically, extended Thorndike's work in instructional analysis. The suggestion underlying this later work was that arranging tasks according to their order of difficulty would optimize learning, especially of the more difficult tasks. Skinner's (1953) prescription for the use of "successive approximations" in instruction represented a refinement of this basic idea. However, neither Skinner nor his immediate interpreters proposed a systematic strategy for generating the order of successive approximations—i.e., the sequence of tasks in instruction. It was not until the 1960s, and Gagné's work on hierarchies of learning (Gagné, 1962, 1968), that any organized theory of sequencing for instructional purposes appeared within the behaviorist tradition.

Learning hierarchies are nested sets of tasks in which positive transfer from simpler to more complex tasks is expected. The "simpler" tasks in a hierarchy are not just easier to learn than the more complex; they are included in— components of—the more complex ones. Acquisition of a complex capability, then, is a matter of cumulation of capabilities through successive levels of complexity. Transfer occurs because of the inclusion of simpler tasks in the more complex. Thus, learning hierarchies embody a special version of a "common elements" theory of transfer.

Hierarchy analysis has come into rather widespread use among instructional designers, particularly in the fields of mathematics and science (see White, 1973). For the most part, the analyses have been of the kind Gagné originally described. Thus, hierarchies for instruction are typically generated by answering, for any particular task under consideration, the question: "What kind of capability would an individual have to possess to be able to perform this task successfully, were we to give him or her only instructions?" One or more subordinate tasks are specified in response to this question, and the question is applied in turn to the subordinate tasks themselves.

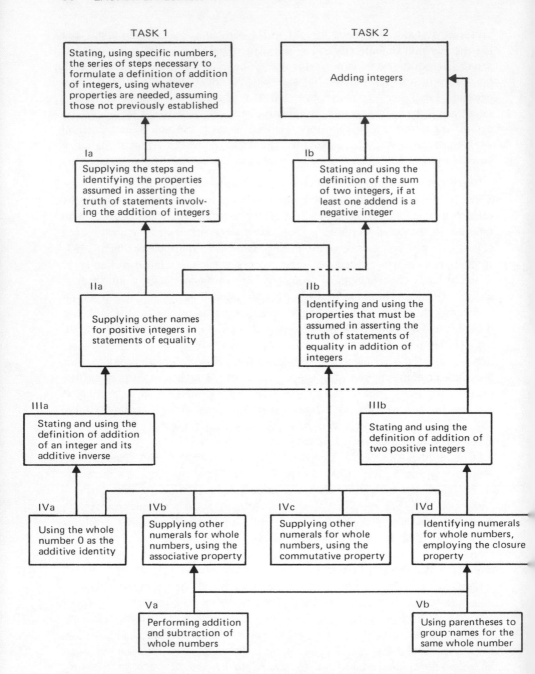

FIG. 1   A learning hierarchy pertaining to the addition of integers. (From "Factors in acquiring knowledge of a mathematical task" by R. M. Gagné, J. R. Mayor, H. L. Garstens, & N. E. Paradise, *Psychological Monographs,* 1962, **76** (Whole No. 526). Copyright 1962 by the American Psychological Association. Reprinted by permission.)

Figure 1 shows an example of one of Gagné's hierarchies. The tasks described in the top-level box are the targets for instruction. Lower levels show successive layers of subordinate capabilities, that is, simpler tasks whose mastery would facilitate learning the more complex ones. Instruction would begin with the lowest-level capabilities not already mastered and proceed upward. The tasks at the low end of the hierarchy can be analyzed further, depending on assumptions about the learner's knowledge. It is assumed that the more elementary capabilities are learned through more elementary types of learning. In other words, implicit in a complete learning hierarchy for a task such as the one shown in Fig. 1 is another hierarchy of "types of learning," progressing from simple S–R learning, through chaining and discrimination, to higher-level concept and rule learning, as shown in Fig. 2. A more complex task such as problem solving would

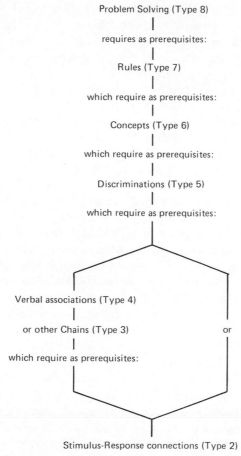

Problem Solving (Type 8)

requires as prerequisites:

Rules (Type 7)

which require as prerequisites:

Concepts (Type 6)

which require as prerequisites:

Discriminations (Type 5)

which require as prerequisites:

Verbal associations (Type 4)

or other Chains (Type 3)   or

which require as prerequisites:

Stimulus-Response connections (Type 2)

FIG. 2 Gagné's hierarchy of types of learning. (From R. M. Gagné, *The Conditions of learning* (2nd ed.), New York: Holt, Rinehart & Winston, 1970. Copyright 1965 by Holt, Rinehart & Winston. Reprinted by permission.)

involve more concept and rule learning and would lead to the discovery of progressively higher-order generalizable rules.

Gagné's hierarchy analyses appear to flirt with information-processing conceptions of psychology, but not to come to grips with them. There is a kind of implicit process analysis involved in the method of hierarchy generation. Presumably, in order to answer the question that generates subordinate tasks, one must have in mind some idea of what kinds of operations—mental or otherwise—an individual engages in when he or she performs the complex task. However, this model of performance is left entirely implicit in Gagné's work.

Gestalt Psychology and the Analysis of Mathematical Tasks

Gestalt psychology was an immigrant in America. In its first generation it spoke a language so unlike the rest of American psychology that it was barely listened to. Now, in a period when we speak easily of cognition and mental operations, the gestalt formulations take on more interest for us. Gestalt theory was fundamentally concerned with perception and particularly the apprehension of "structure." With respect to the complex processes involved in thinking, the concept of structure led to a concern with "understanding" or "insight," often accompanied by a visual representation of some kind. With respect to problem solving, the central concern was with the dynamics of "productive thinking." Several gestalt psychologists, particularly Wertheimer (1959) and his students (Katona, 1940; Luchins & Luchins, 1970), attempted to apply the basic principles of gestalt interpretation to problems of instruction and, in particular, to the teaching of mathematics. It is reasonable to imagine that mathematics, especially geometry, was of particular interest to gestalt theorists because of its high degree of internal structure and its susceptibility to visual representation.

Wertheimer contrasted his theory of productive thinking both with traditional logic and with associationist descriptions of problem solving. Neither of these, he claimed, gives a complete picture of how *new* knowledge is produced by the individual. With respect to teaching, he was concerned that prevalent methods of teaching, with emphasis on practice and recall, produced "senseless combinations" rather than productive problem solving based on the structure of the problem.

Wertheimer's (1959) book, *Productive Thinking*, originally published in 1945, discusses work on several mathematics problems—for example, finding the area of a parallelogram, proving the equality of angles, Gauss's formula for the sum of a series, symmetry of oscillations, arithmetic calculations, and the sum of angles of a figure. Analysis of these tasks, for Wertheimer, consisted of displaying the problem structure on which algorithms are based, rather than analyzing actual performance. Thus, for example, the problem of finding the area of a parallelogram was seen as a problem of "gap fitting"—too much on one side, too little on the other (see Fig. 3). Once the gap is filled and a rectangle formed, a general principle for finding area can be applied. It is recognition of the nature of the

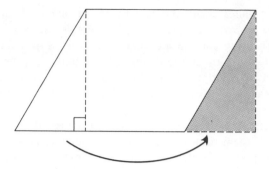

FIG. 3   Wertheimer's area of a parallelogram problem.

problem—the possibility of transforming the parallelogram into a rectangle—that constitutes for Wertheimer "understanding" or "insight." Solutions that follow from this understanding are for him true solutions, elegant ones. Those that "blindly" apply an algorithm, even if the algorithm should work, are "ugly" (Greeno, Chapter 7 of this volume, discusses another example from Wertheimer).

Though Wertheimer talked little about general schemes for instruction, his notions imply the necessity of analyzing tasks into components, perceptual and structural, such that their nature in relation to the whole problem is clear. Only when the true structures of problems are understood can principles derived from them be properly generalized. Whenever possible, it should be left to the student to discover both the problem and its solution. Instruction, if it should be necessary, should proceed in a way consistent with the internal structure of the problem, and in the proper sequence, so that a true understanding is gained by the child, leading to solution. Just how the understanding of components and their part—whole relationships is to be taught is not made clear. Wertheimer suggested that exercises could be introduced which focus students' attention on certain aspects of the problem structure, which should increase the likelihood of achieving insight. He also spoke of certain operations involved in thinking processes—grouping, reorganizing, structurization—from which one might devise ways of teaching.

Piagetian Analyses

In discussing Piagetian task analysis we must consider two quite distinct bodies of literature: (1) Piaget's own work (and that of others in Geneva); and (2) attempts—largely by American and British psychologists—to isolate the specific concepts and processes underlying performance on Piagetian tasks. I will discuss these in succession.

Genevan work   Much of Piaget's own work (on number, geometry, space, etc.) is heavily mathematical in orientation. It seeks to characterize cognitive development in terms of a succession of logical structures commanded by individuals over time. The "clinical method" used by Piaget in his research yields great quantities of raw process data—protocols of children's responses to various tasks and questions. The protocols are interpreted in terms of the child's "having" or "not having" structures of different kinds. Explanation of a task performance for Piaget consists of descriptions of the logical structures that underly it, and of the structures that ontologically preceded and therefore in a sense "gave birth to" the current ones.

Piaget's tasks are chosen to exemplify logical structures that are assumed to be universal. Many of them turn out to involve mathematics, but by and large not the mathematics that is taught in school. One result has been considerable debate over whether the Piagetian tasks should become the basis of the school curriculum, whether they are teachable at all, and whether they set limits on what other mathematical content can be taught (for differing points of view on this matter, see Furth, 1970; Kamii, 1972; Kohlberg, 1968; Rohwer, 1971). Although until recently Piaget's work has not been motivated by instructional concerns, others have tried to interpret his work for instruction. This has often resulted in at least partially competing interpretations.

Piaget's most important contribution to task analysis is probably his pointing out, in compelling fashion, that there are important differences between children and adults in the way they approach certain tasks, the knowledge they bring to them, and the processes they have available. However, his analysis in terms of logic leaves questionable the extent to which his descriptions elucidate the "*psycho*logics" of behavior on these tasks, that is, what people actually *do*. It is certainly the case that for psychologists accustomed to the explicit detail of information-processing analyses, the leap from observation to references concerning logical structure is often difficult to follow in Piaget's work.

Experimental analyses of Piaget's tasks.   Much of the English-language research literature on Piaget has focused on locating specific concepts or component processes underlying the ability to perform well on particular tasks. Conservation tasks have been mostly heavily studied, classification tasks probably next most heavily. There has been relatively little study of tasks characteristic of the stage of formal rather than concrete operational thinking (see Glaser & Resnick, 1972).

Two basic strategies can be distinguished in this research. One is to vary the task in small ways to allow inferences about the kinds of cognitive processes being used. An example of this first strategy is a series of studies by Smedslund (1964, 1967a, b), in which he presented double classification tasks with attributes covered or uncovered, labeled or visually presented. From performance on these variations, he concluded that processing was probably done at a symbolic rather than a perceptual level, that memory was involved, and that some kind of analytic mechanism might be involved in committing perceptions or symbols to memory.

The second research strategy is to instruct children in a concept or process hypothesized to underly performance on some Piagetian task, and then test to see whether they thereby acquire the ability to perform the task. Examples of research of the second kind are Gelman's (1969) study on training conservation by teaching discrimination of length, density, and number; and Bearison's (1969) study inducing conservation by training in equal-unit measurement of liquid quantity. Of the two approaches, the second is more directly interesting in the present context, because the strategy of instruction demands an analysis in terms of instructable components.

Assessment of the Approaches with Reference to Instruction

How do these past approaches to task analysis match the criteria outlined for instructional relevance? To what extent does each address itself to tasks of instructional interest? To what extent do the terms of analysis provide a link to the main body of psychological theory and knowledge? Are instructable units identified? Do the analyses distinguish usefully between performance of learners and of experts?

Instructional relevance. With respect to the choice of tasks, only Thorndike and Gagné show a clear instructional orientation. Their tasks are drawn from school curricula, and where formal validation studies of their analyses occur, they are to a large extent based on the effectiveness of actual instruction in the units identified (e.g., Gagné, Mayor, Garstens, & Paradise, 1962). Wertheimer and the others of the Gestalt school analyze a few tasks drawn from mathematics, but make no attempt to analyze a whole range of subject matter. Further, despite some discussion of productive thinking as a generalized phenomenon of educational concern, there is no analysis of it as such in Wertheimer's work. It seems likely that Wertheimer chose tasks from mathematics that would best lend themselves to analysis in terms of perceptual "Gestalten" rather than selecting those of particular importance to instruction. On the criterion of types of tasks analyzed, Piaget's work is even less directly relevant to instruction. There is, in fact, serious question whether the concrete operations tasks he studied ought to be the objects of instruction, since they are psychological "indicators" of general cognitive status rather than socially important tasks, and since they appear, at least in Western and certain urbanized cultures, to be acquired without formal schooling in the course of development (Glaser & Resnick, 1972). It may be, however, that formal operations need to be taught explicitly, since it is by no means clear that formal operational thinking is universally acquired (Neimark, 1975).

Psychological formulation. Each approach addresses well the analysis of complex tasks in terms of the fundamental psychological constructs relevant to their own times and theories. Thus, Thorndike's analyses describe arithmetic in terms of the basic psychological unit of then-current theory, the associationist bond, and thus suggest specific pedagogical practices drawn from known principles of learning. Gagné's analyses interpret instructional tasks in the terms of behavioral learning psychology: transfer, generalization, and so forth. His concern for the learning of "higher processes" such as rules and principles suggests some sharing of concern with cognitive psychology; however, basic cognitive processes, such as memory and perception, are alluded to only as general abilities assumed not to be instructable or further analyzable. Wertheimer's analyses of mathematical tasks explicitly indicate how gestalt field theory would interpret problem solving and learning in these domains. Finally, Piaget's analyses, like Wertheimer's, attempt to show that performance on complex tasks can be interpreted in terms of underlying structures. For Piaget and Wertheimer, explication of the structures constitutes psychological explanation of the performance. Both are concerned with characterizing the broad outlines of cognitive structures rather than with detailing the *processes* involved in building or utilizing these structures. Only in the experimental analyses of Piagetian tasks do we begin to find attempts to interpret performance more explicitly, that is, in information-processing terms.

Instructability. With respect to the criterion of instructability, Thorndike and Gagné are directly on target. Their aim in task analysis is to facilitate instruction, and the bonds or subordinate capabilities identified are quite clearly described as instructable components. Wertheimer is more difficult to assess with respect to this criterion. His analyses are specific to particular tasks. They do display the basic structure of each task and therefore suggest quite directly ways of teaching that are likely to produce maximum understanding, transfer, and elegance of solution; but there are no general units identified which would be useful across a number of tasks. Piaget's own analyses involve no identification of instructable units. However, a review of studies involving instruction in Piagetian tasks (Glaser & Resnick, 1972) suggests that Piagetian concepts are indeed instructable, or at least lend themselves to analysis into certain prerequisite skills which may be instructable. The studies also suggest how delicate the process of task analysis and instruction is for tasks of any psychological complexity. It is necessary both to identify the appropriate underlying processes or concepts and to find effective ways of teaching them. Identifying one underlying concept will rarely suffice for full success in instructional efforts because there may be several abilities which must be combined, and the absence of any one may lead to failure to learn the target task. Further, "instruction" itself is a very delicate matter. There are no simple rules for constructing situations that will convey the concepts or processes to be taught in a clear way. Even with an appropriate task analysis, the mapping from identified components to instructional strategies remains very much a matter of artful development.

Recognition of stages of competence. Finally, we turn to the novice–expert distinction, the criterion of recognition of stages of competence. On this matter

Thorndike is not very explicit. He recognizes a need for sequencing instruction scientifically, but offers no psychological theory as to how to proceed. Indeed, the impression left is that the difference between novices and experts lies solely in how many bonds have been learned and how well-practiced these are. That there may be important differences in the organization of knowledge for novices and experts is at best only hinted, and not seriously explored. Gagné's particular contribution within the behavioral perspective is a practical method for generating sequences of instructable tasks. In his general notion of transfer—inclusion of simple tasks in more complex ones—Gagné offers a strong suggestion for how to organize instruction for purposes of acquiring higher-order knowledge and skills. Thus, at a certain level, the criterion of recognizing and dealing with differences between novices and experts is explicitly met in learning-hierarchy analyses. Wertheimer's analyses, by contrast, attend not at all to the distinction between novices and experts. The implicit assumption is that behavior in accord with good structural principles is "native" and has simply been stamped out or squelched by the drill orientation of schools.

Piaget, of course, is particularly attuned to changes in the structures available to people at different stages in their intellectual development. In fact, with respect to instruction, Piaget's largest contribution is very possibly the highlighting of substantive changes in competence which occur in the course of development. Piaget's work makes it impossible to ignore differences between performance strategies of novices and experts—whether or not we find Piaget's own analyses convincing or accept his explanations of how these changes occur. By contrast, the experimental or neo-Piagetian work is uneven on this criterion. For the most part, these studies investigate single tasks and look for competence versus incompetence rather than for stages or transformations of competence. There are a few exceptions, largely in recent attempts to interpret changes in performance on Piagetian tasks in terms of information-processing constructs (see Klahr, in press). Investigators have attempted to analyze sequences of Piagetian tasks so that adding one or two simple processes to an individual's repertoire, or modifying extant processes, can be shown to account for successively more complex performances on the Piagetian tasks. This work takes "information processing" as its theoretical orientation and makes heavy use of computer simulation strategies for formal analyses. It thus forms a useful bridge to the second part of this chapter, which is concerned specifically with the present and potential role of information-processing task analysis in instructional design.

INFORMATION-PROCESSING ANALYSES
FOR INSTRUCTIONAL PURPOSES

A major branch of cognitive psychology today carries the label "information processing." As is often the case with an emerging branch of study, it is easier to point to examples of information-processing research than to give a complete or consensual definition of it. Nevertheless, psychologists working in this area tend to share certain assumptions as well as certain research strategies.

Information-processing studies attempt to account for performance on cognitive tasks in terms of actions (internal or external) that take place in a temporally ordered flow. A distinction is generally drawn between data, or *information,* and operations on data, or *processes.* Thus, the concern of information-processing psychology is with how humans act upon (process) data (information). Frequently—but not universally—information-processing models for cognitive tasks are expressed as "programs" for performance of particular tasks. These are often formalized as computer programs whose theoretical validity is judged by their ability to simulate actual human performance.

Most information-processing theories and models find it useful to characterize the human mind in terms of the way information is stored, accessed, and operated upon. Distinctions are made among different kinds or "levels" of memory. While the details and the labels vary, most theories distinguish between a sensory intake register of some kind through which information from the environment enters the system, a working memory (sometimes called short-term or intermediate-term memory) in which the actual processing work goes on, and a long-term (semantic) memory in which everything one knows is stored, probably permanently. Within this general structure, working memory is pivotal. It is only by being processed in working memory that material from the external environment can enter the individual's long-term store of knowledge, and only by entering working memory can information from the long-term store be accessed and used in the course of thinking. Processing in working memory is usually assumed to be serial—one action at a time. Further, working memory is considered to have a limited number of "slots" that can be filled, so that it is only by rehearsing or by "chunking" material into larger units (so that a body of interrelated information takes up a single slot) that loss of information from working memory can be avoided.

Information-processing analyses of instructional tasks share these general assumptions as well as a body of research methods that have been developed for testing the validity of models of cognitive performance. Information-processing analyses are clearly distinguished from behaviorist ones (Thorndike and Gagné in the present case) by their explicit attempts to describe *internal* processing. They differ from the cognitivist Gestalt and Piagetian positions in their attempts to describe the actual flow of performance—to translate "restructuring" or "logical operations" into temporally organized sequences of actions.

In characterizing information-processing analyses of complex tasks, it is useful to distinguish between rational and empirical analyses. Rational analyses are descriptions of "idealized" performances—that is, performances that succeed in responding to task demands, often in highly efficient ways, but not necessarily the ways in which humans actually perform the tasks. Work in artificial intelligence can be considered a form of rational task analysis which is today being applied to increasingly complex kinds of tasks. So can some much less ambitious analyses of simple tasks, some of which are discussed below. Empirical task analyses are based on interpretation of the data (errors, latencies, self-reports, eye or hand movements, etc.) from human performance of a task; the aim of such analyses is to develop a description (model) of processes that would account for those data. In practice, rational and empirical analyses are rarely sharply separated. Rational analyses, for example, may provide the starting point for empirical data collection, leading to an iterative process in which successively closer matches to human performance models are made. Nevertheless, the distinction is a useful one in considering the kinds of investment in information-processing analysis that will be most valuable for instruction.

In the remainder of this chapter, I consider information-processing analyses of several of these kinds. I describe first some of our work in rational process analysis, work that was explicitly concerned with instructional design require-ments. Next, I describe some empirical analyses of the same kinds of relatively simple tasks, and consider the relationship between rational and empirical analysis for instructional purposes. In a final section, I consider the problem of more complex tasks—problem solving, reasoning, tasks that we use as measures of "intelligence" and aptitude—and what the role of formal simulations and empirically studied information process models might be for instruction in such domains.

Rational Task Analysis for Curriculum Design

Rational task analysis can be defined as an attempt to specify processes or procedures that would be used in highly efficient performance of some task. The result is a detailed description of an "idealized" performance—one that solves the problem in minimal moves, does little "backtracking," makes few or no errors. Typically a rational task analysis is derived from the structure of the subject matter and makes few explicit assumptions about the limitations of human memory capacity or perceptual encoding processes. In many cases informal rational task analysis of this kind can serve as a way of prescribing what to teach (i.e., teach children to perform the processes laid out in the analyses), and instructional effectiveness serves as a partial validation of the analysis.

In order to convey the flavor and intent of rational process analysis as applied to instruction, I will describe in some detail part of our own early work on simple arithmetic tasks. This work grew initially out of an attempt to apply learning hierarchy theory to the problem of designing a preschool and kinder-garten mathematics curriculum. We found it necessary, in order to secure agreement among our staff on the probable ordering of tasks, to introduce a method in which the processes hypothesized to be involved in a particular task performance were explicitly laid out (see Resnick, Wang, & Kaplan, 1973). Figures 4 and 5 show examples of the analyses that resulted. The top box in

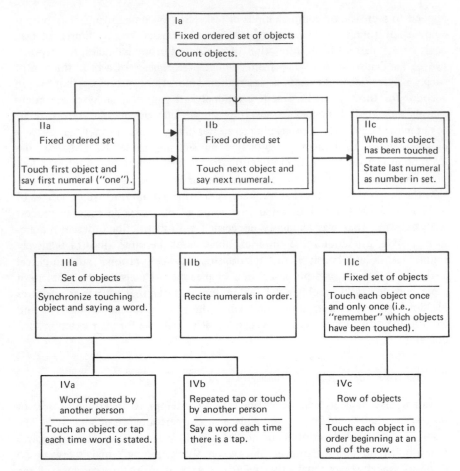

FIG. 4   Analysis of Objective 1-2:C, "Given a fixed ordered set of objects, the child can count the objects." (From "Task analysis in curriculum design: A hierarchically sequenced introductory mathematics curriculum" by L. B. Resnick, M. C. Wang, & J. Kaplan, *Journal of Applied Behavior Analysis*, 1973, 6, 679–710. Copyright 1973 by the Society for the Experimental Analysis of Behavior. Reprinted by permission.)

each figure shows the task being analyzed, the entry above the line describing the presented stimulus and the entry below the line the expected response. The second row in each figure shows a hypothesized sequence of behaviors engaged in as the presented task is performed. Arrows indicate a temporally organized procedure or routine. The lower portions of the charts identify capabilities that are thought to be either necessary to performance (i.e., prerequisite to) or helpful in learning (i.e., propaedutic to) the main task. The identified prerequisite and propaedutic tasks were used to build hierarchies of objectives that formed the basis of a curriculum.

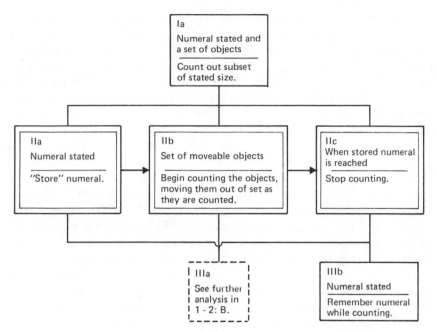

FIG. 5 Analysis of Objective 1-2:E, "Given a numeral stated and a set of objects, the child can count out a subset of stated size." (From "Task analysis in curriculum design: A hierarchically sequenced introductory mathematics curriculum" by L. B. Resnick, M. C. Wang, & J. Kaplan, *Journal of Applied Behavior Analysis,* 1973, **6**, 679–710. Copyright 1973 by the Society for the Experimental Analysis of Behavior. Reprinted by permission.)

At the outset, the process analyses functioned for us as aids in developing prescriptions for instruction. We carried out the kind of research that seemed most directly relevant to that prescriptive function. That is, we looked at the extent to which the analyses generated valid task sequences, sequences which aided learning of the most complex tasks in the set. Two research strategies were involved. First, we conducted scaling studies. In these studies, tests on a number of tasks were given to a sample of the children prior to instruction, and the results were evaluated for the extent to which the tests formed a Guttman scale in accord with the predicted prerequisite relations (e.g., Wang, 1973; Wang, Resnick, & Boozer, 1971). A good approximation to a Guttman scale implied strong prerequisite relations among the tasks—relations that specified optimal teaching orders. A second set of studies (Caruso & Resnick, 1971; Resnick, Siegel, & Kresh, 1971) involved more direct assessment of transfer relations among small sets of tasks. Tasks in a small hierarchy were taught in simple-to-complex and complex-to-simple orders. We then looked at transfer effects on trials to criterion and related measures. These studies showed that teaching in hierarchical sequence was the best way of assuring that most or all of the children in a group learned all the objectives. For the minority who were capable of learning the more complex objectives without intervening instruction, however, "skipping" of prerequisites was a faster way to learn. What these children apparently did was to acquire the prerequisites in the course of learning the more complex tasks. An important instructional question raised by these results is whether we can match instructional strategies to individuals' relative ability to learn on their own—that is, without going through direct instruction in all of the steps of a hierarchy. Before we are likely to answer that question well, however, we will probably need more systematic theories than we now have available of how learning occurs with minimal instruction (cf. Resnick & Glaser, in press).

The kind of task analysis used in these studies served to describe performance in temporally organized sequences and to identify general information-processing abilities, such as perceptual processing (e.g., Fig. 4, IIIc and IVc), memory (e.g., Fig. 5, IIa and IIc), and temporal synchrony (e.g., Fig. 4, IIIa), that are called on in performing a specific complex task. As formal information-processing models, however, the analyses were incomplete because they did not specify every step (for example, stop rules were not typically specified where recursive loops occurred) nor did they explicitly deal with overall control mechanisms or total memory load. In addition, they were not empirically verified as process analyses. Although many observations of performance were made, there was no attempt to match predicted or "ideal" performance against actual performances. The hierarchy tests confirmed the validity of the task sequencing decisions made on the basis of the analyses, but they did not necessarily confirm the details of the analyses. Performance strategies different from those in our analyses might have produced similar sequences of acquisition or transfer effects. Thus, while the scaling and transfer studies met instructional needs quite well, they did not constitute validations of the models' details. For this purpose, the strategies of empirical task analysis are needed.

Empirical Analyses of Specific Tasks

What can empirical analyses suggest about teaching specific tasks? An obvious possibility is that we might use process models of competent performance as direct specifications for what to teach. Such models of skilled performance are potentially powerful. However, these alone do not take into account the capabilities of the learner as he or she enters the instructional situation. I want to describe some experiments we have done that suggest a more indirect relationship between what is taught and how skilled performance proceeds. The experiments suggest that what we teach children and how they perform a relatively short time after instruction are not identical—but neither are they unrelated. They suggest that children seek simplifying procedures that lead them to construct, or "invent," more efficient routines that might be quite difficult to teach directly.

Subtraction In one study (Woods, Resnick, & Groen, 1975) we examined simple subtraction processes (e.g., 5 − 4 = ?) in second- and fourth-graders. The method was borrowed from Groen and others' work on simple addition processes (Groen & Parkman, 1972) and open-sentence equations (Groen & Poll, 1973). That is, we gave children a set of subtraction problems to perform and collected response latencies. Five possible models for performing subtraction problems (of the form $m − n$ = ?; with $0 < m \leqslant 9, 0 \leqslant n < 9$) were hypothesized, and predicted response latencies for each problem for each performance model were worked out based on the number of steps that would be required according to the model. Regression analysis was then used to fit observed to predicted latency functions and thus select the model an individual child was using.

Of five models tested, two accounted for the performance of all but a few subjects:

Decrementing model. Set a counter to m, decrease it n times, then "read" counter. For this model, latencies should rise as a function of the value of n, and the slope of the regression line should reflect the speed of each decrementing operation. This function is shown in Fig. 6.

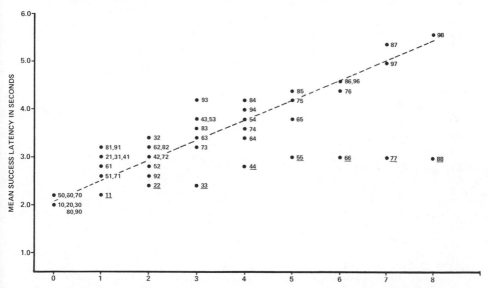

FIG. 6 Plot of reaction times for second-graders solving subtraction problems of the form $m − n$ = ?: Decrementing Model. Numbers beside solid dots denote actual problems (e.g., •54, 65 signifies that problems 5 − 4 and 6 − 5 both had a mean success latency specified by the •). Underlined problems were omitted in the regression analysis. (From "An experimental test of five process models for subtraction" by S. S. Woods, L. B. Resnick, & G. J. Groen, *Journal of Educational Psychology*, 1975, 67(1), 17–21. Copyright 1975 by the American Psychological Association. Reprinted by permission.)

Choice model. Depending on which has fewer steps, perform *either* the decrementing routine (previously described) or another in which a counter is set to n and is then *incremented* until the counter reading matches m. The number of increments is then "read" as the answer. For this model, it is necessary to assume a process of choosing whether to "increment up" or "decrement down." We assume that the choice process takes the same amount of time regardless of the values of m and n. On this assumption, latencies should rise as a function of whichever is smaller, n or $(m - n)$. This function is shown in Fig. 7.

Individual data were analyzed first and a best-fit model selected for each child. Then children were grouped according to the model they fit, and the pooled data were analyzed. All fourth-graders and most second-graders were best fit by the choice model. It seems unlikely that during their arithmetic training the children had been directly taught the choice model for solving subtraction problems. The procedure involved would be difficult to communicate verbally to 6- and 7-year-olds, and might confuse rather than enlighten children at the point of their first exposure to subtraction. Most probably, the children had been taught initially to construct the m set (increment the counter m times), count out the n set (decrement n times), and then count ("read out") the remainder. This algorithm is close to the one described as the decrementing model. The

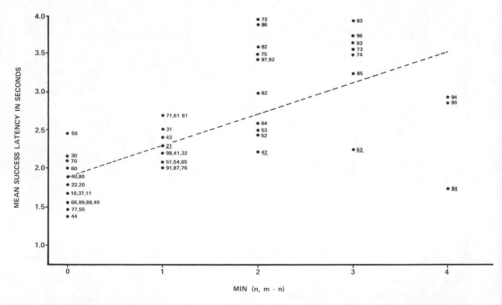

FIG. 7 Plot of reaction times for second-graders solving subtraction problems: Choice Model. MIN $(n, m - n)$ reads "the smaller of n and $(m - n)$." From "An experimental test of five process models for subtraction" by S. S. Woods, L. B. Resnick, & G. J. Groen, *Journal of Educational Psychology,* 1975, **67**(1), 17–21. Copyright 1975 by the American Psychological Association. Reprinted by permission.)

decrementing model is in fact derivable from the algorithm we assume is typically taught, by simply dropping the steps of constructing the m set and actually counting the remainder. Thus, it seems reasonable that a child would develop the decrementing model quite quickly. The choice model, however, cannot be derived from the teaching algorithm in so direct a way. Instead, an invention (the possibility of counting up from n) must be made. This invention is probably based on observation of the relations between numbers in addition and subtraction over a large number of instances. Yet the invention appears to have been made as early as the end of second grade by most of the children.

Addition In another study, Guy Groen and I have been looking more directly at the relation between the algorithm taught and later performance. In the subtraction study we could only guess at what children had been taught, based on our general knowledge of elementary school practice. In the addition study, we controlled the teaching by doing it ourselves. We taught 4-year-olds to solve single-digit problems of the form $m + n = ?$ (where m and n ranged from 0 to 5) by using the following algorithm: (a) count out m blocks; (b) count out n blocks; (c) combine the subsets; and (d) count the combined set. We then kept the children coming back for about two practice sessions a week for many weeks. As soon as each child was performing the addition process smoothly using blocks, we took the blocks away and asked the children to give their answers on a device that allowed us to collect latency data. The children's typical response when blocks were removed was to begin counting out sets on their fingers. Eventually, however, most shifted to internal processing.

Earlier work by Suppes and Groen (1967) had shown that by the end of the first grade, most children added using a choice-type model in which they set a counter to m or n, whichever was larger, and then incremented by the smaller of the two numbers. This is known as the *min* (minimum) model [because the latencies fit min (m, n)]. A few children used a model of incrementing m times, then incrementing n more times, and then reading the counter. We call this the *sum* model [latencies fit $(m + n)$]. The sum model can be derived from the procedure we taught by simply dropping steps (c) and (d) of our algorithm, and it requires no choice. The *min* model, however, requires an invention based on the recognition that sums are the same regardless of the order in which numbers are added, and that it is faster to increment by the smaller quantity.

For five of the six children whose data have been analyzed thus far, it is clear that by the final two test sessions the *min* model gave significant and "best" fit. In general, the trend over blocks of trials was for subjects to be fit well by the *min* model as soon as they stopped counting overtly on most of the trials. It is as if these children discovered commutativity as soon as they were confident enough to stop counting on their fingers!

In the studies just reported children are taught a routine which is derived from the subject matter. After some practice—but no additional direct instruction—

they perform a different routine, one that is more efficient. The efficiency is a result of fewer steps (not, apparently, faster performance of component operations), which in turn requires a choice or decision on the part of the child. A strictly algorithmic routine, in other words, is converted into another routine which turns out to solve the presented problem more efficiently.

A similar finding has been reported by Wallace (1972) in a study of information-processing models of class inclusion. After having received training in the processes revealed by an information-processing analysis, subjects were presented a typical class inclusion task in which they were asked to tell, for example, "Which is more, the red ones or the triangles?" They had been taught to pass through the object array twice, each time quantifying the objects on one of the different value dimensions named and then comparing them to determine which was more. At the posttest administered immediately after training, it was found that some of the children were able to perform the task more efficiently by quantifying on the first pass only objects having only one of the dimensions named by the experimenter. For example, Wallace presented a subject with eight triangles, seven of which were red and one green. Asked "Which is more, the red ones or the triangles?," one subject answered, "There's one green triangle and that makes it more triangles" (Wallace, 1972, pp. 15–16). Since in the class inclusion task the set having only one of the named dimensions is usually the minor subset, this procedure quickly yields the answer. It seems likely that a phenomenon of this kind, that is, the transformation of algorithms by the learner, is more general than we have thought up to now. At least some process data that appear difficult to interpret when averaged over time may show interpretable regularity when early and later phases of performance are examined separately.

Task Structure, Skilled Performance, and Teaching Routines

What are the implications of findings of this kind for instruction? On the face of it, it would seem that we ought to abandon the algorithmic routines suggested by rational task analysis in favor of directly teaching the more environmentally responsive processes that appear to characterize even semiskilled performance. We ought, in other words, to conclude that the initial rational analyses are wrong, since they do not match skilled performance, and that they should therefore not be used in instruction. Rather, we should perform detailed empirical analyses of skilled performance on all of the tasks that a curriculum comprises, and teach directly the routines uncovered in the course of such analysis.

Such a conclusion, I believe, would be mistaken. It rests on the assumption that efficient instruction is *necessarily* direct instruction in skilled performance strategies—rather than instruction in routines that put learners in a good position to discover or invent efficient strategies for themselves. That is what the children did in the studies just reported. They learned a routine but then invented a more efficient performance for themselves. It seems reasonable to suppose—although empirical tests comparing different instructional strategies are needed to draw a strong conclusion—that the teaching routines in these studies were good ones, because they taught the specific skills in a way that called upon children's discovery and invention abilities

To put the case in its most general form, it would seem useful to think in terms of a "triangulation" between the *structure* of a task as defined by the subject matter, the *performance* of skilled individuals on a task, and a *teaching or acquisition routine* that helps novices learn the task. There are three terms in this conceptualization; all three must stand in strong relation to each of the others—thus the image of triangulation. This relationship is schematized in Fig. 8. Most empirical information-processing analyses have been concerned with the relationship between the elements defining the base of the triangle—that is, with the relationship between the structure of the subject matter, or "task environment" (A), and performance (C). Thus, most information-processing task analyses are state theories, describing performance on a given kind of task at a given point in learning or development, but not attempting to account for acquisition of the performance. The rational process analyses that we have developed in the course of our instructional work have been concerned primarily with the structure of the task (A) and an idealized routine that represents the subject matter well and thus prescribes a good teaching routine (B). Our validation studies have in effect been tests of the extent to which the teaching routines and sequences derived through these analyses succeeded in conveying the subject

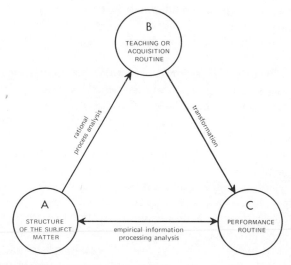

FIG. 8 Relations between teaching routines, performance routines, and structure of subject matter.

matter to learners. The discussion in the past several pages has been concerned with the relationships between teaching routines (B) and performance routines (C). Gaining understanding of the "transformation" processes that link these two routines is a necessary step in completing the triangulation that puts information-processing models into clear relationship with instructional design.

According to this "triangulation" notion, there are three criteria to be met in choosing a teaching routine:

1. It must adequately display the underlying structure of the subject matter.
2. It must be easy to demonstrate or teach.
3. It must be capable of transformation into an efficient performance routine.

The teaching routine, then, is designed to help facilitate acquisition. It provides the connecting link between the structure of the subject matter and skilled performance—which is often so elliptical as to obscure rather than reveal the basic structure of the task.

Teaching routines, in other words, are constructed specifically to aid acquisition. The design of teaching routines may require considerable artistry, and not all routines will be successful in meeting the criteria just laid out. Let us consider some examples. To begin with our own work, the addition routine Groen and I taught is an instantiation of the "union of sets" definition of addition. Thus, it is a mathematically "correct" procedure, and represents the subject-matter structure clearly. The routine is also easy to demonstrate and to learn. Our 4-year-old subjects (who knew only how to count objects when they began the experiment) were performing addition virtually perfectly, using the blocks, after about a half hour of practice. The routine we taught is awkward and slow to perform, however. None of us would like to have to use it in our daily activities, and neither, apparently, did the 4-year-olds. Nevertheless, the data show that the routine is transformable—by a series of steps we can imagine but cannot for the moment document empirically—to the more efficient performance routine of the *min* model. Further, this performance routine exemplifies another aspect of the subject-matter structure, commutativity. Thus, the proposed triangulation is completed. A teaching routine derived by rational process analysis of the subject-matter structure is transformed to a performance routine that reflects an even more sophisticated definition of the subject matter.

The case is similar for the subtraction study. The routine that we presume was taught instantiated a partitioning-of-sets definition of subtraction. The performance routine derived by the children is not only more efficient; it also reflects a more sophisticated aspect of the subject-matter structure, namely the complementary relationship between addition and subtraction operations.

Not all teaching routines meet the criteria enumerated above. Some are awkward to teach; such would be the case, for example, were one to undertake to teach 4-year-olds the *min* model for addition. Others fail to display the subject-matter structure in a way that is transparent to children. This is true, for example, in the case of traditional algorithmic methods of teaching carrying and borrowing that do not display the underlying structure (base arithmetic and its notation) from which the routines are derived.

Sometimes instructional routines are developed in order to display the subject-matter structure but do not meet the transformability criterion—that is, they are not easily mapped onto a performance routine that is efficient and direct. An example of a performance routine that fails on the criterion of transformability is one that was proposed by Bruner (1964) for teaching factoring of quadratic expressions. Bruner was successful in teaching third-graders to perform the factoring operation by creating a "model" of the expression using blocks. As shown in Fig. 9a, the large square is x units long and x wide, thus

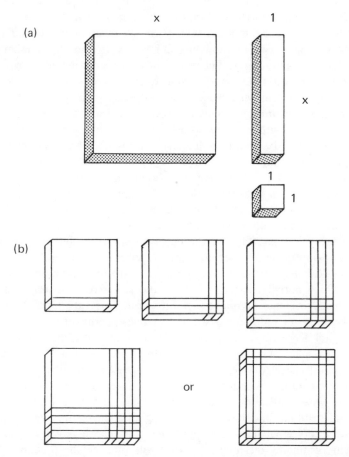

FIG. 9 (a) Three components for quadratic constructions. (b) Squares of ever increasing size constructed with components. (From "Some theorems on instruction illustrated with reference to mathematics" by J. S. Bruner, in E. R. Hilgard (Ed.), *Theories of Learning and Instruction, The 63rd Yearbook of the NSSE* (Part 1). Chicago: Chicago University Press, 1964. Copyright 1964 by the National Society for the Study of Education. Reprinted by permission.)

(x^2). The rod is x units long and one unit wide, thus (x). The small cube is 1×1, thus (1). As shown at the right of the figure (b), children can arrange these three elements in squares which will have equal factors—e.g., $(x + 1)$ $(x + 1)$; $(x + 2)$ $(x + 2)$—and which can also be expressed as quadratics—e.g., $(x^2 + 2x + 1)$; $(x^2 + 8x + 16)$. Allowing children to manipulate the blocks may be excellent for displaying and promoting insight into the structure of the subject matter, but there appears to be no way to transform the square-arrangement routine to a factoring procedure used without the blocks.

Certain other teaching routines in early mathematics do meet the transformability criterion while still representing the mathematical structure. For example, measurement can be taught as a process of dividing into equal units. Wertheimer (1959) did this when he used division of a figure into squares as means of finding its area. Bearison (1969), in a less widely known experiment, induced a generalized conservation concept by showing children how to count the number of 30-ml beakers that were poured into beakers of different sizes, and demonstrating the principle of conservation by pouring equal quantities of liquid into containers of different shapes. This generalized principle of measurement, exemplified in the liquid measurement procedure taught, produced conservation responses in tests of number, mass, length, continuous and discontinuous area, and quantity that lasted for at least six months. Similarly, the number base system (including carrying and borrowing) can be taught using blocks in sizes of one, ten, and one-hundred, placed in units, tens and hundreds columns as in Fig. 10 (cf. Dienes, 1966, 1967a). With these blocks, carrying can be represented by trading or exchanging extra (i.e., more than nine) blocks in a column for a larger block that is placed in the next column. Such an exchange would be necessary for the bottom display in Fig. 10 before the block display could be notated. A reverse exchange operation can be used to represent subtraction. In each of these cases, as the physical representation is dropped, a performance routine can be constructed which initially performs "as if" the representation were present and then gradually becomes more abstracted from it. This is the kind of transformation we believe occurred in our addition teaching experiment.

The general suggestion that I would like to draw from these observations is that most people—even quite young children—use environmental feedback to simplify performance routines. They do not accept the routines they are shown as "givens" but rather as starting points. They invent even when we teach them algorithms. One implication of this line of thinking is that the traditional line between algorithmic and inventive teaching disappears. We are not faced so much with a choice between teaching by rules and teaching by discovery, as with a problem of finding teaching rules that will enhance the probability of discovery—rules that somehow invite simplification or combination with other rules. This way of thinking also draws attention to the extent to which we presently depend, in our normal instructional practices, on this kind of invention and discovery by learners. Our instruction is rarely complete, and rather than

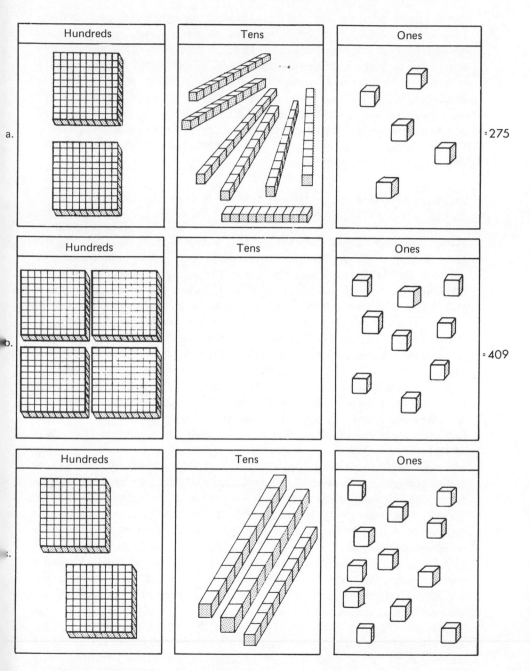

FIG. 10 Block displays for notation problem. (From Resnick & Glaser, in press.)

taking care to point out the simplifying and organizing principles that underlie what we teach, we often choose less than elegant instances and also expect learners to find the underlying principles for themselves. This suggests that differences in learning ability—often expressed as intelligence or aptitude—may in fact be differences in the amount of support individuals require in making the simplifying and organizing inventions that produce skilled performance. Some individuals will seek and find order in the most disordered presentations; most will do well if the presentations (i.e., the teaching routines) are good representations of underlying structures; still others may need explicit help in finding efficient strategies for performance.

Analyzing and Teaching Generalized "Learning to Learn" Abilities

People apparently invent even within the confines of algorithmic instruction. Nevertheless, as just suggested, individuals differ substantially in how good they are at these inventions. Thus, one appropriate concern for instruction is the possibility of teaching general strategies for invention and discovery—strategies that will help learners to be less dependent on the instructor's elegance in presenting particular tasks. An interest in teaching such general "learning to learn" abilities, as they are often called, has been widely expressed by educators and psychologists. However, few successes have been reported, and there is little scientific basis at the present time for such instruction. As in the instruction of any other ability, the first step in teaching general learning abilities is developing a psychological description—a task analysis—of the competence sought. Such analyses are only now beginning to become available.

A growing number of information-processing analyses of problem-solving tasks of various kinds provide a potential basis for instruction. However, it is by no means evident, without further testing and experimentation, that analysis of skilled performance on complex problems can be directly translated into instructional interventions. One test of this possibility has been carried out recently by Thomas Holzman (1975). In an effort to determine the instructability of a generalized pattern detection skill, Holzman looked at an analysis of behavior on series completion tasks that had been carried out earlier by Kotovsky and Simon (1973). The Kotovsky and Simon analysis identified three principal subroutines for discovering the pattern in letter series completion tasks similar to those used on many intelligence tests. These were (a) detecting the "period" of the pattern—that is, the repeating units of a certain number of letters, such as three in the pattern abmcdmefm . . . or four in the pattern defgefghfg . . . ; (b) determining the rule that generates each symbol in the period; and (c) testing the inferred rule to see if it holds for all the letters that have been presented. These subroutines in turn were shown to be dependent upon recognizing three basic relations between items in the series presented: *identity* (e.g., *f* to *f*); *next* in the alphabet (e.g., *f* to *g*); or *backward next* (e.g., *h* to *g*). These three relations exhaust those that were used in the Thurstone (Thurstone & Thurstone, 1941) letter series completion task which the Kotovsky and Simon study used as a basis, although a much more extended and complex list of relations could be used in generating series completion problems.

Based on the Kotovsky and Simon analysis, Holzman taught children from first through sixth grade the strategies for recognizing the three basic relations and for finding periods. Instruction in finding periods was done in such a way as to prevent extrapolation to other subroutines. Children trained in these relations and periodicity subroutines improved significantly on the letter series completion task from pre- to posttest. They also improved significantly more than control children who simply took the pre- and posttest and did not practice the series completion task. Comparisons of particular types of errors for the training and control groups showed that the trained children improved significantly more than the controls on the more difficult relations (e.g., *next* as opposed to *identity*) and on the generally more difficult problems. Control children showed a practice effect, due to experience with the test itself, which was limited largely to improvement on the most easily detectable relation (i.e., *identity*). This study suggests that as information-processing analyses succeed in identifying the processes underlying problem solution, these processes—at least some of them—can be directly taught, and that individuals will then be able to apply them to solving relatively large classes of problems.

What possibilities exist for analyses of problem-solving abilities that are even more general than those Holzman found, and what might these yield as a basis for instruction that would be truly generative of learning-to-learn abilities? Robert Glaser and I have considered this question in another volume (Resnick & Glaser, in press) in which we described several studies of invention behavior in mathematics and related tasks. We argued that the processes involved in problem solving of certain kinds were probably the same ones involved in learning in the absence of direct or complete instruction, and that instruction in those processes might constitute a means of increasing an individual's intelligence.

A model of problem solving was developed in which three interacting phases were identified: (1) problem detection, in which the inapplicability of "usual routines" is noted and a problem or goal formulated; (2) feature detection, in which the task environment (the external situation, which includes both physical and social features) is scanned for cues to appropriate responses; and (3) goal analysis, in which goals are successively reformulated, partly on the basis of external task cues, in order to yield soluble subgoals that contribute eventually to solution of the task as presented. A study by Schadler and Pellegrino (1974) has shown that requiring the subject to verbalize the goals of the problem and his or her strategies for solving it before making overt moves toward solution greatly enhances the likelihood of invention. Along similar lines, it seems likely that ways can be found to make individuals more conscious of the role of environmental cues in problem solving and to teach strategies of feature scanning and analysis. This instruction should enhance the likelihood of their noticing cues that prompt effective actions while recognizing and somehow "deactivating" those that prompt ineffective actions. Extending this general argument of self-regulation as a major characteristic of successful learning and problem solving, Resnick and Beck (in press) have suggested that a similar form of instruction in conscious use of self-questioning and self-monitoring strategies might be an effective way of enhancing reading comprehension abilities.

The specific suggestions that can be offered at this time for instruction of generalized learning abilities are limited, since relatively little work has been done thus far on developing task analyses that characterize these general processes in instructable terms. Rational analysis seems less likely to yield good suggestions for generalized abilities than for specific tasks; thus empirical task analyses seem to be called for. Further, the rigor of formal simulation models seems especially important where the processes are little understood and the task environments loosely structured, as is often the case where problem solving and discovery are called for. Thus, with respect to this most important goal of instruction, it will probably be necessary to engage in the most costly and extended forms of task analysis, that is, those that are formally stated and empirically validated. To the extent that the analyses identify instructable processes, instructional experiments can serve as one of the major forms of empirical validation of the performance models proposed. A mutual interaction between scientific and instructional concerns can thus be envisaged. It is, then, with respect to these general abilities in learning, thinking, and problem solving that information-processing analysis may ultimately have the most to offer to instruction, and instructional efforts to psychological knowledge.

ACKNOWLEDGMENTS

Preparation of this chapter was supported by the Learning Research and Development Center, supported in part as a research and development center by funds from the National Institute of Education (NIE), United States Department of Health, Education, and Welfare. The opinions expressed do not necessarily reflect the position or policy of NIE and no official endorsement should be inferred. I wish to express special thanks to Wendy W. Ford who assisted me at several stages of writing and editing this chapter.

4

Adaptive Instructional Systems: Some Attempts to Optimize the Learning Process

Richard C. Atkinson[1]

Stanford University

INTRODUCTION

One cannot help but question the significance of psychology's contribution to the development of effective instructional procedures. On the one hand, psychology has been very influential in the field of education. In the last 25 years almost every major innovation in education—programmed textbooks, behavioral objectives, ungraded schools, individually prescribed instruction, computer managed and assisted instruction, token economies, and tailored testing to name a few—can be traced to psychology. In many cases these innovations have not been due to psychologists primarily identified with education, but rather to laboratory scientists whose research has suggested new approaches to instruction. Psychology can be proud of that record of accomplishment. But upon closer examination, it is evident that these accomplishments are not as closely linked to psychological research as many might believe. Psychology has suggested new approaches to education, but these suggestions have not led to sustained research programs that have the promise of producing a truly effective theory of instruction. Rather, psychology seems to provide the stimulus for innovation, but innovation that has not in turn led to a deeper understanding of the learning process.

Why has psychology not had a more substantial impact? There are several reasons. The brightest and ablest young psychologists usually are not attracted to educational research, and the research that has been done tends to be piecemeal, not pursuing problems in real depth. This picture may change in the near future due to the limited number of jobs for new Ph.D.s and to society's

[1] Present affiliation: Deputy Director, National Science Foundation, Washington, D.C. 20550.

increasing emphasis on applied research. The more serious problem, however, is that psychologists know a great deal about the acquisition of individual facts and skills, but very little about how these combine to form a meaningful mental structure. Effective methods for acquiring skills and facts are important, but the major problem is the development of knowledge structures that are more than the sum of individual facts. In order to deal effectively with educational problems, we need theories that tell us how knowledge is represented in memory, how information is retrieved from that knowledge structure, how new information is added to the structure, and how the system can expand that knowledge structure by self-generative processes. The development of such theories is under way, and increasingly work in cognitive psychology is moving in that direction. The contributions of Anderson and Bower (1973), Newell and Simon (1972), Rumelhart, Lindsay, and Norman (1972), and Schank (1972) are examples of substantial efforts to develop comprehensive theories of cognition, and it is already evident that this work will have implications for education. Such theories will not simply add another wrinkle to educational research, but will lay the foundations for research encompassing a larger set of educationally significant problems than has been considered in the past.

In this paper I want to review the ongoing work in my laboratory that has implications for instruction. Some of that work represents attempts to deal with the issue of complex knowledge structures, whereas some is more restrictive dealing with the acquisition of specific skills and facts. All of the work involves computer-based programs of instruction used on a daily basis in schools and colleges. These programs can best be described as *adaptive instructional systems*. By that term I mean two things: (1) the sequence of instructional actions taken by the program varies as a function of a given student's performance history, and (2) the program is organized to modify itself automatically as more students complete the course and their response records identify defects in instructional strategies.

Our work on adaptive instructional systems has three foci. One is the development of a course in computer programming for junior college and college students; the second is a course for teaching reading in the first three grades of elementary schools; and the third is a foreign-language vocabulary program being used at the college level. Here I will review research on each of these projects.

INSTRUCTION IN COMPUTER PROGRAMMING

Our first efforts to teach computer programming involved the development of a computer-assisted instruction (CAI) curriculum to teach the AID (Algebraic Interpretive Dialogue) programming language; this course has been used extensively in colleges and junior colleges as an introduction to computer programming (Beard, Lorton, Searle, & Atkinson, 1973). However, it is a linear, "frame-oriented" CAI program and does not provide individualized instruction during the problem-solving activity itself. After working through lesson segments on syntax, expressions, etc., the student is assigned a problem to solve in AID. He must then leave the instructional program, call up a separate AID interpreter, perform the required programming task, and return to the instructional program with an answer. As the student writes a program with AID, the only sources of assistance are the error messages provided by the noninstructional interpreter.

An inadequacy of the AID course, especially for research purposes, is its limited ability to characterize individual students' knowledge of specific skills, and its inability to relate students' skills to the curriculum as anything more than a ratio of problems correct to problems attempted. The program cannot make fine distinctions between a student's strengths and weaknesses, and cannot present instructional material specifically appropriate to that student beyond "harder" or "easier" lessons. In order to explore the effects of different curriculum selection strategies in more detail, we developed another introductory programming course, capable of representing both its subject matter and student performance more adequately. The internal representation of programming skills and their relationships to the curriculum is similar in some ways to the semantic networks used in the "generative" CAI programs developed by Carbonell and others (Carbonell, 1970; Collins, Carbonell, & Warnock, 1973).

The BASIC Instructional Program

An important feature of a tutorial CAI program is to provide assistance as the student attempts to solve a problem. The program must contain a representation of the subject matter that is complex enough to allow the program to generate appropriate assistance at any stage of the student's solution attempt. The BASIC (Beginners All-purpose Symbolic Instruction Code) Instructional Program (BIP) contains a representation of information appropriate to the teaching of computer programming that allows the program both to provide help to the student and to perform a limited but adequate analysis of the correctness of the student's program as a solution to the given problem.

To the student seated at a terminal, BIP looks very much like a typical time-sharing BASIC operating system. The BASIC interpreter, written especially for BIP, analyzes each program line after the student types it, and notifies the student of syntax errors. When the student runs his or her program it is checked for structural illegalities, and during runtime "execution" errors are indicated. A file storage system, a calculator, and utility commands are available.

Residing above the simulated operating system is the "tutor," or instructional program (IP). It overlooks the entire student/BIP dialogue and motivates the instructional interaction. In addition to selecting and presenting programming problems to the student, the IP identifies the student's problem areas, suggests simpler "subtasks," gives hints or model solutions when necessary, offers debug-

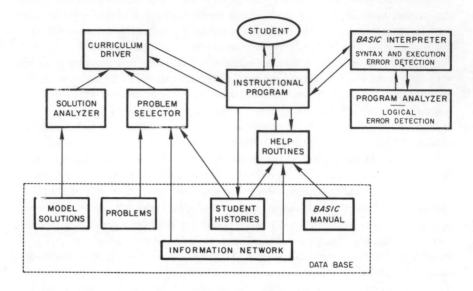

FIG. 1   BIP information flow diagram.

ging aids, and supplies incidental instruction in the form of messages, interactive lessons, or manual references.

At the core of BIP is an information network whose nodes are concepts, skills, problems, subproblems, prerequisites, BASIC commands, remedial lessons, hints, and manual references. The network is used to characterize both the logical structure of the course and our estimate of the student's current state of knowledge; more will be said about the network later. Figure 1 illustrates the interactions of the parts of the BIP program.

The curriculum is organized as a set of programming problems whose text includes only the description of the problem, not lengthy descriptions of programming structures or explanations of syntax. There is no fixed ordering of the tasks; the decision to move from one task to another is made on the basis of the information about the tasks (skills involved, prerequisites, subtasks available) stored in BIPs network.

A student progresses through the curriculum by writing, and running, a program that solves the problem presented on the terminal. Virtually no limitations are imposed on the amount of time the student spends, the number of lines he writes, the number of errors he is allowed to make, the number of times he chooses to execute the program, etc. The task on which the student is working is stored on a stack-like structure, so that he may work on another task, for whatever reason, and return to the previous task automatically. The curriculum structure can accommodate a wide variety of student aptitudes and skills. Most of the curriculum-related options are designed with the less competent student in mind. A more competent student may simply ignore the options. Thus, BIP gives students the opportunity to determine their own "challenge levels" by making assistance available but not inevitable.

BIP offers the student considerable flexibility in making task-related decisions. The student may ask for hints and subtasks to help solve the given problem, or may ponder the problem, using only the manual for additional information. The student may request a different task by name either completing the new task or not, as he or she chooses. On the student's return to the original task, BIP tells him or her the name of the again-current task, and prints the text of the task if requested. The student may request the model solution for any task at any time, but BIP will not print the model for the current task unless the student has exhausted the available hints and subtasks. Taken together, the curriculum options allow for a wide range of student preferences and behaviors.

The Information Network of BIP

Task selection, remedial assistance, and problem area determination require that the program have a flexible information store interrelating tasks, hints, manual references, etc. This store has been built using the associative language LEAP, a SAIL (Stanford Artificial Intelligence Laboratory) sublanguage, in which set, list and ordered triple data structures are available (Feldman, Low, Swinehart, & Taylor, 1972; Swinhart & Sproull, 1971; VanLehn, 1973). Figure 2 presents a

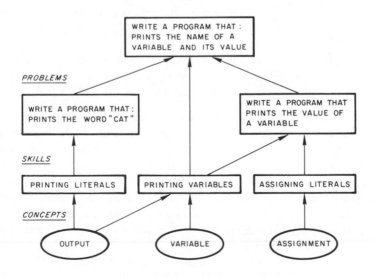

FIG. 2 A segment of BIP information network.

simplified relationship among a few programming concepts, specific observable skills that characterize the acquisition of the concepts, and programming problems that require the use of those skills. The network is constructed using the associative triple structure, and is best described in terms of the various types of nodes:

TASKS: All curriculum elements exist as task nodes in the network. They are linked to each other as subtasks, prerequisite tasks, or "must follow" tasks.

SKILLS: The skill nodes are intermediaries between the concept nodes and the task nodes (Fig. 2). Skills are very specific, e.g., "concatenating string variables" or "incrementing a counter variable." By evaluating success on the individual skills, the program estimates competence levels in the concept areas. In the network, skills are related to the tasks that require them and to the concepts that embody them.

CONCEPTS: The principal concept areas covered by BIP are the following: interactive programs; variables and literals; expressions; input and output; program control—branching; repetition—loops; debugging; subroutines; and arrays.

OPERATORS: Each BASIC operation (PRINT, LET, . . .) is a node in the network. The operations are linked to the tasks in two ways: either as elements that must be used in the solution of the problem, or as those that must not be used in the solution.

HINTS: The hint nodes are linked to the tasks for which they may be helpful. Each time a new skill, concept or BASIC operator is introduced, there is an extra hint that gives a suitable manual reference.

ERRORS: All discoverable syntax, structural, and execution errors exist as nodes in the network, linked to the relevant "help" messages, manual references and remedial lessons.

Clearly in some cases, a hierarchy among skills or problems is implicit; more frequently, however, such a relationship cannot be assumed. By imposing only a very loose hierarchy (e.g., requiring that all students begin the course with the same problem), it is possible to select curriculum and provide assistance on the basis of a student's demonstrated competence level on specific skills, rather than on the basis of a predetermined, nonindividualized, sequence of problems. Students who acquire competence in skills in some manner other than that assumed by subject-matter experts to be standard should benefit most from this potential for individualization.

Upon completion of a task, the student is given a "post task interview" in which BIP presents the model solution stored for that problem. The student is encouraged to regard the model as only one of many possible solutions. BIP asks the student whether he or she has solved the problem, then asks (for each of the skills associated with the task) whether more practice is needed on that skill. In addition to the information gained from this student self-analysis, BIP also stores the result of a comparison between the student's program and the model solution, based on the output of both programs when run on a set of test data. The student's responses to the interview and the results of the program comparison are used in future BIP-generated curriculum decisions. BIP informs the student that the task has been completed, and either allows the student to select the next task by name (from an off-line printed list of names and problem texts), or makes the selection for the student.

An example of the role of the Information Network in BIPs tutorial capabilities is the BIP-generated curriculum decisions mentioned above. By storing the student's own evaluation of his or her skills, and by comparing the student's solution attempts to the stored models, BIP can be said to "learn" about each student as an individual who has attained a certain level of competence in the skills associated with each task. For example, BIP might have recorded the fact that a given student had demonstrated competence (and confidence) in the skill of assigning a literal value to a variable (e.g., $N = 1$), but had failed to master the skill of incrementing a counter variable (e.g., $N = N + 1$). BIP can then search the network to locate the skills that are appropriate to each student's abilities and present tasks that incorporate those skills. The network provides the base from which BIP can generate decisions that take into account both the subject matter and the student, behaving somewhat like a human tutor in presenting material that either corrects specific weaknesses or challenges and extends particular strengths, proceeding into as yet unencountered areas.

The BIP program has been running successfully with both junior college and university students. However, the program is still very much in an experimental stage. From a psychological viewpoint, the principal research issues deal with (1) procedures for obtaining on-line estimates of student abilities as represented in the information network, and (2) alternative methods for using the current estimates in the information network to make instructional decisions. Neither of these issues is restricted to this particular course, and a major goal in the development of BIP is to provide an instructional model suitable to a variety of different subject areas. Two topics must be discussed in relation to this goal: the nature of appropriate subject areas and the general characteristics of the BIP-like structure that make it particularly useful in teaching such subjects.

A subject well suited to this approach generally fits the following description: it has clearly definable, demonstrable skills, whose relationships are well known; the real content of the subject matter is of a problem-solving, rather than a fact-acquiring, nature; the problems presented to the student involve overlapping sets of skills; and a student's solution to a given problem can be judged as adequate or inadequate with some degree of confidence. The BASIC language, as taught by BIP, is one such subject, but the range of appropriate curriculums goes well beyond the area of computer science. For example, elementary statistics could be taught by a similar approach, as could algebra, navigation, accounting, or organic chemistry. All these subject areas involve the manipulation of information by the student toward a known goal, all involve processes that can be carried out or simulated by a computer, and all are based on a body of skills whose acquisition by the student can be measured with an acceptable degree of accuracy.

Because they require the development of problem-solving skills, rather than the memorization of facts, these subject areas are frequently difficult to master and difficult to tutor, especially using standard CAI techniques. One limitation of such standard techniques is their dependence on a "right" answer to a given question or problem, which precludes active student participation in a problem-solving process consisting of many steps, none of which can be evaluated as correct or incorrect except within the context of the solution as a whole. In addition, standard CAI techniques usually consist of an instructional facility alone—a mechanism by which information is presented and responses are judged. This facility can be linked to a true problem-solving facility that allows the student to proceed through the steps to a solution, but the link does not allow the transfer of information between the instructional and the problem-solving portions of the program. The complete integration of the two parts is a key feature of BIP, making it appropriate to instruction in subject areas that have been inadequately treated in CAI.

The most general characteristics of the "network" structure include a representation of the curriculum in terms of the specific skills required in its mastery and a representation of the student's current levels of competence in each of the skills he has been required to use. Individual record-keeping relates each student's progress to the curriculum at all times, and any number of schemes may be used to apply that relationship to the selection of tasks or the presentation of additional information, hints, advice, etc.

An important element of our network structure is the absence of an established path through the curriculum, providing the built-in flexibility (like that of a human tutor) to respond to individual students' strengths and weaknesses as each student works with the course. This can only be accomplished through a careful analysis and precise specification of the skills inherent in the subject matter, the construction of a thorough curriculum providing in-depth experience with all the skills, and a structure of associations among elements of the curriculum that allows for the implementation of various instructional strategies. Instructional flexibility is complemented by research flexibility in such a structure, because the nature of the associations can be modified for different experimental purposes. Once the elements of the network have been established, it is easy, for example, to change the prerequisite relationship between two problems, or to specify a higher level of competence in a given skill as a criterion measure.

The considerable complexity involved in programming this kind of flexible structure imposes a certain limitation. Standard CAI "author languages" are not appropriate to this network approach, and constructing a CAI course on BIP's pattern is not a task to be undertaken by the educator (or researcher) who has no programming support. The usefulness of author languages is their simplicity, which allows subject-matter experts to prepare course material relatively quickly and easily. Most author languages provide for alternative paths through a curriculum, for alternative answer-matching schemes, and so forth; considerable complexity is certainly possible. However, the limits, once reached, are real, and the author simply cannot expand the sophistication of his course beyond those limits.

The programming support required by the network approach, on the other hand, implies (1) the use of a general, powerful language allowing access to all the capabilities of the computer itself, and (2) a programming group with the training and experience to make full use of the machine. It has been our experience that the flexibility of a general purpose language, while expensive in a number of ways, is worth the costs by virtue of the much greater freedom it allows in the construction of the curriculum and the implementation of experimental conditions. For a more complete description of BIP and a review of our plans for further research see Barr, Beard, and Atkinson (1974).

INSTRUCTION IN INITIAL READING
(GRADES 1–3)

Our first efforts to teach reading under computer control were aimed at a total curriculum that would be virtually independent of the classroom teacher (Atkinson, 1968). These early efforts proved reasonably successful, but it soon became apparent that the cost of such a program would be prohibitive if applied on a large-scale basis. Further, it was demonstrated that some aspects of instruction could be done very effectively using a computer, but that there were other tasks for which the computer did not have any advantages over classroom teaching. Thus, during the last four years, our orientation has changed and the goal now is to develop low-cost CAI that supplements classroom teaching and concentrates on those tasks in which individualization is critically important.[2]

Reading Curriculum

Reading instruction can be divided into two areas which have been referred to as "decoding" and "communication." Decoding is the rapid, if not automatic, association of phonemes or phoneme groups with their respective graphic repre-

---

[2] A student terminal in the current program consists only of a Model-33 teletypewriter with an audio headset. There is no graphic or photographic capability at the student terminal as there was in our first system, and the character set of the teletypewriter includes only uppercase letters. On the other hand, the audio system is extremely flexible and provides virtually instantaneous access to any one of 6,000 recorded words and messages.

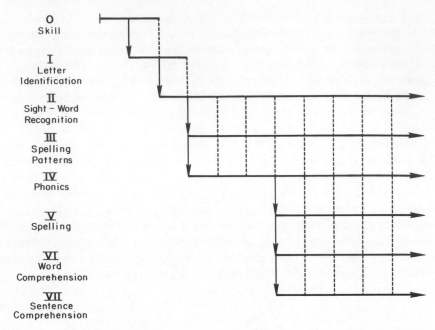

FIG. 3 Schematic presentation of the strand structure. Entry into each strand depends on a student's performance in earlier strands. The vertical dotted lines represent maximal rate contours which control the student's progress in each strand relative to the other strands.

sentations. Communication involves reading for meaning, aesthetic enjoyment, emphasis, and the like. Our CAI program provides instruction in both types of tasks, but focuses primarily on decoding. The program is divided into eight parts or strands. As indicated in Fig. 3, entry into a strand is determined by the student's level of achievement in the other strands. Instruction begins in Strand 0, which teaches the skills required to interact with the program. Entry into the other strands is dependent on the student's performance in earlier strands. For example, the letter identification strand starts with a subset of letters used in the earliest sight words. When a student reaches a point in the letter identification strand where he has exhibited mastery over the letters used in the first words of the sight-word strand, the student enters that strand. Similarly, entry into the spelling-pattern strand and the phonics strand is controlled by the student's placement in the sight-word strand. On any given day, a student may be seeing exercises drawn from as many as five strands. The dotted vertical lines in Fig. 3 represent "maximal rate contours," which control the student's progress in each strand relative to progress in other strands. The rationale underlying these contours is that learning particular material in one strand facilitates learning in another strand; thus, the contours are constructed so that the student learns specific items from one strand in conjunction with specific items from other strands.

The CAI program is highly individualized so that a trace through the curriculum is unique for each student. Our problem is to specify how a given subject's response history should be used to make instructional decisions. The approach that we have adopted is to develop mathematical models for the acquisition of the various skills in the curriculum, and then use these models to specify optimal sequencing schemes. Basically, this approach is what has come to be known in the engineering literature as "optimal control theory," or, more simply, "control theory." In the area of instruction, the system to be controlled is the human learner rather than a machine or group of industries. If a learning model can be specified, then methods of control theory can be used to derive optimal instructional strategies.

Some of the optimization procedures will be reviewed later, but in order for the reader to have some idea of how the CAI program operates, let me first describe a few of the simpler exercises used in Strands II, III, and IV. Strand II provides for the development of a sight-word vocabulary. Vocabulary items are presented in five exercise formats; only the copy exercise and the recognition exercise will be described here. The top panel of Table 1 illustrates the copy exercise, and the lower panel illustrates the recognition exercise. Note that when a student makes an error, the system responds with an audio message and prints

TABLE 1

Examples of Two Exercises Used in Strand II
(Sight-Word Recognition)[a]

	Teletypewriter display	Audio message
Copy exercise		
The program outputs	PEN	(Type pen.)
The student responds by typing	PEN	
The program outputs	+	(Great!)
The program outputs	EGG	(Type egg.)
The student responds by typing	EFF	
The program outputs	////EGG	(No, egg.)
Recognition exercise		
The program outputs	PEN NET EGG	(Type pen.)
The student responds by typing	PEN	
The program outputs	+	
The program outputs	PEN EGG NET	(Type net.)
The student responds by typing	NET	
The program outputs	+	(Fabulous!)

[a]The top panel displays the copy exercise and the bottom the recognition exercise. Rows in the table correspond to successive lines on the teletypewriter printout.

out the correct response. In earlier versions of the program, the student was required to copy the correct response following an error. Experiments demonstrated that the overt correction procedure was not particularly effective; simply displaying the correct word following an error provided more useful feedback.

Strand III offers practice with spelling patterns and emphasizes the regular grapheme–phoneme correspondences that exist in English. Table 2 illustrates exercises from this strand. For the exercise in the top panel of Table 2, the student is presented with three words involving the same spelling pattern and is required to select the correct one based on its initial letters. Once the student has learned to use the initial letter or letter sequence to distinguish between words, he moves to the recall exercise illustrated in the bottom panel of Table 2. Here the student works with a group of words, all involving the same spelling pattern. On each trial the audio system requests a word that requires adding an initial consonant or consonant cluster to the spelling pattern mastered in the preceding exercise. Whenever a student makes a correct response, a "+"sign is printed on the teletypewriter. In addition, every so often the program will give an audio feedback message; these messages vary from simple ones like "great," "that's fabulous," "you're doing brilliantly," to some that have cheering, clapping, or bells ringing in the background. These messages are not generated at random, but depend on the student's performance on that particular day.

When the student has mastered a specified number of words in the sight-word strand, he or she begins exercises in the phonics strand; this strand concentrates on initial and final consonants and consonant clusters in combination with medial vowels. As in most linguistically orientated curricula, students are not required to rehearse or identify consonant sounds in isolation. The emphasis is on patterns of vowels and consonants that bear regular correspondences to

TABLE 2

Examples of the Recognition and Recall Exercises Used in
Strand III (Spelling Patterns)

	Teletypewriter display	Audio message
Recognition exercise		
The program outputs	KEPT SLEPT CREPT	(Type kept.)
The student responds by typing	KEPT	
The program outputs	+	
Recall exercise		
The program outputs		(Type crept.)
The student responds by typing	CREPT	
The program outputs	+	(That's fabulous!)

TABLE 3
Examples of Two Exercises from Strand IV (Phonics)

	Teletypewriter display	Audio message
Recognition exercise		
The program outputs	–IN –IT –IG	(Type /IG/ as in fig.)
The student responds by typing	IG	
The program outputs	+	(Good!)
The program outputs	–IT –IN –IG	(Type /IT/ as in fit.)
The student responds by typing	IT	
The program outputs	+	
Build-a-word exercise		
The program outputs	–IN –IT –IG P– –	(Type pin.)
The student responds by typing	PIN	
The program outputs	+	(Great!)
The program outputs	–IG –IN –IT F– –	(Type fig.)
The student responds by typing	FIN	
The program outputs	////FIG	(No, we wanted fig.)

phonemes. The phonic strand is the most complicated one of the group and involves eight exercise formats; two of the formats will be described here. The upper panel of Table 3 illustrates an exercise in which the student is required to identify the graphic representation of phonemes occuring at the end of words. Each trial begins with an audio presentation of a word that includes the phonemes, and the student is asked to identify the graphic representation. After mastering this exercise the student is transferred to the exercise illustrated in the bottom panel of Table 3. The same phonemes are presented, but now the student is required to construct words by adding appropriate consonants.

Optimal Sequences for Individual Students

This has been a brief overview of some of the exercises used in the curriculum; a more detailed account of the program can be found in Atkinson, Fletcher, Lindsay, Campbell, and Barr (1973). The key to the curriculum is the optimization schemes that control the sequencing of the exercises; these schemes can be classified at three levels. One level involves decision making within each strand. The problem is to decide which items to present for study, which exercise formats to present them in, and when to schedule review. A complete response history exists for each student, and this history is used to make trial-by-trial decisions regarding what to present next. The second level of optimization deals with decisions about allocation of instructional time among strands for a given student. At the end of an instructional session, the student will have reached a certain point in each strand and a decision must be made about the time to be allocated to each strand in the next session. The third level of optimization deals with the distribution of instructional time among students. The question here is to allocate computer time among students to achieve instructional objectives that are defined not for the individual student but for the class as a whole. In some global sense, these three levels of optimization should be integrated into a unified program. However, we have been satisfied to work with each separately, hoping that later they can be incorporated into a single package.

Optimization within a strand (what has been called Level I) can be illustrated using the sight-word strand. The strand comprises a list of about 1,000 words; the words are ordered in terms of their frequency in the student's vocabulary, and words at the beginning of the list have highly regular grapheme–phoneme correspondences. At any point in time a student will be working on a limited pool of words from the master list; the size of this working pool depends on the student's ability level and is usually between 5 and 10 words. When one of these words is mastered, it is deleted from the pool and replaced by the next word on the list or by a word due for review. Figure 4 presents a flow chart for the strand. Each word in the working pool is in one of five possible instructional states. A trial involves sampling a word from the working pool and presenting it in an appropriate exercise format. The student is pretested on a word the first few times it is presented to eliminate words already known. If the student knows the word it will be dropped from the working pool. If not, the student first studies the word using the recognition exercise. If review is required, the student studies the word again in what is designated in Fig. 4 as Exercises 4 and 5.

As indicated in Fig. 4, a given word passes from one state to the next when it reaches criterion. And this presents the crux of the optimization problem, which is to define an appropriate criterion for each exercise. This has been done using simple mathematical models to describe the acquisition process for each exercise and the transfer functions that hold between exercises (Atkinson & Paulson, 1972). These models are simple Markov processes that provide reasonably accurate accounts of performance on our tasks. Parameters of the models are defined as functions of two factors: (1) the ability of the particular student and (2) the difficulty of the particular word. An estimate of the student's ability is obtained by analyzing his or her response record on all previous words, and an estimate of a word's difficulty is obtained by analyzing performance on that

FIG. 4 Partial flow chart for Strand II (sight-word recognition). The various decisions represented in the bottom part of the chart are based on fairly complicated computations that make use of the student's response history. The same recognition exercise is used in both state S_3 and S_5.

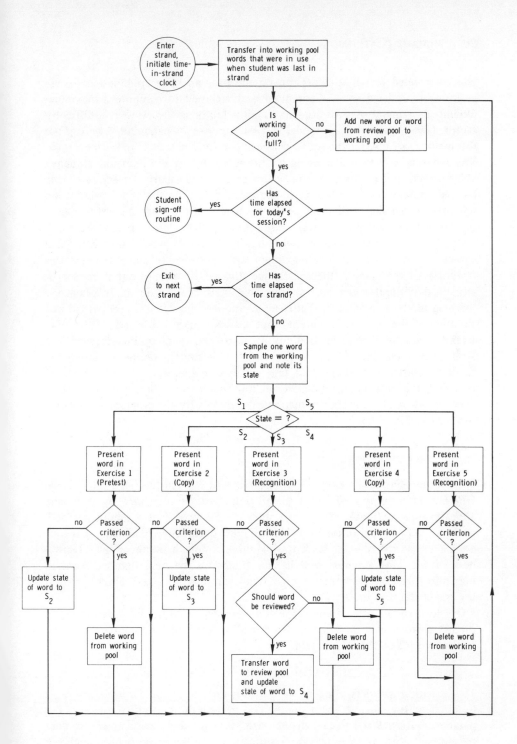

FIG. 4

particular word for all students run on the program. The student records are continually updated by the computer and are used to compute a maximum likelihood estimate of each student's ability factor and each word's difficulty factor. Given a well-defined model and estimates of its parameters, we can use the methods of control theory to define an optimal criterion for each exercise. The criterion will vary depending on the difficulty of the item, the student's ability level, and the precise sequence of correct and incorrect responses made by the student to the item. It is important to realize that the optimization scheme is not a simple branching program based on the student's last response, but depends in a complicated way on the student's complete response history.

Optimization between strands (what has been called Level II) was mentioned earlier in the description of maximum-rate contours. In some respects this optimization program is the most interesting of the group, but it cannot be explained without going into considerable mathematical detail. In essence, a learning model is developed that specifies the learning rate on each strand as a function of the amount of material that has been mastered in each of the other strands. Using mathematical methods of control theory, an optimal instructional strategy is determined based on the model. This strategy defines a closed-loop feedback controller that specifies daily instructional allocations for each strand based on the best current estimate of how much the student has mastered in each strand. An account of the theoretical rationale for the program is presented in Chant and Atkinson (1973).

Optimizing Class Performance

Next let us consider an example of optimization at what has been called Level III. The effectiveness of the CAI program can be increased by optimally allocating instructional time among students. Suppose that a school has budgeted a fixed amount of time for CAI and must decide how to allocate that time among a class of first-grade students. For this example, maximizing the effectiveness of the CAI program will be interpreted as meaning that we want to maximize the class performance on a standardized reading test administered at the end of the first grade.

On the basis of prior studies, the following equation has been developed to predict performance on a standardized reading test as a function of the time a student spends on the CAI system:

$$P(t;i) = A(i) - B(i) \exp[-tC(i)].$$

The equation predicts Student i's performance on a standardized test as a function of the time, t, spent on the CAI system during the school year. The parameters $A(i)$, $B(i)$, and $C(i)$ characterize Student i, and vary from one student to another. These parameters can be estimated from scores on reading readiness tests and from the student's performance during his first hour of CAI. After estimates of these parameters have been made, the above equation can be used to predict end-of-year test scores as a function of the CAI time allocated to that student.

Let us suppose that a school has budgeted a fixed amount of time T on the CAI system for a first-grade class of N students; further, suppose that students have had reading readiness tests and a preliminary run on the CAI system so that estimates of the parameters A, B, and C have been made for each student. The problem then is to allocate time T among the N students so as to optimize learning. In order to do this, it is first necessary to have a model of the learning process. Although the above equation does not offer a very detailed account of learning, it suffices as a model for purposes of this problem. This is an important point to keep in mind; the nature of the specific optimization problem determines the level of complexity that needs to be represented in the learning model. For some optimization problems, the model must provide a relatively detailed account of learning to specify a viable strategy, but for other problems a simple descriptive equation may suffice.

In addition to a model of the learning process, we must also specify an instructional objective. Only three possible objectives will be considered here:

I. Maximize the mean value of P over the class of students.
II. Minimize the variance of P over the class of students.
III. Maximize the mean value of P under the constraint that the resulting variance of P is less than or equal to the variance that would be obtained if no CAI were administered.

Objective I maximizes the gain for the class as a whole; Objective II reduces differences among students by making the class as homogeneous as possible; and Objective III attempts to maximize the class performance while insuring that differences among students are not amplified by CAI. If we select Objective I as the instructional objective, then the problem of deriving an optimal strategy reduces to maximizing the function:

$$f[t(1), t(2), \ldots, t(N)] = \sum_i \left\{ A(i) - B(i) \exp[-t(i)C(i)\ ] \right\},$$

$$t(1) + t(2) + \cdots + t(N) = T,$$

where $t(i)$ is the time allocated to Student i. This maximization can be done using the methods of dynamic programming. To illustrate the approach, computations were made for a first-grade class for which the parameters A, B, and C had been estimated for each student. Employing these estimates, computations were carried out to determine the time allocations that maximized the above equation. For the optimal policy, the predicted mean performance level of the class on the end-of-year tests was 14% higher than a policy that allocated time equally among students (i.e., an equal-time policy, where $t(i) = T/N$ for all i).

TABLE 4
Predicted Percent Gain in the Mean of P and
in the Variance of P When Compared with the
Mean and Variance of the Equal-Time Policy

	Instructional objective		
	I	II	III
Gain in mean of P (%)	14	−15	8
Gain in variance of P (%)	15	−12	−6

This gain represents a substantial improvement; the drawback is that the class variance is roughly 15% greater than the variance for the class using an equal-time policy. This means that if we are only interested in raising the class average, we will have to give the rapid learners substantially more time on the CAI system and let them progress far beyond the slow learners.

Although a time allocation that complies with Objective I does increase overall class performance, other objectives need to be considered. For comparison, time allocations also were computed for Objectives II and III. Table 4 presents the predicted gain in average class performance as a percentage of the mean value for the equal-time policy. Objective II yielded a negative gain in the mean; and so it should, since its goal was to minimize variability, which is accomplished by reducing the time allocations for rapid learners and giving more attention to the slower ones. The reduction in variability for Objective II is 12%. Objective III, which strikes a balance between Objective I and Objective II, yields an 8% gain in mean performance yet reduces variability by 6%.

In view of these results, Objective III would be preferred by most educators and laymen. It offers a substantial increase in average performance while maintaining a low level of variability. These computations make it clear that the selection of an instructional objective should not be done in isolation but should involve a comparative analysis of several objectives, taking into account more than one dimension of performance. Even if the principal goal is to maximize the class average, it is inappropriate in most educational situations to select Objective I over III if it is only slightly better for the class average, while permitting variability to mushroom.[3]

Effectiveness of the Reading Program

Several evaluation studies of the reading program have been conducted in the last few years. Rather than review these here, I would prefer to describe one in some detail (Fletcher & Atkinson, 1972). In this particular study, 50 pairs of

[3] For a more detailed discussion of some of the issue involved in selecting objective functions see Jamison, Fletcher, Suppes, and Atkinson (1975).

kindergarten students were matched on a number of variables, including sex and readiness scores. At the start of the first grade, one. member of each pair was assigned to the experimental group and the other to the control group. Students in the experimental group received CAI, but only during the first grade; students in the control group received no CAI. The CAI lasted approximately 15 min per day[4]; during this period the control group studied reading in the classroom. Except for this 15 min period, the school day for the CAI group was like that of the control group. Standardized tests were administered at the end of the first grade and again at the end of the second grade. All the tests showed roughly the same pattern of results; to summarize the findings, only data from the California Cooperative Primary Reading Test will be described. At the end of the first grade, the experimental group showed a 5.05-month gain over the control group. The groups, when tested a year later (with no intervening CAI treatment), showed a difference of 4.90 months. Thus, the initial difference observed following one year of CAI was maintained, although not amplified, during the second year when no CAI was administered to either group.

No definitive conclusions can be drawn from evaluation studies of this sort about the specific contributions of CAI versus other aspects of the situation. Obviously the curriculum materials used in the CAI program are important, as well as other factors. To do the type of study that would isolate the important variables is too large an undertaking to be worthwhile at this juncture in the development of the reading program. Thus, to some extent it is a matter of judgment in deciding which variables account for the differences observed in the above study. In my view, individualizing instruction is the key factor in successfully teaching reading. This does not mean that all phases of instruction should be individualized, but certain skills can be mastered only if instruction is sensitive to the student's particular difficulties. A reading teacher interacting on a one-to-one basis with a student may be more effective than our CAI program. However, when working with a group of children (even as few as four or five), it is unlikely that the teacher can match the computer's effectiveness in making instructional decisions over an extended period of time.

SECOND-LANGUAGE VOCABULARY LEARNING

In this section, research on CAI programs for second-language vocabulary learning will be discussed. As noted elsewhere in this chapter, the principal goal of our research on computerized instruction has been to develop adaptive teaching procedures—procedures that make moment-by-moment decisions about which instructional action should be taken next based on the student's unique response history. To help guide the theoretical aspects of this work, some years ago we

---

[4] In this study no attempt was made to allocate time optimally among students in the experimental group; rather, an equal-time policy was employed.

initiated a series of experiments on the very restricted but well-defined problem of optimizing the teaching of a foreign-language vocabulary. This is an area where mathematical models provide an accurate description of learning, and these models can be used in conjunction with the methods of control theory to derive precise algorithms for sequencing instruction among vocabulary items. Although our original interest in this topic was primarily theoretical, the work has proved to have significant practical applications. These applications involve computerized vocabulary learning programs designed to supplement college-level courses in second-language instruction. A particularly interesting effort involves a supplementary Russian program in use at Stanford University. Students are exposed to approximately 1,000 words per academic quarter using the computer; in conjunction with normal classroom work this program enables them to develop a substantial vocabulary.[5] Many foreign-language instructors believe that the major obstacle to successful instruction in a second language is not learning the grammar of the language, but rather in acquiring a sufficient vocabulary so that the student can engage in meaningful conversations and read materials other than the textbook.

In examining the work on vocabulary acquisition I will not describe the CAI programs, but will review some research on optimal sequencing schemes that provide the theoretical rationale for the programs. It will be useful to describe one experiment in some detail before considering more general issues.

An Experiment on Optimal Sequencing Schemes

In this study a large set of German–English items are to be learned during an instructional session that involves a series of trials. On each trial, one of the German words is presented and the student attempts to give the English translation; the correct translation is then presented for a brief study period. A predetermined number of trials is allocated for the instructional session, and after some intervening period a test is administered over the entire vocabulary. The problem is to specify a strategy for presenting items during the instructional session so that performance on the delayed test will be maximized.

Four strategies for sequencing the instructional material will be considered. The random-order strategy, (RO), is to cycle through the set of items randomly; this strategy is not expected to be particularly effective, but it provides a benchmark against which to evaluate other procedures. The self-selection strategy (SS), is to let the student determine how best to sequence the material. In this mode, the student decides on each trial which item is to be presented; the learner rather than an external controller determines the sequence of instruction.

---

[5] These CAI vocabulary programs make use of optimal sequencing schemes of the sort to be discussed in this section, as well as certain mnemonic aids. For a discussion of these mnemonic aids see Raugh and Atkinson (1975) and Atkinson and Raugh (1975).

The third and fourth schemes are based on a decision-theoretic analysis of the task. A mathematical model that provides an accurate account of vocabulary acquisition is assumed to hold in the present situation. The model is used to compute, on a trial-by-trial basis, an individual student's current state of learning. Based on these computations, items are selected for test and study so as to optimize the level of learning achieved at the termination of the instructional session. Two optimization strategies derived from this type of analysis will be examined. In one case, the computations for determining an optimal strategy are carried out assuming that all vocabulary items are of equal difficulty; this strategy is designated OE (i.e., optimal under the assumption of equal item difficulty). In the other case, the computations take into account variations in difficulty level among items; this strategy is called OU (i.e., optimal under the assumption of unequal item difficulty). The details of these two strategies will be described later.

The experiment was carried out under computer control; the details of the experimental procedure are given in Atkinson (1972b). The students participated in two sessions: an "instructional session" of approximately two hours and a briefer "delayed-test session" administered one week later. The delayed test was the same for all students and involved a test over the entire vocabulary. The instructional session was more complicated. The vocabulary items were divided into seven lists, each containing 12 German words; the seven lists were arranged in a round-robin order. On each trial of the instructional session a list was displayed on a projection screen, and the student inspected it for a brief period of time; the list involved only the 12 German words and not their English translations. Then one of the items on the list was selected for test and study. In the RO, OE, and OU conditions the item was selected by the computer; in the SS condition the item was chosen by the student. After an item was selected for test, the student attempted to provide a translation by typing it on the computer console; then feedback regarding the correct translation was given. The next trial began with the computer displaying the next list in the round robin, and the same procedure was repeated. The instructional session continued in this fashion for 336 trials.

The results of the experiment are summarized in Fig. 5. Data are presented on the left side of the figure for performance on successive blocks of trials during the instructional session; on the right are results from the test session administered one week after the instructional session. The data from the instructional session are presented in successive blocks of 84 trials; for the RO condition this means that on the average each item was presented once in each of these blocks. Note that performance during the instructional session is best for the RO condition, next best for the OE condition which is slightly better than the SS condition, and poorest for the OU condition. The order of the groups is reversed on the delayed test. (Two points are displayed in the figure for the delayed test to indicate that the test involved two random cycles through the entire vocabu-

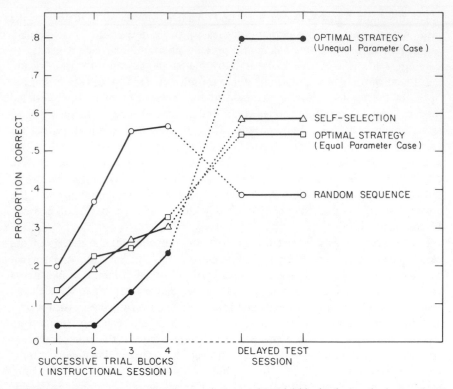

FIG. 5 Proportion of correct responses in successive trial blocks during the instructional session and on the delayed test administered one week later.

lary; however, the values given are the average over the two test cycles.) The OU condition is best with a correct response probability of .79; the SS condition is next with .58; the OE condition follows closely at .54 and the RO condition is poorest at .38. The observed pattern of results is what one would expect. In the SS condition, the students are trying to test themselves on items they do not know; consequently, during the instructional session, they should have a lower proportion of correct responses than students run on the RO procedure where items are tested at random. Similarly, the OE and OU conditions involve a procedure that attempts to identify and test those items that have not yet been mastered and should produce high error rates during the instructional session. The ordering of groups on the delayed test is reversed since all words are tested in a nonselective fashion; under these conditions the proportion of correct responses provides a measure of a student's true mastery of the total set of vocabulary items.

The magnitude of the effects observed on the delayed test are of practical significance. The SS condition (when compared to the RO condition) leads to a relative gain of 53%, whereas the OU condition yields a relative gain of 108%. It is interesting that students were somewhat effective in determining an optimal study sequence, but not so effective as the best of the two adaptive teaching systems.

Rationale for Sequencing Scheme

Both the OU and OE schemes assume that vocabulary learning can be described by a fairly simple model. We postulate that a given item is in one of three states (P, T, and U) at any moment in time. If the item is in State P, then its translation is known and this knowledge is "relatively" permanent in the sense that the learning of other items will not interfere with it. If the item is in State T, then it is also known but on a "temporary" basis; in State T the learning of other items can give rise to interference effects that cause the item to be forgotten. In State U the item is not known, and the student is unable to give a translation.

When Item i is presented on a trial during the instructional session, the following transition matrix describes the possible change in its state:

$$\mathbf{L}(i) = \begin{array}{c} \\ P \\ T \\ U \end{array} \begin{array}{ccc} P & T & U \\ \left[\begin{array}{ccc} 1 & 0 & 0 \\ x(i) & 1-x(i) & 0 \\ y(i) & z(i) & 1-y(i)-z(i) \end{array} \right] \end{array}.$$

Rows of the matrix represent the state of the item at the start of the trial, and columns the state at the end of the trial. On a trial when some item other than Item i is presented for test and study, transitions in the state of Item i also may take place. Such transitions can occur only if the student makes an error to the other item; in that case the transition matrix applied to Item i is as follows:

$$\mathbf{F}(i) = \begin{array}{c} \\ P \\ T \\ U \end{array} \begin{array}{ccc} P & T & U \\ \left[\begin{array}{ccc} 1 & 0 & 0 \\ 0 & 1-f(i) & f(i) \\ 0 & 0 & 1 \end{array} \right] \end{array}.$$

Basically, the idea is that when some other item is presented that the student does not know, forgetting may occur for Item i if it is in State T.

To summarize, when Item i is presented for test and study, transition matrix $\mathbf{L}(i)$ is applied; when some other item is presented that elicits an error, matrix $\mathbf{F}(i)$ is applied. It is also assumed that at the start of the instructional session Item i is either in State P, with probability $g(i)$, or in State U, with probability $1-g(i)$; the student either knows the translation without having studied the item or does not. The above assumptions provide a complete description of the learning process. The parameter vector $[x(i), y(i), z(i), f(i), g(i)]$ characterizes the learning of Item i in the vocabulary set. The first three parameters govern the acquisition process; the next parameter, forgetting; and the last, the student's knowledge prior to entering the experiment.

We now turn to a discussion of how the OE and OU procedures were derived from the model. Prior to conducting the experiment reported here, a pilot study was run using the same word lists and the RO procedure described above. Data from the pilot study were employed to estimate the parameters of the model; the estimates were obtained using the minimum chi-square procedures described in Atkinson (1972b). Two separate estimates of parameters were made. In one case it was assumed that the items were all equally difficult, and data from all 84 items were lumped together to obtain a single estimate of the parameter vector; this estimation procedure will be called the equal-parameter case (E case). In the second case the data were separated by items, and an estimate of the parameter vector was made for each of the 84 items; this procedure will be called the unequal-parameter case (U case). The two sets of parameter estimates were then used to generate the optimization schemes previously referred to as the OE and OU procedures.

In order to formulate an instructional strategy, it is necessary to be precise about the quantity to be maximized. For the present experiment the goal is to maximize the total number of items the student correctly translates on the delayed test.[6] To do this, we need to specify the relationship between the state of learning at the end of the instructional session and performance on the delayed test. The assumption made here is that only those items in State P at the end of the instructional session will be translated correctly on the delayed test; an item in State T is presumed to be forgotten during the intervening week. Thus, the problem of maximizing delayed-test performance involves maximizing the number of items in State P at the end of the instructional session.

Having numerical values for parameters and knowing a student's response history, it is possible to estimate the student's current state of learning.[7] Stated

[6] Other measures can be used to assess the benefits of an instructional strategy; for example, in this case weights could be assigned to items measuring their relative importance. Also costs may be associated with the various actions taken during an instructional session. Thus, for the general case, the optimization problem involves assessing costs and benefits and finding a strategy that maximizes an appropriate function defined on them. For a discussion of these points see Dear, Silberman, Estavan, and Atkinson (1967), and Smallwood (1962, 1971).

[7] The student's "response history" is a record for each trial of the vocabulary item presented and the response that occurred. It can be shown that there exists a "sufficient history" that contains only the information necessary to estimate the student's current state of learning; the sufficient history is a function of the complete history and the assumed learning model (Groen & Atkinson, 1966). For the model considered in this paper the sufficient history is fairly simple. It is specified in terms of individual vocabulary items for each student; we need to know the ordered sequence of correct and incorrect responses to a given item plus the number of errors (to other items) that intervene between each presentation of the item.

more precisely, the learning model can be used to derive equations and, in turn, compute the probabilities of being in States P, T, and U for each item at the start of any trial, conditionalized on the student's response history up to that trial. Given numerical estimates of these probabilities, a strategy for optimizing performance is to select that item for presentation that has the greatest probability of moving into State P. This strategy has been termed the one-stage optimization procedure because it looks ahead one trial in making decisions. The true optimal policy (i.e., an N-stage procedure) would consider all possible item–response sequences for the remaining trials and select the next item so as to maximize the number of items in State P at the termination of the instructional session. Unfortunately, for the present case the N-stage policy cannot be applied because the computations are too time consuming even for a large computer. Monte Carlo studies indicate that the one-stage policy is a good approximation to the optimal strategy; it was for this reason, as well as the relative ease of computing, that the one-stage procedure was employed. For a discussion of one-stage and N-stage policies and Monte Carlo studies comparing them see Groen and Atkinson (1966), Calfee (1970), and Laubsch (1970).

The optimization procedure described above was implemented on the computer and permitted decisions to be made for each student on a trial-by-trial basis. For students in the OE group, the computations were carried out using the five parameter values estimated under the assumption of homogeneous items (E case); for students in the OU group the computations were based on the 420 parameter values estimated under the assumption of heterogeneous items (U case).

The OU procedure is sensitive to interitem differences and consequently generates a more effective optimization strategy than the OE procedure. The OE procedure, however, is almost as effective as having the student make his own instructional decisions and far superior to a random presentation scheme.

The study reported here is one in a series of experiments dealing with optimal sequencing schemes. It was selected because it is easily described and permits direct comparison between a learner-controlled procedure versus procedures based on a decision-theoretic analysis. For a review of other studies similar to the one reported above see Chiang (1974), Delaney (1973), Laubsch (1970), Kimball (1973), Paulson (1973), and Atkinson and Paulson (1972). Some of these studies examine procedures that are more powerful than the ones described here, but they are complicated and difficult to describe without going into mathematical detail. The major improvements involve two factors: (1) methods for estimating the model's parameters during the course of instruction, and (2) more sophisticated ways of interpreting the parameters of the model to take account of both differences among students and differences among items. For example, let $P(i, j)$ be a generic symbol for a parameter vector characterizing student i learning vocabulary item j. In these studies $P(i, j)$ is specified as a function of a vector $A(i)$ measuring the ability of student i and a vector $D(j)$

measuring the difficulty of item j. The problem then is to estimate the ability level of each student and the difficulty of each item while the student is running on the program. In a study reported in Atkinson and Paulson (1972), rather dramatic results were obtained using such a procedure. A special feature of the study was that students were run in successive groups, each starting after the prior group had completed the experiment. As would be expected, the overall gains increased from one group to the next. The reason is that for the first group of students the estimates of item difficulty, $D(j)$, were crude but improved with the accumulation of data from each successive wave of students. Near the end of the study estimates of $D(j)$ were quite precise and were essentially constants in the system. The only task that remained when a new student came on the system was to estimate $A(i)$; that is, the parameters characterizing his particular ability level. This study provides an example of an adaptive instructional system that meets both of the requirements stated earlier in this chapter. The sequencing of instruction varies as a function of each student's history record, and over time the system improved in efficiency by using data from previous students to sharpen its estimates of the difficulty of instructional materials.

CONCLUDING REMARKS

The projects described in this chapter have one theme in common, namely, developing computer-controlled procedures for optimizing the instructional process. For several of the instructional tasks considered here, mathematical models of the learning process were formulated which made it possible to use formal methods in deriving optimal policies. In other cases the "optimal schemes" were not optimal in a well-defined sense, but were based on our intuitions about learning and some relevant experiments. In a sense, the diversity represented in these examples corresponds to the state of the art in the field of instructional design. For some tasks we can use psychological theory to help define optimal procedures; for others our intuitions, modified by experiments, must guide the effort. Hopefully, our understanding of these matters will increase as more projects are undertaken to develop sophisticated instructional procedures.

Some have argued that any attempt to devise optimal strategies is doomed to failure, and that the learner is the best judge of appropriate instructional actions. I am not sympathetic to a learner-controlled approach to instruction, because I believe its advocates are trying to avoid the difficult but challenging task of developing a viable theory of instruction. There obviously is a place for the learner's judgments in making instructional decisions; for example, such judgments play an important role in several parts of our BIP course. However, using the learner's judgment as one of several items of information in making instructional decisions is different from proposing that the learner should have complete control. Results presented in this chapter and those cited in Beard,

Lorton, Searle, and Atkinson (1973) indicate that the learner is not a particularly effective decision maker in guiding the learning process.

Elsewhere I have defined the criteria that must be satisfied before an optimal instructional procedure can be derived using formal methods (Atkinson, 1972a). Roughly stated, they require that the following elements of an instructional situation be clearly specified:

1. The set of admissible instructional actions.
2. The instructional objectives.
3. A measurement scale that permits costs to be assigned to each of the instructional actions and payoffs to the achievement of instructional objectives.
4. A model of the learning process.

If these four elements can be given a precise interpretation, then it is usually possible to derive an optimal-instructional policy. The solution for an optimal policy is not guaranteed, but in recent years powerful tools have been developed for discovering optimal, or near optimal, procedures if they exist. I will not discuss these four elements here except to note that the first three can usually be specified with a fair degree of consensus. Issues of short-term versus long-term assessments of costs and payoffs raise important questions regarding educational policy, but at least for the types of instructional situations examined here reasonable specifications can be offered for the first three elements. However, the fourth element—the specification of a model of the learning process—represents a major obstacle. Our theoretical understanding of learning is so limited that only in very special cases can a model be specified in enough detail to enable the derivation of optimal procedures. Until we have a much deeper understanding of the learning process, the identification of truly effective strategies will not be possible. However, an all-inclusive theory of learning is not a prerequisite for the development of optimal procedures. What is needed is a model that captures the essential features of that part of the learning process being tapped by a given instructional task. Even models that have been rejected on the basis of laboratory investigations may be useful in deriving instructional strategies. Several of the learning models considered in this chapter have proven unsatisfactory when tested in the laboratory and evaluated using standard goodness-of-fit criteria; nevertheless, the optimal strategies they generate are often quite effective. My own preference is to formulate as complete a learning model as intuition and data will permit and then use that model to investigate optimal procedures. When possible the learning model should be represented in the form of mathematical equations, but otherwise as a set of statements in a computer-simulation program. The main point is that the development of a theory of instruction cannot progress if one holds the view that a comprehensive theory of learning is a prerequisite. Rather, advances in learning theory will affect the development of a theory of instruction, and conversely the development of a theory of instruction will influence the direction of research on learning.

ACKNOWLEDGMENTS

This research was supported by the Office of Naval Research, Contract No. N00014-67-A-0012-0054, by National Science Foundation Grant EC-43997, and by Grant MH-21747 from the National Institute of Mental Health.

5

Methods and Models for Task Analysis in Instructional Design

Lee W. Gregg

Carnegie-Mellon University

A theory of instruction must be based on the objectives of the learner and the institutionalized goals of the instructional system. A theory of instruction must also rest upon an adequate formulation of the psychological capacity of the learner. Instructional goals prescribe the domain of tasks to be undertaken by the learner; the psychological capacities of the learner set limits on the size, complexity of the subtasks and the rate of introducing them into the domain.

Each of the first four chapters presents a framework for analyzing tasks from various psychological perspectives. Carroll contrasts strict behaviorism with a currently nonexistent cognitive theory of learning. Calfee takes a statistical view. Resnick eclectically draws from Gagné's hierarchies, Gestalt Psychology, Thorndike, and Piaget to formulate a rational information processing scheme. Atkinson's approach uses optimization procedures to guide instructional design.

In general, instructional design attempts to organize subtask sequences, provide opportunities for learning, and devise ways of evaluating the extent to which the learner acquires proficiency. Notice that these general activities are neutral with respect to methods of analysis and models of the learner. Thus, teachers have been searching continually for new ways to break up tasks into teachable units. The key concepts for many instructors are differentiation followed by integration. If Carroll is right in his assessment of the role behavioral sciences play in education, behavioral objectives will be ignored and soon forgotten. They will become just one more fad thrust on the field. Behavioral objectives may give way to cognitive objectives as defined by Greeno in Chapter 7. If Carroll is right, the naive theories of learning on which many an artful teacher predicates lesson plans will be explained by cognitive theory, but not necessarily extended by it.

Carroll, of course, is right—at least in part. Cognitive theories and information processing models will supplant some of the currently fashionable notions—they have already done so. Furthermore, there is evidence from the set of current chapters of a cumulative body of knowledge dealing with important issues of task analysis and instruction that a lasting contribution will result.

What are the steps in a task analysis? First, we set out to identify component skills such that mastery of the individual skill components assures partial success on the task. We assume that the hierarchy of skills exists and that components are independent. Calfee attacks the issue of independence directly. To the extent that subprocesses like decoding and comprehension can be treated independently, the analysis of components will be successful. One direction that research must take is the identification of the conditions under which tasks may conform to a simple additive hierarchical decomposition. Next in the sequence of analysis, we introduce components one at a time. As Resnick points out in Chapter 3 these components must be teachable. The usual next step in the task analysis requires that we start where the learner is and build on what he already knows and can do. Here the issues revolve around the diagnostic tests for determining the initial state of the learner, and the development of instructional materials that exercise the component. Instructional materials, the teaching routines that Resnick refers to, must provide a basis for integrating the new learning with the old. But the third stage of task analysis attempts to integrate the newly acquired skills into a meaningful whole. Of special concern are the real time constraints. Very often, subtasks that appear to be well learned fall apart when combined in new ways. Think of the feeling of helplessness when you last failed to recall the name of a close friend in performing introductions around a group. Paced recall is not a cognitive task that we are asked to perform frequently.

Are there cognitive theories of learning that can be applied to the job of task analysis? Carroll's review of naive, behavioristic, and cognitive theories of language learning suggests that a cognitive learning theory now exists. Unfortunately, recent work on semantic memory (Norman, Rumelhart, et al., 1975; Quillian, 1967, 1968; Schank, 1972) has been primarily concerned with determining the structure of memory representations. Research on the processes of understanding (Hayes & Simon, 1974 and this volume; Winograd, 1972) assume that a knowledge base is already learned and available. Of course, Greeno has asserted that learning theory and comprehension theory defined in information processing terms are the same thing (Greeno, 1974). My own work on sequential pattern learning (Gregg, 1967), verbal learning (Gregg & Simon, 1967), and serial learning (Gregg, 1972; McLean & Gregg, 1967) leads me to argue that they are not the same. One difference is in the development of intermediate structures in working memory that Greeno has previously described. However, it seems appropriate to stress the similarities between learning and the processes of understanding. Both depend on attention to determine the final outcomes. Both require contiguity of the elements to be associated. The study of comprehension and learning is the study of cognitive organizations.

Although there is no explicit and general cognitive theory of learning, there have been isolated examples pointing potential future directions. The Elementary Perceiver and Memorizer, EPAM, was the first modern theory of semantic memory and showed the main outlines of associative memory structures. Atkinson and Shiffrin's (1968) model for running paired associates learning accentuated the importance of control processes in learning and memory. Just as the role of semantic memory emphasizes structural aspects of representations of knowledge, short-term memory studies emphasize the dynamic operation of control processes in specific tasks. Learning and comprehension, therefore, are similar precisely because they come about from the operation of the human information processing system. His processing limitations determine the rate of acquisition of new information and its availability for use in problem solving.

INDEPENDENCE OF COGNITIVE SKILLS

Are the processes that the human information processing system uses detectable from an analysis of overt behavior in instructional task environments? This is the issue that Calfee examines in Chapter 2.

The method that Calfee proposes is aimed at finding out whether or not processes are independent. Finding they are *not* is not very informative. Since the method does not generate process descriptions, only tests the effects of them, one must create variables to test the hypothesis that a process whose operation may or may not be correctly reflected by the measure, exists. There are two stages at either of which an error can occur. Each stage provides an opportunity for error. One can incorrectly assume that a process exists that transforms a data structure in a certain way. But one can also incorrectly assess the effects of the hypothesized process by failing to define a relevant dependent variable.

Most of the theorizing must go on in advance of and independently of the testing operations suggested by Calfee. Modern inference procedures make it possible to carry out much more powerful analyses of system interactions.

Even though the model of reading proposed by Calfee appears to be correct, the processes must not remain independent for long. The still higher order cognitive processes in speed reading and comprehension cannot depend on simple additive components because selective, intentional use of strategies implies the constructive use of components.

We must distinguish between pedagogically useful packets of information and the information processing mechanisms that may or may not view the materials to be learned in the same way that the instructor views them. Are the human mechanisms really independent? The answer is contingent on the extent to which we can show sequential order in the processing of the information.

INTERACTIONS OF SEQUENTIAL PROCESSES

In any information processing system, there will be a lack of statistical independence among the subprocesses if the output of one processes provides inputs to a later process in the sequence. Since we believe that most cognitive task involving attention are serial, there are few tasks for which a strict independence of the processes is likely. The question is not whether they are independent for they are almost certainly not. The crucial question is, "How are they organized?" How do we study interacting processes? What forms of organization exist?

One of our most popular notions of task organization is the tree structure. The implication is that higher-level elements grow out of well formed lower-level elements. Subtasks are subsumed as components of and precursors to other tasks. But most accounts of learning and analyses of errors during learning suggest that the prior elements are not stable and must change. Even when the learner brings well developed skills to the task, there are confusing periods during which the prior elements are being modified. The notion that prior behaviors are incorporated into higher organizations whole cloth is probably wrong.

Two aspects of the learning process suggest why. First, more complex behaviors usually involve the intergration of serial patterns. Hence, the merging of behavior sequences tends to slur one pattern into another. New patterns result. The distinction between components is changed; and new boundaries are drawn. Second, when more complex behavior patterns are learned, the simpler prior patterns are changed in that the evoking stimuli are different. An example of these kinds of modifications will be seen later.

As Resnick warns, there can be a great deal of difference between competency in early stages of learning and in later stages. One reason, I believe, is that the component skills assume new forms when they merge in higher-order patterns. The organization of more complex skills, whether mental or motor, is analogous to a compiled computer subroutine. Once assimilated into the repertoire there is no need to test each separate instructional during execution. Thus, mental skills take on the properties of automatic motor performance. For example, in playing the piano, practicing left and right hand separately emphasizes sight reading skills, builds habits that are not relevant for the coordinated combination of both parts. When playing the two parts, the places where one must merely check the score can be quite different from those of single-handed and single-minded practice.

In summary, we suppose that location of the tests may change, the size of the perceptual or conceptual unit may vary, and that cues for initiating or sustaining the behavior may be different at different stages of practice.

INDIVIDUALIZATION AND TASK ANALYSIS

Atkinson's approach stresses the idea that the learner must be able to follow flexible pathways through a subject domaine. Optimization of CAI learning tasks is based on a curriculum composed of a network of related tasks and a loose collection of associated skills. In Atkinson's view, subtasks and skills need not be related in a rigidly hierarchical fashion. This in not to say that the instructional materials for CAI are not carefully thought through. Rather, the point is that individual learners can achieve higher performance levels in a variety of ways. For the specific areas of application, there is a "careful analysis and precise specification of the skills inherent in the subject matter." Thus, for Atkinson the subject matter defines the structure of tasks; the learner acquires skills that are inherent, i.e., determined by the task demands.

Optimization is based on an empirical procedure to assess transfer of training. Thus, it is possible for a student to shift from one strand to another based on performance within the first strand. Control of the process is guided by a model of learning that provides a complete response history which then in turn feeds a Markov model. The optimization procedures are based on empirical results of transfer and acquisition using simple models of the performance during learning. Trial by trial selection of items and exercises procedes from a determination of each student's ability and each item's difficulty. At the most global level, optimization is over the allocation of student time to each strand.

In these procedures, Atkinson has captured the crucial questions of instructional design that each teacher asks:

1. What items and exercises should I give?
2. How should the student's time be distributed over the different classes of work?
3. How should the resources available for instruction be allocated among the students?

Atkinson shows how far one can go toward answering these questions with relatively simple models of performance during learning. His experiments on the optimum sequencing of vocabulary items indicates the kind of gains one can expect from the systematic selection and presentation of items for study. Improvement of the order of 50 and 100% are, indeed, impressive results. Atkinson points out that comprehensive theories of learning are not necessary to produce important differences in rate and degree of learning.

I view Chapter 4 by Atkinson as a landmark for CAI applications. In it we see three important demonstrations of the state of the art in appropriate applications of computer based instruction. First, the Basic Instructional Program (BIP) represents an appropriate use of the computer as a problem solving tool. The learner masters a programming language under the direction of the system which assesses his or her level of problem-solving skill and tutorially guides the learner through increasing levels of skilled performance. It has been several years since I leveled the criticism that most CAI work did not use computers in ways for which they were intended (Gregg, 1970). Clearly that comment cannot be applied to Atkinson's work. The second part of Atkinson's chapter describes his analysis of the reading task and it's acquisition. Here a sophisticated analysis of the skills required in reading is presented and a series of exercises within each strand defined. Although on a trial by trial basis, the model that determines the sequence of learner experience is a powerful application of decision theoretic ideas to transfer from strand to strand in a complex structure based on task analysis. In that earlier criticism, I said that it seemed a waste to use computers as glorified memory drums. Atkinson's program for the instruction in initial reading bears no resemblance to so stupid a machine. Perhaps the only legitimate criticism that remains is that certain complex cognitive tasks that require understanding will require complex cognitive analyses. In the chapters that follow, models of semantic memory, sentence comprehension, and understanding written problem instructions point the way for these new developments.

SUBJECT STRATEGIES AND TASK ANALYSIS

Resnick's review of concepts underlying the analysis of instructable components poses several challenges. The issue is how to combine components logically to produce the desired behavior of presumably higher complexity. Instructional design rests on the premise that a sequence of component tasks can be identified and then mastered in some order to produce behavior. The integration can have logical implications. The ideas of Osherson (1974) on logical grouping capture the hierarchical nature of performance combinatorics, but not the order information that I have stressed so heavily in this discussion.

The reason I believe serial order is so important is evident when we consider that a subject strategy consists of a sequence of cognitive acts involving shifts in attention and transformations of objects. Thus, in any problem-solving task or learning situation, a complete description of the psychological problem space must include the representation of the specific objects and the set of operators to be applied. In a later chapter, Simon and Hayes discuss problem isomorphs where superficially distinct problems map onto the same problem space. Hence, differences in problem-solving performance can be attributed to a failure to find an efficient representation for the task. But here I am talking about performing an identical task where only the instructions to the learner vary.

In a recent, unpublished experiment by Gerritsen, Gregg, and Simon, the subjects were instructed in three strategies. All other conditions of the experiment were the same. The strategies, however, caused the subjects to attend to different aspects of the problem as it was being solved. Both the stimulus information and the transformation rules were different for each strategy.

The experimental task was similar to Restle's (1970) serial pattern learning task. The problem was displayed before the subject consisting of a digit from one to six and a series of 3, 4, or 5 letters which stood for the symbolic operators: T was transpose, add one; M was mirror, obtain the sevens compliment; and R was repeat. The subjects responded by pressing buttons labeled with the values one to six on a panel in front of them.

The three strategies were called the Doubling, Recompute, and Pushdown Methods. Each specified a different information processing sequence and each resulted in quite different response measures and error patterns. In fact, performance on the task varied by a factor of 3 to 1, from 2244 msec per response for the Recompute Method to 721 msec per response for the Doubling Method. Such robust effects from instructions alone argue that any attempt to identifying skill components must be certain of their implementation in terms other than task variables.

CONCLUSIONS

The moral of this research story is simply that subject strategies are crucial to an understanding of cognitive performance. One way of viewing the entire problem of instructional task analysis is to say that the goal is to specify a complete set of subject strategies sufficient to the task, to map feasible strategies onto the current information processing skills of the learner, and finally to develop instructional methods and materials such that the learner acquires those strategies that have the greatest educational value.

Resnick, in Chapter 3, showed that children will invent strategies and these may be more efficient than those derived by curriculum designers. Chapter 7 by Greeno will show that we can teach better or worse strategies. The challenge for instructional design is clear.

6

Notes on a Cognitive Theory of Instruction

David R. Olson

Ontario Institute for Studies in Education

My purpose in this chapter is to discuss five general points presented in chapters of Carroll, Atkinson, Calfee, and Resnick that underlie the discussion or development of a theory of instruction.

First, I want to indicate my opinion as to the current status of the enterprise. I believe that a theory of instruction is a legitimate scientific goal and that such a theory has as examplars some impressive local successes (e.g., Atkinson's work). However, it is easy to overestimate its current status. As it now stands, the theory of instruction is very primitive and not at all at a stage requiring complex mathematical descriptions for its expression. Considerations of the nature of performance, the nature of knowledge, the nature of the communicable and instructable, and the nature of experience—some of which have been raised by Carroll and Resnick as well as by others (cf. Olson & Bruner, 1974)—are conceptual issues that must be faced in the attempt to construct such a theory.

At the more specific level of optimal design, that is, research directed to the production of an explicit instructional program designed to achieve a particular educational goal, the achievements to date are more impressive. Programs designed to achieve a particular goal, such as those described by Atkinson, Resnick, and Calfee (Chapters 4, 3, and 2, respectively, of this volume), and others such as *Sesame Street* (Palmer, 1975) can be described quite precisely and achieve their goals quite successfully.

But what is the relation between specific instructional programs, the problem of design, and a general theory of instruction? Atkinson raised this point in regard to the "depth" of the theory based on the set of parameters found to be relevant to the optimization of a particular instructional program. The 'theory' is, as I understood him, primarily an equation optimizing the particular set of parameters for that set of tasks. The problem is that that equation would not be generalizable to a new, quite different set of tasks. How then do we get to a general theory of instruction that would apply to the vast array of things that are taught to all sorts of learners by a vast array of means? It is about this general theory of instruction that we know so little.

Stated in another way, the relation between particular procedures and general theory may be conceived in terms of the relation between *design* and *theory*. In the analysis of instruction are we concerned primarily either with the problem of designing effective instructional systems (cf. Richards, 1968, 1974) *or* with the construction of a theory that would make explicit the nature and consequences of the experiences managed by formal institutions such as schools. And it is difficult to serve these two goals at the same time.

Second, I want to consider what a "cognitive" instructional theory would look like. If we simply adopt "behavioral objectives" or if instructional theory is concerned only with optimization, cognitive theories are, to say the least, as luxury. What could a cognitive theory add? As Carroll pointed out, cognition means knowledge. A cognitive theory would be concerned with the nature of human knowledge, how it is represented and how it is acquired. But in instruction, we are not concerned with all knowledge but rather with that knowledge which is of such social value that the society creates an institution to guarantee that it is transmitted to every child growing up in that society. What is that knowledge and what are the means at our disposal for conveying it?

Carroll argued that a theory of instruction that takes seriously the nature and acquisition of knowledge would make instuction more effective. Calfee and Resnick by their research programs show that they agree. And they may be right. But in being right they would be indistinguishable from any behaviorist or social engineer. Again, then, what could cognitive psychology add?

Cognitive psychology could be concerned, not with prediction and control and optimization, but rather with "understanding." Objective knowledge, borrowing from Popper (1972), is a record of the culture's solutions of important problems. As such, knowledge complements the adaptive resources given to us through the genes and those acquired through our own personal experiences. This knowledge is coded in terms of the symbol systems of the culture, particularly natural language. Such knowledge is shared and therefore social in nature. In content and in structure and in social significance this knowledge is distinctive from that acquired via direct practical activity; presumably the processes involved in the extraction of such knowledge are distinctive and the consequences of the acquisition of this knowledge are unique. A theory of instruction, therefore, is needed for more than simply improving the power of our procedures; it is needed to help make explicit just what it is we are doing to children and adults in the process of socializing them. Then we will be in a position to decide which of these effects are worthwhile as well as which means are effective.

To summarize this point: instructional theory should be concerned not only with optimization, control, or the achievement of behavioral objectives but also, and more basically, with making explicit the nature and the consequences of the transmission of socially useful knowledge. Once these processes are explicit they are subject to rational consideration, as Popper (1972) has argued. So we require a theory of instruction that would cast into theoretical terms what is already going on in the schools, and elsewhere, in the name of instruction and what is being altered with the introduction of new types of programs whether they be activity programs, or CAI, or whatever.

Third, I would like to consider instruction as the communication of explicit, formalizable routines. This point is related to Resnick's interesting suggestion that good instruction may trade off communicability with formal adequacy. I recently published an article titled "What is worth knowing and what can be taught? (Olson, 1973)" in which I argued that much of the knowledge most worth having—making discoveries, speaking convincingly, writing effectively, and various social and ethical skills—cannot be taught explicitly because the algorithm underlying them (if indeed there are such algorithms) are not known. Many that are known are too complex to communicate easily (consider, for example the passive transformation in English). Yet, in another sense, these important skills may be 'taught' by providing demonstrations and by providing sessions for repeated practice accompanied by appropriate feedback.

To summarize this point, some knowledge is formalizable—an algorithm for adding, for example, and can be taught explicitly. But other, more complex skills, including many socially valued skills, cannot be taught explicitly and they may have to be 'taught' through demonstrations or *modeling* and/or through making allowances for learning through trial and error or *muddling*. And a theory of instruction is going to have to specify the nature and the role and the consequences of modeling and muddling as well as the more explicit intervention which, for the sake of alliteration, we may call *meddling*.

Fourth, consider the relation between knowledge and skill or knowledge and performance. Carroll raised this issue in regard to the linguist's distinction between competence and performance. Cognitive psychology contrasts with behaviorist theory in assuming that knowledge can be wrested from the purpose for which it was acquired and the context in which it was acquired and cast into more general symbolic form, thus rendering that knowledge applicable to a much wider range of problems.

Schools clearly got carried away with the assumption that the acquisition of theoretical knowledge, what Ryle (1949) called propositional knowledge, was the sine qua non of education, perhaps giving some legitimacy to student's current protest against the value of being stuffed with "irrelevant" knowledge.

This issue hangs critically upon an understanding of how knowledge relates to performance. Friere's book *The Pedagogy of the Oppressed* (1972) makes the case that the only liberating knowledge is knowledge acquired by *praxis*—action coupled with reflection. Perhaps useful knowledge must be acquired in the context of action. Minimally, a cognitive theory of instruction must indicate how knowledge is related to performance both in its acquisition and its subsequent use.

Fifth and finally, I want to argue in a preliminary way that the *means* of instruction are not simply instrumentalities in instruction. This point is based on the concept of the bias of communication (McLuhan, 1964; Innis, 1951). The way, the means by which one is taught, biases what is learned in a way that has largely escaped detection. I have recently argued, (Olson, 1974) following the leads of Havelock (1974), Goody and Watt (1968), Bruner, (1966) and others, that the particular reliance in our culture on the use of language out of the context of practical action has put a distinctive mark on both our cultural patterns and our cognitive processes. Specifically, the use of written prose as a means of instruction recruits and develops a set of mental competencies that are general to a wide range of intelligent performances. To illustrate, the fact that we learn Chemistry from textbooks which utilize the peculiar language of explicit written prose results not only in some knowledge of chemistry but also of literary skills of a high level. These skills—the ability to see the logical implications of written statements, and more importantly, the ability to formulate general statements from which true inferences can be drawn—are mental skills of great importance and generality. But because they are a specialized set of skills, they are appropriate only for some kinds of tasks; and they may lead us to undervalue other, equally important but different skills such as those involved in the arts or, for that matter, those involved in common-sense judgments. Instructional theory will have to account for the nature of means before it can be regarded as a general theory.

It is this somewhat vague, general, and preliminary level of conceptual analysis that, I believe, will yield new understanding of the nature of instruction.

Part II

PROCESS AND STRUCTURE IN LEARNING

As the anatomist, with his microscopical study of the stomach, may finally suggest the ways for cooking more digestible food, so the experimental psychologist will combine and connect the detailed results more and more, till he is able to transform his knowledge into practical educational suggestions. . . . Single disconnected details are of no value for such a practical transformation; and even after all is done, this more highly developed knowledge will be but a more refined understanding of qualitative relations—never the quantitative measurement which so many teachers now hopefully expect [Münsterberg, 1898].

7

Cognitive Objectives of Instruction: Theory of Knowledge for Solving Problems and Answering Questions

James G. Greeno

The University of Michigan

A great deal of progress has been made in recent years toward the understanding of many cognitive processes. Psychological theories that have been developed and tested deal with perception, memory, thinking, and language processing at a level of detail and specificity that is an order of magnitude beyond the theoretical concepts available only a few years ago.

My purpose in this chapter is to show how some of this body of theory can be used in the formulation of instructional objectives. The motivation for this is quite simple. The goal of instruction is that students should acquire knowledge and skills of various kinds. A rich set of concepts has been developed in scientific psychology that can be applied to analyze the structure of knowledge and cognitive skills. Thus, it should be possible using those concepts to carry out analyses of the knowledge and skill that are desired as outcomes of instruction. It may be expected that the explicit statement of instructional objectives based on psychological theory should have beneficial effects both in design of instruction and assessment of student achievement. The reason is simple: we can generally do a better job of accomplishing something and determining how well we have accomplished it when we have a better understanding of what it is we are trying to accomplish.

The view I am taking has much in common with the opinions of many educational psychologists (such as Anderson & Faust, 1973) who recommend that instructional goals be formulated as behavioral objectives. In the view taken here, development of instructional objectives begins with consideration of the kinds of tests used to assess whether students have acquired the knowledge intended as the outcome of learning. But rather than just specifying the behaviors needed to succeed on such tests, cognitive objectives are developed by analyzing the psychological processes and structures that are sufficient to produce the needed behaviors.

There is an important psychological assumption implicit in the position taken here. I am assuming that the goals of instruction, including aspects of conceptual understanding, can be inferred from the tasks that students are expected to perform during instruction and, following instruction, on tests. If this is accepted, then it follows that a theory specifying cognitive structures and processes sufficient to perform those tasks is a candidate hypothesis about what the instruction is trying to produce. Of course, any candidate that is proposed can and should be questioned regarding issues of substance. I am confident that the specific features of the objectives I will present here can be improved, although I have tried to incorporate reasonable psychological assumptions into these illustrative cases. However, the general kind of description offered here should be taken as a completely serious proposal about what the goals of instruction are like. It may be that when we see what kinds of cognitive structures are needed to perform criterion tasks, we will conclude that something important is missing; but if that is the case, it also will be important to identify a more adequate set of criterion tasks in order to ensure that instruction is promoting the structures we think are important.

I have chosen three substantive domains in which to develop illustrative cognitive objectives of instruction. The first is elementary material in fourth-grade fractions; the second is introductory material in high-school geometry; and the third is some material from introductory college psychology dealing with auditory psychophysics. None of these is developed to anything near a complete and detailed set of objectives; however, I hope that I have developed a sufficiently specific example in each case to make the enterprise credible. One reason for choosing these three examples is that they represent instruction carried out at widely different age levels. I believe that our current stock of concepts and techniques in cognitive psychology is adequate to the task of analyzing instructional objectives from elementary school through college, and my choice of examples is meant to back up that belief.

A related point about the choice of examples is that they illustrate some important broad relationships between knowledge that is imparted to students of different ages. The knowledge needed to do computations with fractions seems to involve a simple kind of algorithmic skill that can be expressed easily with flow charts. Suppes and Morningstar (1972) developed similar models for analysis of addition, subtraction, and multiplication; Suppes (1969) has called these automaton models. Tasks used for instruction in high-school geometry require a more complicated set of procedures and knowledge structures. Knowledge that is required for geometry can be represented as a production system, including mechanisms that are found in current theories of problem solving (e.g., Newell & Simon, 1972) for setting goals and searching in a problem space. The problem-solving system uses numerous procedures of the kind taught to elementary-school students, so knowledge of the first kind is embedded in the more complex structures required for the more mature learning.

The instructional objectives for college psychology seem to require still another level of complexity. Understanding auditory psychophysics requires acquisition of a complex network of concepts of the kind we are familiar with in theories of semantic memory (Anderson & Bower, 1973; Kintsch, 1974; Norman, Rumelhart, & Group, 1975; Quillian, 1968) and performance on many criterion tasks (such as essay examinations) requires a procedure for generating paragraphs in answer to complex questions. We are just now beginning to explore the kinds of cognitive capabilities needed to produce structured verbal output at the level of paragraphs (e.g., Abelson, 1973; Crothers, 1972; Frederiksen, 1972; Rumelhart, 1975). The mechanisms of generating explanations apparently share significant features with mechanisms of generating solutions for problems, but there are also significant differences, due at least in part to the more open-ended quality of the task.

EXAMPLE 1: FRACTIONS[1]

Much of the work on fractions required of students involves carrying out calculations such as finding equivalent fractions, adding and subtracting fractional numbers, and finding common denominators. Ability to carry out those calculations is a minimal objective of instruction, and it can be represented in a psychological theory as a flow chart showing the component processes of the procedure. In general, the procedure is not unique—there are more ways than one to calculate the correct answer. Alternative procedures can be represented in different models, or incorporated in a single nondeterministic model that allows different branches to be taken.

Procedural Representation of a Concept

Figure 1 shows a procedure for adding two fractions. The upper part of the diagram shows a procedure for finding fractions with a common denominator that are equivalent to the numbers given in the problem. The lower part sketches the operation of checking the answer and reducing if necessary.

If the procedure shown in Fig. 1 is accepted as a psychological model of adding fractions, then it is a candidate for an instructional objective in the elementary mathematics curriculum. The concept of adding fractions is a procedure, and a goal of instruction is to have students acquire that procedure as part of their cognitive equipment. The idea of representing a concept as a cognitive procedure

[1] I have been privileged to participate in a number of discussions of children's learning of fractions with my colleague Joseph Payne and his students. Many of the opinions and judgments that I have about fractions have been developed in those discussions, although Payne and his group surely should not be held responsible for faults in my understanding.

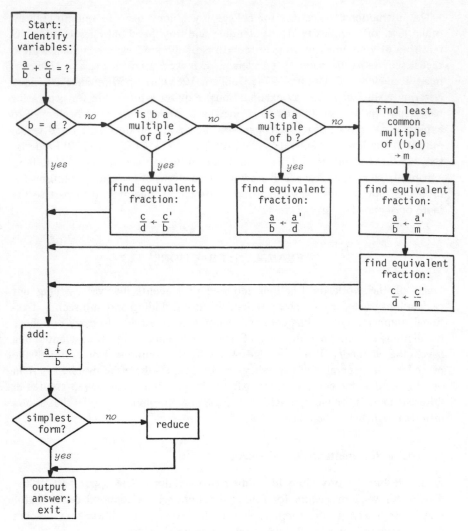

FIG. 1 Procedure for addition of fractions.

is familiar in recent theoretical work. Examples include Hunt's (1962) analysis of categorical concepts as procedures for classifying stimuli, and Winograd's (1972) theory of language understanding, where concepts are procedures for identifying objects and answering questions about their locations.

Cognitive Representations of Quantity

Procedures like Fig. 1 can compute answers, but they lack conceptual understanding of a kind that many educators would want students to acquire. Texts such as the one by Payne, May, Beatty, Wells, Spooner, and Dominy (1972) include numerous exercises like the one shown in Fig. 2, for which the student is to fill in the blanks of "___ out of ___ pieces are shaded." Other exercises present sets of discrete objects, such as a row of circles, some of which are colored differently from the others, with a question "___ out of ___ circles are red." The intent is for students to begin by seeing fractional quantities represented pictorially, as parts of regions or as subsets.

An important issue in the theory of mental computation is the way in which quantitative information is represented. A procedure like Fig. 1 is neutral with regard to the representation of quantity — that is, quantities could be represented in a variety of ways and the procedure could be designed to work on any of them. I suggest that the instructional objective reflected in exercises like Fig. 1 can be represented in a theory about the ways in which fractional quantities are represented.

I will distinguish here among three representations of quantity; there probably are more, but these seem to be the main possibilities involved in elementary instruction. The first representation is just an ordered alphabet of numerals. Students can count, and the list produced by counting provides a precedence relation on the numbers. Basic operations of addition, subtraction, multiplication, and division may also be stored as relations on numbers—for example, "five times three equals 15," may be in cognitive structure as a sequence of verbal associations.

A second representation involves actual or imagined quantity, the number of items in a set. A system could be designed with a counting mechanism for assigning a number to any set, but with operations of addition, multiplication, and so on carried out on sets rather than directly on numbers. For example, to find 5 × 3, imagine a set of five objects, then imagine three of those sets, and count the total number of objects in the three sets.

A third representation uses geometric forms, and quantity is represented as the spatial extent of a form. Addition and subtraction can be represented as moving to the right or left on a number line. To multiply 5 × 3, imagine a rectangle divided vertically into five sections, where the measure of each section is taken to be one. Then the rectangle is made three times as large—imagine two more rectangles just below the first one with the three rectangles concatenated, forming a single large rectangle. The total measure of the large rectangle is 15, as

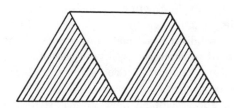

FIG. 2   Diagram representing a fraction spatially.

could be confirmed by counting all the sections of size equal to the original sections.

It would not be realistic to suppose that arithmetic operations are generally carried out by anyone as operations on sets or regions. No one multiplies 9 × 7 by imagining nine objects, each reproduced seven times, and counting the total; we remember that 9 × 7 is 63. However, teachers and writers of texts apparently feel that it is useful to introduce procedures for manipulating quantity as operations on spatial representations or on representations of sets. If Piaget (1965) is correct, addition and multiplication of numbers depend on the same basic cognitive operations as additive and multiplicative combinations of sets (and, we might suppose, regions—though that may involve some additional sophistication about space and geometry; see Piaget, Inhelder, & Szeminska, 1960). With or without Piaget's theory, it is reasonable to assume that students' acquisition of basic arithmetic concepts is aided by connecting those concepts with operations on sets and spatial quantity, since they have observed many of those changes in their experience.

When fractions are introduced, they can be related either to diagrams showing geometric shapes divided into pieces, or to diagrams showing sets of objects of different kinds. Fractions can also be defined for the students as a combination of operations including a multiplication and a division (Dienes, 1967b), although this would generally be done in connection with diagrams involving sets or regions. I will not try to present a full analysis here of all the relative advantages of various ways of presenting fractions. My goal will be to show that the cognitive representation of quantity can play an important role in procedural representations of mathematical concepts. I believe that the formulation of psychological theories involving different representations gives some new clarity to the issues involved in choosing a way to present mathematical concepts, and I will illustrate this with some discussion of the issue regarding fractions. However, this discussion should be seen as an illustration of a way in which cognitive objectives can be used in discussion of alternative instructional methods, rather than firm advocacy of a particular method.

Alternative Objectives with Differing Representations

The plan of the rest of this section is as follows: I will present three models that find equivalent fractions when the denominator of the fraction to be computed is a factor or a multiple of the fraction given. One of the models incorporates a process of generating a unit region and operates on that region by forming subregions either by subdividing or collecting pieces of the region. A second model uses a process of generating sets, forming subsets by partitioning the set and generating members. The third model is a simple algorithm for computing equivalent fractions using operations of multiplication and division defined on numbers. The reason for developing these models is to show how theoretical analysis of a task can provide specific psychological characterizations of alterna-

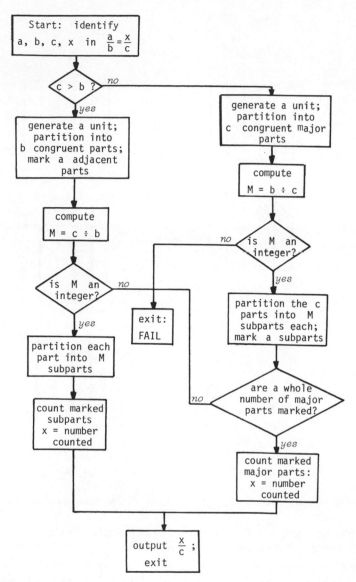

FIG. 3 Procedure for finding equivalent fractions, using spatial representation of fractional quantity.

tive instructional goals. I will also give some tentative discussion regarding implications of the different models for acquiring other concepts related to equivalent fractions.

A model that uses spatial processing of a region is shown in Fig. 3, and Fig. 4 shows traces of the program as it solves two problems. This model and the ones

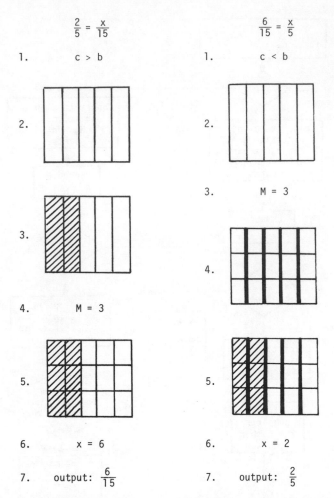

$$\frac{2}{5} = \frac{x}{15}$$

1.   c > b

2.

3.

4.   M = 3

5.

6.   x = 6

7.   output: $\frac{6}{15}$

$$\frac{6}{15} = \frac{x}{5}$$

1.   c < b

2.

3.   M = 3

4.

5.

6.   x = 2

7.   output: $\frac{2}{5}$

FIG. 4   Traces of the procedure for equivalent fractions using spatial representation.

that follow assume that the problem has been formulated so that one denominator is a multiple of the other, and the answer is an integer. If these conditions are not satisfied, these processes return failure. The representation of fractions in Figs. 3 and 4 is like the one shown in Fig. 2, and a reasonable curriculum would use introductory exercises like Fig. 2 as preparation for learning the structure of Fig. 3.

Figure 5 shows a model of finding equivalent fractions using a process that includes a mechanism for generating sets, members of sets, and subsets. A trace of the program's solution of two problems is shown in Fig. 6.

A third model of finding equivalent fractions is given in Fig. 7. This represents a simple algorithm for finding the correct answer, without the involvement of any imagery or diagrams.

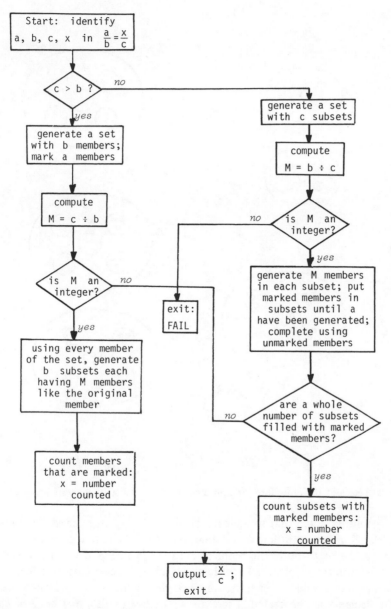

FIG. 5 Procedure for finding equivalent fractions, using set theoretic representation of fractional quantity.

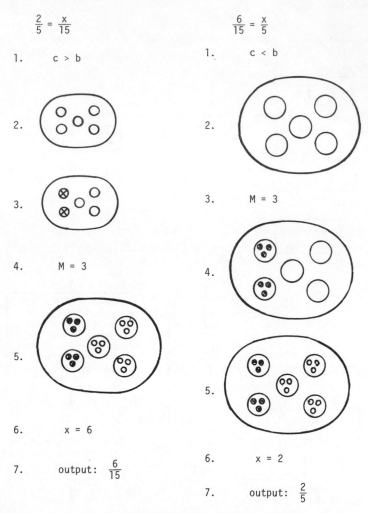

FIG. 6 Traces of the procedure for equivalent fractions using set-theoretic representation.

It should be noted that some features of processing assumed in these models are based on my intuition rather than on any data that I am aware of. For example, the first step in the problem $6/15 = X/5$ in Fig. 5 when it noted that $c < b$ is to imagine (or draw) a set having c subsets as elements. In effect, I have assumed that a subject generates abstract place-holders that will become sets when elements are generated. There are alternative models that are also plausible. For example, one might assume that initially a set with b elements is generated; then they are grouped into subsets having $M = b/c$ elements in each subset; then the elements in a of the subsets are marked; and finally X is found by counting the marked elements. As far as I know, the choice I have made in showing Fig. 5 rather than the model sketched above is an arbitrary one.

Two comments should be made about these arbitrary features of processing that are incorporated in theories presented here. First, in many cases experimental tests of the models could be developed to distinguish between alternative models, if it were considered important to distinguish between them empirically. Second, it may not be critical to distinguish between models differing in processing details if the details lack important implications for quality of student performance in instructional situations, or the ability of students to progress to further stages of knowledge and understanding. The variations that I have thought of within the three classes of models that I have presented seem relatively unimportant to me as regards instructional implications.

However, I think the differences among the three models diagrammed in Figs. 3, 5, and 7 probably are significant in connection with students' ability to use concepts of fractional quantity in later learning and in situations that arise in experience. It is a reasonable hypothesis that procedures like those of Figs. 3 and 5 are important in applying fractions in situations that arise in experience. The argument is as follows: in situations involving continuous quantity (such as

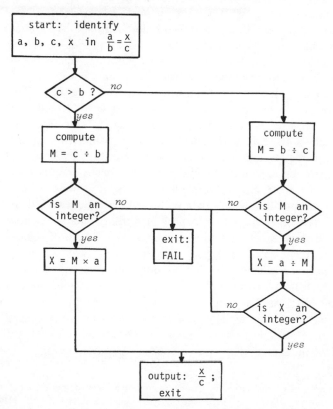

FIG. 7 Procedure for finding equivalent fractions, operating directly on numerical representations.

fractions of cups of substances used in cooking) and in situations involving sets of discrete units (such as fractions of individuals in a group who favor a certain action) there is quantitative information. It is likely that a person will have a cognitive representation of this information in the form of a spatial representation of continuous quantities, or a set-theoretic representation of discrete units.[2] Then procedures that can use those representations directly are more likely to be applied than procedures that require translation from those representations to numerical representations, such as Fig. 7 would.

The other consideration involves acquisition of further structures involving fractional quantities. There are reasons to expect that the spatial representation involved in Fig. 3 may provide a better basis for understanding addition and subtraction of fractions than the operations on sets involved in Fig. 5. Note that if Fig. 3, the two equivalent fractions (such as $\frac{2}{5}$ and $^6/_{15}$) are represented in the spatial domain as equal quantities. In the set-theoretic representation a change in the denominator involves a change in the number of elements in the set; this means that the relationship that is preserved between equivalent fractions does not correspond to an invariant quantity.

Now consider adding two fractions such as $\frac{2}{5} + \frac{1}{4}$. It clearly is possible to do that in either representation, but it seems more natural in the spatial representation where changes to common denominators do not require changing the spatial size of the unit. In the set-theoretic representation, fractions with different denominators have different numbers of elements in the total sets—for example, $\frac{2}{5}$ involves a set with five members, while $^6/_{15}$ involves a set with 15 members. Thus, it might be expected that when students have learned to think about fractional quantities as parts of regions, they might more easily learn addition and subtraction of fractions than if they learned to think of fractional quantities as subsets. This expectation has some support in a study by Coburn (1973), who compared two instructional sequences for introducing fractions. In one condition, fractions were introduced with diagrams of regions, with a fractional quantity corresponding to the part of the whole region shaded or marked in some way. The other condition involved presenting fractions as ratios, primarily of numbers of objects in different sets (such as the ratio of squares to circles, where there might be five squares and eight circles). Both sequences included a unit on addition and subtraction of fractions, although the ratio group required some instruction on part—whole relations prior to learning about adding and subtracting fractions. The two groups did equally well in addition and subtraction of fractions with equal denominators and on other general problems involving fractions. However, in addition and subtraction of fractions having unequal denominators, there was a substantial advantage favoring the group

---

[2] There is evidence that persons represent quantitative information in spatial images, even when the information is presented verbally; see DeSoto, London, and Handel, 1965; Huttenlocher, 1968; Potts, 1972.

receiving the introductory material based on regions rather than ratios of the numbers of members in sets.

The hypotheses developed here about alternative representations and addition or subtraction of fractions also seem to favor the spatial model regarding transfer to other topics, such as decimals. Representation of fractions as subsets implies that equivalent fractions are equivalent relations between quantities that are not equivalent, and when applications involve equivalent quantities there may be a conceptual difficulty produced by the set-theoretic representation. On the other hand, numerous concepts and applications involving fractions apparently call for understanding of the kind of invariant relation involved in the set-theoretic representation. This seems to be the case for multiplication and division of fractions, and for many applications involving percentages (cf. Begle, 1967).

It seems surely to be the case that the desired outcome of instruction included both the models shown as Figs. 3 and 5, and the model of Fig. 7 as well, since that provides for efficient computation. There are important psychological and pedagogical questions regarding relations among different representations of quantity. I will not try to develop an analysis of those relationships here. It would have to be largely speculative at this stage of our knowledge, but considerable attention is being given in current research to problems that should provide substantial clarification of this issue.

Conclusion

The examples worked out here for fractions have the feature of all task analyses in showing in some detail what it is that students must do in order to perform successfully on exercises and tests. The knowledge needed corresponds to procedures for carrying out computations, and at least in the present treatment, concepts such as addition of fractions and equivalent fractions are a form of procedural knowledge. The procedures can be defined on different representations of fractional quantity, and alternative models of the concept of equivalent fractions were presented, based on representations involving spatial extent, numbers of elements in sets, and simple numerical representation. Implications of the differences among the models were suggested.

EXAMPLE 2: EUCLIDEAN GEOMETRY[3]

As students progress in mathematics training they are expected to carry out tasks that are more complex and require greater skill in solving problems. Plane

[3] I am grateful for the assistance of John Greeno and Katie Greeno who provided thinking-aloud protocols of their solutions of problems in geometry. We worked through the section of parallel lines in a text by Clarke (1971), intended for preparation of students for the British ordinary-level examinations.

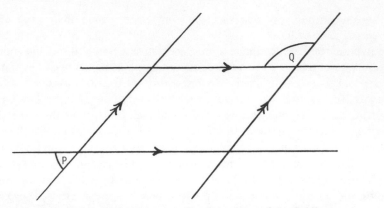

FIG. 8   Diagram for a problem in angles and parallel lines.

geometry, taught in the ninth or tenth grade, requires sophistication in problem-solving procedures that is qualitatively different from that represented in the instructional goals for fractions.

The major new requirements involve mechanisms for creating goals as part of the process of solving problems. In most exercises in elementary arithmetic, some numbers are presented and a procedure is specified—for example, "Add $\frac{2}{3}$+ $\frac{3}{4}$." In many exercises given in high school geometry, a situation is presented and a goal is specified, and the student is required to supply a set of procedures for achieving the goal. In order to understand what students must know in order to succeed on problems of this kind, we need to use concepts taken from the theory of problem solving, where goal-directed search mechanisms have been analyzed (Newell & Simon, 1972).

Consider the diagram shown in Fig. 8; the question is, "Given that $P = 30°$, find Q." This kind of problem is given is a geometry course when students have studies parallel lines with transversals, and before they have the theorem that opposite angles in a parallelogram are equal. Solution requires relating angle Q to some other angle in a diagram which in turn in related to angle P, or finding some longer chain of angles related to each other. A solution found by one subject uses the angles marked in Fig. 9. Angle A and angle P are congruent, because they are corresponding angles, so $A = 30°$. Angles A and B are congruent for the same reason, so $B = 30°$. Angles B and Q are supplementary because together they form a straight angle; thus, angle Q is shown to have measure $Q = 180° - 30° = 150°$.

Knowledge for Solving Problems

I will now present hypotheses about the knowledge students need to solve problems in geometry of angles and parallel lines. There are three main components of the theory. First, there is a representation of students' ability to

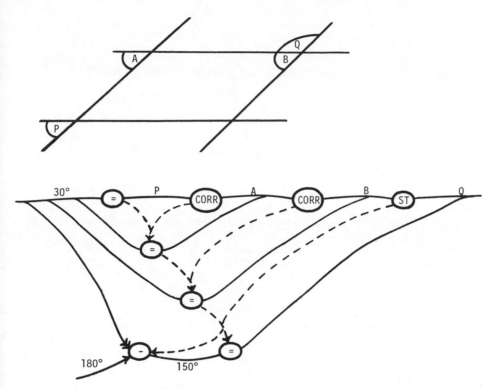

FIG. 9 Additional angles used in solving the problem (Fig. 8) and diagram showing relations between angles and quantities used in the solution.

recognize relations between angles based on their locations relative to each other and to parallel lines. A second component represents students' knowledge of propositions such as, "corresponding angles are congruent." The third component is a mechanism that sets goals and selects components of the knowledge structure that are needed in solving specific problems.

Recognition of relations. To solve a problem of the kind shown in Fig. 8, one requirement is that students learn to identify relevant relations between pairs of angles. A standard exercise involves presentation of a diagram like Fig. 10, with instructions to "Find four pairs of corresponding angles, eight pairs of alternate angles, and four pairs of verticle angles." The performance required of students is that they be able to identify certain patterns of relational properties. The relevant psychological theory is the theory of pattern recognition.

In current theories of pattern recognition it is assumed that recognition consists of identifying a learned pattern of features (Feigenbaum, 1963; Hunt, 1962; Selfridge, 1959). The knowledge required to recognize patterns is a network of feature detectors, linked together in an appropriate way. Figure 11

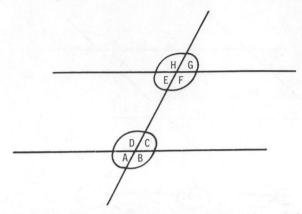

FIG. 10   Diagram for identification of angles having various relations.

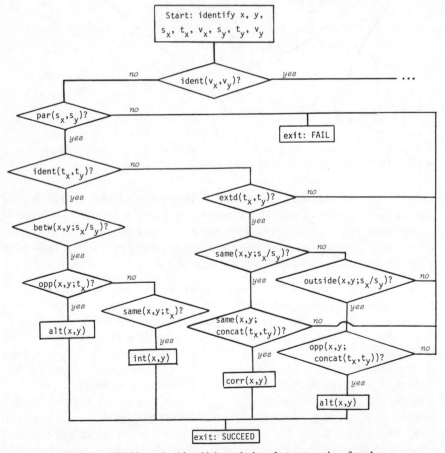

FIG. 11   EPAM net for identifying relations between pairs of angles.

shows part of a network for identifying relations between angles. The relations shown are alternate angles, interior angles (on the same side of the transversal), and corresponding angles. These are relations between angles with different vertices, having two sides that are parallel. The notation used refers to sides of angle x as s_x and t_x, and the vertex of angle x as v_x, and similarly for angle y. Note that at the top of the diagram there is a test to determine whether the angles being tested have a single vertex. A positive outcome here would send the system off to components not shown here, where vertical angles and adjacent complementary or supplementary angles would be identified.

The system shown in Fig. 11 has the form of an EPAM net (Feigenbaum, 1963). To illustrate the recognition system, follow the tests that would occur for a pair of corresponding angles, such as D and H in Fig. 10. First, the angles have different vertices. They do have a pair of sides that are parallel, so $\mathrm{par}(s_x, s_y)$ is positive. Their remaining sides are not a single segment, so $\mathrm{ident}(t_x, t_y)$ is negative. However, the side of angle H is a straight-line extension of the side of angle D, so $\mathrm{extd}(t_x, t_y)$ is positive. The angles are both above their respective parallel sides, so $\mathrm{same}(x, y; s_x / s_y)$ is positive, and both are on the left side of the transversal, so same $[x, y; \mathrm{concat}(t_x, t_y)]$ is positive. The system thus arrives at $\mathrm{corr}(x, y)$ and exits with success.

In EPAM, feature tests are carried out serially, in a fixed order. I will present some considerations shortly that question this aspect of the model, and I do not consider that a critical feature of the theory. The important psychological idea is that a system for recognizing patterns is a network of feature tests, and students must acquire such a network as part of their knowledge of geometry.

Network of propositions. Students also learn numerous propositions involving relations among angles. For example, "corresponding angles are congruent," and "adjacent angles that form a straight angle are supplementary." A set of propositions in memory is commonly represented as a network in which nodes represent concepts and links represent relations among the concepts (Anderson & Bower, 1973; Kintsch, 1974; Norman *et al.,* 1975). Several propositions from geometry are shown in Fig. 12.

First, consider connections in the network where nodes are linked by dashed lines. An example is (VERT X Y) → (CONG X Y), vertical angles are congruent. Sometimes there are three properties involved, as where (RT X) and (RT Y) and (CONG X Y) are all joined; the proposition is that if X and Y are both right angles, then X and Y are congruent.

The dashed arrows in Fig. 12 correspond to inferences that can be made or conclusions that can be taken. For example, the student can conclude that X and Y are congruent if it is known that X and Y are vertical angles. The propositions shown in Fig. 12 thus correspond to productions in the sense of Newell and Simon (1972), for each proposition has a condition and an action component. The condition is given at the tail (or tails) of an arrow, and the action is given at the head.

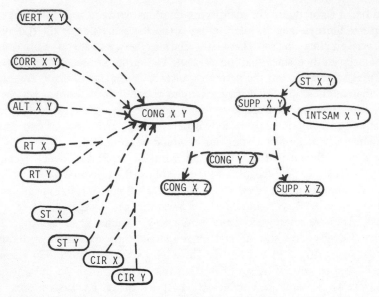

FIG. 12   Network of propositions corresponding to productions used in solving problems about angles and parallel lines.

The representation in Fig. 12 simplifies the situation in an important way. The nodes there represent states of affairs that correspond to propositions. It is useful in considering problem solving to unpack those propositions and represent them as relational structures. This is done in Fig. 13. There, dashed lines still represent inferences that can be made, but they are inferences that derive a proposition from other propositions. Each proposition consists of one or more elements (frequently angles) and a property or a relation involving the element(s). Figure 13 also represents several propositions about the measures of angles. For example, in upper right corner there is the proposition, if X and Y are complementary angles, then the measure of X plus the measure of Y is $90°$. In the upper left corner are represented some complicated but important propositions about the measures of concatenated angles; for example, if angles $A, B, \ldots, K$ are concatenated to form angle X, then the measure of X is equal to the sum of the measures of $A, B, \ldots,$ and K. Note that there is no specific notation to distinguish between the angle X and the measure of angle X. When an element goes through an arithmetic relation ($=$, $+$, or $-$) it is understood that the element is the measure of an angle.

Now return to Fig. 9, and consider the network that represents the relations among angles in the diagram used in obtaining the solution. Initially, the information is given that $P = 30°$, and the problem is to find the measure of Q. The solution is obtained as follows: First, angle A is noticed, and since A and P are corresponding angles, the measure $30°$ is assigned to A. Next, angle B is noticed, and since A and B are corresponding angles, the measure 30° is assigned to angle B. Finally, since B and Q form a straight angle, the measure of Q is 180° − 30° = 150°. Note that each of these inferences is represented in the diagram by a dashed line. The solution of the problem is shown as a connected relational network that satisfies the requirement of connecting Q with a quantity—that is, assigning a measure to Q. Each step in solving the problem corresponds to a proposition found in the network of propositions shown in Fig. 13.

Problem-solving procedures.   Knowledge structures like those represented in Fig. 11 and Fig. 13 are necessary for a student to solve geometry, but they are not sufficient. An additional requirement is a system for interpreting a problem, setting goals, and selecting productions from the knowledge base for use in generating the relations needed for solution of the problem. The ideas to be presented here are an attempt to use intuitions about problem solving that have been recognized for many years, especially by Duncker (1945), Selz (1913), and Wertheimer (1959). When a problem is understood, the person perceives certain structural relations among components of the problem. However, the structural pattern is not complete, and that is why there is a problem. Thus, problem solving can be seen as a process of modifying a structure in order to complete a pattern. Recent contributions to the theory of problem solving have developed formal representations of goal-directed pattern matching (Hewitt, 1969; Wino-

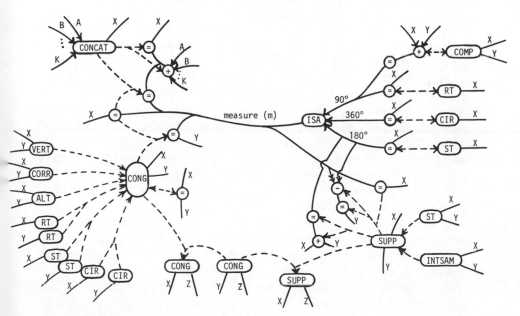

FIG. 13   Network of productions showing propositions as links between relations in component propositions.

grad, 1972) and search for operators or productions that achieve progress toward solution of a problem (Ernst & Newell, 1969; Newell, 1972b; Newell & Simon, 1972).

Problems in the geometry of parallel lines and angles can be solved by a system that can satisfy goals consisting of patterns that may be matched in the problem situation. The system keeps a list of angles whose measures are known, and a list of relations between pairs of angles that have been found during the process of problem solving. The system knows about quantitative relations such as (CONG X Y), X and Y are congruent, and (SUPP X Y), X and Y are supplementary. It also knows about geometric relations such as (CORR X Y) and (VERT X Y), which it can evaluate using feature tests such as those in Fig. 11, and it knows which quantitative relation can be inferred from each geometric relation, as shown in Fig. 12.

A problem is presented in the form of a diagram, a goal, and some given information. The system assimilates the given information and sets the goal as presented. For the problem shown in Fig. 8, the structures are

$$(\text{MEAS } P \text{ 30})   (\text{GOAL} * (\text{MEAS } Q \text{ ?NUM}))$$

(My notation here is a mixture of Newell's (1972b) notation for a production system oriented toward problem solving, and the simplified PLANNER syntax used by Winograd (1973). The asterisk marks the current goal of the system, and is replaced by % if the goal is set aside temporarily while another goal is attempted. A pattern such as (MEAS Q ?NUM) specifies a property or relation first, then the objects that have the property or relation. A question mark indicates a gap in the pattern, and the goal is to find some object that satisfies the gap. For example, ?NUM indicates that the gap is to be filled by a number.)

The system works by evaluating its current goal. There are several kinds of goal, each corresponding to a procedure. The procedure succeeds if certain specified conditions are found in the data structures containing list of known measures and relations on angles. If a goal succeeds, the system carries out an action called ASSIGN which adds an appropriate entry to the data structure and deletes the accomplished goal from the goal structure. If the goal fails, a new goal is created and the old goal is saved. The system tries to accomplish specific goals first, then retreats to weaker goals that can produce results of possible use to the stronger goals that have failed earlier.

As an example, when (GOAL * (MEAS Q ?NUM)) is evaluated, each angle with known measure is examined to see whether it is part of a structure in which a quantitative relation links the known angle with angle Q. The procedure used is a variant of the MATCH process used in HAM (Anderson & Bower, 1973). If such a structure were found, the procedure would return a structure of the form (QR Q NUM) Where QR is the quantitative relation found (CONG, COMP, SUPP, or CIR), and NUM is the numerical value of the known angle found in the structure. If the goal succeeded, the system would carry out the action ASSIGN-MEAS, creating a data structure in which Q would be assigned a measure equal to NUM if the relation found were CONG, or 90 − NUM if QR were COMP, or 180 − NUM if QR were SUPP, or 360 − NUM if QR were CIR. In solving the problem of Fig. 8, the goal of assigning measure fails initially, so the system takes the action (SETGOAL (?QREL Q ?ANGM).

Now the goal structure is the following list:

$$((GOAL * (?QREL \ Q \ ?ANGM))(GOAL \ \% \ (MEAS \ Q \ ?NUM)))$$

Again, the system examines the angles with known measure, hoping to create a structure in which a quantitative relation links angle Q with a known angle. This goal succeeds if there is a data structure in which Q is linked to a known angle through one of the geometric relations (CORR, VERT, ST, . . .) from which a quantitative relation can be inferred. Again, no such relation is found, so the system tries to create one, setting up

$$(GOAL * (?REL \ Q \ ?ANGM)).$$

This goal examines the angles with known measure, testing the features of each one in relation to Q using the recognition network shown in Fig. 11. This fails, since P, the only known angle, has no side that is either identical to a side of Q or a straight-line extension of a side of Q.

The system has failed in all its attempts to directly link Q with an angle that has known measure. It then retreats to the following goal:

$$(GOAL * ((MEAS \ ?ANG \ ?NUM)(NEARER \ Q \ ?ANG \ ?ANGM))).$$

This goal tries to assign measures to some angle that can be found in the diagram that is nearer angle Q than some angle whose measure is already known. The property NEARER is defined on a path consisting of transversals between parallel lines. The procedure takes P (still the only known angle) and works through its list of geometric relations until it finds one that it can pair with P and match the features of the pair with the pattern needed to identify the relation. In the diagram of Fig. 8, all the geometric relations can be found for angles paired with P; presumably the one that is found is the one at the top of the system's list of relations. (Note that trying to find an angle fitting a specific relation involves activating a terminal node in the recognition network and testing the pattern of features connected to that node, rather than working down the network from the top. The process is again analogous to the MATCH process in HAM (Anderson & Bower, 1973). in this case the probe received by MATCH is the angle P and a terminal node that names a relation.)

The goal finds angle A and identifies the relation (CORR P A), then returns the structure (CONG A 30). This leads to assigning measure 30 to angle A in the list of known angles. Now the system returns to its previous goal (?REL Q ?ANGM). With a new known angle is the list, a geometric relation with Q might be found, but it is not. (Note that all the features of corresponding angles are present except the last one requiring that the angles be on the same side of the transversal.) This causes the system to recreate the goal ((MEAS ?ANG ?NU-

M)(NEARER Q ?ANG ?ANGM)), which succeeds through finding (CORR A B) and returns (CONG B 30); then the system assigns measure 30 to angle B.

Now the system returns to its goal (?REL Q ?ANGM) again, and this time it finds a known angle related to Q; the goal now returns (ST Q B) and this structure is entered in the list of known relations. Now the preceding goal (?QREL Q ?ANGM) is reactivated and it succeeds, returning (SUPP Q B). Finally, the system returns to the initial goal (MEAS Q ?NUM) and this succeeds; the last act is to assign measure 150 to angle Q.

The preceding illustrates the process of problem solving. I will now present a brief description of the general features of the problem-solving system. At the highest level, the procedure is a production system that takes a goal as a condition, and evaluates the goal as an action. Then the outcome of evaluating the goal becomes part of the condition, and an action of creating a data structure is carried out if the goal succeeded; otherwise, a new goal is created. At this level, the model represents general skills involved in problem solving, including such strategies as trying to find a direct link between data and unknowns, and then if that fails working on something more complicated.

The procedures for evaluating goals incorporate knowledge about the relational properties and propositions involved in the task domain. Each evaluation procedure looks at data structures that represent relations among components of the problem, and determines whether other needed relations can be inferred. This amounts to a production system functioning at the level of specific inferences made during the process of solving a problem. As an example, the process of evaluating the goal (?QREL X ? ANGM) and the procedure (ASSIGNQREL) is equivalent to the following set of productions:

(GOAL * (?QREL X ?ANGM))   and   (GOAL % (MEAS Y ?NUM))   and
$\qquad$ (RT X Y) $\rightarrow$ (COMP X Y)
$\qquad$ (ST X Y) $\rightarrow$ (SUPP X Y).
$\quad$ (CIRCLE X Y) $\rightarrow$ (CIR X Y)
$\qquad$ (VERT X Y) $\rightarrow$ (CONG X Y)
$\qquad$ (CORR X Y) $\rightarrow$ (CONG X Y)
$\qquad$ (ALT X Y) $\rightarrow$ (CONG X Y)
(INTSAM X Y) $\rightarrow$ (SUPP X Y).

That is, when the goal structure is as shown in the first line, and the data structure contains the element on the left of one of the other lines, then the element on the right of that line can be created.

Pattern Recognition and Constructions

In many geometry problems, the material presented does not permit a solution; the problem solver must supply additional lines. An example of such problems is in Fig. 14; given that AB is parallel to CD, find an equation connecting X, Y,

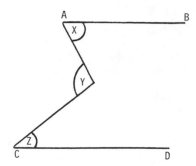

FIG. 14 Diagram for a problem
requiring a construction.

and Z. One solution is obtained by constructing a parallel to AB through the
vertex of Y, creating angles Y_1 and Y_2. Then $(\text{ALT } X Y_1) \rightarrow X = Y_1$ and $(\text{ALT } Z Y_2) \rightarrow Z = Y_2$, giving $Y_1 + Y_2 = X + Z$, and then $(\text{CONCAT } (Y_1 Y_2)Y) \rightarrow Y = Y_1 + Y_2$, so $Y = X + Z$.

The interesting psychological question is how the problem solver thinks of
making the construction. One way for this to happen would be to arrive at the
goal of finding a relation between X and Y, test the features of some relation,
and find a partial match. In fact, one subject solving this problem said, "If there
were a parallel line here, then X and Y would be equal."

In order to solve problems requiring constructions, the problem-solving system
should be able to detect partial patterns, and should have productions for
completing patterns by adding new points and lines in the problem. Recognition
of the need for a construction is similar to the understanding of a problem—it
involves matching components in the problem with a stored problem and finding
a gap or a partial mismatch. The idea sketched here of constructions related to
subgoals and pattern recognition is quite similar to Gelernter's (1963) treatment
of the problem, where constructions are developed when subgoals have failed,
and a frequent cause of failure has been the absence of a feature that can be put
into the problem with an available construction theorem. The present discussion
has considered only the process of recognizing that a construction would be
useful; actual mechanisms for making constructions have been described by
Scandura, Durnin, and Wulfeck (1974).

Meaningful Solution Structures

Gestalt psychologists such as Duncker (1945) and Wertheimer (1959) emphasized the desirability of teaching students meaningful solutions of problems,
rather than rote, mechanical forms of solution. The concept of meaningfulness
in problem solving has generally depended on the intuitions of authors and
readers. Perhaps some progress can be made toward pinning the concept down
by examining the relational networks that represent alternative solutions to
problems.

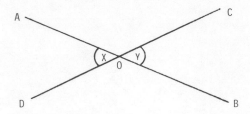

FIG. 15 Diagram for the problem of vertical angles.

I will discuss one of the problems that Wertheimer (1959) considered, the problem of vertical angles. I will present analyses of two solutions that Wertheimer presented to illustrate his distinction between meaningful and rote solutions. These solutions will be compared, and two distinguishable criteria of meaningfulness will be suggested.

Figure 15 gives notation for the problem of vertical angles. Given that AB and CD are straight lines that intersect at 0, prove that X and Y are congruent.

A typical statement of the proof goes as follows:

1. $X + \angle A0C = 180°$, since they form a straight angle.
2. $Y + \angle A0C = 180°$, for the same reason as (1).
3. $X + \angle A0C = Y + \angle A0C$, since they both equal 180°.
3. $X = Y$, since $\angle A0C$ can be subtracted from both sides of (3).

A graph showing the relations in this proof is shown in Fig. 16.

Wertheimer criticized this proof as being rote and mechanical. His evidence that students fail to grasp important relations included the observation that when asked to recall the proof, students often write $X + \angle A0C = 180°$, $Y + \angle B0D =$ and then become puzzled.

An alternative proof that seems to fit Wertheimer's criterion of meaningfulness could be stated as follows:

1. $\angle A0B$ and $\angle D0C$ are congruent, since they are both straight angles.
2. X and $\angle A0C$ form $\angle D0C$ by concatenation.

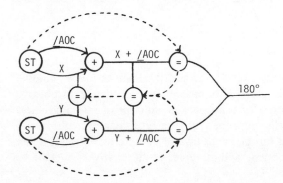

FIG. 16 Diagram of a solution of the problem of vertical angles primarily using algebraic relations.

3. Y and $\angle A0C$ form $\angle A0B$ by concatenation.
4. X and Y are congruent, because they form congruent angles when they are concatenated with the same third angle.

A diagram showing this proof is shown in Fig. 17.

There are two apparent differences between Fig. 16 and Fig. 17. First, Fig. 17 is slightly simpler than Fig. 16. Second, Fig. 17 uses only geometric relations and properties, while most of the relations in Fig. 16 are algebraic. It seems reasonable to suppose that both of these properties relate to meaningfulness of a solution.

One sense of the concept of meaningfulness involves coherent structure. We would say that a student has better understanding if all components of a problem are linked closely with many other components, rather than each element being connected with only one or two other components. In general, closer linking will correspond to simpler structure. In Fig. 17, the congruence of X and Y is derived in one step from the congruence of $\angle D0C$ and $\angle A0B$, combined with the concatenations involving X and Y with $\angle A0C$. In Fig. 16, the route to $X = Y$ is slightly more circuitous, involving equality of two quantities because they both equal $180°$, and an algebraic operation on the expressions $X + \angle A0C$ and $Y + \angle A0C$.

It should be noted that the simplicity of a certain kind of solution is well defined only with respect to a fixed set of productions. A simpler structure than Fig. 16 would apply to a subject who had a production

$$(X + A = M) \quad \text{and} \quad (Y + A = M) \rightarrow (X = Y).$$

It seems to agree with intuition that a student with a richer set of complex productions would have a better understanding of problems than a student who had to work out many sequences of small steps. On the other hand, this shows that the question of meaningfulness cannot be decided on grounds of simplicity

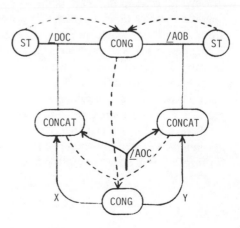

FIG. 17 Diagram of a solution of the problem of vertical angles using geometric relations.

in favor of one kind of solution rather than another, since either can probably have a complex or a simple version, depending on the complexity of a person's knowledge.

The second feature distinguishing Figs. 16 and 17 is the extent to which they use geometric relations, rather than algebraic operations. I think that this may have been what Wertheimer had in mind in referring to understanding structural relations in this problem, rather than applying an algorithm in a way that often might seem arbitrary in the sense of lacking motivation in the domain of the problem.

The distinction can be made rigorous if we define two problem spaces, one having productions that we call geometric, the other having productions that we call algebraic. A problem in geometry can be solved entirely in the problem space of geometry, if an appropriate set of productions exists there and they are found and applied. Alternatively, there may be a mapping of some geometric properties and relations into the domain of algebra. These could be translations of properties, or they could involve productions that take geometric properties as conditions and create algebraic objects as actions. When objects are created that can satisfy the conditions of algebraic productions, then problem solving can go on in the problem space of algebra. After an appropriate set of productions has been applied, a translation back to geometric objects can be carried out, if it is needed. (Strictly speaking, the solution in Fig. 16 is incomplete. A final step using the proposition, "if two angles have equal measure, they are congruent," would finish the job.)

The distinction between solving a problem in its own problem space and translating into another for purposes of computation probably is subject to considerable blurring, especially if we consider the result of experience in applying productions from one domain to solve problems in another. It seems likely that any pair of productions of the form $A \rightarrow B$, $B \rightarrow C$, if used often enough, would soon lead to the existence of a production $A \rightarrow C$. By a similar process of fusion, it seems likely that a student who has applied algebraic operations many times to geometric quantities (spatial representations of angles, areas, and so on) would probably have what amounted to a set of productions for manipulating geometric quantities, without explicit translation into algebraic operations. Clearly, the question of meaningfulness of a problem solution is relative to the specific set of productions that a problem solver has available, whether we consider meaningfulness as solving in the problem domain or as producing as a solution a well-integrated relational structure.

I have some anecdotal evidence that achievement of the apparently more meaningful solution in fact depends on the student's having a general production for manipulating quantities of the form

$$(\text{CONCAT } (A \ B) \ X) \quad \text{and} \quad (\text{CONCAT } (A \ C) \ Y)$$
$$\text{and} \quad (\text{CONG } X \ Y) \rightarrow (\text{CONG } B \ C).$$

One subject with whom I have worked on this problem did not know how to prove that vertical angles are congruent when we began. I gave the steps of a proof stating the two sums that equal 180°, making a single equation, and obtaining the equality by subtracting the same quantity from both sides of the equation. About two weeks later, I asked the subject whether she remembered the proof; she did not. Then I gave some different examples involving concatenation of quantities. One example involved weighing suitcases by holding them and standing on a scale. If two suitcases produce the same weight when they are combined with a person, the suitcases must be of equal weight. The other example involved distances from city to city given on a map. If the distance from Liverpool to London via Birmingham equals the distance from Birmingham to Dover via London, then the distance from Liverpool to Birmingham must equal the distance from London to Dover. With these items of background, the subject generated the proof of equal vertical angles. Then she solved Wertheimer's transfer problem where the angles shown are overlapping right angles, and she remembered the proof about vertical angles on two later occasions—one two days later and the other seven months later.

This anecdote does not provide sufficient evidence for any definite conclusions about exact structural relations in the problem of vertical angles. It does illustrate a use of the theoretical analysis in identifying the cognitive component needed to solve special problems. In this case, if my analysis is correct, the needed component is a production dealing with combinations of quantity in a general way, rather than with specific geometric concepts.

Conclusion

Geometry represents at least two levels of knowledge that are more complex than are involved in the simple kinds of computation involved in elementary fractions. The recognition network needed to identify relations between angles involves a concept in the form of a procedure for processing stimulus features. That seems no more complex than the procedures for finding equivalent fractions and other similar operations in elementary arithmetic. However, the inferences needed to solve problems require a network of propositional knowledge corresponding to productions that take properties and relations as conditions and generate new relations as actions. And the system requires general knowledge of relations between goals, to select propositions in a way that will lead to solutions to problems that are presented.

The general analysis of problem solving as recognition of partial patterns provides a framework for analyzing the process of recognizing the need for a construction in a geometric problem. The framework also provides a way of comparing solutions of problems that partially clarifies the troublesome concept of meaningfulness in problem solving.

EXAMPLE 3: AUDITORY PSYCHOPHYSICS

The tasks to be considered in this third section require yet another increase in the complexity of performance by a student. Nearly all problems given in high school mathematics are well-defined problems in the sense that they present a specific goal and a specific set of premises or data to work from. In many situations students are asked to produce paragraphs or brief essays as answers to questions. While many questions require only simple retrieval of factual information from memory, others present ill-defined problems (Reitman, 1965) in which the student must generate more than a path of operations leading to a goal.

The material that I will consider in this last section is part of the content of introductory college psychology, and the selection of content for this discussion is taken from the introductory text by Lindsay and Norman (1972). I do not intend to suggest that the kinds of complex semantic processing that I will discuss here are confined to college-age adults. The processes are required whenever a person generates complex substantive material, as in the telling of stories, and much of that is done by quite young children. Certainly, complex question answering is expected of students in junior high school and high school in many of their courses.

Semantic Networks

A structure of concepts and relations can be represented conveniently as a network, and a majority of investigators use such a representation to characterize the knowledge required for answering questions (see especially Anderson & Bower, 1973; Kintsch, 1974; Norman et al., 1975). The notation that I will use here is similar to that of Norman et al. (1975), which also is included in Lindsay and Norman's (1972) text and is used in Norman's chapter in this volume. I have, however, reversed the roles of elements and relations, partly to be consistent with my earlier discussion and partly because some of the discussion of this material is helped by having attention focussed on relations rather than on concepts as the main components of the structure.

The content of psychophysics includes concepts from physics, biology, and psychology. Most of the information given by Lindsay and Norman about the physics of sound is shown in Fig. 18. Most of the relations shown such as ISA, HAS, and CAUSE have been used frequently in many discussions of semantic memory. ISA denotes category membership. HAS denotes a relation of property attribution, which takes several forms not distinguished here such as having parts (components of a complex wave) and having units (such as Hertz for frequency).

The representation of Fig. 18 is, of course, highly schematic. A complete description would include many distinctions not made in the diagram, and would require elucidation of several components. In general, the concepts and

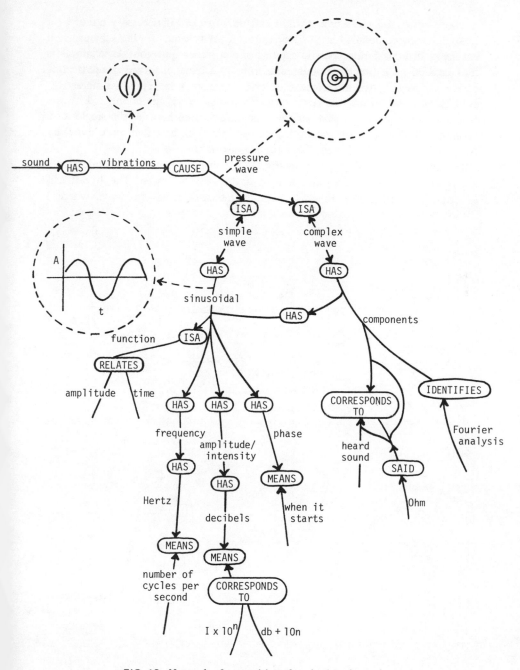

FIG. 18 Network of propositions for physics of sound.

relations correspond to schemata that can be unpacked if necessary either by a theorist for more detailed analysis or (in a different sense) by the subject when necessary in considering specific aspects of a topic or question. An example is the concept of a function, which is a general schema involving a relation of correspondence between members of two or more sets. Thus the node RE-LATES and the presence of two variables whose values are connected by the function are expected as parts of the schema indicated here by the single term "function." This kind of conceptual embedding is discussed in more detail by Norman, Gentner, and Stevens in Chapter 9 of this volume.

The dashed lines and diagrams in Fig. 18 involve concepts whose understanding apparently includes production of a diagram or image. The hypothesis involved here is similar to that used in the section on fractions, where I

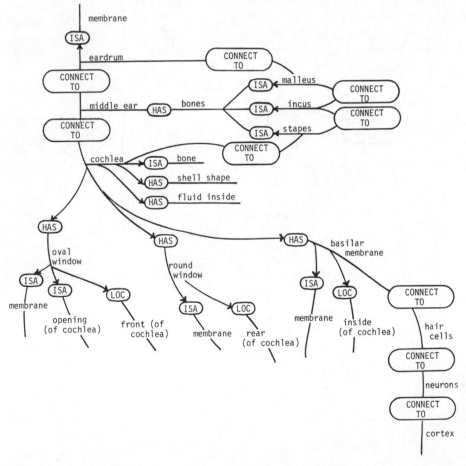

FIG. 19 Network of propositions for anatomy of hearing.

presented the idea that some processing can be mediated by use of a representation of quantity either in spatial or set-theoretic terms. The use of generative processes involving images for question answering has been noted before, notably by Jorgenson and Kintsch (1973) and by Norman (1973). Norman's discussion is especially pertinent. His example involved generating a floor plan, and subjects used rules based on general properties of rooms and buildings, even when this led to mistakes in the specific task they were engaged in.

Just as many of the nodes in Fig. 18 represent concepts that are not spelled out in detail, the diagrams presented there only sketch the representation that we would hope students acquire regarding sound waves. The procedure for generating the image of a sine wave should be connected to the concepts of frequency and amplitude in ways that I have not worked out in detail, and the properties of the various diagrams involving concepts of vibrations, a pressure wave, and a sinusoidal function all should be related to each other in definite ways not specified here. Analysis of these cognitive structures would be a task well within the technical capabilities available at present, although some new understanding would probably be achieved by developing detailed models here, as with other domains.

Figure 19 shows a semantic network containing the main concepts of anatomy connected with hearing. This figure seems entirely straightforward; however, note that HAS has yet another meaning here (the cochlea is characterized by some of its properties, and by some of its parts), and the relation CONNECT TO refers to rather different kinds of anatomical relations (the way in which the malleus is connected to the incus is quite different from the way hair cells are connected to neurons).

Figure 20 shows a network of concepts that refer to events that occur when a sound wave produces a neural reaction in the brain. The descriptions of properties of neural responses of different kinds are severely abbreviated here, and good knowledge of these would involve quite an intricate structure of interrelationships.

An important feature of Fig. 20 is its inclusion of concepts from both Fig. 18 and Fig. 19. The knowledge structure that we expect students to acquire is a synthesis of all three of these networks. It should be noted also that the knowledge shown in Fig. 20 should relate strongly to the student's general knowledge about neural processes, as well as general concepts of anatomy and physics.

Process of Answering Questions

Many questions can be answered by a relatively simple process of retrieving factual information that is stored in memory. For example, Fig. 19 contains the answer to the question, "which bone of the middle ear is connected to the ear drum?" A process for retrieving facts from memory has been developed in detail

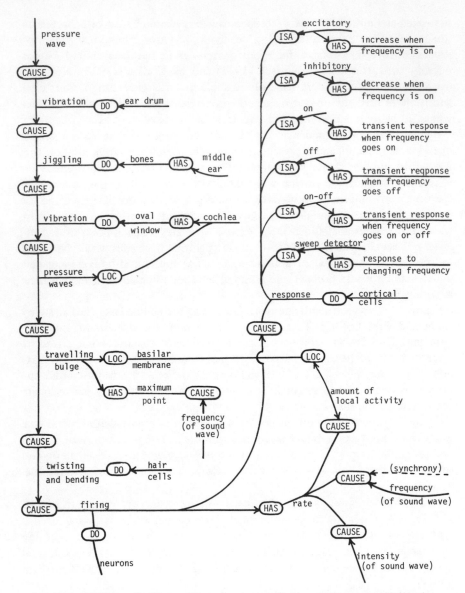

FIG. 20 Network of propositions about events that occur when a sound is heard.

by Anderson and Bower (1973); it involves entering the memory structure at components mentioned in the question (in this case, middle ear, bone, and ear drum) and searching for a match to a specified structure. If a match is found, the information is retrieved in the form of a propositional structure containing the answer required. In this example, the matching structure would contain the links

(ISA malleus bone) (CONNECT-TO malleus cochlea), and the answer would be "the malleus."

The process of retrieving facts from memory can be seen as a kind of pattern matching; in fact, the mechanism proposed in the preceding section for pattern matching in problem solving was borrowed from Anderson and Bower's (1973) discussion of fact retrieval. Some information resides in memory as a substructure of a person's knowledge. A question is asked, and the question contains components that match components of the stored information. The person retrieves the pattern, including components that were not in the question, and the new retrieved components constitute an answer to the question.

Less specific questions can be asked, and their answers require some selection and judgment by the person who answers. "What is the basilar membrane?" could be answered (from Fig. 19), "a membrane in the cochlea, connected to hair cells," or (from Fig. 20), "the thing that has a travelling bulge caused by pressure waves in the cochlea," or a number of other possibilities, including a combination of the two mentioned above. One thing a student must do is decide how much information is needed: "tell me about sound waves," can call for a brief paragraph or a 30-page article or a book. Also, the degree of specificity required in an answer sometimes is uncertain. In some contexts, the question, "where is the basilar membrane?" might be answered best with "in the ear," but in other contexts, "in the cochlea" might be more appropriate (cf. Norman, 1973). Clearly, there are some important principles of social psychology operating in the answering of most questions, in which the answerer applies assumptions about the knowledge structure of the asker in deciding what kind of information is most relevant to the question. This is understood well by students who often spend some time during examinations trying to judge "what the instructor wants" as an answer to a question.

One class of questions used frequently in examinations seems to raise a special set of theoretical questions. These are questions requiring explanations of phenomena or relationships. A relatively simple example is the question, "explain how pressure waves in the cochlea produce firing of neurons." To arrive at an answer, a student should generate a sequence of components each involving a CAUSE relation. A mechanism like the one described for finding the measure of an angle in Fig. 8 would be suitable. The process might start by setting a goal of finding an event that causes firing of neurons, then checking whether that matched the "pressure waves in the cochlea" taken from the question, and if not, searching back further until a path of causal links had been established. As in the case of problem solving, successful performance depends both on having appropriate knowledge structures and having an appropriate strategy for generating goals that drive the pattern matching and search processes needed to obtain an answer.

More complicated processes are needed for a question such as the following: "A recording is made of a performance on a pipe organ. When the recording is played at high volume, a certain passage sounds uniform in loudness, but when the volume is decreased, the low and high notes sound much softer than the notes in the middle range. Explain why this occurs." Lindsay and Norman (1972) present the information needed to answer this question. It involves the fact that loudness is caused jointly by intensity and frequency; decreasing the sound level makes a very large decrease in loudness of low and high frequency sounds, but a smaller decrease in loudness at medium frequencies.

The first requirement placed on a student by the question about loudness and frequency is to comprehend the question. This requires considerable knowledge in the subject of psychophysics, and use of that knowledge in a sophisticated system for constructing an interpretation of the information given in the question. This is not the place to go into the theory of language understanding in detail, but recent contributions to that theory (Simon & Hayes, this volume; Schank, 1972; Winograd, 1972) make it clear that a mechanism for understanding a message makes critical use of knowledge about the meanings of concepts contained in the message and relations of those concepts to other concepts in the person's knowledge structure.

But beyond comprehension, the student who answers the question must also have a system for generating an answer that provides an explanation. One of the things students need to learn is what counts as an explanation of something, and that is definitely nontrivial when the thing to be explained is a complex functional relationship. We do not have a theory worked out yet to characterize just what is involved, but it seems probable that the mechanism will involve principles like those used by Abelson (1973) concerning the organization of belief systems and by Rumelhart (1975) concerning the organization of stories. The student must know that an explanation requires certain components. Most explanations either relate the explanandum to some general principles or describe a mechanism that performs in the way to be explained (I am not concerned here with the question whether these are fundamentally similar, or whether other kinds of answers can be explanations as well.). Thus, an explanation is organized according to rules, and these rules constitute a schema that must be part of the student's knowledge.

When a schema for "explanation" is activated along with a structural description of the relationship to be explained, a search can be conducted for relevant information in memory. I expect that the explanation given by many people would be mediated by a graph of equal-loudness contours, such as the one shown in Fig. 21. A student who knows about the joint dependence of loudness on frequency and intensity could have that knowledge in the form of a program for generating a graph showing the relationship. To use the diagram, the student would need further procedures for interpreting the information produced when the graph was generated. In this case, a uniform decrease in sound level corresponds to a horizontal line moving from a high level on the graph downward for some distance. An explanation of the relative softening of low and high frequencies would note that a decrease in sound level passes a greater number of

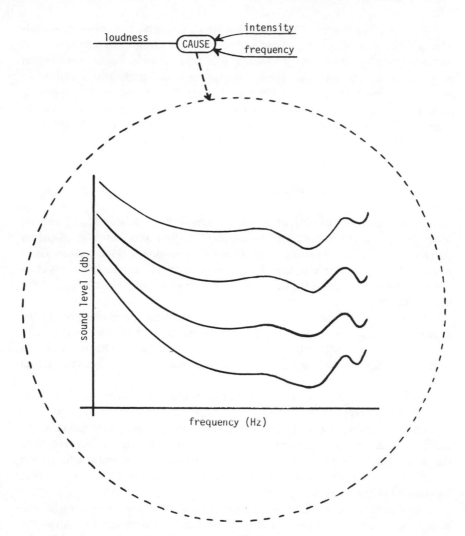

FIG. 21 Graph representing knowledge about the way in which loudness depends jointly on sound intensity and frequency.

contours at low and high frequencies than at medium frequencies, and this corresponds to a greater decrease in loudness at the extremes than in the middle range.

Conclusion

In this section I have taken up issues that are at the edge of available theoretical concepts in cognitive psychology. The theory of semantic networks is quite well developed and serves to represent knowledge structures of the kind we try to teach in many expository subjects such as psychology. We test students' knowledge by asking them questions, and to perform successfully they are required to understand the questions and generate appropriate answers. A substantial beginning has been made in the theory of language comprehension, and some promising suggestions are available regarding generative processes in question answering. The available theories do not take us as far in this area as do the available theories of problem solving, but enough is understood to permit a rough sketch of the kinds of processes that probably are involved.

GENERAL CONCLUSIONS

My goal in carrying out this work was to explore the applicability of current concepts and theories in cognitive psychology to topics actually taught in classroom instruction. The results have been encouraging. I think we can assert confidently that our state of knowledge and understanding in cognitive psychology has now developed to the point where meaningful contact can be made with the content of instruction.

In this chapter, the concepts and techniques of cognitive psychology have been applied to analyses of instructional tasks. Task analysis has been a major activity of educational psychologists for some time, and Resnick's chapter 3 in this volume provides a review and discussion of instructional task analysis in relation to cognitive psychology.

Careful attention to components of instructional tasks is potentially helpful in at least three ways. First, it aids in the design and evaluation of curriculum materials. Secondly, it constitutes useful knowledge for teachers who have the task of training students in the skills and understanding that are represented in the theoretical analyses. Third, it probably would constitute useful information for students who have the task of acquiring the skills and understanding represented in the analyses.

An important question is whether task analyses that are more strongly embedded in general psychological theory, as I have attempted to embed the illustrations developed in this chapter, will be of increased usefulness in the practice of instruction. It would be pleasant to have strong reasons for a positive response to that question, but it seems to me that such an evaluation must come from the potential users of the product, not from one who proposes to offer the product for use. A further impediment to enthusiasm now is the fragmentary nature of the illustrations of detailed task analysis based on cognitive theory. A more reasonable evaluation may be possible when we can display a relatively complete analysis of the knowledge desired as the outcome of instruction in some subject such as fractions or geometry or psychophysics. Perhaps the conclusion can be drawn from the present work that it is reasonable to undertake such an analysis using concepts that are currently available in cognitive psychology. Of course, we should expect that an effort to apply current theories will show some needs for changing the theories. But we have apparently reached a state of knowledge and understanding that provides a reasonable starting basis for development of instructional objectives based on general psychological theory.

ACKNOWLEDGMENTS

This work was supported by a fellowship from the John Simon Guggenheim Foundation. I am also grateful for the hospitality of the Department of Experimental Psychology, University of Oxford, where I was a visitor during the time I carried out this work.

8

Impression Formation, Discrepancy from Stereotype, and Recognition Memory[1]

Ray Hyman

University of Oregon

The background for the research in this chapter includes an interest in the "prepared mind" (Hyman, 1961, 1964a). Under what conditions, for example, do preconceptions and prior knowledge about a problem interfere with the restructuring necessary to achieve a solution and under what conditions do they help? A particular form of this question is concerned with the role of discrepancy from prototypes in guiding the course of inquiry and contributing to the growth of knowledge (Brunswik, 1959; Gombrich, 1961; Hyman, 1964b; Kuhn, 1962; Mischel, 1971).

The motivation of the current research program is to find experimental paradigms to study the operations of schemata and discrepancies from prototypes in science, art, and everyday affairs. On the one hand, such schemata contribute to distortions of reality, missed discoveries, resistance to innovation, and other tendencies to assimilate new input to preconceived viewpoints. On the other hand, they are necessary precursors to the recognition of important problems, to the detection of anomalies, and to their own eventual adaptation to the disturbing discrepancies.

Although the experimental paradigm described here is directed primarily to such practical issues, both the paradigm and the questions it was designed to answer overlap with current research in psycholinguistics, verbal memory, and cognitive psychology. This overlap might be taken as an encouraging sign of a narrowing gap between issues of how we acquire knowledge in the real world and issues being studied by contemporary cognitive psychology.

The paradigm is based on the impression-formation task used in studies of person perception (Hastorf, Schneider, & Polefka, 1970; Warr & Knapper,

---

[1] The experimental data were collected by Janet Polf and W. Tram Neill, who also contributed both to the design and the analysis of the results.

1968). In the present version, the subject is presented with the description of a hypothetical individual (see Table I for examples). The description consists of the name of the individual, the discipline in which he is currently majoring (Accounting, Law, or Social Work), and a character sketch written around ten adjectives or traits. The subject's task is to read the description, form a coherent impression of the individual described, and then circle those adjectives on a checklist that appropriately describe the individual.

After performing this task with a small number of sketches, the subject is unexpectedly tested for his memory of the actual adjectives used in the description of each hypothetical individual. In the experiment to be reported, the test is for recognition memory. Using the same list of adjectives as was employed for the impression task, the subject now indicates which ones he believes were in the sketch of a given individual as well as his rated confidence in the judgment.[2]

The independent variable in the present experiment is the degree to which the sketch of a hypothetical individual is discrepant from the sterotype of the category to which he is assigned. The degree of discrepancy is determined operationally by having a normative sample of judges rate the similarity of the individual described in each sketch to the stereotype for each of the majors.

Schemata, Prototypes, and Stereotypes

We assume that our subjects possess *schemata* for the categories consisting of Accounting, Law, and Social Work students.[3] We view the schema for a given category as a system or set of criteria by means of which the subject can either generate or recognize instances that are members of the category. For the impression formation task, we further assume that the schema also includes an ideal or representative instance of the category—the *prototype*—which is employed as a standard against which new instances are compared.

A schema for the category of Law Student, for example, would consist of a prototype of a typical law student along with rules and criteria that specify the type and range ·of permissible transformations that can be performed on this

---

[2] The literature on memory indicates that the effects that we want to explore within this paradigm will most likely show up in free or cued recall rather than in recognition memory (cf. Kintsch, 1970). Nevertheless, we employed only recognition memory in our initial experiment. One reason for this choice was the hope that we could obtain many more interesting indices of how the discrepancy from stereotype in the initial descriptions eventually showed up in later recognition. In our subsequent studies we plan to use recall, or a combination of recall and recognition.

[3] The concept of "schema" has been used in a variety of ways and has acquired a variety of connotations within the field of psychology (for examples see Attneave, 1957b; Bartlett, 1932; Evans, 1967; Northway, 1940; Oldfield, 1954; Reed, 1973; Woodworth, 1938). In this chapter only some of these varied connotations are intended. We make no assumptions, for example, about how the schemata originate nor about the specific mechanisms by which they operate.

prototype. When a prototype for a given category is shared by members of a subculture, as are the prototypes for the majors used in this experiment, then we call the prototype a *stereotype.*

Properties of the Impression Formation Task

The impression that the subject forms on the basis of a small set of traits seems to correspond closely to Bartlett's notion of a schema (Bartlett, 1932). Bartlett's use of the concept of "schema" has been criticized as being vague and inconsistent (Northway, 1940; Oldfield & Zangwill, 1942). One problem is that what Bartlett was pointing to, while real enough, is elusive and hard to describe. Rather than being a clearly delineated cognitive structure, Bartlett's schema seems to be a diffuse, quasi-affective "organized setting" within which the subject tries to make sense of material to be assimilated or to be recalled.

Apparently, the subjects readily form impressions on the basis of a few items of information about an individual. Because there is a great deal of inter-and intra-subject consistency in the impressions that are formed, social psychologists attribute an "implicit personality theory" to their subjects. (Hastorf *et al.,* 1970). These implicit personality theories, in the realm of interpersonal perception, seem to play a role much like Schank's (1972) system of conceptual dependencies.

What is of interest for the purposes of the present research is the fact that subjects form coherent impressions even when given information that is internally inconsistent.[4] A major objective of this research program is to study the differential effects upon memory of achieving such coherent impressions of information that vary in their internal consistency or compatibility. Thus, we attempt to experimentally manipulate the degree of inconsistency while ensuring that the subject will be able to achieve a coherent impression.

The adjectives chosen by the subject to indicate his impression provide two kinds of information about his "inferences" from the description he is given. First, they indicate the relative influence-upon the subject's initial impression of the assigned major and the character sketch. Second, they provide a baseline for subsequent memory of the sketch. We can evaluate the relative influence upon memory of those adjectives contained in the sketch and those used by the subject in his initial impression.

Zangwill (1972) cites some studies which demonstrate that what the subject reproduces in recall depends heavily upon his initial response to the original

---

[4] After having conducted this experiment, we have discovered that subjects do not always form an integrated impression. In the experiment by Gollin (1954) less than one-fourth of the subjects attempted to integrate or find a coherent basis for apparently discrepant information about a given person. The remaining subjects focussed on one aspect of the information while ignoring the discrepant aspect or included both aspects without attempting to reconcile them.

stimulus. Northway (1940) similarly argues that what the subject reproduces in serial reproduction tasks is not the original stimulus but his initial perception of that stimulus. And the Russian psychologist, Smirnov (1973) concludes that the perception of the original material proceeds at two levels. One is the level of actual details and the other is the level of a more abstract impression which we achieve in our effort to comprehend the material. This notion is much like that of the schema-with-correction theme as employed by Attneave (1957b) and Posner and Keele (1968, 1970). The important point is that memory may be guided as much, if not more, by the general impression formed at time of initial exposure as by actual content of the stimulus.

METHOD

Stimulus Materials

The stimulus materials consisted of three personality sketches, each attributed to a hypothetical individual. Each sketch was written around a set of ten adjectives selected on the basis of a normative study in which 12 judges were presented with a list of 11 occupational majors such as Physical Education, Accounting, Law, Medicine, Etc. The judges were instructed to imagine the typical graduate student who would be majoring in each of these areas. For each such typical major, the judges went through Anderson's list of 555 adjectives (Anderson, 1968) and circled each one that they felt to be descriptive of that individual. On the basis of the agreement among the judges, six nonoverlapping sets of 10 adjectives were selected for the construction of six separate sketches. Each sketch was written to fit the stereotype of a particular occupational major. An attempt was made to employ adjectives that were unique to a single major, that were not strongly negative on rated likeableness, and for which a reasonable number of equivalent synonyms existed on the list. The three sketches used in the present study, each paired with the occupational major to which it is most appropriate, are listed in Table 1.

The perceived similarity of each sketch to each major was measured in a second normative study employing 53 judges, all of whom were drawn from the same population as the subjects in the experiment. The judges formed an impression of the individual described in each of the six sketches. Immediately after reading each sketch, each judge described his impression of the target person by checking the appropriate adjectives on a 200-word checklist. This 200-word checklist had been constructed from Anderson's list of 555 by eliminating those adjectives that were never or rarely used in the first normative study. A set I, defined as the normative impression for a sketch, was derived for each sketch from these initial descriptions. Each adjective that was circled by 60% or more of the judges was included in the impression set I for that sketch.

TABLE 1
The Stimulus Materials: The Three Personality
Sketches Employed in
This Experiment[a]

MICHAEL DECKER

Michael Decker is currently doing graduate work in Law. During his senior year in high school, Michael Decker's school counselor wrote the following description of him based upon interviews and psychological tests:

Michael is an *ambitious* person who often is *impulsive* and *daring* in his thinking and actions. Being *skeptical,* he tends to be *outspoken* in his opinions. He tackles problems in an *aggressive* manner. He is both *talkative* and *forceful* in his social interactions. Although possessed of a *fiery* temperament, he is quite *shrewd* in his dealings with others.

ROBERT CAYWOOD

Robert Caywood is currently doing graduate work in Accounting. During his senior year in high school, Robert Caywood's school counselor wrote the following description of him based upon interviews and psychological tests:

Robert is basically a *cautious* and *thrifty* person. His outlook is *materialistic* and his classmates probably regard him as *insensitive.* In tackling any assignment he is *orderly* and *thorough.* Because he is *serious* and *unassuming,* he appears to be socially *withdrawn.* Both politically and in other ways he is a *conformist.*

ANDREW FLEMING

Andrew Fleming is currently doing graduate work in Social Work. During his senior year in high school, Andrew Fleming's school counselor wrote the following description of him based upon interviews and psychological tests:

Andrew is both a *warm* and *idealistic* person. Basically a *trusting* individual, he is *patient* and *sympathetic* in dealing with people. His classmates describe him as *generous* and *considerate.* He is genuinely *tolerant* of other viewpoints and *sincere* in his desire to listen. Andrew readily agrees that his outlook is *sentimental.*

---

[a]Each sketch is paired with the occupational major to which it is most appropriate in terms of judges' ratings. The ten key adjectives are italicized in each sketch: they were not italicized in the actual stimulus materials.

Next, the judges directly rated the similarity of the sketch to the typical graduate student in each of 10 occupational majors. The ratings were made on a 7-point scale with "1" indicating "very similar" and "7" indicating "very dissimilar." Note that that these ratings provide us with a measure for our basic independent variable: the "similarity-to-stereotype" for each possible sketch-major combination.

Finally, the 53 judges indicated their impressions of each of the 10 occupational majors by checking items on the 200-word checklist described above. A set *M,* defined as the stereotype for a major, was constructed from those adjectives endorsed by more than 60% of the judges for a given major.

From these normative data, the three sketches and the three occupational majors to be used in the present study were selected. Table 2 shows the combinations of the majors and sketches used with each experimental condition

TABLE 2
The Major-Sketch Pairings Used
in Each of the
Experimental Conditions[a]

Experimental condition	Sketch Name		
	CAYWOOD	FLEMING	DECKER
A	Accounting (2.0)	Law (4.1)	Social work (4.8)
B	Social work (6.2)	Accounting (5.6)	Law (2.2)
C	Law (3.8)	Social work (1.2)	Accounting (4.6)

[a]The columns indicate the sketch name and the rows the experimental condition. Each cell indicates the assigned major for the condition. The numbers in parentheses are the average ratings of similarity-to-stereotype for each major-sketch pairing. The ratings were made by judges on a 7-point scale such that "1" indicates "very similar" and "7" indicates "very dissimilar."

along with the similarity-to-stereotype ratings for each major-sketch combination.[5]

The Adjective Check List

The construction and the composition of the adjective list, which is the constant instrument upon which all the impressions and recognition judgments are mapped, are very important. A new checklist of 91 adjectives was constructed by selecting items from three sets—the character sketch itself, C; the generalized impression of the sketch, I; the stereotype of an occupation major, M—appropriate to one of three sketches or the three majors. We attempted to get an even distribution of adjectives among the subsets formed by the sets C, I, and M and their complements. The greatest set overlap is between the stereotype for Social Worker and the impression for Fleming (10 of 22 adjectives); the least is between the stereotype for Law and the impression for Decker (2 of 24

[5]Ideally, the arrangement of sketches, assigned majors, experimental conditions, and relative similarity-to-stereotype would form a Greco-Latin square with each of these four factors orthogonal to one another. We could not achieve such complete orthogonality with the present set of three sketches and majors. In fact, out of the total set of six sketches and majors that we started with, we could form only one balanced Greco-Latin square with a subset of three. But this subset had undesirable features such as strong overlap between two of the sketches and a very wide range of discrepancy in one condition and practically no range in discrepancy for another. The selection employed here is consequently a compromise. There is confounding between the moderate and extreme levels of discrepancy in that Law is never paired with the most discrepant case in any of the three experimental groups while Accounting is paired with the most discrepant case in two of the conditions. The contrast between the least discrepant case and the other two levels of discrepancy, however, is orthogonal to the other three factors.

adjectives). The stereotypes for Law and Accounting share two adjectives out of a total of 25 between them. Table 3 may help to clarify what was accomplished in the two normative studies that supplied the sketches, the majors, and the checklist for the present experiment.

The checklist was constructed so that a number of comparisons could be made from subject's responses. Table 4, for example, illustrates the partition of the checklist relevant to the analysis of responses to the major-sketch pairing of (Fleming, Social Worker). Table 4 provides such information as the following: both Andrew Fleming and the typical major in Social Work are considered to be kindly and pleasant; Fleming is considered to be good-humored and broad-minded, but these traits are not part of the stereotype of the Social Worker. On the other hand, the typical student in Social Work is described as accessible and dedicated, adjectives which are not part of the general impression of Fleming. Also, even though the adjective idealistic is used in the sketch of Fleming, the majority of judges did not check it as part of their impression of him. Later we will add two more cross paritions of the check list for more detailed analyses—one includes the list of adjectives included in the other two sketches and the other includes those adjectives actually checked by a subject as descriptive of the combination (Fleming, Social Worker).

TABLE 3
The Normative Studies and Their Yields

Study 1: 12 judges

Judges describe each of 11 occupational majors on a 555-word checklist (Anderson, 1968).

Results:

(i) Six nonoverlapping sets of 10 adjectives, each set appropriate to a different one of 6 majors. A character sketch is written around each set.
(ii) A reduced list of 200 adjectives.

Study 2: 53 judges

Judges

a. Describe the 6 sketches on 200-word checklist.
b. Rate each sketch for similarity to stereotype of 10 occupational majors on scale from "1" (very similar) to "7" (very dissimilar).
c. Describe each of the 10 occupational majors on the 200-word checklist.

Results:

i. normative impression set of adjectives for each sketch.
ii. rated similarity of each sketch to each major.
iii. stereotype set of adjectives for each major.

From these results, the three sketches and the three majors were selected and the 91-word checklist was constructed.

TABLE 4

The Partition of the Checklist Relevant to
Analyzing the Results for the Pairing
(Fleming, Social Work)[a]

$C\bar{I}'\bar{M}'$	$CI\bar{M}'$	$CI'\bar{M}$	CIM
idealistic	sentimental	(empty)	patient
	trusting		sincere
	generous		sympathetic
			tolerant
			warm
			considerate

$\bar{C}'I\bar{M}'$	$\bar{C}'IM$	$\bar{C}\bar{I}'M$	$\bar{C}\bar{I}\bar{M}'$
good-humored	kindly	accessible	accurate
soft-hearted	pleasant	adaptive	analytical
trustworthy	sensitive	dedicated	careful
broadminded	sociable		cautious, etc.
cheerful	thoughtful		
congenial	acceptant		
cooperative	charitable		
emotional	earnest		
gentle	friendly		
	helpful		

[a]C stands for the set of adjectives in the sketch for Fleming; I stands for the set of adjectives in the normative impression of this sketch; and M stands for the set of adjectives in the stereotype of Social Work. $\bar{C}$, $\bar{I}$, $\bar{M}$ stand for the complements of these sets.

Subjects.   Forty-seven subjects, taking undergraduate psychology courses, were asked to participate in an experiment on impression formation for which they would be paid $3.00. They were told that the experimental session would take between $1\frac{1}{2}$ to 2 hr.

Procedure.   Each subject was given a booklet with detailed instructions. Each subject could go through the entire experimental session at his own pace. Total time varied from 30 to 90 min. The subject was told that he would be reading three brief sketches, each describing a different person. He was to form an impression of the person described and then record which adjectives on the accompanying lists seemed to fit his overall impression. He was to read a sketch for as long as he felt necessary. He was to think about what the person was like overall. Once he felt he had formed an impression of the person, he was to turn the page to the list of adjectives. Without looking back to the sketch, he was to read down the list of adjectives. Whenever he encountered a word that seemed to fit his idea of what the person was like, he was to circle it. The subject did this for each of the three sketches in turn. The instructions were repeated prior to each sketch.

Upon completing the checklist for the third sketch, subject came upon the following instructions:

> In the first part we asked you to form an impression of a person on the basis of the description we supplied to you. At that time we did not tell you that you were to remember anything about the description. But in this second part of the experiment, we are going to ask you to remember as best you can those adjectives that were actually in the descriptions we supplied to you. We are aware that your ability to recognize that an adjective was or was not in the sketch of a given person cannot be done with absolute certainty.

Detailed instructions about how to employ the 6-point rating scale followed. For each adjective, subject was to circle "1" if he was very confident that the word *did* appear in the sketch; "2" if he was reasonably confident that the word did appear; "3" if he was slightly confident that it *did* appear; "4" if he was slightly confident that the word *did not* appear, etc. We did not allow a neutral category on the scale because our preliminary experiments indicated that subjects tend to overuse the middle category.

The subject then turned the page and encountered the list of 91 adjectives with the rating scales beside each one. At the very top of the page was the name and major of the major-sketch combination that he was trying to remember. When he completed his ratings for one sketch, he turned the page to a repetition of the instructions in case he needed to refresh his memory for them. He then turned to the recognition task for the second sketch; and then finally to the last sketch.

The experiment was conducted in a large classroom with the subjects seated such that all could be monitored by three experimenters who were present throughout the session.

RESULTS

The results are based upon the data from 44 of the 47 subjects distributed as follows; 14 in Condition A, 15 in Condition B, and 15 in Condition C (Three subjects failed to follow instructions).

The Impression Formation Task

Figure 1 summarizes the data of how the subjects used the checklist categories to describe their impressions of the sketches. The categories C' (the sketch adjectives), $\overline{CI}$ (adjectives in normative impression, but *not* in sketch) and K (adjectives in the other two sketches) and Base (all the remaining adjectives) were employed because they consisted of identical adjectives for a given sketch and all three category assignments. The data are pooled across the three sketches. The first value on the abscissa is the average similarity-to-major for the 3 cases in which each sketch was assigned to its most compatible major; the second value is the average for the 3 cases in which each sketch was assigned to its next most compatible major; the third point is the average for the 3 cases in which each sketch was assigned to its least compatible major. At all three levels of similarity-to-stereotype, subjects use about 80% of the adjectives that were in the target person's sketches to describe their impressions. Almost as frequently, they employ adjectives that are normative associates of the sketch (category CI). The "baseline" category tends to elicit somewhat more usage than do the adjectives in the other two sketches. This is partly due to the fact that the baseline contains adjectives in the stereotype categories and, for each sketch, the adjectives in the closest or more appropriate stereotypic category tend to be employed in the impression task with almost as much frequency as are the adjectives in the $\overline{CI}$ category (approximately 70% as compared with approximately 75%).

Figure 1 shows that subjects do tend to use the adjectives from the normative impression in making their own descriptions of the sketch. It also seems to indicate that the descriptions were affected very little by the degree of discrepancy from stereotype. Figure 2 shows the tendency to employ adjectives during the impression formation task that come from the three stereotype categories on

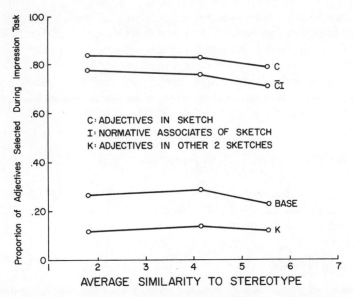

FIG. 1 Proportion of adjectives selected from various categories of the checklist during the impression-formation task. The similarity-to-stereotype along the abscissa is based on the averaged normative ratings for the three sketches at each of the three levels of relative discrepancy from stereotype. The normative ratings are on a scale ranging from "1," very similar to the stereotype of the assigned category, to "7," very dissimilar to the stereotype. Each point is based on the data from 44 subjects.

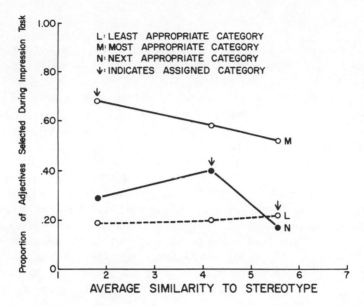

FIG. 2 Proportion of adjectives selected from the three stereotype categories on the checklist during the impression formation task. The abscissa has the same meaning as in Fig. 1. The arrows indicate the assigned category.

the checklist. The top line on the graph, for example, shows the tendency to use adjectives in the most appropriate category (the stereotype which is closest to the sketch) when that category is the assigned one and when it is not. Here it looks as if the tendency to use adjectives from the appropriate stereotype is greater when that is also the assigned stereotype. Although this is a reasonable and expected finding, not too much reliance should be placed upon it because it is mainly due to one sketch.

With one exception, the tendency to use adjectives from the various stereotype categories seems to be determined almost entirely by the similarity of the sketch to the stereotype rather than by the assignment of the sketch to a major. The exception is for the intermediate case. In this latter case it does appear that assigning a sketch to a major that is moderately discrepant (rather than extremely discrepant) does result in an enhanced tendency to use adjectives in this category to describe the impression. Although this finding of some assimilation to the stereotype for the moderately deviant assignment is consistent with our predictions, the effect is rather small and local (in the sense that it does not seem to affect other categories of the description).[6]

---

[6] Subsequent analyses of individual adjectives and a replication experiment with a much larger sample confirms the fact that the assignment of a major to a sketch affects both the impression and the recognition task. The analysis by large categories of adjectives masks this effect because many of the adjectives do not discriminate because they are easily rejected as being irrelevant to a particular sketch.

The Recognition Task

The dependent variable for evaluating the subject's recognition memory for the adjectives in the sketches is simply the average rating for the various categories of adjectives.

Figure 3 summarizes the basic results on the recognition task. As in the preceding two figures the results are displayed as a function of the average similarity to the stereotype. Here too, the relative discrepancy between sketch and assigned major has little effect.

Figure 3 displays the recognition ratings broken down by the six categories formed by splitting each of the three categories C (sketch adjectives), $\overline{C}I$, and B (baseline) into those adjectives used by S in his own description (D) and those not used in his own description ($\overline{D}$). For both the D and the $\overline{D}$ categories, the subjects consistently tend to rate the adjectives that were actually in the sketch as more likely to have been in the sketch than they do the adjectives in the normative associates ($\overline{C}I$). In Fig. 3 this effect is larger for those adjectives in the subjects' descriptions than for those that are not. We do not consider this interaction "significant," however, because it is due mostly to one sketch and does not exist in the other two.

The normative associates, in turn, tend to be rated as more likely to have been in the sketch than the adjectives in the base set. This effect is approximately of

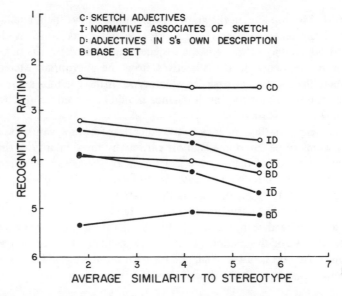

FIG. 3 Recognition rating as a function of average deviation from stereotype. The ordinate represents the rating scale which ranged from "1," very confident that adjective was in the sketch, through "6," very confident that adjective was *not* in the sketch. Each point is based on the data from 44 subjects.

the same size for both the adjectives used by the subjects in their descriptions of the sketches and for those not used in their descriptions. Finally, for each of the three categories, the adjectives actually used in the subjects' descriptions of their sketch impressions tend to be consistently rated as more likely to have been in the sketch than those not used by the subjects in their descriptions.

Figure 3 suggests, then, that the recognition ratings can be explained or accounted for by three approximately additive main effects. One effect is due to the adjective actually having been in the sketch; another effect is due to the adjective being a member of the impression of that sketch generated by a group of judges; the third effect is due to the adjective being one of those actually used by the subject in his description of the immediate impression he formed of the sketch-major combination. Our analysis of variances on the three sketches confirms this impression. The reader should compare Fig. 3 with Fig. 1 to note how closely the recognition data mirror the descriptions made during the impression formation task.

DISCUSSION

This chapter examines one of a contemplated series of studies that will explore the usefulness of the impression-formation task as a paradigm for investigating issues related to the restructuring of memory and the acquisition of knowledge. Two issues of concern in the present experiment are the role of the subject's immediate impression upon his subsequent memory for the sketch and the effect of assigning the sketch to compatible or discrepant majors. The data suggest that neither the subject's initial impression nor the major to which the hypothetical individual was assigned have any appreciable affect upon his recognition memory for which adjectives actually were included in the sketch. Instead, two approximately additive components appear to determine the subject's tendency to judge an adjective as having been in the sketch. One component is whether or not the adjective actually did occur in the sketch. And the other component is whether the adjective belongs to the set of normative adjectives that judges have checked as characteristic of the individual described in the sketch.

The analysis of variance indicate that the subject's confidence ratings can be accounted for by three additive main effects. One main effect results from the adjective's having been in the sketch. The second results from the adjective being a member of the normative impression set generated by the sketch. The third main effect is due to whether the adjective was or was not in the subject's own immediate description of the impression created by the sketch-major combination.

The lack of any interaction between the checklist categories and the usage of adjectives in the impression task along with the parallel outcomes from both the impression and recognition tasks suggests that we have two dependent variables which both reflect the same effects. The fact that one dependent variable is obtained prior to the other apparently does not have any effect on the outcome.

The use of "determine" in the preceding paragraphs was not intended to indicate causality. While it makes sense to view the occurrence of an adjective in the stimulus sketch as "causing" an increment in recognition memory for that adjective, it makes much less sense to treat the normative category of adjectives in the sketch impression as a causal agent. Presumably the adjectives in the sketch cause the subject to generate or retrieve a category or schema for describing the individual in the sketch. This personal category or impression then becomes the source or causal agent for increasing the subject's tendency to falsely recognize an adjective as having been in the sketch. This personal impression is partially correlated with both the normative impression of the sketch and with the subject's choice of adjectives in the impression task.

It is possible that the effect of the subject's immediate impression of the stimulus might show up in recognition memory with a longer interval between stimulus presentation and subsequent testing for retention. As mentioned in the introduction, it is even more likely that such an effect will show up in recall rather than recognition. The data on memory for visual form (Riley, 1962) and various attempts to replicate and elaborate Bartlett's work (Zangwill, 1972) indicate that reproduction and recall are heavily influenced by the subject's initial response to a stimulus but that recognition memory may or may not be a function of this initial reaction.[7]

The most important result is the fact that recognition memory seems to be strongly influenced by two approximately additive components. Possibly there is also a slight influence of the stereotype of the assigned major. Future studies will investigate how these components fare over longer intervals of retention and in terms of other indices of retention. From the work on pattern recognition (Hyman & Frost, 1974; Posner & Keele, 1968, 1970) and from some of the work on semantic memory (Barclay, 1973; Bransford, Barcley, & Franks, 1972; Bransford & Franks, 1971); we would expect that with increasing retention intervals or with heavier memory loads the memory of the specific adjectives or details of the sketch would fade to zero or to a negligible level while the tendency to base the memory upon the general impression will remain stable. The so-called "reconstructive" aspects of the memory will then dominate subsequent retention. Whether this latter result is seen as a defect or a virtue of memory will depend upon the task and the goals set by the experimenter, the educator, or the student. It is interesting to note that in the pattern-recognition studies it is considered a virtue to respond in terms of a generalized impression or abstracted

---

[7] Since the present experiment was reported we have completed a new study in which we used both recall and recognition measures. The recall scores show the same pattern of results as do the recognition.

image, whereas in recognition—memory performance is scored in terms of ability to discriminate the actual details from the general impression.

Our manipulation of discrepancy from stereotype represents only one of many possible ways to manipulate discrepancy. Our majors "Law Student," "Accounting Student," and "Social-Work Student" are by no means mutually exclusive. The set of adjectives in the stereotype for an Accounting Major include descriptors such as "analytical," "careful," "consistent," "methodical," "systematic," etc. Almost all of these descriptors seem to deal with work habits and ways of coping with problems. Not a single adjective in this stereotype list for Accountant refers to interpersonal relationships.

The adjectives in the stereotype for Social Work major, on the other hand, include such descriptors as "accessible," "adaptive," "acceptant," "charitable," "friendly," "helpful," "kindly," "sensitive," etc. With practically no exceptions these traits all deal with interpersonal relationships. Thus, there is no incompatibility between the stereotypes of the major in Accounting and the major in Social Work. In thinking of an Accountant major, one does not typically consider his interpersonal relationships and vice versa. But there is no reason why an individual cannot simultaneously fit the stereotypes of a student in Accounting and a student in Social Work. One way to create true discrepancy is to work with mutually exclusive categories or to deliberately construct sketches which contain adjectives that are antonyms of those adjectives that describe a given stereotype.

Another related problem with the categories we have used is that they are quite broad in their inclusiveness. Our hypotheses about relative discrepancy from stereotype were based on the idea that the category of each of the majors was bounded in the sense that descriptions of individuals who were quite different from the stereotype would be viewed by the subjects as definitely not a member of that category. It was hoped that the sketches that were intermediate in similarity to the stereotype would be seen as quite different from the stereotype but still within the permissible bounds of variation from it. Actually, our categories seem to be relatively unbounded. Although the subjects do seem to have coherent and shared ideas of what the typical or prototypical student in each occupational major is like, they also probably see these categories as relatively unbounded in that any sort of student can choose to major in any of these areas. Possibly we would have more clearly bounded categories if we assigned sketches to the actual occupations rather than to students who are training for that occupation.

Still another reason why the assigned major had little effect upon the impression and the recognition tasks might be the fact that the sketches were written so as to be internally coherent and cohesive. The sketches generated a consistent impression of an individual without any help from the assigned major. It is possible that the assignment will have a noticeable effect only when the stimulus is vague, ambiguous, or internally contradictory (cf. Bransford & Johnson, 1973 for related evidence). In the studies of labeling and memory for visual form (Riley, 1962) the stimulus objects are typically ambiguous.

A major purpose of this chapter is to indicate the promise of the impression-formation task as a paradigm for the experimental investigation of a variety of questions related to the restructuring of memory, the acquisition of new information, the assimilation of new inputs to existing representations, and the accommodation of existing representations to fit the new inputs. From our preliminary experiments and from our experience with the experiment discussed here, we are encouraged by many features of this paradigm. For one thing, the subjects say that they find the task meaningful and quite relevant to their daily activities. For another thing, individual behavior is surprisingly consistent and well predicted from population norms collected on moderately sized samples.

Using the same stimulus materials and paradigm, we plan to study the effects on other indices of memory such as recall and the effects of longer retention intervals. Other extensions of this work will involve changing the manner of manipulating discrepancy from prototype as well as changing the stimulus materials. For example, we plan to make sketches internally ambiguous in the sense that the adjectives used will be drawn from two or more different stereotypes. The assignment of the sketch to one or the other of potentially relevant categories should result in relatively more emphasis on the relevant subset of adjectives both in forming the impression and in subsequent memory.

ACKNOWLEDGMENTS

This research was supported by the Advanced Research Projects Agency of the Department of Defense and was monitored by the Air Force Office of Scientific Research under Contract No. F44620-73-C-0056.

9
Comments on Learning Schemata and Memory Representation

Donald A. Norman
Donald R. Gentner
Albert L. Stevens

University of California, San Diego

Consider what happens when a person learns a complex subject matter. By complex, we mean something that takes a considerable amount of time to learn—time measured in weeks and months, not in hours or days. Complex topics contain a large structure of information composed of the relevant concepts and processes that make up the topic. A large amount of time is necessary just to incorporate such a mass of material into a person's memory structure. Moreover, sheer rote acquisition of the concepts is not enough. The material must be structured in such a way that relevant concepts can be related properly to one another. The procedures must be learned well enough that they can be performed when needed, and more important, so that they can be performed when the situation is not quite the same as when the concept was learned.

Before we can make much progress towards the understanding of how complex topics are learned, we need to know about the organization of knowledge within human memory. We contend that our relative lack of knowledge about the learning process is a direct reflection of our relative lack of knowledge about the structure of human memory. Things are changing, however. Psychology is now coming to understand memory structure better. In turn, we are now starting to get a better understanding of the process of learning.

In this chapter we examine some current ideas about memory structure and show their relevance toward the study of learning. We discuss the organization of basic memory units around *frames* or *schemata* and more especially, the way by which a person comes to modify these units. The overall result of this endeavor, to us at least, is both exciting and disappointing. It is exciting because it appears to show how recent work in the study of cognitive systems can potentially be of value to our deeper understanding of the problems involved in education. It is disappointing, because when we are done, it can be said that all that has been accomplished is the statement of old knowledge and understanding into a new terminology. Despite all this, we are optimistic that the new terminology, coupled with our understanding of cognitive processes can eventually lead to a deeper understanding of learning.

MEMORY REPRESENTATION

Semantic Networks

A number of workers in the field of human memory have recently been developing formal representations for the knowledge within memory. Most of the models that we are interested in here are described as *semantic neworks*. Following the work of Quillian (1968), they are all characterized by a directed, labeled graph structure, such as those shown if Figs. 1, 2, and 3. We call our version of a semantic network an *active structural network* to emphasize that the representation is both active and passive. It can contain general procedures that can be executed whenever functional knowledge must be used (This work is reported in Norman, Rumelhart, and the LNR[1] research group, 1975: from now on we refer to this work as "LNR"). Although we will base our discussion on this work the comments will apply to all semantic network representations.

Basically, the semantic network provides a means of representing knowledge. It is a new tool in psychology. Previously, our formal models have been abstract: a mathematical learning model, for example, talks of the probability or the strength of some association between two elements, but the elements are usually part of a large homogeneous set. With semantic networks, we look at the structure of very particular items.

The Internal Components of Verbs

Consider, for example, how a child might come to learn language. In the work of the LNR research group, the meanings of verbs can be decomposed into underlying primitive elements. Thus, some verbs specify only STATIVE components; others are more complex, specifying CAUSE and CHANGE. When we say that;

(1)   The skier went to the top to the mountain.

there is a change of location of the skier—as shown in Fig. 1.

---

[1] The acronymn LNR represents the research group at the University of California, San Diego which has studied these issues. The group was originally formed and supervised by Peter Lindsay, Donald Norman, and David Rumelhart: hence, LNR.

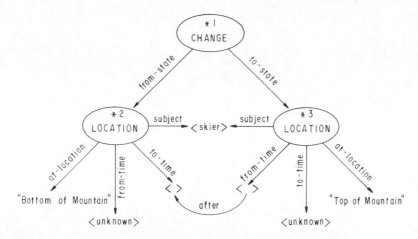

FIG. 1 The skier went to the top of the mountain.

The figure shows the decomposition of the verb "went" into its more basic underlying components, i.e., its network structure. Network structures are composed of nodes and ordered, labeled relations connecting these nodes. In Fig. 1, the ovals represent modes that are token instances of propositional structures, the angular brackets (e.g., skier) represent nodes that are token instances of concepts, and the phrases enclosed in quotation marks (e.g., "bottom of mountain") represent network structures for the concepts described by the phrases, but which we have not shown in detail in the figure in order to maintain the clarity of the diagram. In the LNR active structural network, there are four different types of node structures, two of which are shown in Fig. 1. The numbers of the token propositional nodes have no meaning: they are used solely to facilitate the discussion of these nodes.

Figure 1 can be interpreted in a straightforward manner by starting with node *1, the oval labeled CHANGE. This indicated that some change of states has taken place: the relations leaving node *1 describe the states that are involved. The CHANGE takes place from a state shown by the node *2: This node says that its subject (a skier) was located at the "bottom of mountain" from some unknown time to some time not specified (but indicated by the unnamed node shown as angular brackets). The result of the change is the state represented by node *3: the skier is now as location "top of mountain." Notice that the time he was located at the top of the mountain is not specified, except to indicate that it is later than the time at which he was no longer at the bottom of the mountain.

A more complex verb is one that implies causality: say "to give." If we say

(2)   Suzette took the skis from Henry.

we mean that Suzette did something that caused the skis to change from Henry's possession to her possession. We illustrate this sentence with the structure shown in Fig. 2.

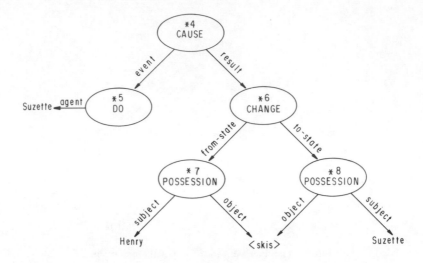

FIG. 2   Suzette took the skis from Henry.

Note that these structures provide frameworks for subsequent knowledge. Each structure is a memory *schema:* it allows us to organize the material that we learn later on. Thus, if we learn that

(2B)   She promised to return them by morning.

we know that there is an obligation to return the skis. From that we can deduce that she got them from Henry with his permission, and in fact, we expand the framework for the knowledge to something like that shown in Fig. 3. Note that we add the new knowledge directly to the framework for the old. Not only did we have a convenient way of modifying the structure for the previous episode according to the framework provided by the schema for the first sentence, but we have now modified the structure into one that is equivalent to "borrow." Suzette borrowed the skis. It is easy to see how other statements could have modified the structure to indicate that

Suzette stole the skis (no permission was granted)
Suzette purchased or rented the skis (she paid money for them)
Suzette got the skis by asking Peter to pick them up for her (expanding the
    DO statement).

Developmental Studies

The schemata provided by this form of structural analysis turn out to be rather powerful. Dedre Gentner (1975) shows how a number of the verbs of possession can be analyzed in this way. More important for present purposes, she reports on experiments which show that a person's memory of the actual verb used in a

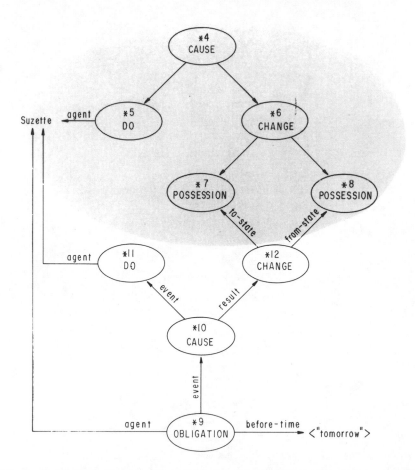

FIG. 3 *In shaded areas:* Suzette took the skis from Henry. *Not shaded:* She promised to return them by tomorrow. *Total structure:* Suzette borrowed the skis from Henry promising to return them the next day.

sentence will vary systematically with the other information provided, much in the manner of the illustrations we have already provided.

Gentner has also studied the order in which these structures are learned. If we look at Fig. 4 we see the underlying components that she has analyzed for the structures of the verbs "give, take, buy, sell, spend money, trade." Gentner shows how one can derive an ordering for the acquisition of the underlying components, and therefore for the verbs themselves. In fact, she has performed the necessary experiments. She seated children in front of tables which had two dolls (Bert and Ernie) and she asked the children to make one doll buy, sell, give and take toys from the other. The details are reported in her paper, but the important aspect is that the developmental sequence of acquisition followed the expectations rather nicely. See Fig. 5. You might note that the structures of

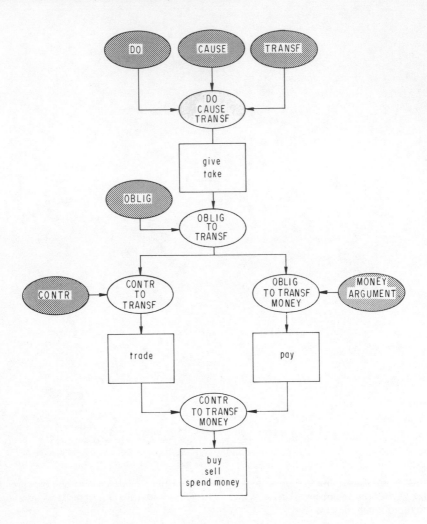

FIG. 4 The relationships among the concepts underlying the verbs "give," "take," "pay," "buy," "sell," and "spend money." The semantic components and the states that permit full understanding of the verbs are represented by the shaded ovals. Age of the acquisition of the verbs proceeds vertically, youngest age at the top. (From Gentner, 1975.)

these verbs are reasonably complex. The time course of the acquisition of the verbs follows the theoretical ordering of their complexity. It takes children approximately 5 years to progress from the state in which they use words like "give" and "take" properly to the point where they use the entire set of possession verbs shown in Fig. 4 properly. The structural network descriptions for these verbs show why this long time period might be necessary. Children must learn about a number of different concepts—some dealing with social

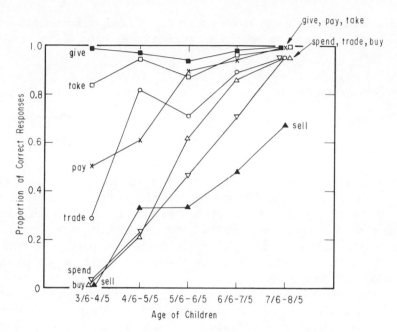

FIG. 5 Probability of correct use of verb versus age of children. (From Gentner, 1975.)

conventions, some dealing with language, and others dealing with the physical properties of objects and locations. All these concepts must be understood, and then, for the proper linguistic labels to be assigned, they must be interrelated in the manner shown by the network structures. Once the schema for the inter-relations is acquired, then the linguistic use can be appropriate to the situation. Note that the schemata capture the interdependence of nonlinguistic phe-nomena. Concepts such as OBLIGATION, CAUSE, and DO are not verbal or linguistic concepts: these schemata and the network presentations are not restricted to linguistic concepts.

We could go on, but for present purposes it is not necessary. Suffice it to say that it is possible to demonstrate how similar structural representations can be formed for visual scenes (Palmer, 1975: in the LNR volume) and for stories (Rumelhart, 1975).

SCHEMATA

The Structure of Schemata

A schema provides a framework on which to interrelate different elements of information about a topic into one conceptual unit.

A schema consists of statements about the important features of the unit, the functions of the unit, rules for selection and rules for use.

Functional schemata will often contain a conditional statement and sets of events that are to be performed according to the status of the conditional state.

The Selection of Schemata

Schemata are selected for use according to their similarity to the situation.

The Modification of Schemata

By relaxing the restrictions of arguments of a schema, it is often possible to apply it to a new situation. We give two examples of this later. A schema must specify the proper set of conditions to which it can apply. When a schema is misapplied, the relevant modification is the imposition of restrictions, so that the schema will not be misapplied in the future. It is possible to combine a number of schemata into a single, higher-level schema which can then be applied to a more complex situation.

In learning by analogy, the student basically selects a schema with an appropriate organization, even if it is for an inappropriate topic area. If this schema is already well learned and easily applicable to situations for which it is normally appropriate, then it provides a useful frame for the understanding of the new topic. By proper instruction, it can be modified to apply to the present situation. For example, we find it useful to introduce computers and computer programs by drawing on the student's knowledge of plays and scripts. We explain that the script is replaced with the concept for a program and the performers with the computer. This use of old schemata constitutes a powerful way to introduce new information about a complex and unfamiliar area.

Examples

Here we present three examples that demonstrate different aspects of the process of learning and teaching. All illustrate the ways by which teacher and student use schemata. First, we show that one use of knowledge schemata is to allow for intelligent guesses, even when very little is actually known about the specific concept under consideration. This point is illustrated in what we call *The Mayonnaise Problem*. Second, we show how the prior existence of schemata relevant to the topic matter that is being studied can be both a help and a hindrance to the student. We call this *The White Sauce Problem*. Finally, we discuss how a person acquires and modifies schemata, basing successive new understandings of the topic being studied on modification of the old schemata for that topic. We call this *The Jump Problem*. The first two examples are presented reasonably briefly, for they act more as enjoyable, light examples than as profound statements of major theoretical substance. The last example, the Jump Problem is presented in more detail, for although the work presented here represents only the beginning steps in our studies, it does raise issues on which we wish to concentrate our attention in future research.

Example: The mayonnaise problem.   The study of cooking provides a useful example of the difficulty of learning complex subjects, especially the use of previously acquired schemata. To a noncook, the combination of ingredients in mayonnaise is not at all an obvious one. First, no heat is applied. Second, the basic components do not match most people's conceptions of what it should take to make a smooth, white, creamy substance we know as mayonnaise. It is for this reason that it is interesting to ask naive subjects just what they expect mayonnaise to be made of. They are forced to use the closest schema that they have: one that has some properties in common with mayonnaise. Their responses give us some insight into how much a person can warp a schema to a foreign situation. We claim this use of schemata through analogy is very widespread. In Table 1 we present protocols collected from two naive subjects who were forced to specify how to make mayonnaise.

TABLE 1
Protocols for Mayonnaise Problem

Protocol of the experimenter (DAN) and CN, an 8-year-old female

DAN: How do you make mayonnaise?

CN: How you make mayonnaise is you look at a cookbook.

DAN: OK, but without looking at a cookbook, can you guess what it is that's inside of mayonnaise?

CN: Uh.

DAN: How you would make it?

CN: Uh Butter—uh let me think (5-sec pause) hmm (10-sec pause) whipped cream very very very fine—ly whipped so it's smooth. That's probably how you make it, just with whipped cream, very very very very fine and smooth.

DAN: Anything else?

CN: You might add a little taste to it.

DAN: Taste of what?

CN: (10-sec pause) Sort of a vanilla taste.

DAN: Suppose I said that mayonnaise is made from egg yolk—and oil. What would you say?

CN: I would say it's very very—wrong.

DAN: Why?

CN You can't just make mayonnaise out of egg yolks and water—I mean and oil.

DAN: Why not?

CN: Because of taste and smoothness and stuff like that.

Protocol of the experimenter (DAN) and GB, an adult male psychology professor

DAN: How would you make something like mayonnaise?

GB: Mayonnaise? How do you make mayonnaise? You can't make mayonnaise, it has to be bought in jars. Mayonnaise. Um. You mix whipped cream with, umm some mustard.

The mayonnaise protocols illustrate that previously developed schemata can be applied to new problems, not necessarily in appropriate fashion, of course. The determinants of which schemata get applied are the features which come from what is known: in this case, the features of the end result. The problem is that the relevant properties of egg and oil and their interactions (that they can form a white creamy substance) are not part of any stored schema, so the correct answer cannot be derived. As the examples illustrate, mayonnaise has properties which make it look more like certain dairy products than the result of mixing the yolks of eggs with oil.[2]

The point of this exercise is simple (perhaps too simple for the space it has occupied). We believe that this use of old schemata thru analogy is all pervasive and powerful. Although the sauces derived by our two subjects are not at all mayonnaise, they are intelligent creations, and they are not bad sauces for some purposes. Normally, this creative use of an old schema for a novel purpose is an essential use of the creative process of discovery.

Later we return to this issue. We believe that the mayonnaise problem is an example of "functional reasoning". Here is what we believe is involved:

1. No knowledge of the components of mayonnaise existed.
2. It is known that mayonnaise is smooth, creamy, off-white in color. Its taste is known (and it is somewhat acidic).
3. General schema:
   Blends of foods blend their properties.
   Texture: sour cream or whipped cream yields a color that is too white and a taste that is not right.
   Correction: add yellow-spicy—acidic mustard.

So we have:

Selection of schema by analogy.
Modification towards goal.

This is reasoning by analogy. In functional reasoning we claim there must be one more step: the schema has variables in it, and any concepts that fulfill appropriate range restrictions on those variables may be used in the solution of a problem.

Example: The white sauce problem. One important component of the process of learning and teaching is that of communication. The teacher has the

---

[2] To make mayonnaise, one puts 2 egg yolks in a mixing bowl with one teaspoon of vinegar or lemon juice. Seasonings may be added (dry mustard, salt, white pepper). Then, while beating vigorously with a wire whip, oil is added, drop by drop, until the mixture is thick and creamy (about $1/3$ cup of oil). More oil is then added in a slow steady stream (all the while beating vigorously). When $1-1\frac{1}{2}$ cups of oil have been added, mix in a second teaspoon of vinegar or lemon juice.

task of conveying a particular knowledge structure to the student. The learner has the task of deducing just what structure is intended by the teacher, as well as the additional task of adding the new information to his previous knowledge in such a way that it can be referred to and used at a later time. Many of the problems of learning and teaching can be understood as problems in this communication process. Learning, however, is unlike most simple communications in that the structures to be acquired can be complex, and it is not always clear just how they are to fit together. Moreover, the differences in the knowledge shared among the participants in a learning situation are often considerably greater than in simple discourse.

In many ways, this aspect of the learning process is actually a problem. First, there is the problem of identifying the appropriate referent—of determining just what topic is under consideration. Second, there is the problem of so specifying the information being acquired and incorporating it within the memory structure that it can be recovered when later it is needed.

Social conventions govern the form of the interactions between a teacher and a student, with certain well-formed conventions about the nature of the interactions and questions that normally take place. A private tutorial allows for more interaction than does a seminar. In turn, lectures allow few opportunities for the communicative aspect of the learning process to take place.[3]

One aspect of this communicatory process is that the same teacher may use quite different procedures to teach the same material to two different students. In our studies of the tutorial dialogues between beginning students and tutors and advanced students and tutors, the difference is expository style is clear: the tutor tends to lecture the beginner; with an advanced student, things are more like a relaxed conversational interchange of information. Books reflect this difference, for the style of the book depends upon the level of the student which it is addressing. One example readily available comes from a comparison of the recipes in an elementary cookbook with the recipes of an advanced cookbook. Thus, one recipe for mayonnaise in a book intended for advanced cooks takes exactly six sentences (67 words) and a list of ingredients. Essentially the very same recipe for a beginning cook is around 13 times longer; three pages of text or about 900 words and a list of ingredients.[4]

---

[3] A textbook allows no interaction, of course, although in some sense the use of branching, teaching machine texts or simple computer assisted instructions sequences do recover some aspects of the communication. The recent work by Carbonell (1970, 1971) and Collins, Warnock, Aiello, and Miller (1975) and Brown, Burton, and Zdybel (1973) adds communication to computer-aided instruction by providing the computer system with a semantic network of knowledge about the topic matter and allowing it to interact in a tutorial fashion with the student.

[4] The advanced example comes from "Masterpieces of French Cuisine" by Amunatequi (1971), and the introductory example from "Mastering the Art of French Cooking" by Child, Bertholle, and Beck (1961).

One technique we have used to explore the processes of learning and teaching is that of tutorial instruction. For these tutorial studies we picked the topic of French cooking—to be exact, the subset of techniques involved in the making of the family of white sauces. This topic is well suited for our purposes: complex enough that it constitutes a challenge for the learner, sufficiently self contained that one can hope to learn a considerable amount within a reasonable amount of time. Moreover, it is easy to find well motivated students and teachers. (We concentrated the sessions on the coverage provided by Child, Bertholle, & Beck, 1961, pp. 54-93.)

Suppose you set out to teach someone the family of French white sauces. How should you present it? How does one get across the entire network of inter-related concepts?

When an advanced cook tutors a beginner, there is a tendency to lecture at first, describing the overall family of sauces. Then, when the overview description has been completed, the beginner's lack of understanding often surfaces, causing a fumbling, exploratory interaction in which each tries to understand what the other is thinking.

Table 2 shows a small excerpt from such a tutorial. The advanced tutor (T) has finished a twenty minute lecture on the white sauces. He concludes by saying; "and I think that's all there is to say." The student (S) has been following, making appropriate comments along the way. But now, unexpectedly, the student asks a question which indicates that she does not understand the overall pattern of sauces. The tutor is disturbed, and there follows a period in which the tutor tries to straighten out the concepts. This is a portion of that conversation. It starts with the student attempting to summarize her understanding of the sauces.[5]

The tutorial shown in the table illustrates a problem with reference. If the student finds a partially correct referent, errors may go undetected. In this case, it seems that the student originally had a concept for white sauce (the standard American white sauce): heat together butter and flour and then add milk. This fits easily with the new use of the term "white sauce." But French white sauces can also be made from fish or chicken stocks without milk or cream. This new procedure does not fit the student's existing memory structures, and a good deal of confusion ensued until the tutor was able to straighten it out. It was only when the discrepancy between her previous conception of white sauce and the French conception was explicitly mentioned that she began to make sense out of her lesson. The interesting thing about this tutorial session was that for the first 20 minutes, neither tutor nor student realized that there were any problems. It came as somewhat of a shock to both participants to realize that there were vast confusions, and the entire session lasted for 45 minutes beyond the point where

[5] We thank J. Lustig, S. Schane, and F. Wightman for serving as tutors and tutees.

TABLE 2
Beginning Student and Advanced Cook Tutorial[a]

S:	We start out with two different white sauces, veloute and Bechamel—and Bechamel is with—milk did you say?
T:	Right.
S:	Veloute is with egg yolk and cream so it's richer.
T:	Uh—no. Bechamel is with milk, veloute is with stock. That's the basic difference.
S:	Oh that's right. We made the veloute into Parisienne.
T:	Either the Bechamel . . .
S:	OK.
T:	or the veloute can be a Parisienne.
S:	What American cooks mean when they say a white sauce is—Bechamel. They mean a roux with—
T:	Milk.
S:	Milk.

(The problem here is that the student confused her knowledge of American white sauce with the related but different concept of the French family of white sauces. The tutor again reviewed the concepts involved in the sources. The student tried to review:)

S:	(long pause) OK. (long pause) If you

	take—a—sauce made with stock instead of milk and cream, and add egg yolks I—is that ever done?
T:	That's a Parisienne.
S:	The Parisienne doesn't have to start with the veloute.
T:	The veloute is—
S:	Has—cream or milk.
T:	No—no—the veloute is the roux and the stock.
S:	I keep—I keep mixing that up. The veloute is stock—and then cream—
T:	The Bechamel is the milk—base. (pause) And from both of those you can get to Parisienne by adding egg yolks and cream.
S:	OK.

(At this point the tutor reviewed the concepts. The student summarized the problem:)

S:	I'm confused because Bechamel is what I originally learned as a white sauce and a white sauce is a large class with all these different kinds of sauces.
T:	That's right.

[a]Roux: A mixture of flour and butter that serves as a thickening agent. Lightly cooked (for white sauces), browned to make brown roux.

Stock: Clear or brown liquid, usually made from chicken or fish (white stocks) or meat brown stocks).

Bechamel: A basic white sauce made with roux and milk.

Veloute: A basic white sauce made with roux and white stock.

Enrichment: The addition of butter, cream, or egg yolks.

the tutor had intended to end the session by saying, "and I think that's all there is to say."

This section shows one aspect of the communication between teacher and student: the difference between the student's prior conception of the topic and the actual one to be learned. This prior conception guides the student into some erroneous assumptions, hindering the final acquisition of the concepts.

Example: The jump problem. This last example is the most serious of the three we wish to describe. What we want to discuss is how a student acquires a schema for a concept, discovers places where it does not operate in an appropriate fashion, and then modifies the schema. We feel that the most important cognitive structures that we should study are those that allow the discovery of the inappropriate aspects and change them. We will say more about this later. Alas, we will not be able to say it well or precisely.

In our studies, we took students at the University of California, San Diego who had no previous experience with computers and put them in front of a visual (television) display and a typewriter keyboard. They were given a series of examples in programming in the language FLOW, starting off with some basic principles. At times, the students were asked to type a particular program into the computer and then to predict the result of that program. After the student had predicted the result of the sample program, he could have the computer perform the program and observe the result displayed on the screen in front of him. At times, we asked the students to write new programs that would accomplish some goal.

The computer language is very simple. For the aspects illustrated in this chapter, only two principles need to be understood:

All programs consist of an ordered set of commands (in the examples here, most programs are only 2 or 3 lines long).
Each line of the program is numbered for easy reference.

In this section we illustrate some of the problems in developing an accurate schema for one of the commands of the language FLOW. We follow the course of one student who is learning to use the command "Jump to . . . ." She has just previously learned to use the command "Print" in several different programs, but no program was longer than two lines and most contained only a single use of the "Print" command. In this section, we are primarily concerned with the examination of the interaction between the student's understanding of the concepts as represented by the schemata that she has developed and the program that she is creating. We trace the development of the schema for "Jump to" through successive stages of experience with different programs that result from the schema.

We start watching the student at the point where she has been asked to type the following program, Program 1, onto the display terminal.

Program 1:   010 Print "Rochelle"
               020 Jump to 010

Experimenter: This program will make the computer repeat the printing of the word "Rochelle." What do you think the output will look like?

Student: The computer will print the word "Rochelle" twice.

The answer is consistent with the ordinary sense of the word "repeat." It is also consistent with the student's prior experience, for in previous programs where there were no Jump statements and where at most there were two print statements, any program that repeated the same printout printed the same word twice. If we could characterize this student's schema for the purpose of the "Jump to" instruction, it probably would look something like this:

Schema 1:   If the instruction is "Jump to n," then the computer does instruction number n.

Now the student was instructed to run Program 1. When she did so, the output that appeared looked like this:

RochelleRochelleRochelleRochelleRochelleRochelleRochelleRochelleRo . . .

Student: I guess it keeps repeating until someone tells it to stop.

By her comment, the student has clearly learned something more about the "Jump" statement. To test what she had learned, we aksed her to enter a new program into the computer and to predict its outcome.

Program 2:   010 Print "Hi"
               020 Print "Rochelle"
               030 Jump to 010

Experimenter: What do you think this program will do?

Student: Its first instruction is to print "Hi" so it will do "Hi," then it will (pause) there's no space, so it will just go "HiRochelle" for the second instruction. And then it will go back to the first instruction which was Print "Hi," so it will just write "Hi" until we tell it to stop.

We see from this example that the student has modified Schema 1 into a new form, something like this:

Schema 2:   Do each instruction in order unless the instruction is a JUMP-TO. If the instruction is JUMP-TO n, then continue doing instruction n until told to stop.

Note that this schema, even though incorrect, is perfectly consistent with everything the student has seen up to this point. She has derived her notion of sequential order of execution from earlier programs and has used it here to predict the first two elements of the output. From Program 1 she has seen that the Jump-to in that program caused the instruction to be repeated. Hence, she developed Schema 2.

The test of the student's schema came when she was asked to run Program 2. Here is what happened:

HiRochelleHiRochelleHiRochelleHiRochelleHiRochelleHiRochelle . . .

Once again the result was not what was expected. Once again the schema for "Jump" had to be modified.

> Student: When you say jump to the first instruction, it will go to that and then I guess it goes to the second one and if there isn't a second one it will just keep repeating the first one. Otherwise it will repeat both.

This is a rather complicated and highly conditionalized notion, but it is perfectly consistent with all examples she has seen. When she was asked to describe how the computer actually performed Program 2, she provided a correct line by line description. Her schema now might be characterized like this:

> Schema 3:   Do each instruction in order unless the instruction is "Jump to."
> If the instruction is "Jump-to n," then begin doing instructions at number n.
> If there are no more instructions, stop.

Again, we tested her knowledge by asking her to type a specified program and to predict the result:

> Program 3:   010   Jump-to 030
> 020   Print "Hi"
> 030   Print "Rochelle"

> Student: The computer will go to the third instruction and print "Rochelle" then to the second and print "Hi" and then to the third again and print "Rochelle."

The actual result is this:

> Rochelle

Only the one word is printed, and then the program halts. Why did the student predict what she did, when according to Schema 3, she should have been able to predict the result properly? Evidently she has other schemata about the operation of the computer. Many students seem to believe that every statement must be executed at least once, and this schema could apply here. If so, this causes a conflict with Schema 3, which might possibly be resolved by a reversion to one of the earlier schemata for "Jump." Whatever the reason, it was a simple matter for the student to modify her schema for "Jump." When she saw that the output was the single word "Rochelle," she was readily able to determine why:

> Student: The first instruction tells it to go on to the third and then there is no instruction to tell it what to do so it stops.

Now, finally, she seems to have a complete and correct schema for the "Jump" instruction. When given two more tests, she predicted the results correctly:

> Program 4:   010   Print "Hi"
> 020   Print "Rochelle"
> 030   Jump-to 020

The predicted and correct result is:

> HiRochelleRochelleRochelleRochelleRochelleRochelleRochelleRochelle . . .

This shows that the student doesn't believe that each repetition needs to be the same.

> Program 5:   010   Print "Hi"
> 020   Jump-to 010
> 030   Print "Rochelle"

The predicted and correct result is

> HiHiHiHiHiHiHiHiHiHiHiHiHiHiHiHiHiHiHiHiHiHiHiHiHiHiHiHiHi . . .

This program shows that she understands that not every line need be followed.

These examples point out the ways in which a student formulates hypotheses about the concepts which are being taught, applies those hypotheses, and modifies them when necessary. Learning appears to be organized around small, simple schemata that can be applied to situations wherever deemed appropriate. Part of the task we must face is to determine how a person comes to acquire, apply, and modify these schemata.

Learning by Modification of Existing Schemata

To transform the examples of the use of schemata that we have presented here into a viable, useful theory of learning, we need to specify with more precision just what it is that takes place when a schema is selected, used, and then modified. We are not ready to report much information here, but we can tell you of some related work that seems relevant.

First, consider what kinds of structure a person needs in order to be able to modify his schemata. The student needs to be able to compare the results predicted by a given schema with the results that actually occur. Then he needs to determine the points of mismatch, and then correct that mismatch. Thus, he needs a process with some access to the procedures which it is examining and modifying. This is no simple feat.

The problem of learning through errors is, of course, a well known one. Seymour Papert and his educational group at the Artificial Intelligence Laboratories at MIT have made a big issue of this form of learning. Debugging, is what Papert calls it—the process of eliminating the errors or bugs in one's own knowledge. The skills of debugging are clearly important ones. Papert believes it is perhaps even more important to teach a child how to debug his own knowledge than to teach him the knowledge itself. The implication is that if a child knows how to learn, then he can get the knowledge by himself. We find that this philosophy strikes a sympathetic chord: Why do we not attempt to teach some basic cognitive skills such as how to organize one's knowledge, how to learn, how to solve problems, how to correct errors in understanding: these strike us as basic components which ought to be taught along with the content matter.

There has been some work in the Massachusetts Institute of Technology Artificial Intelligence Laboratories on the mechanisms necessary for transforming schemata that were in error into better ones. One of the best known examples of this work was performed by Winston (1973). Winston showed his system figures of block structures. The system would develop network representations for the structures (very similar in form to the structural networks of the LNR representation). Winston's system corrects schemata by comparing the representations for the various objects and noting the differences. The network gets modified according to the nature of these differences. In fact, Winston shows how the most important aspect of the training sequence is the *near miss:* the appropriate form of deviation from the schema.

Now without exception, everyone we have ever talked to who is either in the field of education or in learning gets very angry when we tell them of Winston's work. "That's nothing very remarkable," they sputter, "why if you go look at any elementary education text, or the work of . . . " etc. We agree, but disagree. Winston's work is not important for the concept of the near miss. What is important is that he has managed to develop a formal procedure for representing certain kinds of knowledge and then for changing that representation when it is found not to be appropriate. It is one of the most sophisticated examples of a learning program of which we are aware.

More recently at The Massachusetts Institute of Technology, Sussman (1972) and Goldstein (1973) have taken another step closer to the development of learning procedures. They have managed to develop systems that can correct programs, find the errors, and modify them appropriately.

We are still not at the point where psychological models can be developed around these formalizations of schemata, and the suggested mechanisms for modification, but we believe that we are close.

SOME GENERAL COMMENTS

Learning involves the acquisition of new cognitive structures built upon old, previously acquired structures. Such a statement, by itself, says little that has not been said many times before. What we believe might be new is some understanding of the underlying representation of these structures.

The overall structure for a concept matter is not yet known. In this chapter we have discussed some extremely simple knowledge frameworks: for verbs, for simple recipes, and at the level of verbal description, for a programming language. At this point we wish to speculate upon two or three issues relevant to the acquisition and use of these schemata. First, some comments upon theory. Second, some comments on what should (or could) be taught. Third, some brief comments on the problem of communicating the relevent structures to the student.

On theory   What has been shown here is very incomplete. It certainly is a far distance away from what we claimed to be interested in: the learning of comples topics. We need to specify how we interrelate all the information. We still need a lot of work on this problem. We think the important principle is that the material is organized around schemata. There does not seem to be a homogeneous network structure. Rather there seems to be well structured means for organizing the information, and for functional procedural definitions. Moreover, the schemata provide means for applying the structures to new and to unusual situations.

On what might one teach   Two general principles seem applicable:

Introduce the general framework for the material that is to be learned.
Build upon the general knowledge that previously existed.

One different form of knowledge that we believe to be important is to teach learning skills:

The student should know how to evaluate and modify his schemata.

In the examples shown above, it has been important that existing schemata could be modified. This is true whenever a schema is inappropriate either because one simply doesn't know enough or because one is reasoning by analogy.

In general, one has to know how to understand the nature of this reasoning process to be effective at doing it. We have been impressed with Papert's teaching of "debugging skills"—we believe he is correct when he places heavy emphasis on this.

Functional reasoning   Collins, Warnock, Aiello, and Miller (1975) have demonstrated some nice examples of what they called "functional reasoning," reason in which knowledge is deduced from general principles. The most interesting cases occur when the person doing the reasoning is not aware that he knows any relevant general principles. What in fact happens, we believe, is two things. First there is something akin to our mayonnaise example: reasoning by analogy. Second, comes the examination of several examples and a generalization. A general principle can be considered to be one in which the schema has many of its constant terms replaced with variables (the variables will have constraints placed upon the set of concepts which may be used to fill them).

The process by which one takes specific knowledge about a particular instance of a concept or of an experience and generalizes it to apply to a larger class of experiences is one that needs a good deal of study. One suspects that this generalization process is at the heart of much of our everyday operations in which new situations must be dealt with by the experience gained from old ones. Learning by analogy, learning by modification of existing schemata, the use and interpretation of metaphor, and functional reasoning would all appear to be related examples of this generalization of knowledge. As we gain in our understanding of the structures of human memory and in the ways by which the knowledge structures are acquired, modified, and used, we will come to enrich our understanding of learning, of teaching, and of the human use of knowledge.

ACKNOWLEDGMENTS

This research was supported by the Advanced Research Projects Agency and the Office of Naval Research of the Department of Defense and was monitored by ONR under Contract No. N00014-69-0200-6045.

10
Abstract Conceptual Knowledge: How We Know What We Know

Robert E. Shaw

Center for Research in Human Learning
University of Minnesota

Buford E. Wilson

Behavioral Studies Program
Governors State University

INTRODUCTION

The task of developing a psychology of instruction is formidable because we must first understand the nature of knowledge, how it is acquired, under what conditions it might be taught, and the signs by which its attainment might be celebrated. Of course, our task would be foredoomed if every area of knowledge were so distinctive in its requirements on the human mind that completely different cognitive processes were invoked in each case. If so, then the most help educators might realistically expect from psychologists would be a pluralism of principles consisting of independent sets of heuristic tricks, especially tailored for each area of pedagogical focus.

Clearly, the working hypothesis which best serves both psychology and education assumes that knowledge-gathering processes of mind are essentially the same across all disciplines, that any differences will be in detail rather than principle. Let us then begin by posing the central problem for a cognitive theory of instruction in a way that presupposes this working hypothesis: *what is the nature of the general cognitive capacity that underlies all knowledge acquisition?* It is to this question that this chapter is addressed.

THE ABSTRACT NATURE OF CONCEPTS

A basic characteristic of human intelligence is the ability to formulate abstract conceptual knowledge about objects and events. Abstract conceptual knowledge is exemplified when we can deal appropriately with novel instances of a concept, that is, when our knowledge goes beyond just those instances experienced.

There is abundant evidence that our knowledge of language must be abstract given the novelty that must be dealt with. Indeed, the role of novel events in language has long been recognized by linguists. Sentences are almost always novel events. To verify this fact you need only pick at random a sentence in a book and then continue through the book until the sentence is repeated. Unless you have picked a cliché or a thematic sentence, it is unlikely that the sentence will reoccur. We readily admit that most sentences are novel, but what about the elements from which sentences are constructed? These elements must be the same in order for us to understand sentences. Further examination, however, shows that words too are typically novel events. The apparent physical sameness of words is an illusion supported by the use of printing presses. If we consider handwriting, we find a great deal of variation in the construction of letters and words. The novelty of words becomes even more clear when we think of the same word spoken by different speakers, male and female, child and adult, or by the same speaker when he is shouting or whispering. Words, like sentences, are typically novel events. To say that words are novel events may be incorrect in some instances. We have heard our friends use the same words many times, our own names being a case in point. The importance of the argument for novelty is to illustrate that this repetition is not necessary for our understanding of words; thus our ability to recognize words is not a function of having experienced that particular *physical event* before.

Greenburg and Jenkins (1964) demonstrate an even more striking example of the capacity to deal with novel instances of a class. They found that English speakers could deal appropriately with novel sequences of English phonemes. Sequences of Phonemes in English are subject to powerful constraints described by rule structures for syllable and word formation. If we randomly sample strings of English phonemes we will produce three types of strings: strings which are actual English syllables or words; strings which violate the rules for English syllables and word construction and therefore are not English syllables or words; and finally, strings which are in accord with English rule structure, but are not found in English. Given only consonant–vowel–consonant (CVC) strings we all recognize *cat* as an actual English word and *cah* as clearly not an English word. However, what about the strings *dib* and *lutt?* Both of these CVCs are in accord with English rules of syllable construction. *Dib* is in fact an actual English word. Consequently, Greenberg and Jenkins constructed a measure of distance from English, based upon the rules of English syllable construction, which accurately predicted subjects' judgments of novel strings of phonemes. The subjects' judgments about novel strings of phonemes were consistent and predictable on the basis of linguistic rules for syllable construction in English.

This research clearly demonstrates that the knowledge, on the basis of which English speakers recognize and construct English syllables and words, is abstract in the sense that it is not knowledge of particular physical events, but rather knowledge about systems of abstract relationships. One's ability to recognize sequences of phonemes not experienced before as acceptable or unacceptable English strings demonstrates knowledge of rules of sequencing of phonemes, that is, abstract conceptual knowledge which allows us to recognize and produce novel events.

But phonemes too are abstract classes of events which cannot be specified in terms of common physical elements. Research in the perception of speech has shown that the same phonemes are specified by different physical events in different contexts and that the same physical event can specify different phonemes in different contexts (Fant, 1964; Liberman, Cooper, Shankweiler, & Studdert-Kennedy, 1967). So, with phonemes too, the basis of recognition is knowledge of a code or system of relationships, not knowledge of particular physical elements. As we have seen, breaking language events into smaller and smaller elements does not result in a level of analysis based upon particular physical elements. Rather, at each level we find still another system of abstract relations which is necessary to specify the nature or meaning of particular physical events.

Similarly, we are able to recognize a melody played on a piano even though previously we have only experienced instances of that melody played on other instruments, or by an orchestra, or even hummed. To do so, therefore, we must have an abstract concept of the melody that specifies the isomorphism existing among the various instances. Often we are able to recognize that a painting is executed in the style of impressionism or by a particular artist, say Cezanne, even though we have never seen that particular work before. To do so we must have an abstract concept that specifies the style of the school or artist such that the instances, novel ones included, are seen as similar. Thus, there seems to be ample reason to conclude that concepts are not necessarily based upon knowledge of particular physical events, nor upon physical units, elements, or features, since instances of many concepts are only abstractly related.

GENERATIVE CONCEPTS

Due to their generality, abstract concepts apply to a potentially infinite equivalence class of instances. However, this fact poses a serious problem for a cognitive theory bent upon explaining how they are acquired. Since one's experience is with but a sample of the entire set of instances to which such concepts refer, several puzzling questions arise: First, how can experience with a subset of objects or events lead to knowledge of the whole set to which it belongs? There is a problem of explaining how *some* part of a structure can be equal to the whole structure. Indeed, the claim that *some* can, under certain circumstances, be equivalent to *all* seems to involve a logical contradiction. That it does not, fortunately for cognitive theory, can be amply illustrated in many different areas of conceptual knowledge. In a moment, we will illustrate this fact from examples drawn from three distinct fields—mathematics, linguistics, and perceptual psychology.

A second crucial question that must be answered, given a precise answer to the first, concerns the nature of the subset that can provide the knowledge necessary to deal with the entire set. Will just any subset of instances do, or must the subset be a certain size or quality? In other words, how do instances of a concept qualify as exemplary cases of the concept? A precise answer to this last question has quite obvious implications for the selection of effective instructional material for teaching concepts.

Generative concepts in mathematics. In mathematics the concept of an infinite set provides a structure for which it is true that a proper subset is equal to the total set. Cantor proposed this definition of the infinite when he discovered that a subset of all natural numbers, such as the even integers, can be placed into a one-to-one relationship with the total set of integers. But a more relevant case for our purposes is the problem of providing a precise description for an infinite class of objects. By a precise description is meant a finite specification of every instance of the infinite class.

A moment's reflection suffices to conclude that so-called *nominal* concepts are quite inadequate for this purpose since it is impossible to ostensively define an infinite class, say by pointing to each element. Hence the label "infinity" could not be consistently applied since finite enumeration will not discrimate between classes just a little larger than the ostensive count and ones infinitely larger.

For similar reasons so-called *attributive* concepts of infinite classes are not possible since the attempt to abstract common features from all members of such classes fails. If not every member of an infinite class is surveyed by a process of finite abstraction, then a potentially infinite number of cases may exist which fail to exibit the attribute common to the finite subset actually experienced. Thus, the learning of concepts that refer to classes with a potentially infinite number of members such as trees, people, red stars, cannot be adequately explained by a cognitive process involving finite abstraction. The process of abstraction postulated to explain the acquisition of abstract concepts must work in some other way. As a mill for abstract knowledge, it must take a finite set of exemplars as grist for producing concepts of infinite extension.

This problem has perplexed philosophers for many centuries, leading some empiricists and nominalists to propose that in fact no concept of an infinite class is really possible. Their argument was based upon the belief that since finite abstraction is the means by which all concepts are formed, then the concept of the infinite must be a negative concept referring only to our ignorance regarding the exact size of a very large class which had been indeterminately surveyed by the senses. This belief constitutes a refusal to recognize the creative capacity of human intellignece and led the empiricists to a theory of knowledge founded upon associative principles—principles which define knowledge as nothing more than the association of memoranda of past sense impressions—what Dewey (1939) rightfully called "dead" ideas because they cannot grow.

Infinite structures can only be represented by finite means if the finite means are creative, in the sense that a schema exists by which the totality of the structure can be specified by some appropriate finite part of the structure. Such a schema by which the whole can be generalized from an appropriate part can be called a *generative* principle, while the appropriate part can be called a generating substructure or just *generator* for short. That a structural totality can be specified by a generator *plus* a set of generative principles can usually be verified by the principle of mathematical induction.

Consider the problem of how one comes to know the concept of natural numbers. Two stages seem to be involved: one must first learn the set of numerals 0, 1, 2, . . . , 9 as well as a system of syntactic rules by which they may be concatenated to form successively ordered pairs (e.g., 10, 11, . . . , 99), triples (e.g., 100, 101, . . . 999), etc. The number of numerical strings is, of course, potentially infinite. Hence the numeral set 0, 1, 2, . . . , 9 constitutes the generator which potentially yields all possible well-ordered numerical strings when the appropriate generative rules of the grammar are applied.

The second stage in acquiring the concept of natural numbers entails *inter alia,* not only knowledge of the grammar for numerical labels, but knowledge of the *closure* of arithmetic operations by which (*a*) any number can be shown to be a logical product of an arithmetic operation applied to a pair of numbers e.g., $1 + 0 = 1$, $1 + 1 = 2$, $1 + 2 = 3$, . . . ,and (*b*) any logical product of numbers always yields numbers.

Indeed, it does not take children long to realize that any combination or permutation of the members of the generator set (0, 1, 2, . . . , 9) yields a valid number. For example, is 9701 an instance of the concept of natural number? Of course, you will recognize it as a valid instance. But how do you know? Have you ever seen this number before? Does it matter? Unless it is part of an old phone number, address, or some serial number that you have frequently dealt with, then you probably have no idea whether it is a familiar or novel instance of the concept of natural number. Nevertheless, one knows immediately that it is an instance, presumably because one's knowledge of strings of numerals is as abstract as that for English sentences.

Generative linguistic knowledge. A similar line of argument can be developed with respect to the best way to characterize a speaker's knowledge of his native language. The problem is: "how do we acquire the linguistic competence to comprehend sentences that have never before been experienced?" For instance, it is unlikely that you have ever experienced the following sentence: *the impish monkey climbed upon the crystal chandelier, gingerly peeled the crepes from the ceiling, and threw them at the furious chef.* This fact, however, in no way diminishes your ability to recognize it as a grammatical, if novel, sentence.

Whatever the precise details, it seems clear that the child acquires generative knowledge of his language from limited experience with a part of the whole corpus that is potentially available. Furthermore, on the basis of this limited experience, he is able to extrapolate knowledge about sentences never before experienced by him, as well as knowledge about those never before experienced by anyone.

Presumably, the child's immediate linguistic environment consisting of his or her family and local aspects of his culture, provides him with a generator set of exemplary structures from which he educes the generative principles by which all other sentences are known. Chomsky (1965) has argued that a transformational grammar provides the operations defining the mapping of the generator set of clear case utterances onto the corpus of all utterances; other theorists disagree. However, no one disputes the fact that the acquisition of language requires cognitive schemata that are truly generative in nature.

It is also worth noting that during acquisition specific memory for sentences experienced seems to play no necessary role in the process. Several lines of research support this contention. Sachs (1967) demonstrated that subjects were unable to recognize syntactic changes in sentences that did not change their meaning as readily as they were able to detect changes in meaning. This suggests that people often do not remember the explicit form of sentences experienced. Other researchers (e.g., Blumenthal, 1967; Mehler, 1963; Miller, 1962; Rohrman, 1968) argue that rather than the surface structure of sentences being remembered, it is the deep structural relations specified by current transformational grammars that characterize the abstract conceptual knowledge retained in memory.

One important insight that emerges from a study of such cases is that for generative concepts there are no truly novel instances. There are only those instances that are actual, because they belong to a generator set, and those that are potential, because they lie dormant among the remaining totality of instances. Consequently, the only difference between actual *versus* potential instances is whether the instance has been made manifest by application of the generative principle. Once done so, a newborn instance bears no marks of its recent birth to denote that it is new rather than old.

If the above reasoning is valid, we are able to formulate our first empirical hypothesis: *if people obtain abstract concepts then they will not necessarily be able to recognize novel instances of the concept as being novel; that is, instances in the generator set of a concept (i.e., clear-case exemplars) will not always be distinguishable from those instances never before experienced.*

In the next section we review some of the research recently completed at the University of Minnesota which lends plausibility to the hypothesis that generative systems theory provides a precise description of the function of the cognitive capacity by which we obtain abstract concepts.

EXPERIMENTS ON GENERATIVE CONCEPTUAL SYSTEMS

The problem of how people learn abstract conceptual systems is by no means new to psychology. Sir Fredric Bartlett (1932), in his classic book *Remembering,* realized that what people learn must be some kind of an abstract system or schema rather than a discursive list of simple instances. Clearly concepts can be learned from a small set of very special instances, what might be called *prototypes* or exemplars of the concept. Considerable research has shown this to be the case. However, in doing so some curious results were uncovered. Furthermore, the attempt to characterize precisely the nature of prototypic instances sufficient for the learning of a given concept proved more elusive than expected.

Attneave (1957a) demonstrated that experience with a prototype facilitated paired-associate learning involving other instances of the concept. In related research Posner and Keele (1968) found that subjects were able to classify correctly novel dot patterns as a result of experience with classes to patterns which were abstractly related to the novel instances, i.e., related by statistical rules rather than by feature similarity. Later, Posner and Keele (1970) isolated the following properties of the conceptual systems which enabled subjects to classify novel instances of the classes of dot patterns: (1) this conceptual system was abstracted during initial experience with the classes of patterns, and (2) although derived from experience with patterns, it was not based upon stored copies of the patterns. One week after the original experience with the patterns, the subjects' ability to classify the patterns actually seen earlier had decreased, while their ability to classify "new" prototypic patterns surprisingly had not. This result supports Bartlett's view by strongly suggesting that these "new" instances were classified in terms of a highly integrated system of abstract relations (a conceptual system) rather than being mediated at the time of classification by memory of individual patterns.

The question then is: "how can a subset of instances of a class be used to generate the entire class?" One avenue that we are investigating is to see what insight the concept of group generator may give into the generative nature of conceptual systems.

The notion of a group generator can be understood intuitively by carefully studying the illustrations of the generator and nongenerator sets of stimuli used in the experiment reported below, page 207. One should notice that the *generator* set consists of cards whose relations define the displacements figures undergo when orbiting around the center of the card, that is, when the ordered sequence of cards specifies orbiting. On the other hand, the *nongenerator* set of stimuli consists of cards that are physically similar to those in the generator set, differing, however, in that no sequence of these cards is sufficient to specify the orbiting concept. At most they specify a displacement of four figures over the diagonal path running from the upper left to the lower right hand corners of the card.

In the next section a more formalized account of the group generator notion is presented.

The Concept of Group Generator

Many examples of the generative property of mathematical groups exist. For instance, for each integer n, it is possible to construct a group having exactly n elements (a group of order n) by considering $1, a, a^2, a^3, \ldots, a^{n-1}, a^n$, where $a^0 = a^n = 1$ and the operation is ordinary algebraic multiplication. Such a group is called *cyclic* because the initial element (a^0) is identical to the terminal element (a^n); the symbol a is called a *generator* of the group, since every group element is a power of a, that is, $a \times a = a^2, a \times a^2 = a^3, \ldots, a \times a^{n-1} = a^n = a^0$.

The (integer) representation of the concept of a group with a generator is but one application of this abstract system. As another example, consider the rotational (cyclical) symmetry of a square. Let each vertex of the square be labeled (1, 2, 3, 4,) and represented as the bottom row of a matrix. Then let each position initially occupied by these vertices be similarly labeled and represented in the top row of the same matrix:

$$\text{positions } (P) \quad (1 \quad 2 \quad 3 \quad 4)$$
$$\text{vertices } (V) \quad (1 \quad 2 \quad 3 \quad 4)$$

We now define a 90° clockwise rotation of the square as follows:

$$\begin{pmatrix} 1\ 2\ 3\ 4 \\ 1\ 2\ 3\ 4 \end{pmatrix} \overset{90°}{\Rightarrow} \begin{pmatrix} 1\ 2\ 3\ 4 \\ 4\ 1\ 2\ 3 \end{pmatrix}$$

The 360° rotation of the square can be similarly represented as four 90° rotations:

$$
\overset{\text{I}}{\begin{pmatrix} 1\ 2\ 3\ 4 \\ 1\ 2\ 3\ 4 \end{pmatrix}} \overset{90°}{\rightarrow}
\overset{\text{II}}{\begin{pmatrix} 1\ 2\ 3\ 4 \\ 4\ 1\ 2\ 3 \end{pmatrix}} \overset{180°}{\rightarrow}
\overset{\text{III}}{\begin{pmatrix} 1\ 2\ 3\ 4 \\ 3\ 4\ 1\ 2 \end{pmatrix}} \overset{270°}{\rightarrow}
\overset{\text{IV}}{\begin{pmatrix} 1\ 2\ 3\ 4 \\ 2\ 3\ 4\ 1 \end{pmatrix}} \overset{360°}{\rightarrow}
\overset{\text{I}}{\begin{pmatrix} 1\ 2\ 3\ 4 \\ 1\ 2\ 3\ 4 \end{pmatrix}}
$$

The configurations I–IV are the group elements representing all the possible configurations of a square that can be generated by a product of $90°$ rotations. This can be summarized in tabular form as follows:

X	I	II	III	IV
I	I	II	III	IV
II	II	III	IV	I
III	III	IV	I	II
IV	IV	I	II	III

From inspection of the table it is clear that I is the identity element and that every element has an inverse, e.g., II $\times$ IV = I, III $\times$ III =I, etc. To illustrate the group operation, ($\times$), by which these products of rotations in the table above were computed, consider the way in which one proves that the element IV is the inverse of element II since their product II $\times$ IV yields the identity element I (a $0°$ or $360°$ rotation).

$$\text{II} \qquad\qquad \text{IV} \qquad\qquad \text{I}$$

$$\begin{pmatrix} 1 & 2 & 3 & 4 \\ 4 & 1 & 2 & 3 \end{pmatrix} \times \begin{pmatrix} 1 & 2 & 3 & 4 \\ 2 & 3 & 4 & 1 \end{pmatrix} = \begin{pmatrix} 1 & 2 & 3 & 4 \\ 1 & 2 & 3 & 4 \end{pmatrix}$$

In general, to multiply one array by another do the following: Replace the value of the vertex in a given position in the first array with the value of the vertex found under the position with the corresponding value in the second array. For instance, in the above example, II $\times$ IV = I, the products are computed as follows: V_4 in P_1 of II is replaced by V_1 in P_4 of IV; V_1 in P_2 of II is replaced by V_2 in P_1 of IV, etc., where V_i and P_i denote the appropriate vertex and position.

More importantly (for our purposes), the group of rotations for the square has two generators, namely II and IV. Either of these, if multiplied iteratively by itself, yields all elements of the group. Thus, II^2 = III, II^3 = IV, II^4 = I, II^5 = II and similarly, IV^n yields III, II, I, IV, respectively. This generative property is not trivial since neither I nor III are generators of the group; I^n = I since it is the identity and III^n alternates between I and III, never producing II or IV because III is its own inverse. Many other groups have nontrivial generators. A most important group is that of perspectives of solid objects. The fact that, for many objects, a few perspectives provide sufficient information to specify their total shape suggests a way in which perceptual systems, like conceptual ones, may be generative. (Shaw, McIntyre, & Mace, 1974)

The basic strategy for testing the applicability of the group-generator description in explaining generative conceptual systems is to construct acquisition sets which either are or are not generators specifying the total class of instances referred to by the concept. This suggests the following hypothesis:

> If the information specified in the group generator acquisition set is sufficient to allow subjects to generate the entire class, subjects should then treat novel instances of the class in a fashion similar to the way they treat experienced instances of the class. In contrast, the subjects who are given a non-generator acquisition set should treat experienced and new instances of the class differently.

A Generative Concept Experiment

To investigate the above hypothesis Wilson, Wellman, and Shaw constructed a system consisting of four, simple geometric figures (a *cross*, a *heart*, a *circle*, and a *square*) orbiting alone through the four corner positions of a square card. This allows for the construction of sixteen distinct stimuli (i.e., four figures X four positions = 16 cards). These sixteen cards provide the underlying set over which the concept of *orbiting* can be defined by an appropriate ordering of the cards. Moreover, the system of relationships among the cards determined by the discrete orbiting of the figures, logically specify a group of transformations (displacements) that is isomorphic with the geometric group of 90° rotations of the square discussed earlier. By definition two specific groups (e.g., the *orbiting* and *rotation* groups denoted above) are abstractly equivalent if some third group can be found to represent each. The numeric arrays, I–V with the operation X, constitute such a group.

The sixteen cards which provide the underlying set for the "orbiting" group can be represented by the numeric arrays I–IV as follows: let the top row of the array specify the corner positions on a stimulus card while the bottom row specifies the figures that occur in those positions. In this fashion, the columns of the arrays I–IV, reading from left to right, denote all sixteen cards in the set underlying the concept of orbiting. In the rotation case, each relationship between adjacent arrays specifies the new positions assumed by the vertices of the square as it rotates discretely through 90°; by contrast, in the orbiting case, the relationship between adjacent arrays now provides a summary of the new positions assumed by each of the orbiting figures from card to card. In other words, the orbiting of a figure can be thought of as a rotation around an axis point outside the figure. Hence they have the same group multiplication table and are abstractly equivalent.

The sequence of cards specifying a generator for the 16-card set used in the acquisition phase of the experiment for one group of subjects is shown in Fig. 1.

Notice that the first four cards constitute the columns of array I while the second four cards constitute the columns of array II. To see that these eight

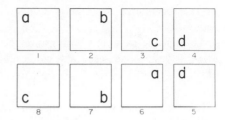

FIG. 1 Group generator acquisition set.

cards qualify as a generator for the total set of cards one need only multiply them together in the iterative fashion as discussed earlier. By consulting the group multiplication table one immediately verifies that multiplying array II (or IV) by itself a sufficient number of times yields all the arrays, I–IV, and therefore, is a generator for the total set of cards. Also by consulting the table, one can verify that iterative multiplication of array III by itself yields only I and III and, therefore, does not qualify as a generator for the group of sixteen cards.

There is a sense, however, in which III is a generator that specifies an abstract concept; namely, since the geometric figures occur in all four positions across cards, if they are treated equivalently, then they do specify the entire set. In order to minimize the *degree of abstraction* (i.e., generality) of the nongenerator acquisition set, eight cards were selected in which the figures occurred in only two positions, rather than four positions specified by III. This selection guaranteed that the nongenerator acquisition set could not specify the entire concept (set) at any level of abstraction. (Although it does contain the generator for a system of diagonal relationships.) The cards in this new nongenerator acquisition set used in the experiment are shown in Fig. 2.

During recognition both groups were shown the eight cards they had experienced during acquisition *plus* the remaining eight novel instances of the system. Additionally, both groups were shown nine cards which did not fit the system, that is, noncases. The noncases were constructed by using inappropriately colored geometric forms, forms occurring in the center of the card, and forms which were oriented differently on the card than those in the system, for example, a 45° rotation from the perpendicular. The recognition set, therefore, consisted of 25 cards, 8 "old" cards, 8 "new" but appropriate cards and 9 "noncases." Subjects were shown each of the 25 cards one at a time and asked

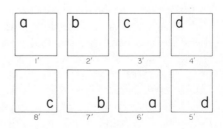

FIG. 2 Nongenerator acquisition set.

to rate each card as "old" or "new," that is, as one they had seen during acquisition.

As might be expected both groups consistently rated the old items as old and identified the noncases as new cards. The generator acquisition set subjects rated old cards as old on 80% of the cases and the noncases as new on 99% of the cases.

The two groups were strikingly different, however, in their judgments of the new but "appropriate within-the-system" cards. The "nongroup generator" subjects correctly identified these new instances as new on more than 90% of the cases. In marked contrast, the "group generator" subjects rated the new cards as being old 50% of the time. That is, their judgments of the new but appropriate instances were at a chance level. On 50% of their judgments, subjects identified the novel instances of the system as cards which they had experienced during acquisition. This group could clearly discriminate system from nonsystem cards, as shown by their rejection of the noncases; but they could not consistently discriminate experienced instances of the system from novel ones.

Two conclusions can be drawn from these results:

1. During acquisition subjects are acquiring information about the abstract relations existing between the items in the acquisition set. That is, they are gaining more information than can be characterized by copies of the individual cards they experienced.

2. The information specified by the group generator is sufficient to allow subjects to generate the entire system. This supports the claim that these subjects' knowledge of the system of orbiting cards is indeed generative.

The fact that subjects in the generator group could not consistently discriminate between previously experienced and novel instances of the system, strongly suggests that subjects are acquiring an abstract relational concept which defines a class of events, not simply information about the specific instances they had experienced. Furthermore, this result also suggests that these subjects acquired a knowledge of an event (the orbiting of cards) that is truly generative. (More about this type of event conception will be said in the next section.)

Assuming that subjects are acquiring abstract relational systems from experience with the generator acquisition set rather than specific memory of experienced instances, the question arises as to the effect of more experience with the acquisition set. Conceptions of memory based upon the abstraction of static features, or copies of the experience events, would predict that more experience with the acquisition set would facilitate subjects' recognition of new instances of the system as actually new, that is, as not before experienced. If, instead of storing copies of the experienced instances or abstracting the common attributes of the instances, subjects are acquiring information about the abstract relations among these instances in the system, more experience with the acquisition set would not necessarily result in an increased ability to recognize new instances of the system as being novel. As subjects better acquire the abstract relational system they would be more able to discriminate instances of the system as being novel. As subjects better acquire the abstract relational system they would be more able to discriminate instances of the concept from noncases. However, the novel instances of the system may be more difficult to discriminate as new precisely because they are instances of an abstract relational system

To investigate this possibility, four additional groups were run, two with each of the two types of acquisition sets. One group experienced the generator acquisition set twice, and a second group three times. Similarly, a third experienced the nongenerator acquisition set twice and the fourth group experienced it three times. Following the acquisition phase, all groups were tested for recognition.

In the nongenerator groups, the greater amount of experience with the acquisition set resulted in an increased ability to recognize the new instances of the system as new. The subjects who experienced the acquisition set three times were able to recognize the new instances as new on 100% of the cases. The nongenerator subjects were able to consistently identify new instances of the concept as new after one presentation of the acquisition set, and the subjects given more experience with the nongenerator acquisition were even more accurate in this discrimination. However, the results obtained with subjects who experienced the group-generator acquisition set were quite different. Not only were these subjects unable to identify novel instances of the system as new, but additional experience with the acquisition set decreased the subjects' ability to recognize new instances as being new. As stated earlier, the subjects who experienced the acquisition once accepted the new instances as old 50% of the time. Subjects who experienced the acquisition set twice before recognition identified the new instances as old on 75% of their judgments, and the subjects who experienced the generator acquisition set three times identified the new but appropriate instances of the system as old on over 80% of their judgments. All of these subjects continued to correctly recognize the old instances as old and reject the noncases as not before experienced.

These results provide strong evidence that subjects are acquiring information about an abstract system of relations and not simply information about the static properties or attributes of the experienced instances. If subjects' judgments were based solely upon the attributes or static features of the experienced instances, the subjects would be able to recognize new but appropriate instances as being new and increase experience should enhance this recognition. As we have seen the results were not obtained. On the other hand, if subjects are acquiring a generative conceptual system, then, instances which are appropriate to the system would be recognized as familiar. As the abstract conceptual system is better learned the subjects' would be more likely to recognize novel instances of the system as belonging to the system and, therefore, identify them as old.

It should be noted that these data provide strong support for our hypothesis, namely, that knowledge of a subset of the instances of a concept was in fact tantamount to knowledge of all instances of the concept. When the system was well learned, subjects could not distinguish old from novel instances. Clearly, experience with the group-generator acquisition set was in this case tantamount to experience with the entire system.

Finally, it should be noted that in these experiments subjects were *not* instructed to find relations between the individual instances, nor were they told that they would be tested for recognition. Rather, subjects were instructed that we were studying short-term memory of geometric forms. Their task was to reproduce, by drawing each card in the appropriate acquisition set after performing an interfering task. In this case, the abstraction of the systematic relations between instances of the system appears to be automatic in the sense that it was not intentional.

EVENT CONCEPTS AS GENERATIVE KNOWLEDGE

In this section we present evidence in support of the contention that event concepts are abstract in nature and therefore generative.

Shaw, McIntyre, and Mace (1974) argue that perceiving the nature of events involved the detection of sufficient information to specify their *affordance* structure. The term "affordance" is borrowed from James Gibson (1966) and refers to the invariant perceptual information made available by objects and events that specifies how animals and humans might adapt to their environments.

The affordance structure of events consists of two necessary components: the transformation over which the event is defined (the transformational invariant) and the structures which undergo the change wrought by the application of the transformation (the structural invariant). The transformational invariant must be perceptually specified in the acquisition set if the dynamic aspects of the event are to be identified (e.g., that the event is of x running, rolling, growing, smiling, etc.), while the structural invariant must be perceptually specified if the subject of the event is to be identified (e.g., what x is: *John* runs, the *ball* rolls, the *flower* grows, *Mary* smiles, etc.).[1] A set of instances of an event is not an

[1] Perhaps a better way to clarify the difference between structural and transformational invariants is as follows: given that John runs, John walks, John smiles, John loves, the subject of all these events is John; the subject's structure is what is common or invariant and, hence, is the *structural* invariant of all the events denoted. On the other hand, given the following events: John runs, Bill runs, Mary runs, Jill runs, then there is no common subject. All we know is that some object with a minimal structure to support the operation *to run* is involved. The operation on the minimal structure x is the transformational invariant. But note that even here to define that transformation presupposes some minimal structural invariant as its necessary support. A similar argument for the necessity of postulating minimal transformational invariants in order to define structures can also be given. For these reasons the affordance structure of events, inclusive of actions and objects, necessarily requires both structural and transformational invariants for its definition. Since in ecological science there are only affordance structures, that is, animal–environment, or subject–object relations, the affordance concept is a universal semantic primitive that deserves careful study by cognitive psychologists.

exemplary set and, therefore, does not constitute a generator set for the event, if it fails to provide perceptual information sufficient to specify both the transformational and structural invariants. To summarize this hypothesis:

> *All necessary conditions being satisfied, a person will acquire the concept of an event when presented with an acquisition set of exemplary instances (a generator set) because such a set provides the minimal perceptual information sufficient to specify the affordance structure of the event.*

In the experiment discussed in the previous section we showed how a certain subset of object configurations qualified both formally and psychologically as the generator set for an event concept, that of an "orbiting" event defined over geometric forms. Thus, the group generator description does seem to offer a viable means of making explicit the manner in which abstract conceptual systems may be creative.

The abstract concept derived from perceiving the orbiting of the stimulus figures can be analyzed as follows: The generator set in the acquisition phase of the experiment consisted of stimulus configurations sufficient to specify a subgroup of the displacement group, namely, the orbiting group. This set of stimuli constituted the structural invariant of the event while the group operation (orbiting) constituted the transformational invariant of the event. The subjects succeeded in obtaining the concept of this event by detecting these two invariants which taken together constitute the affordance structure of the event.

The orbiting group itself provides a description of the relevant aspects of the abstract concept of the event. Thus construed, the perceived meaning of the event *is* the orbiting group interpreted over the stimulus structures presented. Consequently, we see no way or reason to avoid the conclusion that in all event perception situations the existence of an abstract concept is entailed. Under this view, the generator for the abstract event concept is that set of instances which conveys sufficient perceptual information to specify both the transformational and structural invariants defining the event. The meaning of this invariant information for the human or animal perceiver is the affordance structure of the event.

In our opinion, this analysis argues in favor of the hypothesis that perception is a direct apprehension of the meaning of events insofar as their affordance structure is concerned. Since abstract concepts are generatively specified by (i.e., abstractly equivalent to) their exemplary instances (generator set), their acquisition can also be considered direct, requiring no augmentation by voluntary inferential processes. Similarly, no constructive cognitive process need be postulated to explain how abstract concepts are built up out of elementary constituents as argued by the British Empiricists since such elementary constituents play no necessary role in the definition of the concept.

Have we made too much of the apparent success of the generative systems approach in a single line of experiments? It is important to ask whether the same analysis can be applied to a variety of experimental phenomena. We explore this possibility in the next section.

Perceiving the Affordance Structure of Elaborate Events

So far we have presented an example involving an event whose affordance structure can be formally described by very simple group structures, i.e., orbiting. We would now like to discuss two complex events whose affordance structures, although more elaborate, still seem amenable to generative systems theory.

The shape of nonrigid objects. Theories of object perception usually attempt to explain the perception of objects and patterns which do not change their shape over time. However, a truly adequate theory must also explain the origin of concepts of events where object configurations or the shape of objects undergo dynamic change. Shaw and Pittenger (*in press*) have conducted a series of experiments designed to explore this problem The assumption behind the research is this:

Shape is considered to be an event-dependent concept rather than an absolute property of static objects. This is contrary to the traditional view that identifies shape with the metric-Euclidean property of *geometric rigidity under transformation,* that is, the fact that under certain transformations (e.g., displacements) the distances between points on an object do not change. Unfortunately, this definition is too narrow since it fails to apply to a manifold of natural objects which remain identifiable in spite of being remodeled to some extent by various "nonrigid" transformations (e.g., growth, erosion, plastic deformation under pressure).

Biomorphic forms, such as faces, plants, bodies of animals, cells, leaves, noses, inevitably undergo structural remodeling as they grow, although their transforms retain sufficient structural similarity to be identified. Such forms, like geological structures under plastic deformation or archaeological artifacts under erosion, are relatively nonrigid under their respective remodeling transformations. Since the property of geometric rigidity is not preserved by any of these, it cannot provide the invariant information for their identification. Clearly, then, a new and more abstract definition of shape must be found upon which to develop a theory of object perception that is broad enough in scope to encompass all objects—rigid as well as nonrigid ones. Consequently, the following definition was decided upon: *Shape, as an event-perception concept, is to be formally construed to mean the sum total of invariant structural properties by which an object might be identified under a specified set of transformations.*

This definition should sound familiar since it is but a restricted version of the definition of the affordance structure of objects given earlier. But notice, that by this definition the geometric rigidity of an object under displacement is but one of the many kinds of structural invariants possible. By a careful study of the perceptual information used to identify human faces at different stages of growth (i.e., age levels), it was hoped that the generality and fruitfulness of the event-perception hypothesis might be further tested.

Perceiving the shape of faces as a growth event. Faces, no less than squares or other shapes are dynamic events since their affordance structure (e.g., shape) is derived from a growth process (the transformational invariant) which preserves sufficient structure (structural invariant) to specify the identity of the face of the person undergoing the aging transformation (growth). In a similar fashion, different people at the same stage of growth, can be perceived as being at the same age level because growth produces similar effects over different structures (Pittenger & Shaw, 1975). These common effects constitute the information specifying the transformational invariant of the growth process. Thus, each transformation can be identified by the style of change wrought over various objects to which it is applied.

In addition to empirically discovering the invariant information specifying the identity of the structures over which an event is defined, a problem of equal weight for the event perception hypothesis is to isolate the invariant information specifying the transformation by which the dynamic aspect of an event is defined. Both of these informational invariants must be found in every event perception experiment if the affordance structure of the event being studied is to be experimentally defined. Pittenger and Shaw conducted the following experiments in an attempt to discover the affordance structure of the growth event defined over human faces. The biological literature suggests two classes of transformations for the specification of the transformation of skull growth: strain and shear. A strain is a geometric transformation which, when applied to a two-dimensional coordinate space, changes the length of the units along one axis as a transformation of the units along the other axis. For instance, a strain transformation can take a square into a rectangle or vice versa. On the other hand, a *shear* is a geometric transformation which transforms the angle of intersection of the coordinate axis, say from a right angle to something less or more than a right angle. Such a transformation might take a square into a rhombus. Consequently, Pittenger and Shaw constructed a set of stimuli by having a computer apply different degrees of these two transformations to a human facial profile, and then by photographing the computer plotted transforms of the given profile. Three experiments were run to test the hypothesis that the perception of age level is derived from information made available by growth events.

To illustrate the application of these transformations to faces, we will describe the production of stimuli for the first experiment. The stimuli were produced by applying combinations of these transformations globally to a two-dimensional Cartesian space in which the profile of a 10-year-old boy had been placed so that the origin was at the ear hole and the y axis was perpendicular to the Frankfurt horizontal (a line drawn tangent to the top orb of the ear hole and the bottom orb of the eye socket).

The formula used for the shear transformation in producing the stimuli expressed in rectangular coordinates was $y' = y$, $x' = x + \tan \theta y$, where the $\tan \theta$ is the angle of shear and x', y' are new coordinates. The formula for the strain transformation used, expressed for convenience in polar coordinates, was $\theta' = \theta$, $r' = r(1 - k \sin \theta)$, where r is the radial vector and θ is the angle specifying direction from the origin. Here k is a constant determining the parameter value of the strain. Thus in producing the stimuli $\tan \theta$ and k are the values to be manipulated for varying the amount of shear and strain, respectively. (For a detailed discussion of this approach see Shaw & Pittenger, in press.) The calculations were performed by computer and the profiles drawn by a computer-driven plotter.

The initial outline profile was transformed by all 35 combinations of seven levels of strain ($k = -0.25, -0.10, 0, +0.10, +0.25, +0.35, +0.55$) and five levels shear ($\theta = -15°, -5°, 0°, +5°, +15°$). These transformations are not commutative. Shear was applied first. The resulting profiles are shown in Fig. 3.

These shape changes approximate those produced by growth. We hypothesize that the changes are relevant to perception in two ways; they are a sufficient stimulus for the perception of age while at the same time leaving information for the identity of the face invariant. The reader will note, however, that profiles on the extreme values for each variable are quite distorted. These values were

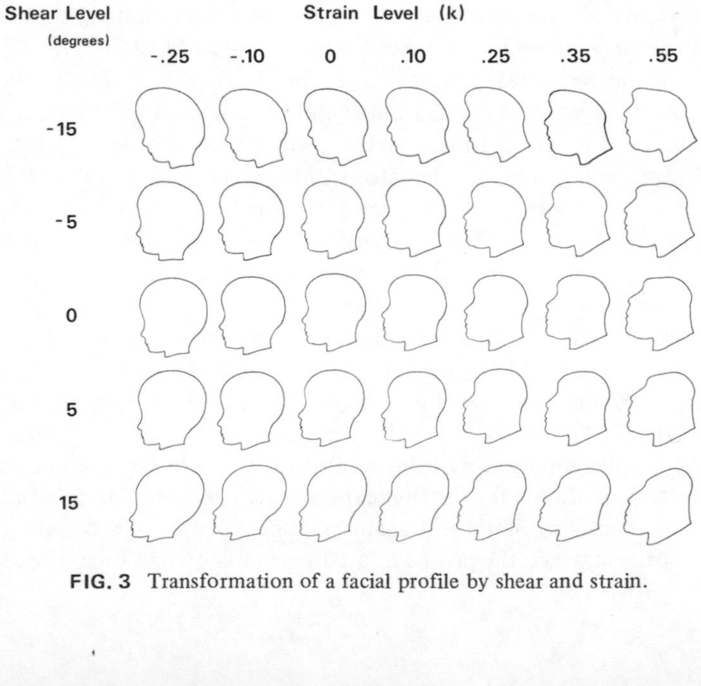

FIG. 3 Transformation of a facial profile by shear and strain.

chosen to test the supernormal stimuli hypothesis. Supernormal stimuli are produced by exaggerating some relevant aspects of a stimulus. Ethologists claim that such stimuli lead to exaggerated responses (Tinbergen, 1951).

Experiment 1

To test the effects of the shape changes induced by shear and strain the profiles shown in Fig. 1 were presented by slide projector to the subjects in a task requiring magnitude estimates of age. The subjects were instructed to rate the ages of the profiles by choosing an arbitrary number to represent the age of the first profile and assigning multiples of this number to represent the age of succeeding profiles relative to the age of the first. Twenty subjects were asked to rate the 35 slides resulting from the transformations described above. The results were straightforward. Using a Monte Carlo technique Pittenger and Shaw found that 91% of the judgments made by the subjects agreed with the hypotheses that the strain transformation produced monotonic perceived age changes in the standard profile. On the other hand, using the shear transformation to predict judgments produced only 66% agreement. Since strain was by far the strongest variable of age change, we decided to test the sensitivity of subjects to very small changes in profiles due to this transformation.

Experiment 2

Sensitivity to the shape changes produced by the strain transformation was assessed in the second experiment by presenting pairs of profiles produced by different levels of the transformation and requiring subjects to choose the older profile in each pair. A series of profiles was produced by applying strain transformations ranging from $k = -0.25$ to $+0.55$ to a single profile, where k is the coefficient of strain used in the equation controlling the computer plots. Eighteen pairs of profiles were chosen; three for each of six levels of difference in degree of strain. The pairs were presented twice to four groups of ten subjects. Different random orders were used for each presentation and each group. Subjects were informed that the study concerned the ability to make fine discriminations of age and that for each pair they were to choose the profile which appeared to be older. During the experiment they were not informed whether or not their responses were correct. By correct response we mean the choice of the profile with the larger degree of strain as the older.

Several results were found. An analysis of variance on percentage of errors as a function of difference in strain showed a typical psychophysical result—a decline in accuracy with smaller physical differences and an increase in sensitivity with experience in the task. However, two other aspects of the results are more important for the question at hand. First, subjects do not merely discriminate the pairs consistently but choose the profile with the larger strain as the older profile with greater than chance frequency; in the first presentation the larger strain was selected on 83.2% of the trials and the second, on 89.2% of the trials. In each presentation, each of the 40 subjects selected the profile with the larger k as older on more than 50% of the trials. In other words, the predicted effect was obtained in every subject. A sign test showed the change probability of this last result to be far less than .001. Thus, the conclusion of the first experiment is confirmed in a different experimental task. Second, sensitivity to the variable proved to be surprisingly fine.

Experiment 3

A third experiment was designed to determine if a structural invariant existed by which individual identity might be perceived as follows. We have all had the experience of recognizing someone we know as a child years later when they have grown to maturity. As a preliminary test of preservation of identity under the strain transformation, profile views of the external portions of the brain cases of six different skulls were traced from x-ray photographs and subjected to five levels of strain. Five pairs of transformed profiles were selected from each individual sequence; the degree of strain for members of three pairs differed by 0.30 and those of the other two pairs by .45 values of k. A profile of a different skull was assigned to each of the above pairs which had the same degree of strain as one of the members of the pair. Slides were constructed of the profile triples such that the two profiles from distinct skulls which had the same level of strain appeared in random positions at the bottom. Thirty subjects were presented the slides and asked to select which of the two profiles at the bottom of the slide that appeared most similar to the profile at the top. The overall percentage of errors was low: for the 30 sets of stimuli presented to 30 subjects, the mean error was less than 17%, with no subject making more than 33% errors. Since no subject made 50% or more errors, a sign test on the hypothesis of chance responding (binomial distribution) by each subject yields a probability of far less than 0.001. Indeed, in another set of studies, Pittenger and Shaw also found that people are quite able to rank order by age photographs of people taken over nearly a decade of growth from pre- to post-puberty years.

The results of these three studies provide support for two important hypotheses: the strain transformation due presumably to growth, not only provides the major source of the relevant perceptual information for age level, but also leaves invariant sufficient perceptual information for the specification of the individual identity of the person by the shape of the head alone.

These experiments also support the contention that the perceived shape of an object is not simply the shape of a static, rigid object, but is rather a higher order structural invariant which remains relatively unchanged by the events (i.e., transformational invariants) into which such objects may enter. Further dramatic support for this claim is provided by the fact that the identity of human faces is preserved under elastic transformations as distinctive from growth as artistic characterization. The success of political caricaturists rests on their ability to satirize a political figure by exaggerating distinctive body or facial features without obscuring the identity of the famous or infamous personage depicted. Indeed, there is evidence that such an artistic redition of complex structures facilitates their indentification (Ryan and Schwartz, 1956). But will the event perception hypothesis apply equally well to still more elaborate events in which complex transformations are defined over a variety of structures?

Perception of a tea-making event. Recently, at the Center for Research in Human Learning, Jerry Wald and James Jenkins have been investigating the generative nature of an elaborate event: the act of preparing tea. To study this event 24 photographs were taken depicting the various steps involved in the preparation of tea. These stimuli were presented to subjects following the same experimental design used in the "orbiting" event experiment discussed earlier. Sixteen of these 24 pictures were used as an acquisition set portraying the tea-making event to subjects. Later, these 16 pictures, plus the remaining 8 from the original set, were shown to the subjects, who were asked to indicate whether the picture was new or one which occurred during acquisition. The subjects were unable to distinguish the new but appropriate pictures of the event from the pictures they had actually experienced during acquisition. Once again we see that a partial subset of the possible instances of an event can specify the entire event.

The general results found in this experiment were essentially the same as those found in the case of the "orbiting"-event experiment reported earlier. Namely, it was again found that subjects were very good at recognizing as new pictures which were physically similar to those in the acquisition set but inappropriate as elements in the event. For example, if a type of movement or direction of movement inappropriate to the event portrayed during acquisition was depicted, subjects classified the picture as new. Clearly, the knowledge which subjects gained during acquisition was knowledge of an abstract system of relations, that is, an event, not knowledge of exact copies of the exemplars specifying the event. Additional support for the contention that subjects are acquiring a generative system of relations is provided by the finding that subjects who were provided more experience with the acquisition pictures were even more likely to mistake the novel but appropriate instances for those actually seen.

GENERAL CONCLUSIONS, AND IMPLICATIONS FOR INSTRUCTION

Each of the event perception experiments discussed is not only amenable to a generative systems explanation but seems to require it. The range of events surveyed, from simple events such as orbiting objects, to more elaborate events involving growth of human faces and the preparation of tea, suggests that the ability to formulate abstract concepts is a basic cognitive capacity underlying knowledge acquisition. This characterization of knowledge acquisition has several important implications for a theory of instruction.

The most general implication concerns how we should conceptualize the nature of those situations in which we accrue useful knowledge about our natural, cultural, social, and professional environments. If the majority of our experiences in these areas involve encounters with either novel instances of old events or fresh instances of new events, then the goals on instruction must go beyond concern for how particulars may be learned. Rather, the primary goal should be to train people to exploit more efficiently their cognitive capacity to assimilate knowledge that is abstract and, therefore, generative.

Moreover, if adaptive responding to even ordinary events, such as recognizing faces or making tea, entails generative knowledge of abstract relationships, then this is all the more true for dealing with higher forms of knowledge in such fields as science, philosophy, mathematics, art, history, or law. Acquisition of knowledge in all areas is a result of abstraction over well chosen instances of events, the exemplars which instantiate the generator sets for the concepts involved. Accepting these conclusions, what potential impact might such a cognitive theory of knowledge have upon current educational practices?

1. Programs of instruction should primarily consist of lessons in which students are furnished with direct experience with those core concepts of the field. As we saw in the case of the experiments reported, the abstraction of generative systems requires first-hand experiences with those exemplary instances of a concept that constitute its generator set. However, our educational institutions typically, and sometimes exclusively, use the "lecture" technique by which students are made passive recipients of the conclusions or implications drawn from another person's experience, where in actuality some version of the experience itself would be a much better form of instruction. Instruction, which takes the form of learning facts or principles about some concept x, is not a substitute (although it may be a useful supplement) for acquiring direct experience about concept x, even if presented in some analogical or simpler prototypical form. This is why some courses of study wisely rely heavily upon laboratory or field experience. Indeed, every classroom should be a "laboratory" for first-hand, rather than second-hand experiences.

There is little new in the above observations regarding the preference of active participation in the learning process over passive reception of material to be learned. What is new, however, is the insight that the generative capacity to formulate abstract concepts may be naturally engaged when the student experiences a very special subset of exemplars, namely, the generator. Therefore, the selection of the exemplars of a concept to be taught is a very different affair, requiring the joint efforts of cognitive psychologists and instructional experts.

2. Another, related implication of the generative characterization of conceptual knowledge is to offer a new theory of the transfer of training effects so desirable throughout the educational progress of a student. How do old concepts facilitate the learning of new ones; and how does new information become integrated with existing information?

Since the generative nature of knowledge has not been seen as implying a core cognitive capacity, both specific and general transfer have been seen as a secondary, spin-off effect of learning specific reactions to specific objects or events. We have attempted to show throughout this chapter why this characterization of learning is backwards. The generative cognitive capacity that is responsible for transfer is not derivative from or based upon knowledge of exact replicas or copies of experiences. It is the abstractness of concepts that accounts for the generality or transfer of conceptual knowledge gained in one situation to new situations. Transfer, therefore, is inherent in the acquisition of abstract concepts.

3. A final implication of this theory for instruction related to the selection of criteria for evaluating performance as an indicant of the state of conceptual knowledge attained by the student. This has proven to be a most difficult and, somewhat surprisingly, a most controversial issue. The proposed theory suggests why this is so.

A major source of difficulty in the evaluation of the knowledge a student has acquired is to know what types of performance count. There are several performance levels students may attain due to either their sophistication in an area, their motivation, or the nature of the concepts to be learned. First, and easiest to evaluate, is the ability to verbalize, or articulate in some other overtly demonstrable form, exactly what they know about a topic. Unfortunately, this level of performance is exhibited inadequately by most people and tends to be rare except for simplistic cases where a rote memorization of particulars is appropriate. Such knowledge, however, is not necessarily generative in nature and, thus, its successful evaluation poses no guidelines for an adequate evaluation of students' abilities to use abstract conceptual knowledge.

A second and more frequently exhibited performance level is that the student has attained useful knowledge of a topic but is unable to articulate what he or she knows. Clearly, a very important goal of education is to bring a novice in some subject matter area up to the level of an expert. Indeed, often we would be very happy if our pedagogical attempts had even more limited success in that the student somehow learned to make sound judgments although remaining unable to articulate the basis for the judgments.

This state of affairs, rather than being rare among experts, is actually very common. Few experts can specify, in algorithmic clarity, the reasoning process they go through in order to arrive at a sound judgment with respect to a problem in their area of expertise, although they may present a learned rationalization afterwards. Many art connoisseirs are able to distinguish styles of artists, categorize according to era, culture or school, various artifacts presented to them without being able to say beforehand the criteria they use. Similarly, chess masters intuit outcomes of games and strategies of opponents without being able to specify a priori criteria for doing so. Indeed, in all areas of knowledge, to be an expert is synonymous with the ability to render objectively sound judgments without necessarily being able to specify every step in the ratiocinative process involved. If it were not so difficult to do so, educating novices to the level of experts would only require rote memorization of algorithmic judgmental procedures applied to rotely memorized banks of data.

The intuitive judgments of experts do, of course, promulgate from a knowledge basis, but one that is usually more tacit than explicit. In short, expert judgments are a by-product of generative systems of knowledge rather than of inert data banks of factual information. Consequently, in our effort to evaluate how much closer to an expert's judgmental ability education has moved novices, we want to assess primarily the degree of generative, tacit knowledge they have obtained and not just their explicit knowledge of itemized facts. Based on the current theory and findings, we suggest that the following questions should be answered by any knowledge evaluation procedure:

a. Can the student identify the same set of clear-cases of the concept that a majority of experts agree upon? This includes also the ability to distinguish non-cases from true cases.

b. Will the student, once tutored in the concept area, select a prototypical instance of the concept from a recognition set of instances as being most likely an instance previously studied, even though it was, in fact, never seen?

c. Can the student deal with novel instances of the concept with the same facility shown with familiar ones? And corollary to both (b) and (c):

d. Does the repeatedly tutored student display an inability to recall whether he or she has seen relevant particulars about the concept area before, while at the same exhibiting considerable confidence that irrelevant particulars were not seen before? This is a very important criterion for determining if the student has indeed built up tacit knowledge structures that are not accessible to conscious articulation. In fact, the proportion of false positives in recognition tests may provide the only way to determine whether an inarticulate student has nevertheless gained sufficient knowledge for making sound intuitive judgments (on the assumption, of course, that a comparison of the students' judgments with that of experts is not directly feasible).

Obviously, there is still much work to be accomplished before drawing any final conclusions about the proposed theory. It already exhibits, however, in our opinion, sufficient promise in both theoretical and practical areas to merit further development by both cognitive and educational psychologists.

ACKNOWLEDGMENTS

Preparation of this paper was supported in part by a Career Development Award to Robert Shaw from the National Institute of Child Health and Human Development (1 K04-HD 24010), in part by a post-doctoral trainee-ship awarded to Buford Wilson by the same agency and by grants to the University of Minnesota, Center for Research in Human Learning, from the National Science Foundation (GB-17590), the National Institute of Child Health and Human Development (HD-01136), and the Graduate School of the University of Minnesota. The paper was completed while the senior author was a fellow at the Center for Advanced study in the Behavioral Sciences to whom our heartfelt thanks are given for its support.

11
Toward a Theory
of Instructional Growth

S. Farnham-Diggory

University of Texas at Dallas

From 1967 to 1971, when I was writing *Cognitive Processes in Education* (Farnham-Diggory, 1972), I was largely alone in attempting to relate informa- tion-processing psychology to education. That has now changed, and the chapters in this volume represent important new contributions to the area. The chapters also reveal awareness by this group of distinguished scientists of what a big job they have undertaken. Really understanding educational problems, really analyzing the psychological processes involved, really distilling and applying psychological principles, are enormously complex tasks—only recently under- taken by theorists capable of coping with them. Prior to the last decade, the best theoretical minds in the business were working on problems derived from relatively simple learning theories of the day. Such theories were not adequate for the proper study of instructional behavior, although they were challenging in other ways. Finally, there emerged a theoretical framework—the information- processing framework—complex enough to fit the real world of education. As a result of this development, and of the caliber of scientific though it is fostering, the next 10 or 15 years of psychological research should produce major new insights into instructional issues.

For this to happen, however, our theories must push well beyond the descrip- tive level—which is to say, they must generate testable predictions that a smart educator, flying by the seat of his pants, would not be likely to make. As Carroll (Chapter 1, this volume) has noted, most educational theory today has the form of cultural tradition passed on by word of mouth. Educators trust this tradition because it provides them with hand-holds. But we know it will not get them where a good theory will get them. The relation between intuitive practice and good theory is analogous to crossing a stream by following a personal map from rock to rock, and crossing by means of a properly engineered bridge. Unfortunately, much of psychology, purporting to build the bridge, may be merely using a different language to describe the process of getting from rock to rock. We can see this by attending to the descriptions of good educators who are not familiar with psychological jargon.

An especially useful and humbling book in this regard is one written by a man named Charles Allen (1919), described on the flyleaf of his book as "Sometime Agent for Industrial Training of Boys and Men, Massachusetts Board of Education, and Superintendent of Instructor Training, U. S. S. B. [United States Shipping Board] Emergency Fleet Corporation." Mr. Allen was born in 1862, and this book, which was obviously a culmination of 30 or 40 years of experience, was published in 1919. Although some of the Pavlovian, Watsonian, and Gestalt psychological principles were around at that time, Allen was innocent of them. He told it like it was, without benefit of any such newfangled nonsense. The title of his book sets the straightforward tone. It was called "The Instructor, the Man, and the Job." Let me give you some examples of Allen's instructional wisdom:

> Whatever the instructor intends to put over to the learner must be given to him in some order; it cannot be given to him all at once. This brings up the question as to . . . whether there is not a *best instructional order* . . . and, if so, how it can be determined.
> . . .
> An effective order of instruction . . . presents certain characteristics among the more important of which are:
>
> 1. The different teaching jobs . . . are so arranged that . . . each succeeding job extends the learner's knowledge and skill, but does not call for a different sort of knowledge and skill.
> 2. Jobs that require the learner to think of the least number of different things at once come first and jobs that require the learner to think of the most different things come last.
> 3. The jobs are arranged according to the difficulty of learning how to do them rather than according to the order in which they would be done in getting out a finished product . . . That is, the order is an *instruction* order, not a *production* order.
>
> . . . An illustration of a course of instruction which does not meet these conditions would be the following procedure . . . Where two rivet holes do not come together 'fair', they must be reamed to a common size. This is usually done with a pneumatic or electric drive . . . A group of men after having been cautioned as to the control of the machine were placed in compartments of the ship to ream out all holes that required reaming. These holes were, of course, all sizes, fair and unfair . . . Some could be reamed in easy positions and some required difficult positions. Under these conditions the learner was immediately put up against jobs of all sorts of difficulty, since he took the holes as they came. He worked in this way until he had learned to ream. Under these conditions the learner had to learn too many things at once, reducing the probability that he would thoroughly grasp any one thing, causing a state of mental confusion and slowing up the learning operation . . . Under a properly arranged order of instruction the work would have been so laid out that holes of different degrees of fairness would have been marked so that the learner first learned to ream the fairest hole, then the next

fairest hole, and so on up to the most unfair hole that he would ever have to work on. Moreover it is very unlikely that one compartment would afford enough samples of holes of all degrees of fairness, so that instead of keeping him in one compartment till all holes were reamed, he should have been carried from one compartment to another as the demands of the training required . . . Keeping the gang that is under instruction in one compartment till it is all reamed up gives good *production* conditions; such an arrangement is an example of bad *instructional* conditions.

As between the two methods of training given above, the latter would train a reamer much faster, make a better workman of him, keep him in a much better frame of mind while he was under training and turn him out with a much better attitude towards his job [Allen, 1919, pp. 78–80, italics his].

We can list many psychological principles contained in Allen's specifications. From 1918, four decades of discrimination learning theory would have been applicable. But would it have done any more for Allen than he could have done for himself—even experimentally? Without benefit of stimulus–response jargon, Allen could have, and probably did, run a crew through the ordered procedure that he recommended, run another crew through the unordered procedure, and measure resulting work skills and attitudes—sufficiently well to make money-saving decisions about training procedures. Traditional discrimination learning theory would not have expedited such an empirical program very much. It would not have built a bridge, but would merely have renamed some of the empirical procedures. Can modern information-processing psychology do any better? Can it provide new information, new guidance which a smart instructor would not be able to get for himself? Or are we also just renaming some phenomena?

Let me give you another example. Allen outlined in detail the necessary steps for performing what we would call a task analysis. For any given block of skills (for example, those of house carpentry), the instructor was to decide what the *progression factors* were (Allen's term). What had to be increased? What had to be decreased? For example, fear of working at a height had to be decreased in house carpenters. Accuracy of measurement and placement had to be increased. The number of operations to be remembered and performed had to be increased.

Having designated these progression factors, the instructor was then to allocate jobs which matched the levels of progression. For example, the very first job should keep the man on the ground, require easy, gross measurements, and only a few operations. Paper work met those specifications—the man stands on the ground, hangs up creosoted paper, cuts it off at the bottom, and nails it on. At an intermediate level, Allen got the man up on a stage or scaffolding, and had him do clapboarding—which required more precise measurement and a larger number of operations. At an advanced level, the man was placed on the roof, nailing down shingles.

The instructor was to work this out by putting all the carpentry jobs on file cards, and fitting them into a diagram like that shown in Fig. 1. The Os refer to checkpoints, or tests, which the man must pass before he moves on to the more advanced levels.

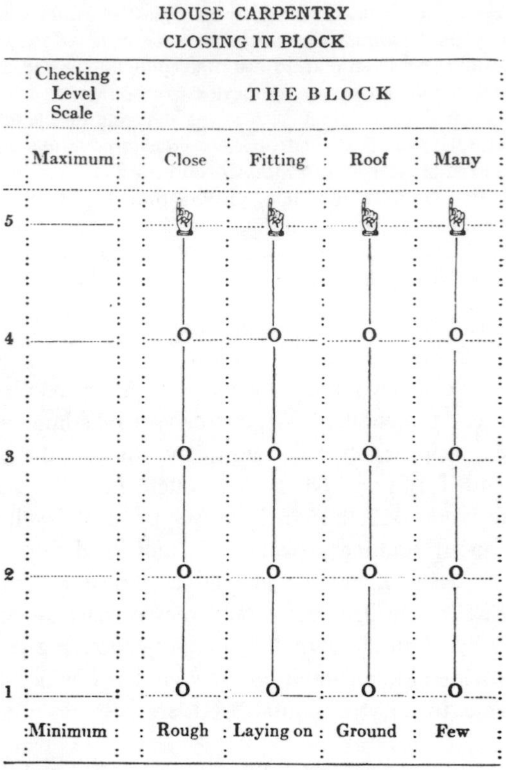

HOUSE CARPENTRY
CLOSING IN BLOCK

FIG. 1 Task analysis chart used by Allen in designating steps in the training of house carpenters (Allen, 1919, p. 90).

The question again is: do our modern methods of task analysis really add anything to this? Or have we merely restated in fancier and more detailed jargon what good instructors already know? That is, are we *helping* these instructors in any way?

Two brief final examples, more cognitive in nature. Allen talks about the need to teach special technical terms and skills on the job, rather than in some preliminary classwork—which is what he says most lazy, inexpert instructors would rather do. Allen calls this knowledge *auxiliary material,* and says:

. . . If [auxiliary material] is given him in advance of the job he has nothing to 'tie' it to; it makes but little impression. If it is given him after the job he has not been given it when he has a chance to *apply* it. In either case, what 'tying' he can do will be to such a general idea of the situation as he may get from such general knowledge of the job as he may have picked up somehow . . . a pretty weak thing to tie to . . . In order that he shall think of the thing in question when he should, he must have gotten it in connection with some operation, so that, whenever he performs that operation the thing, say 'shooting the tool,' will come up in his mind in connection with that part of the job. It is the failure to recognize this fact that makes so much 'preliminary work in the fundamentals' of so little value; general talks on safety first are given and then, when the men on the job do exactly what the instructor warned them not to do, he wonders what is the matter and calls them stupid. He puts up lessons on fractions, and then finds that his men do not know how to use fractions on the job; he teaches trade terms in advance of their use and, when they come up on the job, the men do not know their terms. In all these cases, the trouble is that the instructor, who has plenty of trade experience to tie to, forgets that the learner has little or none; it is another case of the instructor thinking of the problem with his own brain and not putting himself in the place of the learner [Allen, 1919, p. 103].

Allen calls this correct method of instruction the *tying up* method, and provides specifications for exactly how the instructor is to carry this out, how he should decide what the auxiliary material is, how he should time its introduction on the job, and so forth.

A final example has to do with the very interesting perceptual problem of how you know a rivet is *hot enough.* Before introducing this problem Allen discourses on what we would now term *the Socratic method* of questioning. Allen might not have known that term, but he did know his man had to be taught to think, and that the only way to do that was to get his mind going.

In explanation it may be stated that, in riveting, the rivets are driven hot. They are heated in a small portable furnace or forge. A part of the job of the 'heater boy' is to pick out rivets at the right heat for driving. If too hot they are 'burned' and should not be driven. If too cold they will not drive properly . . . The heater boy is paid for knowing *how* to pick out a rivet at the right heat.

. . . In planning a lesson the instructor has three questions to answer. First, what are the ideas to be put over in the teaching unit? Second, what is the teaching base or 'jumping-off point' (J.O.P.) that is proposed to be used? Third, what ideas already in the learner's mind does the instructor intend to utilize in carrying the learner up to the J.O.P.? . . . A few general rules can be given.

Work from the qualitative or general notion to the quantitative or exact notion, always ask 'how' or 'what' before asking 'how much' . . . General ideas should be presented before specific ideas. For example, the idea that the rivet must be at a certain heat to be right will be put up before the idea that the right color is just under a white heat.

. . . In order to put over these ideas, the learner must be made to have in his mind a certain group of ideas or a picture to serve as a foundation for the building on of the new idea contained in the teaching unit. In this particular lesson, a good J.O.P. is to have the learner thinking of the problem of knowing when a rivet is hot enough.

[To build up the J.O.P., the instructor is to ask such questions as the following:]

First Idea. (A rivet)

1. Have you ever seen a rivet?
2. Can you tell a rivet from a bolt?

. . .

Second Idea. (A hot rivet)

1. Could you pick up a rivet that you found lying around the yard?
2. Could you tell a very hot rivet from a cold rivet without touching it?

. . .

Third Idea. (A rivet heated enough)

1. Can a rivet be heated to different heats?
2. Would it make any difference what heat a rivet has, provided it is hot?

3. Hasn't the heater boy got to know somehow when the rivet is at the right heat?
J. O. P. How does he know when a rivet is just hot enough?
. . .
[Training then includes such experiences as:]
(Place rivets in fire.) Have each boy pick out correctly heated rivets, meantime asking such questions as are suggested below, of the other boys.
Bill; Pick out a correctly heated rivet.
Sam; Did he do it?
Jack; How do you know he did it?
Tom; You pick out a rivet.
Jack; You watch him.
Sam; Pick out another one.
Bill; That wasn't right, was it?
Jack; Pick out a burnt rivet.
Carry on work of this kind until satisfied each boy knows a properly heated rivet [Allen, 1919, pp. 184–195].

The question is: can we, 50 years later, improve that instructional program through our knowledge of the psychological principles involved? The answer, I think, is *yes*. While it is true that psychologists do not pay enough attention to the work of good educators, it is also true that educators have not been able to solve many of their own problems, or even to recognize when some of the solutions were at hand in their own experience. The fact that we recognize the importance of Allen's insights is a sign that our own theories are mature enough to match up to good instruction, and move it further along.

Let us consider some of the principles this volume has offered.

DYNAMIC THEORETICAL MODELS

All four of the chapters under discussion here stem from dynamic theoretical positions. They are concerned with changing conceptual fields. Shaw and Wilson (Chapter 10, this volume) have attempted to account for the well-known human capacity to generate unlimited new instances of a concept. Where does the criterial rule come from? How is it learned? Shaw and Wilson argue that it is discovered inductively as a result of experience with a critical set of conceptual exemplars—the *generator set*. They present data showing that subjects will learn an abstract system of relations, not merely a list of static properties, if they practice on the generator set. Although Allen (1919) undoubtedly recognized this principle, he was far from formulating precise predictions regarding its nature. Instructionally, the implication is straightforward and important: if you can teach only one case of a complex concept, which one will you choose? The research carried out by Shaw and Wilson, along with that of the other prototype theorists, Rosch (1973a,b), Reed (1973), and Lockhead (1970, 1972) points toward the day when that question can be answered scientifically rather than intuitively.

The Hyman study (Chapter 8, this volume) begins, in effect, where the Shaw and Wilson study ended: with a fully formed concept, that of a *professional role.* Hyman was concerned with the power of such a stereotype to distort recognition memory for trait adjectives. This, again, is a dynamic theoretical conception. Hyman's data show that concepts actively influence recognition memory. In Allen's world, that could mean false recognition of a heated rivet whenever a trainee held a strong preconception of appropriate rivet characteristics. True, Allen was prepared for false recognitions, and he structured the instructional situation accordingly. But Hyman's research points the way toward exact scaling of characteristics that a student must learn to notice, and exact predictions about the extent to which prior learning will affect detection skills.

The LNR network, as described by Norman, Gentner, and Stevens in this volume (Chapter 9) and elsewhere (e.g., Norman, 1973; Lindsay & Norman, 1972) is a fully dynamic theory of how memory is modified by the new demands that are made upon it. In the LNR network (as in the networks of Collins & Quillian, 1972; Schank, 1972; and Anderson & Bower, 1973) concepts can be represented as object-relation-attribute constellations. These constellations are not fixed, but can be formed and re-formed as the occasion demands. Norman, Gentner, and Stevens provide several examples of the mental restructuring that takes place during tutorials. The interaction between the experimenter and the student in the Jump Problem (pp. 192–193, this volume) would probably have been especially appealing to Allen. One imagines that he would have admired the systematic protocol analysis, the step-by-step printout of changes in the student's programming rule. Such detailed analysis is the theoretical groundwork necessary to the discovery and bracketing of critical teaching moments. Eventually, we should be able to define Allen's J.O.P. ("jumping off point") as rigorously as we can define the critical heat of a rivet.

Greeno (Chapter 7, this volume) illustrates an application of LNR theoretical principles to a lesson in psychophysics. Again, we see how knowledge can be represented as a set of dynamic interrelationships. Greeno also asks, in this section of his chapter, what higher-order goals and constraints affect student performances. Essentially, we can say that there are rules affecting entry into, and use of, the conceptual network (Lindsay & Norman, 1972). Before answering a question about the facts of psychophysics, one must answer the question: What kind of an answer does the instructor want? Nowhere are such meta-strategies considered by Allen.

Additional facets of Greeno's chapter will be discussed in a later section.

In summary, we can say that our modern technological and theoretical capacity to *represent changing conceptual states* is a major advance in instructional theory. By virtue of this capacity, we can work toward the precise specification of (a) key instructional concepts that will have maximal viability and generality; (b) the rate at which new information will be assimilated to, or distorted by, old information; (c) critical teaching moments; and (d) rules governing the way in which organized knowledge is accessed.

Now we turn from consideration of dynamics to consideration of structures.

THE SCHEMATIC FRAME

Each of the chapters under discussion here has evidenced concern with mental organizations described as *schemata*. It is clearly the case that all cognitive theories of instruction will postulate higher-order schemes governing both the learner's potential and the teacher's strategies.

Shaw and Wilson have discussed the relational schemata underlying judgments of aging. As infant faces were geometrically transformed, certain feature relationships remained invariant. This invariance could be called the *identity schema;* the transformational invariants themselves comprised the *aging schema.*

Hyman has suggested that schemata function as intervening stages in a recognition task. The perception of a trait, or a trait name, evokes a broad personality stereotype. This stereotype, in turn, increases the probability that other traits associated with it will be noticed, and even falsely recognized. Norman, Gentner, and Stevens consider schemata to be the basic units of memory. For learning to have occurred, relevant schemata—that is, schemata similar to those activated by the learning situation—must have been modified or recombined. Their "Mayonnaise Problem" illustrates how subjects summon schematic analogs to cope with task demands. Mayonnaise must be made of something that looks white and tastes spicy, hence it must be made of whipped cream and mustard. Greeno's higher-order issues are actually schematic issues. Selecting the right form for an answer to a question is selecting a schema; deciding how specific to be, is deciding about the potential application of a schema; learning "what counts as an explanation of something [p. 156]" is learning that "an explanation is organized according to rules, and these rules constitute a schema that must be part of the student's knowledge [p. 156]."

Formulations of this type, and the experiments delineating them, have moved modern instructional science well beyond Allen's "tying up method." However, because we try to educate masses of students simultaneously, there remain massive discrepancies between the available schemata of learners, and information presented by teachers. That is one aspect of what J. McV. Hunt (1961) has called "the problem of the match."

There are many different ways in which the term *schema* is now being used throughout psychology. Although this must trouble theoretical purists, it has an important implication: it indicates widespread scientific attention to the fact that our heads contain higher-order units and capacities. Almost everyone, it seems, has left his little S–R links by the wayside.

But there is one aspect of behaviorism that cognitians have not left behind: the distinction between *competence* (or knowledge, or learning) and *performance.*

PERFORMANCE PROGRAMS

With deceptive ease and fluency, Greeno (Chapter 7, this volume) has provided us with a feast of performance models for lessons in fractions and geometry. Flow charts, or production systems—choose the one that is most appropriate for your theory of a task, and of what happens when that task is taught. For cognitive psychologists, this is a powerful and exciting hypothesis-generating exercise. For educators in search of a ready-made bridge, it is often dismaying. What is the use, they ask, of all this hypothetical formalism?

There are two answers to that. First, there is no other way of representing a complex instructional situation. Believing that it can be represented more simply is an illusion. True, we have not yet developed a complete instructional science, but we are never going to develop one until we raise our heads from the sands of oversimplification. Like the molecule, the gene, and the galaxy, the human mind is very complicated. We will never fully understand it or devise appropriate ways of educating it until we have a theory that is detailed enough to model it. The fact that we have trouble understanding such theories does not alter the fact that we need them, and that they represent a proper use of hypothetical formalism.

The second answer to a "what's the use . . . ?" question concerns the ability of human beings to construct response programs (Newell, 1972a). We need complex models of the type Greeno describes to account for the fact that no two people ever respond to the same situation in the same way, as well as for the fact that no one can exactly duplicate his own responses. We are endlessly constructive and inventive. Modeling our capacities in this respect is an extremely complicated issue.

Consider the subject in Shaw and Wilson's "orbiting" card experiment. The mathematical system described on pages 204–205 represents an abstract logical structure. But clearly it does not represent what the subject is doing mentally as he performs the experimental task. How might we represent those mental processes? The reader is invited to select a modeling schema from Greeno's menu and apply it to the Shaw and Wilson experiment—the point of the exercise being to discover that subjects exposed to the generator set must have built a different representation of the stimulus, because they saw different stimuli. Subjects shown the nongenerator set saw hearts, crosses, circles, and squares in only two positions on the cards. Subjects shown the generator set saw the same stimuli in all four positions. To understand the subsequent confusion manifested by subjects shown the generator set, we must understand how they represented, or failed to represent, the information—compared to subjects in the other condition. Mathematical group theory does not predict the construction of differing mental representations. For that, we need psychological theories (e.g., EPAM, Simon & Feigenbaum, 1964.; Gregg & Simon, 1967).

In the case of Hyman's experiment, what were the subjects actually doing? They were remembering words in a recognition paradigm. How was the prototype—the Social Worker or the Lawyer—supposed to be activated during the task itself? This is not specified, nor was the experiment designed to test such specifications—e.g., to test the possibility that a trait label which was never seen, but which was generated entirely by the stereotype, might take longer to recognize (signifying a longer sequence of mental operations). In the absence of a performance theory of this type, we are compelled to wonder if Hyman's results are not simply another manifestation of a fact reported in 1960 by Wishner: that trait clusters display intercorrelations that are independent of personality constructs. The subject's false recognition of trait names may reflect the associative structure of the language, rather than the psychological structure of his mind.

The problem with the performance of subjects in the studies reported by Norman, Gentner, and Stevens plagues all the "networkers." How do we account for the fact that the network was not infinitely activated? Since every concept is potentially related to every other concept, what prevents those relationships from firing? Somewhere, in a model of the subject's performance, there must be a task objective, rules governing the recruitment of skills and concepts, and tests of their applicability and value.

As a way of organizing the issues, consider Fig. 2.

Any subject, performing any experimental task, is an "assembler" of his own knowledge, orienting skills, mental operations (such as comparing or inferring) and self-management tactics. To respond to a task, he must detect features of the situation, or summon feature memories of some kind. He will (if he is over the age of 2 or 3) probably also use words and syntactic rules. He must call up well-practiced motor skills, such as writing or talking. The way he puts all these together—his rules and strategies for doing so—constitute his performance pro-

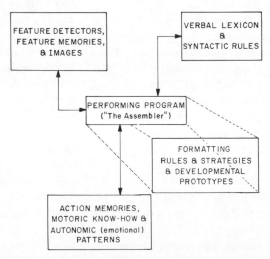

FIG. 2 The structural components of complex behavior.

gram, one which may or may not match up to the experimenter's theory of what such a performance program should entail.

With reference to the question: why *three* systems, feature, verbal, and action? The answer is simply that we seem to be constructed that way. Our perceptual skills, our feature-noticing skills, are not the same as our linguistic skills. We cannot substitute percept for word. Nor can we substitute percept or word for action and related physiological phenomena. This design for humans has some theoretical advantages which may or may not have had evolutionary significance. For example, the fact that a motor skill can run itself off automatically means that perception is freed for other monitoring operations. The fact that words are separable from percepts can produce discrepancies that are important discrimination cues: how else can we learn that all "green leafy vegetables" are not lettuce? Bruner (Bruner, Olver, & Greenfield, 1966) has reviewed much additional evidence—although his own theoretical integration of it has been somewhat different from the model shown in Fig. 2.

In addition to these three systems, we have a stock of special programming operations—problem-solving heuristics, classification abilities, operations in the Piagetian sense, serializing capacities, and so forth. These are not conscious strategies, but are fast, habitual, management routines.

Figure 2 is essentially a scheme for organizing and comparing complex behavior, rather than a theory. It is especially useful in the analysis of pedagogical situations. For example, consider the "White Sauce Problem" in Chapter 7 by Norman, Gentner, and Stevens. What program was the student expected to assemble? Answers to questions about French sauces. What sort of language was involved? Labels like *Bechamel, Veloute, roux,* as well as familiar words like *sauce, white,* and *milk.* What features—actual perceptual experiences—were involved? None, in this lesson. (That was, Allen would no doubt have suggested, one of the problems.) Similarly, the involvement of the motor system—stirring, disintegrating lumps, gradual pouring—was missing from the lesson. Although the authors found the tutee's verbal confusions theoretically interesting, one wonders if they represented anything more significant than the fact that differences in consistency, coloring, and flavoring among members of the French sauce family were not discriminated, because the necessary nonverbal cues were never experienced.

CONCLUSIONS

Overall then, what do we know that would really have been new to Allen? Our best theorizing right now—and it is very good indeed, as the chapters in this volume reveal—is with reference to models of competence, of knowledge-structures. Because they are dynamic models, they represent the human potential for the combination and recombination of ideas, rather that the static architecture of lexicon. But we are still not devoting enough theoretical effort to the development of models of performance. Whether we are addressing tasks of learning, recalling, recognizing, generalizing, or evaluating—we are not yet adequately modeling what subjects *do*. Allen was concerned with performance. We are much better than he was in specifying the characteristics of a well-stocked head. But he was still ahead of us in specifying the characteristics of learning and teaching as active processes.

ACKNOWLEDGMENTS

The preparation of this paper was supported in part by Public Health Service Grant No. MH-07722 from the National Institute of Mental Health.

12

It's the Thought that Counts: New Approaches to Educational Theory

J. R. Hayes

Carnegie-Mellon University

The chapters in this section are very closely related. All of them are concerned with the application of ideas of cognitive psychology—ideas still in the state of rapid development—to the problems of instruction. For example, all are concerned, at least in part, with the processes by which new information is stored on long-term memory and with the implications of these processes for instruction. In pursuing this concern, the authors draw on what is now one of cognitive psychology's most active areas, the modeling of semantic memory. The area includes work by such authors as Quillian (1969), Schank (1972), Anderson and Bower (1973), Kintsch (1972), and, of course, the Norman, Rumelhart, and LNR group (1972), represented in this volume by Norman, Gentner, and Stevens. Further, Greeno makes use of goal structures embodied in a production system representation in a manner similar to recent work of Newell and Simon (1972).

There is necessarily as air of tentativeness about much that is said in these chapters because the authors are attempting to point out new directions rather than simply giving better specification to the old.

COGNITIVE OBJECTIVES

I find Greeno's proposals especially exciting. He has taken of the difficult task of defining cognitive objectives in education—objectives intended to replace the more traditional behavioral objectives. To specify a behavior objective for instruction, we state a particular set of behaviors we want the students to be able to perform after instruction, e.g. to solve a specified class of arithmetic problems, or to answer questions about a chapter in a history text. To specify a cognitive objective, we state a set of changes we want the instruction to bring about in the students' cognitive processes, e.g. acquisition of a particular algorithm for division or the assimilation of a body of historical fact to information already in long-term memory.

Since Greeno does not discuss the relative merits of cognitive and behavioral objectives at any length, it seems appropriate to do so here. One of the most important advantages of cognitive objectives is that they tend to focus our attention on the underlying cognitive processes to a greater extent than do behavioral objectives. An example from my own teaching experience will illustrate the point.

Several years ago, I was involved in the teaching of elementary calculus to a group of college students who rated themselves "poor" in mathematics ability. Some of these students had a peculiar sort of difficulty in solving algebra problems. In problems where the task was to "express X in terms of Y" given a set of four or five relations, e.g. $R = Z^2$, $X = R + 3$, etc., a student might combine relations and draw inferences without apparent pattern. Student performance improved considerably when they were taught some elementary planning procedures for identifying what relations were useful in a given problem and in what order they should be considered. The difference, of course, lay not in the answer that the student produced but rather in the *processes* he used to search for the answer.

I do not know with any certainty why the students had failed to learn the planning procedure for solving such problems prior to college, but the following account is at least plausible. For very simple problems involving just two or three relations, the trial and error procedure may work quite will in the sense that the problem requires no more than two or three trials before a successful solution is achieved. If, in learning algebra, the students solved only short problems, it might by very hard for the teacher to determine whether the students were using trial-and-error or some more efficient procedure. It would not be surprising then if at least some students never progressed beyond trial and error. Now, it is not impossible in principle to deal with this problem using behavioral objectives. What one would need to do is to be sure that the students could solve problems which resemble in all important aspects the problems they will eventually be required to solve. The difficulty lies in knowing what the important aspects are. It is exactly at this point that knowledge of the underlying cognitive processes is important and that the superiority of cognitive objectives becomes most apparent. Without an understanding of the cognitive processes it is often very difficult to judge just what sort of behavior we ought to require of our students.

I encountered another example illustrating the same point when I was doing research on the use of visual imagery in elementary mathematics (Hayes, 1973). One of my subjects reported that he thought of each of the digits as having a set of points that he used as "counting points." For example, the digit "3" had three counting points each located at one of the leftward projections of the digit, the digit "4" had four counting points also located at well specified positions on the digit, etc. When the subject added a pair of numbers such as "5" and "7," he would say "Five," and then looking at each of the counting points on the digit "7" in turn, say "six, seven, eight, . . . " until at the last counting point, he arrived at the answer "twelve." When I asked the subject how he had learned this method of adding, he told me that he used to count on the digits with his pencil until his teacher forbade him to do it. He then switched to performing the same processes with eye fixations. Clearly, the teacher had achieved her behavioral objectives but she had failed to have any important influence on the underlying cognitive processes.

The scope of the task that Greeno is tackling is apparent in the set of three examples he used as illustrations. The first example concerns the understanding of fractions by primary school students; the second, understanding of psychophysics at the college level. For each example, Greeno provides a model of what he believes to be the underlying cognitive processes, drawing as necessary on modern analysis of good structures, perceptual processes, and semantic memory. The details of these models, of course, may need to be modified as more knowledge accumulates, but the general direction in which Greeno is heading seems just right.

ASSIMILATION OF NEW INFORMATION

As we noted above, all four of the authors are concerned, from various points of view, with the assimilation of new information into memory. Shaw and Wilson focus on the logical structure of the information being stored while the others focus on the integration of new knowledge with information already in memory.

Shaw and Wilson propose an interesting hypothesis for concept learning. As I understand it, they propose that a set of instances will be sufficient to allow a subject to infer the whole concept if the differences between instances imply a set of operators which is a generator set for the whole concept. Actually, Shaw and Wilson are not fully explicit about the process by which operators are inferred from instances. I have assumed that differences between instances must be important for that process. An operator is a generator for the whole concept if, by applying it repeatedly to an instance of the concept, it will generate all of the instances of the concept. For example, suppose that the concept is the set of four 90° rotations of a square. The pair of instances

is sufficient to allow the subject to infer the whole concept because the difference implies a 90° rotation operator and this operation is a generator of the set of four rotations. However, the pair of instances

is not sufficient because the difference between the two instances implies a 180° rotation operator which is not a generator of the set.

The experimental results which Shaw and Wilson report are consistent with their hypothesis, but they do not as yet provide a convincing demonstration of its correctness.

While Hyman's experimental observations are confined to the area of person perception, it is clear that his theoretical focus and that of Norman et al. are quite similar. Both are primarily interested in the way in which a person's acquisition of new knowledge is conditioned by the current structure of his or her memory. In particular, both investigators are concerned with the way in which new information is assimilated to schemata or organized bodies of knowledge in memory.

Hyman's chapter provides an interesting illustration of the problem of assimilating information to scientific schemas. His experiment is intelligently designed and well carried out. One expects, before reading the results, that it will demonstrate the influence of schemas in memory. But it doesn't—the experiment fails. Hyman isn't discouraged, nor do we feel he should be. We believe as he does that if one persists, it will be possible to find many experiments which illustrate the point about schemas. This incident, though, reminds us that the point is a vague one. It isn't that schemas always influence memory in measurable ways under specified circumstances—it is only that schemas sometimes influence memory under circumstances which we cannot as yet specify. Clearly we need what Norman, Gentner, and Stevens are trying to provide—a good process model for schemas.

DIRECT TRAINING OF COGNITIVE SKILLS

In considering the application of psychology to instruction, it seems most natural to think about what the teacher or the designer of instructional materials should know about the student. However, in this volume, Greeno, Norman, Gentner, and Stevens, and Resnick have all independently suggested that we should consider the importance of what the student knows about his own cognitive processes and the extent to which we can change these cognitive processes by direct training. Greeno says that knowledge of cognitive processes " . . . probably would constitute useful information for students [p. 158]."

Norman says, " . . . if a child knows how to learn, then he can get the knowledge by himself . . . " and he asks, "Why do we not attempt to teach some basic cognitive skills such as how to organize one's knowledge, how to learn, how to solve problems, how to correct errors in understanding [p. 000] ."

Resnick says " . . . it seems likely that ways can be found to make individuals more conscious of the role of environmental cues in problem solving, and to teach strategies of feature scanning and analysis [pp. 79–80] ." Such instructions would enhance the likelihood of their noticing cues that prompt effective action. Similar ideas are being championed by Papert at the Massachusetts Institute of Technology.

This topic is dear to my own heart, since Steven Rosenberg and I recently designed and taught a course which was intended to teach problem-solving skills to college students. Our objective was to provide a course that would help students to increase their problem-solving skills by direct training. In designing the course, we made liberal use of the work of others—notably of Polya (1957) and Wickelgren (1974) on the teaching of problem solving and of Newell and Simon (1972) on the analysis of problem-solving skills.

The students who elected the course were distributed through the four colleges of the University. There were 6 students from Fine Arts, 12 from engineering, 12 from science, and 12 from humanities and social science. While this mix created difficulty in finding common ground on which to discuss some topics, it was in general perceived as beneficial both by us as instructors and by the students because of the diversity of points of view which it brought to class discussions.

The course consisted of three sections: a Diagnostic section, lasting about three weeks, a Theory–Practice section of eight weeks, and a Transfer section of two weeks.

The Diagnostic section was designed to serve two functions. First, it was designed to provide the student with information about the current state of his problem-solving skills. Second, it was designed to teach him procedures for examining his own problem-solving processes. In all, five techniques were used to accomplish these objectives. First, a self-report form was used to obtain the students' own inventory of his strengths and weakness in problem solving. Second, a problem-solving test including a very wide variety of problems (logical problems, imagery problems, writing problems, etc.) was administered and each student was given feedback about his own performance as compared to other students in the class. Third, each student was required to record time usage data over one-week period as a means of assessing work habits. Mean values for number of hours spent in study and in various other activities were reported so that students could assess their own performance against the group mean. Fourth, students were asked to keep problem-solving diaries in which they recorded step by step accounts of their own problem-solving behavior on homework assignments for later analysis. Fifth, some of the techniques of protocol analysis were demonstrated in class and practiced in small group sessions.

The theory practice section consisted of two major activities which ran concurrently—a series of lectures on the theory of problem solving and the students' skill improvement project.

The skill improvement project was the most important single aspect of the course. On the basis of information gained during the diagnostic section, the student was expected to identify a skill that he wanted to improve and to design a project which would improve it. Thus, the student had to devise a way for measuring his initial state of skill, generate a plan for improving the skill which drew on materials discussed in the course, and measure his final state of skill. Areas chosen included skills in logical problem solving, time management, chess, imagery, memory, and many others.

A second part of the Theory–Practice section was a teaching experience. We felt that by teaching a skill that he understood well, the student would be required to do a careful analysis of that skill in order to communicate it to others. Student feedback would provide him with information about the adequacy of his analysis. In general, we found that the teaching task worked quite well as a pedagogical device. Students reported that they did come to understand their own skills better.

The third part of the Theory–Practice section was the course of lectures which ran concurrently with the skill improvement project. Here we attempted to provide breadth rather than depth on the theory that the interested student could explore any topic of special interest to him in greater depth.

For example, the lecture topics included the following:

1. An overview of problem-solving techniques including trial and error, learning, heuristic search, planning, pattern recognition, and a number of other methods.
2. A discussion of the importance of representations in problem solving, illustrations of how changes in representation can turn a difficult problem into an easy one, and discussion of the procedures for constructing representation.
3. The management of short-term memory including demonstration of the constraints imposed on problem solving by the limitations of short-term memory, and the demonstration of techniques for avoiding these limitations.
4. The importance of long-term memory (for example, of factual world knowledge) for problem solving and techniques for storing information.
5. The nature of rule induction and some techniques for inducing rules.
6. The nature and use of hypothetical reasoning.
7. Techniques for decision making and the limitations of the human as a decision maker.

8. The nature of planning and its importance in problem solving.
9. Perceptual processes and imagery in tasks such as chess and mental arithmetic.
10. The function of mathematical notation in problem solving.

In the final section of the course, the students were asked to identify what, if anything, they had learned in the course that was applicable to their own area of special interest, and to report that learning in form of concrete instances. It was here that we hoped that both we and the students would learn in what respects the course was of practical use and in what respects if failed in its objectives. In general, the results were quite encouraging, as we will see below.

EVALUATION OF COURSE EFFECTIVENESS

To evaluate the effectiveness of a course of this sort is rather difficult since the students were working in a number of diverse directions. Nevertheless, by examining the student improvement projects and transfer reports, we can identify three general areas in which students report definite improvements in problem-solving skills.

1. Improvements due to increased awareness of own cognitive processes.
2. Improvements due to increased diagnostic skills.
3. Improvements in generalize problem solving skills.

One of the most influential aspects of increased awareness of own cognitive processes appeared to be the distinction between trial and error and other types of solution procedure. Four of the students commented independently that the distinction had clarified their thinking about problem solving. One, an electrical engineer said " . . . my self improvement project taught me that although it is not esthetically pleasing to me, trial and error solutions are sometimes more efficient. I have used this knowledge to more effectively solve problems in my fiance and marketing courses." Another electrical engineer commented " . . . I have always used hypothetical reasoning to some extent but never realized exactly what it was."

Three of the psychology students applied diagnostic skills they had learned in class to the process of analyzing case studies. Reading through a case study line by line, they recorded their current judgement as to what was important and what was not important as they proceded. Then, they read the case study again and recorded their importance judgements a second time. They used the difference between the first and second judgements as a clue to the determinants of their clinical judgements.

Improvements in problem solving due to generalized problem-solving skills appear in a number of forms. A psychology major used imagery techniques to improve her ability to memorize. Applying her skill to the game of concentration, she became good enough so that her friends refused to play with her. More practically she applied the technique to remembering appointments, shopping lists, learning the Greek alphabet.

Several students reported gains due to improvements in planning and organization. A physics student said, "Working problems in this course has helped me to work problems in physics, not because they are the same types of problems, which they are not, but because of the orderly methods I have developed as a result." A psychology student reported, "The first skill I was able to transfer was being able to clearly identify the problem. Later the same student said, "In both tasks, I set up the problem, pointed out what it was I was going to solve, and then in an organized manner found out the details that were essential to solve the problem." A math student reported, "Outside of math, I found planning good in writing papers for a history class. It was the first time I had ever been able to successfully use an outline to write a paper."

A chemistry student reported, "There were other ways of improving my labs through time management. For example, there was one U.V. spectrophotometer available for the third experiment and everyone had to use it. By doing the third experiment first, I was the only one on the machine and didn't have to wait in line." " . . . In this way, I finished up my set of experiments a week and a half ahead of everyone else."

Six students reported applications of knowledge about perceptual processes and imagery. A music major analyzed the structure of musical notation in relation to pattern recognition processes in reading music. A physics major improved his ability to visualize complex molecules in biochemistry. Several electrical engineers noted the close analogy between the recognition of patterns in chess and the recognition of patterns in analysis of circuit diagrams.

Three students reported that they had used decision making procedures discussed in class in practical application—one to choose an apartment, one to choose a graduate school, and one to identify the winner in a Miss America contest.

While results such as these are complex and incomplete, and probably contaminated by the fact that students often like to say encouraging things to their teachers, we are, nonetheless, encouraged that our course really did help the majority of our students both by increasing their knowledge of their problem solving-processes and by providing them with new problem solving skills.

In summary, the major themes in the chapters we have reviewed—establishment of cognitive objectives for instruction—direct training in cognitive skills—study of the assimilation of information to memory schemes—constitute important directions for the interaction of cognitive psychology with instruction. Clearly it will be many years before the details are worked out. When they are, however, both cognitive psychology and the science of instruction will be richer for it.

Part III

FUNDAMENTAL PROCESSES IN COMPREHENDING AND UNDERSTANDING INSTRUCTIONS

I must confess that a man is guilty of unpardonable arrogance who concludes, because an argument has escaped his own investigation, that therefore it does not really exist. I must also confess that, though all the learned, for several ages, should have employed themselves in fruitless search upon any subject, it may still, perhaps, be rash to conclude positively that the subject must therefore pass all human comprehension. Even though we examine all the sources of our knowledge and conclude them unfit for such a subject, there may still remain a suspicion that the enumeration is not complete or the examination not accurate [Hume, 1748/1955].

13
Verbal Comprehension in Instructional Situations

Marcel Adam Just
Patricia A. Carpenter

Carnegie-Mellon University

The main medium for the acquisition of knowledge is probably verbal comprehension. The central importance of comprehension skill is recognized by our educational institutions, and therefore comprehension is often used as a criterion skill for measuring achievement and aptitude. In this chapter, we will report on our investigation of one aspect of verbal comprehension, namely, the mental processes that underlie sentence comprehension. Our research focuses on the information a person extracts from a sentence, on the internal representation of that information, and on the mental operations that are applied to the representation. Our aim is to specify the parameters of the information-processing system in simple comprehension tasks. We will validate our theoretical proposals by accounting for response latencies in a task where people decide whether a sentence is true or false. Then we will examine verbal comprehension in a number of other tasks, showing how the same fundamental processes are common to these various situations.

This chapter consists of three sections. First, we will outline an information-processing model that accounts for response latencies in verifying simple and embedded affirmative and negative sentences in which the negative sentences contain the explicit negative, *not*. Second, we will show that the same model explains how people interpret simple instructions that contain implicitly negative lexical items like *except, different,* and *forget*. Third, we will examine two tasks that occur in educational tests of verbal comprehension—sentence completion and reading comprehension—in order to show how performance in these tasks can be analyzed within the same theoretical framework.

AN INFORMATION-PROCESSING MODEL
OF SENTENCE VERIFICATION

The Internal Representation

Understanding a sentence involves internally representing the information that the sentence contains. It is likely that the format of the internal representation is propositional, a relational structure consisting of a predicate and one or more arguments. We will use the conventional notation, (*PREDICATE, ARGUMENT*), to denote a proposition. In this notation part of the representation of a simple declarative sentence like *The dots are red* is (*RED, DOTS*), meaning redness is predicated of the dots. Since predications can be affirmed or negated, the entire representation of this affirmative sentence is (*AFF, (RED, DOTS*)). A negative sentence like *The dots aren't red* is represented as (*NEG, (RED, DOTS*)). *AFF* and *NEG* are embedding markers that denote the affirmative or negative polarity of the predication. This form of representation allows us to combine simple propositions to represent more complex sentences. For example, *It is fortunate that the dots are red* can be represented as (*FORTUNATE, P*), where *P* is the simple proposition (*AFF, (RED, DOTS*)).

The internal representation of a sentence is not necessarily linguistic in nature. The verbal symbols in these representations, for example, *DOTS,* are used to denote more abstract entities. In fact, research on sentence-picture verification suggests that there may be a level of representation that is neither linguistic nor pictorial in nature but can represent information from either domain (Chase & Clark, 1972; Clark & Chase, 1972). For example a picture of red dots may be represented (*RED, DOTS*).

The detailed form of the representation of various kinds of sentences has not yet been empirically verified. For example, the research on the linguistic factors that determine the psychological predicate-argument structure has only begun (cf. Halliday, 1967; Hornby, 1972). Moreover, there are cases where various representations are formally equivalent and the selection of one particular form is really arbitrary. Nevertheless, this conventional notation is sufficient for the current model and promises to be flexible enough to accommodate a variety of linguistic structures (cf. Kintsch, 1972).

The same sentence may be represented differently in different situations. This follows from the assumption that the representation contains the information that a person extracts from a sentence. What information is extracted depends on the preceding sentences, the situation in which the sentence is embedded, and the listener's previous knowledge. The role that context plays in how a sentence is represented suggests an important distinction between the psychological notion of an internal representation and the traditional linguistic notion of deep structure.

The Task

We have recently proposed a model to account for the mental processes underlying the verification of affirmative and negative sentences (Carpenter & Just, 1975). The situation that originally gave rise to the model is a simple task in which a person must decide whether a sentence is true or false of a picture. For example, Just and Carpenter (1971) presented sentences like *The dots are red* or *The dots aren't red,* as well as pictures of red dots or of black dots. Thus, the sentences could be affirmative or negative, and true or false. A person was first shown the picture, and then timed as he or she read the sentence and decided whether it was true or false. The results of this study showed that it took longer to verify negative sentences than affirmative sentences by a certain amount of time, called *negation time.* In this particular study, the negation time was a little more than two-fifths of a second. The study also showed that affirmative sentences were verified faster when they were true than when they were false, while negative sentences were verified faster when they were false. The difference in verification time between the true and false sentence was opposite in sign but equal in magnitude for affirmative and negative sentences. This time, called *falsification time,* was a little more than one fifth of a second in this study. These two results, the latency advantage of affirmative sentences, as well as the interaction between affirmative—negative and true—false, were also found in a number of previous studies (Chase & Clark, 1972; Clark & Chase, 1972; Gough, 1965, 1966; McMahon, 1963; Trabasso, Rollins, & Shaughnessy, 1971; Wason & Jones, 1963).

The Mental Operations

In this section we will outline a model that accurately predicts the verification times for these simple affirmative and negative sentences. We will show that it also accounts for the verification of embedded sentences. Moreover, the main features of the model will serve as a basis for our examination of comprehension processes in instructional situations.

The main focus of the model is on the operations that compare the sentence and picture representations. The model postulates that the corresponding constituents from the two representations are retrieved and compared, pair by pair. Moreover, the number of these retrieve and compare operations is assumed to be the primary determinant of the pattern of verification times. Figure 1 shows a flow chart for the proposed process. The propositional structure of the representations provides an ordering relation on the constituents. This ordering determines the sequence in which constituents are compared. Inner propositions are compared before polarity markers. An *AFF* marker in a sentence representation is assumed to match the absence of a marker in the picture representation, since

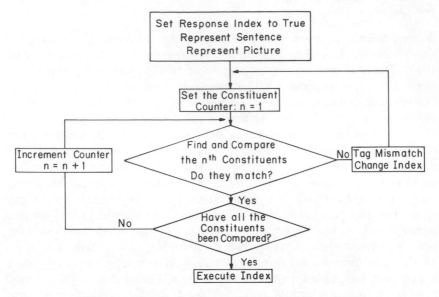

FIG. 1 A flow chart of the constituent comparison model.

pictures are generally encoded affirmatively. The "find and compare" process is a serial, iterative operation that can be applied to representations with multiple embeddings. This iterative operation will allow the model to be generalized without additional assumptions.

The central assumption is that whenever two corresponding constituents from the sentence and picture representations mismatch, then the entire comparison process is reinitiated. To prevent the process from looping forever on mismatching constituents, we assume that the first time a mismatch is discovered, the two constituents involved are tagged, so that on subsequent recomparisons the two will be treated as a match.

Since mismatches cause the comparison process to be reinitiated, the total number of comparison operations, and consequently the total latency, increases with the number of mismatches. Moreover, a mismatch that occurs later in the comparison process results in more recomparisons than a mismatch on earlier constituents. Thus, the total latency is a function of both the number of mismatches and their locus in their respective representations.

A response index records the matches and mismatches between constituents. The index has two possible states, *true* and *false*. At the beginning of each trial, its initial state is *true*, and each mismatch causes it to change its state. The time spent in changing the response index (and tagging mismatching constituents) is assumed to be negligible relative to the time to perform the find and compare operation.

TABLE 1
Representations and Predictions for the
Four Information Conditions[a]

	True affirmative	False affirmative
Sentence:	The dots are red.	The dots are red.
Picture:	Red dots	Black dots
Sentence representation:	(AFF, (RED, DOTS))	(AFF, (RED, DOTS))
Picture representation:	(RED, DOTS)	(BLACK, DOTS)
	+ +	− index = false
	response = true	+ +
	k comparisons	response = false
		$k + 1$ comparisons

	False Negative	True Negative
Sentence:	The dots aren't red.	The dots aren't red.
Picture:	Red dots	Black dots
Sentence representation:	(NEG, (RED, DOTS))	(NEG, (RED, DOTS))
Picture representation:	(RED, DOTS)	(BLACK, DOTS)
	− + index = false	− index = false
	+ +	− + index = true
	response = false	+ +
	$k + 2$ comparisons	response = true

[a]Plus and minus signs denote matches and mismatches of the corresponding constituents. Each horizontal line of plus and minus signs indicates a reinitiation of the comparison process.

When the model is applied to the proposed sentence and picture representations in the Just and Carpenter experiment, it can account for the latencies in the four conditions. In the simplest case, the true affirmative, there are no mismatches between the sentence and picture representations, as shown in Table 1. The first comparison, between the inner propositions, results in a match. The second comparison, between polarity markers, also results in a match (Recall that *AFF* marker in the sentence representation is presumed to match the absence of any polarity marker in the picture representation). Thus after a total of two constituent comparisons, the truth index is still set to *true,* and this response is executed. The number of constituent comparisons in the true affirmative case serves as the base line for the other conditions, and will be referred to as k. Here, k equals 2.

In the false affirmative condition, the inner propositions of the sentence and picture mismatch. The mismatch will reinitiate the comparison process, causing one extra comparison above the base number. Table 2 shows the consequences of this mismatch in detail. The mismatching constituents are tagged and the

TABLE 2
A Trace of the Operations in Verifying a False Affirmative

| | Stimulus sentence: *The dots are red.* |
| | Stimulus picture: A set of black dots |

Operations	
Initialize response index to *true*	
Represent sentence	(AFF, (RED, DOTS))
Represent picture	(BLACK, DOTS)
1. Compare first constituents	
Tag sentence constituent	(AFF, (M))
Tag picture constituent	(M)
Change index to *false*	
Reinitialize comparison process	
2. Compare first constituents	+
3. Compare second constituents	+
Respond with content of index	*False*
Number of comparisons	$k + 1$, where $k = 2$

response index is set to *false*. After the reinitiation, the tagged inner constituents are compared, and they match. The next comparison, between the polarity markers, also results in a match. So, the response *false* is executed after a total of $k + 1$ constituent comparisons.

In the false negative condition, there will be a total of $k + 2$ comparisons, due to the mismatch on the second constituent, the polarity markers. This mismatch will cause the response *false* to be executed. For the true negative condition, both the first and the second constituents mismatch, so that the response *true* will be executed after a total of $k + 3$ constituent comparisons. Both of these cases are summarized in the bottom half of Table 1.

The model postulates that verification latencies should be a direct function of the number of constituent comparisons. The number of comparisons, and hence the latency, should increase linearly from true affirmative (k), to false affirmatives $(k + 1)$, to false negatives $(k + 2)$, to true negatives $(k + 3)$.

The results of the experiment, as well as the best fitting straight line, are shown in Fig. 2. The predictions of the model fit the data quite well. The model accounts for 98.0% of the variance among the four means. The slope is 215 msec per constituent comparison.

Only one parameter, the time to find and compare a pair of constituents, is necessary to characterize the processing in these four conditions. Elsewhere (Carpenter & Just, 1975), we have tested the detailed predictions of the model and shown that it can also account for the latencies in many other similar

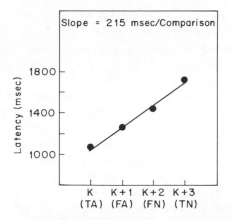

FIG. 2 The fit of the constituent comparison model for the four information conditions. (Data from Just & Carpenter, 1971, Exp. II).

experiments (i.e., Clark & Chase, Expts. I, II, & III, 1972; Gough, 1965, 1966, Expt. II; McMahon, 1963, Trabasso *et al.*, Expt. IX, 1971). Thus, the current model provides a parsimonious explanation of performance in these tasks. Although parsimony is desirable, the model should be evaluated on the basis of its ability to offer a rigorous formulation that is both a plausible mental process and can incorporate a wide variety of empirical results. This ability will be demonstrated in each of the following sections. The nature of the propositional representation, particularly the embedding feature, should allow the model to be generalized to more complex sentences without additional modifications. This property of the model was tested by examining embedded affirmative and negative sentences.

A Test of the Model

To further test the model, the scope of the negative was systematically varied. Other factors, like the sentence length and the picture, were kept constant. The scope of a negative is defined as the range of constituents to which it applies (Jackendoff, 1969; Klima, 1964). The affirmative sentences used in the experiment included the superordinate clause *It is true that* . . . (e.g., *It is true that the dots are red*) and could be negated in two ways. With one type of negation, the negative has a small scope, namely the inner predication: *It is true that the dots aren't red.* This will be called predicate negation. The second type of negation has a larger scope since the negative is in the superordinate clause where it applies to the entire inner proposition: *It isn't true that the dots are red.* This type of negation will be called denial. Denials should take longer to process than predicate negatives because the mismatch will occur on a constituent that is compared later. The exact predictions can be derived by examining the hypothesized representations for these sentence types and their interaction with the comparison process.

The representation of an affirmative sentence like *It's true that the dots are red* may be the same as for the simple sentence *The dots are red*, namely, *(AFF, (RED, DOTS))*. The rationale is that the embedding clause *It's true . . .* does not change the truth value and so it can be ignored. To demonstrate this point, consider a concatenation of this type of clause, e.g., *It's true that it's true that it's true . . . the dots are red*. The number of such embedding clauses is irrelevant to the truth value of the proposition. Similarly, the embedding affirmative proposition may be deleted from the representation of a predicate negative sentence like *It's true that the dots aren't red,* so that the representation would be *(NEG, (RED, DOTS))*. However, the representation of a denial like *It isn't true that the dots are red,* must include the negative embedded clause. Here the embedding clause does affect the truth value of the sentence. Thus, denial sentences might be represented like *(NEG, (AFF, (RED, DOTS)))*. The pictures would be represented as simple propositions like *(RED, DOTS)* or *(BLACK, DOTS)*. Table 3 shows examples of the representations in the six conditions.

The experiment was verification task in which the person was timed while he read a sentence, looked at a picture, and then decided whether the sentence was true or false of the picture. There were 24 subjects.

The predicitions of the model can be derived by examining the flow chart model in Fig. 1 and the representations in Table 3. The predicted number of operations necessary to verify a true affirmative is k; for a false affirmative it is $k + 1$; for a false predicate negative it is $k + 2$; for a true predicate negative it is $k + 3$; for a false denial it is $k + 4$; and for a true denial it is $k + 5$. The verification latencies should increase linearly with the proposed number of operations. A linear increase in latencies among these six conditions will constitute strong support for the constituent comparison model and the notion of a single underlying iterative operation.

The results showed that, as predicted, the mean latencies increased linearly with the number of hypothesized constituent comparisons. More precisely, latencies increased an average of 200 msec for each additional constituent comparison (Standard Error = 23 msec). Figure 3 shows this result, along with the best fitting straight line. The model accounts for 97.7% of the variance among the six means, $F(1, 115) = 171.17$, $p > .01$. The residual 2.3% is not significant, $F(4, 115) = 1.01$. The root mean squared deviation (RMSD) of 52 msec is small relative to the 200 msec parameter. This analysis confirms the major hypothesis that verification time increases linearly with the number of constituent comparisons.

The error rates for the six conditions were correlated with the latencies ($r = .98$), as is shown in Fig. 3. This correlation indicates that the probability of error

TABLE 3
Representations and Predictions for the Six Information Conditions[a]

	True affirmative	False affirmative
Sentence:	It's true that the dots are red.	It's true that the dots are red.
Picture:	Red dots	Black dots
Sentence representation:	(AFF, (RED, DOTS))	(AFF, (RED, DOTS))
Picture representation:	(RED, DOTS)	(BLACK, DOTS)
	+ +	− index = false
	response = true	+ +
	k comparisons	response = false
		$k + 1$ comparisons

	False predicate negative	True predicate negative
Sentence:	It's true that the dots aren't red.	It's true that the dots aren't red.
Picture:	Red dots	Black dots
Sentence representation:	(NEG, (RED, DOTS))	(NEG, (RED, DOTS))
Picture representation:	(RED, DOTS)	(BLACK, DOTS)
	− + index = false	− index = false
	+ +	− + index = true
	response = false	+ +
	$k + 2$ comparison	response = true
		$k +$ comparisons

	False denial	True denial
Sentence:	It isn't true that the dots are red.	It isn't true that the dots are red.
Picture:	Red dots	Black dots
Sentence representation:	(NEG, (AFF, (RED, DOTS)))	(NEG, (AFF, (RED, DOTS))
Picture representation:	(RED, DOTS)	(BLACK, DOTS)
	− + + index = false	− index = false
	+ + +	− + + index = true
	response = false	+ + +
	$k + 4$ comparisons	response = true
		$k + 5$ comparisons

[a]Plus and minus signs denote matches and mismatches of the corresponding constituents. Each horizontal line of plus and minus signs indicates a reinitiation of the comparison process.

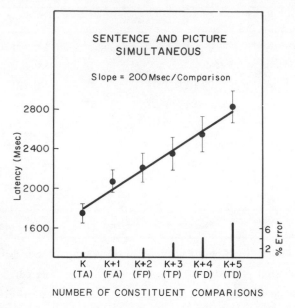

FIG. 3 The fit of the constituent comparison model for the six information conditions.

increases with the number of hypothesized operations. This suggests that the probabilities of error in the comparisons are additive.

The model is able to predict the processing time for these six conditions on the basis of a single parameter: the time to find and compare a pair of constituents. These results strongly support the hypothesis that a single iterative operation accounts for the processing of affirmative and negative sentences. The embedded representation, combined with the iterative comparison operation, allow the model to account for the two scopes of negation without additional assumptions.

A further control study showed that the representation and processing of the sentence is determined by its semantics, rather than by its surface structure. To show this, we compared the processing of sentences that had the same constituent structure but different surface structures. In this control study, the inner propositions of the sentences were embedded in two ways: the same way as the previous experiment (e.g., *It's true that the dots aren't red*) and with the embedding clause at the end of the sentence (e.g., *That the dots aren't red is true*). Both of these kinds of sentences are postulated to have the same constituent structure. However, the position of the negative in the surface structure has been changed. If the results of the basic experiment can be replicated with the new sentences, then the results cannot be due to position of the negative morpheme in the surface structure. The new stimulus sentences were: Affirmative—*That the dots are red is true;* Predicate negative—*That the dots aren't red is true;* and Denial—*That the dots are red isn't true.*

This control study showed the two types of surface structures were processed similarly. Both types of sentences showed a linear increase in latency as the number of comparisons increased. Regardless of whether the negative morpheme occurred near the beginning or end of the sentence, denials took about 500 msec longer to verify than predicate negatives. This result shows that the underlying constituent structure rather than order of negatives in the surface structure determines processing time, and constitutes further support for the proposed representations for the two kinds of negative sentences.

The mental processes described by this model are not specific to the sentence-verification paradigm, but occur in a large number of situations that involve verbal comprehension. These more general processes involve relating the information from a sentence to information from a second source, such as the listener's previous knowledge of the world. For example, in order to agree or disagree with a statement, it is necessary to compare the statement to a representation of one's own belief. In order to answer a *Wh* question (e.g., *Who painted the fence*), the information provided in the question (e.g., that someone painted the fence) must be compared to previous knowledge before the interrogated constituent can be retrieved. In order to acquire new information through a verbal medium, the old information in the communication will serve as a basis to which the new information is added. The determination of which information is old can only be made if the sentence representation is compared to previous knowledge. In the next section of this chapter, we will show that these comparison operations also occur when we follow simple instruction. Thus, the basic kinds of operations described by the model are part of a large class of comparison operations that occur very commonly when we comprehend linguistic material.

The mental operations described by the model are not specific to the processing of explicitly negative sentences, but rather they occur in the processing of a variety of semantic structures. Elsewhere, we have shown how the model accounts for semantic structures such as negative quantifiers like *few*, particular and universal quantifiers like *some* and *all* (Just, 1974), counterfactual clauses like *Mary would have left* . . . (Carpenter, 1973), and active and passive sentences like *The car hit the truck* and *The truck was hit by the car* (cf. Carpenter & Just, 1975). Next we will show how the model also accounts for the processing of instructions that contain implicitly negative predicates.

COMPREHENDING IMPLICITLY NEGATIVE INSTRUCTIONS

A number of predicates like *forget, thoughtless, disagree,* and *absent* are considered implicitly negative (cf. Clark, in press; Just & Carpenter, 1971; Klima, 1964). For example, we may define *forgot* as *didn't remember* or we may think of *absent* as *not present,* and so on. By contrast, we do not generally think of *remembered* as *didn't forget.* This suggests that there may be an asymmetry in how we internally represent pairs of lexical items like *remember* and *forget;* an implicitly negative item like *forget* may be internally represented as a negation of *remember.* This hypothesis can be tested by examing the data from a number of comprehension studies that have used such implicitly negative predicates. Two types of studies provide relevant data. The first type involves sentence verification tasks where the stimuli contained implicitly negative predicates. In the second type of study, the implicit negatives were in the instructions given to the subject. If predicates like *forget* are represented as negatives, then their processing should conform to the constituent comparison model.

Remember—Forget

The implicitly negative predicate *forget to* presents an interesting opportunity for examining the comprehension of negation. Not only is this predicate negative, but the proposition embedded in it is also negative. For example, the sentence *John forgot to let the dog out* directly implies that John did not let the dog out (Karttunen, 1971). Thus one can study how people extract information from the implications of implicitly negative predicates. In a study by Just and Clark (1973, Expt. II), subjects were presented with an affirmative sentence (*John remembered to let the dog out*) or an implicitly negative one (*John forgot to let the dog out*) and then were timed as they verified the probe sentence (e.g., *The dog is in*) as true or false of the implication of the parent sentence. The relevant information from a sentence like *John forgot to let the dog out* is that the dog is not out. This may have been represented as (*NEG, (OUT, DOG)*). The information from a sentence with *remembered to* would be represented as (*AFF, (OUT, DOG)*). This sentence representation would be compared to a representation of the probe, like *The dog is in,* represented (*AFF, (IN, DOG)*). The model predicts that verification latencies should increase linearly from true—*remembered,* to false—*remembered,* to false—*forgot,* to true—*forgot.* The data conform very nicely to predictions of the model, which accounts for 94.6% of the variance among the four conditions, as shown in Table 4. This result shows that the implications in implicit negatives are processed similarly to explicitly negative sentences.

Present—Absent

A similar kind of verification task provides evidence that indicates *absent* is internally represented as a negation of *present.* Sentences like *The star is present* or *The star is absent* were verified against pictures that either contained a star (*) or a plus (+), Clark (in press). If *absent* is internally represented as a negative, then a sentence like *The star is absent* might be represented as *(NEG, (PRESENT, STAR)).* This representation would be compared to the representation of the picture, either *(PRESENT, STAR)* or *(PRESENT, PLUS),* in this experiment. These representations can be used to generate the predictions of the

TABLE 4

Observed (and estimated) Latencies for Executing Affirmative and Implicitly Negative Instruction

Reference	Example of implicitly negative instruction	Variance accounted for by model (%)	Time per comparison (msec)	Number of constituent comparisons			
				k TA	$k+1$ FA	$k+2$ FN	$k+3$ TN
remember–forget (Just & Clark, 1973)	If John forgot to let the dog in, then the dog is out, T or F?	95.0	285	2814 (2890)	3252 (3175)	3536 (3461)	3670 (3746)
present–absent (Clark, in press)	The star is absent, T or F?	94.8	169	1463 (1506)	1749 (1675)	1823 (1844)	2002 (2013)
same–different (Seymour, 1969)	Are the word and shape different, Y or N?	98.8	82	678 (667)	736 (749)	824 (831)	922 (913)
agree–conflict (Trabasso et al, 1971)	Does the color name conflict with the color patch, Y or N?	99.4	108	828 (836)	959 (944)	1046 (1052)	1159 (1160)
synonymous–unrelated (Clark, in press)	Are the two words unrelated, Y or N?	99.8	145	1117 (1121)	1266 (1266)	1423 (1410)	1547 (1555)

model. The latencies should increase linearly from true–*present,* to false–*present,* to false–*absent,* to true–*absent.* As Table 4 shows, the model accounts for 94.8% of the varience among the four means, with an estimated 169 msec per constituent comparison. Thus, the results support the hypothesis that in this task, *absent* is interpreted as an implicit negative. Moreover, the quantitative relations among the four latencies support the idea that there is a serial retrieval and comparison of constituents from the internal representations of the sentence and picture.

The next several experiments are tasks in which the instructions contained implicit negatives. We will show that the comparison process postulated by the model for sentence verification also explains how people understand and execute simple instructions.

Same–Different

One experiment that used negative instructions involved comparing a word (either the word *circle* or *square*) to a picture (of either a circle or a square) (Seymour, 1969). One group of subjects was given an affirmative instruction; they were asked to respond "yes" if the word and the picture had the same meaning and to respond "no" otherwise. Another group of subjects was given a negative instruction: respond "yes" if the word and picture are different, and "no" otherwise. The instruction involving the predicate *different* may have been represented with a negative: respond "yes" if the picture is *not* the same as the word–*(NEG, (IS,X)),* where the symbol X takes the value denoted by the word. For example, when the word was *circle,* it would be coded into the instruction as *(NEG, (IS, CIRCLE)).* Then, this representation would be compared to the picture representation. If the picture was a square, the comparison between the representation of the instruction and the representation of the picture, *(IS, SQUARE),* would result in a "yes" response. If the instruction were compared to a picture of a circle, the comparison would result in a "no" response. Each time an instruction with *different* is executed, the subject is essentially processing a negative construction. Therefore, the model predicts that latencies should increase linearly from "yes"–*same,* to "no"–*same,* to "no"–*different,* to "yes"–*different.* As Table 4 shows, the model accounts for 98.8% of the variance among the four means, with a slope of 82 msec per constituent comparison. This supports the hypothesis the *different* is internally represented as an implicit negative. Moreover, the results show that the mental processes involved in executing instructions can be explained by the model for sentence verification.

Agree–Conflict

A very similar experiment by Trabasso *et al.* (Expt. X, 1971) can be analyzed to test whether the predicate *conflict* is internally represented as a negative. The task was to compare a word (either *orange* or *green*) to a picture that was colored either orange or green. One group of subjects was given an affirmative instruction: judge whether or not the word and the picture agree. Another group was given an implicitly negative instruction: judge whether or not the word and picture conflict. The instruction involving *conflict* might be represented as *(NEG, (IS, X))*, where the symbol *X* would take the value of the color word presented during the trial. For example, suppose the word orange were presented; it would be coded into the instruction as *(NEG, (IS, ORANGE))* and then compared to the picture. If the picture were colored green, the comparison between the representation of the instruction and the representation of the picture, *(IS, GREEN)*, would result in a response of "yes." If the instruction were compared to an orange picture, it would result in a response of "no." These representations lead to the prediction that the latencies should increase linearly from "yes"–*agree*, to "no"–*agree*, to "no"–*conflict*, to "yes"–*conflict*. As Table 4 shows, the model accounts for 99.4% of the variance among the four means, with an estimate of 109 msec per constituent comparison. This supports the hypothesis that the processes involved in following simple instructions with *agree* and *conflict* are the operations of representing, retrieving, and comparing constituents.

Synonymous–Unrelated

The lexical item *unrelated* may also be represented as an implicit negative. To test this hypothesis, Hayden and Clark asked people to judge the semantic relation between two words that had the same meaning (e.g., *large* and *big*) or different meanings (e.g., *large* and *tidy*) (reported by Clark, in press). One group of subjects was given an affirmative instruction: judge whether or not the two words are synonymous. Another group was given an implicitly negative instruction: judge whether or not the two words are unrelated. The instruction with *unrelated* may have been represented like the implicit negatives *different* and *conflict: (NEG, (MEANS, X))*, where *X* takes on the value of one of the two words presented in a trial. For example, suppose the pair *(large–tidy)* were presented. The first word might be coded into the instruction, *(NEG, (MEANS, LARGE))*. The second word would be coded as *(MEANS, TIDY)* and then compared to the representation of the instruction. In this case, the response would be "yes." If the second word were *big*, the response would have been "no." The model predicts that latencies should increase linearly from "yes"–*synonymous*, to "no"–*synonymous*, to "no"–*unrelated*, to "yes"–*unrelated*. As Table 4 shows, the model accounts for 99.8% of the variance among the means, with an estimate of 145 msec per constituent comparison. This supports the hypothesis that *unrelated* is represented and executed as a negative instruction. As in the cases of *different* and *conflict*, the negative item *unrelated* takes longer to execute and causes the "yes" response to take longer than the "no" response.

Except

In a very different kind of task, Jones (1966a, b, 1968) examined how people execute instructions that contain the implicitly negative word *except*. In these tasks, people would read an affirmative instruction like "Cross out the numbers 1, 3, 4, 6, 7," or a negative instruction like "Cross out all the numbers except 2, 5, 8." Then they were given a sheet that was filled with digits 1 to 8 in random order and timed while they performed the task. The two instructions require the same overt responses; but if *except* is a negative, the two instructions will cause very different mental operations. We hypothesized that the instruction with *except* is represented as: *(NEG, (IS, 2 or 5 or 8))*. Each digit encountered on the page would be represented *(IS, X)*, where *X* takes the value of the digit. The digit will be crossed out if there are two mismatches between the two representations. This would happen if *X* took the value 7, for example. By contrast, the affirmative instruction would be represented *(AFF, (IS, 1 or 3 or 4 or 6 or 7))*. Each digit encountered on the page would be represented as *(IS, X)* so the digit would be crossed out if there were no mismatches. The negative instruction took a significant 13 sec longer to execute, and resulted in significantly more false positive errors (crossing out digits that weren't supposed to be crossed out).

In a second experiment, Jones equated the number of digits to be represented in an instruction. The positive instruction was "cross out the digits 3, 4, 7, 8." The negative instruction was to "cross out all members except 1, 2, 5, 6." Again, the negative instruction took much longer to execute (by 100 sec) and resulted in more false positive errors. Thus, executing a negative instruction, even in a very different kind of task, takes significantly longer than executing the equivalent affirmative one. This is consistent with the hypothesis that mismatches between the internal representation of an instruction and the representation of some second source of information, will lead to longer latencies.

The preceding analysis makes it clear that certain single words are internally represented by two components—an affirmative core as well as a negative component. While we cannot specify a priori whether or not a word is internally represented as a negative, our model does provide a procedure to discriminate negative lexical items from affirmative items. If the verification latencies for a suspect word are shorter for false than for true, then we infer that word is being represented and processed as a negative in that situation. Thus, the results cited above show that *forget, different, unrelated, conflict,* and *except* are represented as negatives. The same kind of analysis can also exonerate suspect words. For example, *small* is not processed as a negation of *large;* it is represented as an affirmative (Carpenter & Just, 1972; Just & Carpenter, 1971).

Other Instructional Examples

Comprehending an instruction can be a major source of difficulty in performing an everyday task. We sometimes encounter complex instructions where there is no conceivable pupose for their complexity. The following notice from the Internal Revenue Service (Form 4918) provides an example (italics added):

ANY QUESTIONS ABOUT THIS NOTICE?

In the event we *failed* to give you credit for a Federal tax deposit or any other payment you made, please accept our apology and be guided by the following:

1. If the payment *not* credited was made within the last four weeks or so, we will credit it soon. You need *not* write us. Just subtract the payment we *haven't* included.

2. If the payment *not* credited was made more than four weeks ago, subtract it from the balance due . . .

3. If you have paid the entire balance due within the last four weeks, please *disregard* this notice.

Please send us an explanation if the balance is *incorrect* for any reasons *other than* payments we *haven't* credited.

Explanation of Penalty or Interest Charges

Your return was *not* filed and your tax was *not* paid by the due date. The combined penalty is 5 percent of the tax *not* timely paid for each month of part of a month the return was late, *but not* more than 25 percent.

This notice is *not* the result of an audit of your return. When we select a return for audit, we notify the taxpayer.

Presumably the IRS is not interested in testing our comprehension skills.

In other situations, the purpose of a complex instruction is precisely to assess comprehension skills, as illustrated by the following item (Personnel Test, Form D., E. F. Wonderlic, 1922):

Count each Z in this series that is followed by an F next to it if the F is not followed by an S next to it. Tell how many Z's you count.

ZFZSEYZFSYFZFFSYSZFEZFSFZYFZFY

This is an extremely easy task if one comprehends the instruction, which could have been simplified as follows: *Count the occurrences of the sequence (/Z/, /F/, /non-S/) in this series.*

There are other situations where the purpose of complex instructions is not clear. The following example is taken from an aptitude test for prospective students of management science (Graduate Study in Management: A Guide for Prospective Students, 1974)

Directions: Each of the data sufficiency problems below consists of a question and two statements, labeled (1) and (2), in which certain data are given. You have to decide whether the data given in the statements are sufficient for answering the questions. You are to blacken space

A. if statement (1) ALONE is sufficient, but statement (2) alone is not sufficient to answer the question asked;

B. if statement (2) ALONE is sufficient, but statement (1) alone is not sufficient to answer the question asked;

C. if BOTH statements (1) and (2) TOGETHER are sufficient to answer the question asked, but NEITHER statement ALONE is sufficient;

D. if EACH statement ALONE is sufficient to answer the question asked;

E. if statements (1) and (2) TOGETHER are NOT sufficient to answer the question
   asked, and additional data specific to the problem are needed.

Example: In $\triangle PQR$, what is the value of x?
   (1) $PQ = PR$
   (2) $y = 40$

Answer: C

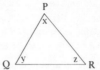

This kind of instruction seems to be testing both the ability to comprehend
instructions, as well as knowledge of geometry and logic. Incorrect answers
could be caused by any of these three sources. The relative contribution of
comprehension difficulties can be assessed by rewriting these instructions in a
simplified format.

Revised Directions: Answer *YES* or *NO* to each of the following questions.
   In $\triangle PDR$, can you deternine the value of x if all you know is that:
   (1) $PQ = PR$? (Answer is *NO*)
   (2) $y = 40$? (Answer is *NO*)
   (3) $PQ = PR$ and $y = 40$? (Answer is *YES*)

These examples illustrate how successful performance in a test may depend on
comprehension skills in decoding the instruction, as well as the content skills
that the test ostensibly taps. Thus, both components may enter into the test
scores that can often predict future academic performance. It may turn out that
the predictive ability of the test is partially due to the comprehension skills it
taps, rather than the content skills. If the test is being used only for actuarial
purposes, the relative loadings of the two factors are irrelevant. However, if the
testing is for diagnostic purposes, then it it necessary to assess the relative
contribution of comprehension skills before remedial action can be taken (cf.
Hunt, Frost, & Lunneborg, 1973). This may prove to be a fruitful approach to
test construction.

In many situations, the primary purpose of an instruction is to inform, to help
people perform correctly and efficiently. For example, instructions on income-
tax forms or in repair manuals should be constructed to minimize comprehension difficulties. A theory of sentence comprehension such as we have outlined
suggests the kinds of problems that may arise in representing and executing
various kinds of instructions. The theoretical approach also suggests ways of
making everyday instructions easier to comprehend.

EDUCATIONAL TESTS OF VERBAL COMPREHENSION

Sentence-Completion Tasks

Another domain in which we can apply our information processing analysis is
the sentence-completion task, which often appears in tests of academic achieve-

ment or ability. This task involves choosing one of several alternatives that "best" completes a sentence frame. Consider the following example:

Beauty is only skin-deep, but ___ goes all the way to the bone.
a. disease   b. blood   c. ugliness   d. fright   e. liniment
(Answer: c)

Although performance in this task depends to some extent upon an adequate vocabulary, much of the processing can be explained in terms of the processes described by the comprehension model.

Many of the items in a sentence-completion test have structures that are basically like the example above. These items consist of two parallel clauses of the same syntactic type, although there may be a negative lurking in one of them. The missing item is a constituent of one of the clauses. The connective between the two clauses is either affirmative (e.g., *and*) or negative (e.g., *but*). The polarity of the connective, as well as the presence of a negative in one of the clauses, determines whether the missing item should be an antonym or synonym of the corresponding constituent in other clause. In the example above, the negative connective *but* is a cue that the answer is an antonym of *beauty*.

A number of examples will give the flavor of the kinds of sentence completion items that involve negative connectives, like *yet, but, unlike, whereas,* and *although* (taken from a booklet, *Preparation for college board examinations* by Henry Regnery Co., 1972, pp. 107–126):

Unlike his cousin, the artist, who was colorful, whimsical, and erratic, the teacher was prosaic, _____ , and consistent.

a. infallible   b. commonplace   c. objective   d. disorganized   e. subtle

Though he was romantic and sensual in his outlook, his life was one of ___.

a. profligacy   b. naivete   c. austerity   d. virtuousity   e. maturity

These conditions are not ___ the nature of women but have grown up in spite of it.

a. intrinsic to   b. paramount in   c. compelling in   d. immutable in   e. extrinsic in

Early in the 19th century, in the South, it had become the fashion to raise only one staple crop, whereas in the North the crops were ___.

a. diversified   b. unstable   c. fallow   d. uniform   e. wild

In this game he was an amateur, not an expert, and thus, for the first time, became a(n) ___ instead of a man of action.

a. connoisseur   b. spectator   c. lawyer   d. pragmatist   e. authority

Linguistic analyses of the clausal conjunction *but* show that it involves incongruence between the two clauses. For example, *but* may be used if there is a lexical contrast between the two clauses, e.g., *Mary likes school but John hates it.* A second use of *but* involves a contrast between what is stated and what the speaker believes to be the usual connection between the two clauses, e.g., *Bill is a politician but he's honest* or *Dick is a veterinarian but he doesn't like dogs* (cf. Lakoff, 1971; Gleitman, 1969; Dik, 1968). Other connectives like *instead, although, in spite of, however,* and *yet* conjoin similar kinds of contrasting clauses.

In an experimental investigation of the completion task, Osgood and Richards (1973) asked subjects to complete sentences like *X is beautiful ___ dumb* or *X is old ___ slow,* with *and* or *but.* The two adjectives in the sentence either had the same or opposite affective polarity, which was determined a priori with the semantic differential. As the linguistic analysis would predict, incongruence between the two lexical items was a more favorable environment for *but,* whereas congruence was a more favorable environment for *and.*

The comparison model suggests the processes that might underlie performance in this completion task. First the sentence is parsed into two parallel clauses. Then the constituents of the clauses, including the coordinate conjunction and polarity markers, are checked serially for their polarity. The number of negatives determines whether it is a synonym or antonym of the provided constituent that is output as a response.

This model of processing can be tested with data collected during the sentence completion task. Hoosain (1973) measured latencies while people completed sentences like those in the Osgood and Richard's task, and he also varied the number of explicit negatives in the sentence. For example, a sentence could involve adjectives of similar affective polarity (e.g., *Eve was mild___nice*) or opposite affective polarity (e.g., *Carl was troubled___happy*), and could contain either no negatives at all, one negative (e.g., *Eve was mild___not nice*) or two negatives (e.g., *Eve was not mild___not nice*).

As might be expected, latencies increased as the number of negatives in the sentence increased from zero to one to two. Furthermore, latencies were shorter when the two adjectives were congruent in affective polarity. This difference was not affected by other factors, such as the number of extra operations caused by the presence of additional negatives. The results are completely consistent with a process that serially checks the constituents of the sentence. The presence of a negative results in a mismatch between the sentence representation and the affirmative frame with which it is compared. Such mismatches cause extra operations, whose durations are additive. Thus, the basic processes involved in this sentence-completion task are quite similar to the ones involved in comprehending and verifying sentences, although the control structures may be different for the two tasks. Processes in both tasks involve serially examining the constituents of representations, encountering mismatches, and consequently performing additional mental operations. This analysis has attempted to show that performance on a common item from a test of verbal skills can be analyzed in terms of underlying mental operations found in other comprehension tasks.

Potential Applications: The Reading Comprehension Test

In this section, we will try to outline the kinds of representations, retrieval and comparison operations in another task involving verbal comprehension: the reading comprehension test. This task is much more complex than the other ones that we have analyzed. The reading comprehension test involves reading a passage, usually 150-500 words long, and then answering 8 to 12 multiple-choice questions about the passage. The instructions are to first skim the passage then read the questions and return to the passage for information when it is necessary. The time allotted to read the passage and answer all the questions is usually 5 to 15 minutes. We studied this task by having three subjects express their strategies and thoughts aloud while they performed several reading comprehension tests. Thus, this section represents a potential extension of the general approach, rather than an empirically confirmed model.

During the initial reading of the paragraph, the theme or central proposition of the passage is generally extracted and represented. Our subjects indicated they had represented the thematic information by their ability to answer the questions about the theme without looking back at the passage. In other studies, it has been shown that if subjects are kept from knowing the theme, both comprehension and memory for the passage suffers (Bransford & Johnson, 1973; Dooling & Lachman, 1971). Also, when recognition memory for individual sentences in a passage is tested, there is a much higher false-alarm rate for distractor sentences that contain the theme (Singer & Rosenberg, 1973). (See also Hyman, Chapter 8, this volume). These results indicate that the thematic information plays a central role in the representation of the passage.

The initial representation of the passage also contains information about higher-order relations that exist between the thematic proposition and subsidiary propositions. These are relations such as causality and temporal order of events, which are sometimes cued by words like *because, consequently, after, before,* and so on. The representation of individual propositions linked by higher-order relations can be accommodated by a number of representational schemes (cf. Crothers, 1972; Kintsch, 1972; Rumelhart, Lindsay & Norman, 1972; Schank, 1972). Subjects often stored the occurrence of such higher-order relations without storing the content of the subsidiary proposition. For example, after the initial reading a subject might remember that the consequences of a certain event were listed, but be unable to recall the specific instances.

The third kind of information extracted during the initial reading is a representation of the information development in the passage. Subjects seemed to store information that could act as a pointer to a particular part of the passage when a question required specific information. In a sense, the printed passage was used as an external memory, and the internal representation served as an indexing system for that external memory. Our subjects often knew where to look in the passage for specific information. For example, if a question alluded to a specific fact, the subject would say "I remember something about that just before the end" or " . . . that appeared in the middle." Then, he would proceed to search through the appropriate part of the passage. Of course, some of these strategies are probably due to the task conditions, which emphasize speed, but permit subjects to look back. In summary, it appears that after the initial reading, our subjects had a record of the location of certain information in the passage, as well as the main theme and a list of some relations between the theme and subsidiary propositions.

Our approach to the reading comprehension test is to focus on representing, indexing, retrieving, and comparing information. Although our approach de-emphasizes the obvious factor of vocabulary, i.e. previous knowledge of the words in the passage, experimental evidence suggests that such de-emphasis may be justified. Tuinman and Brady (1973) showed that thorough pretraining on vocabulary items from the reading passage did *not* raise the comprehension scores of children in grades four to six. While some minimal knowledge of the vocabulary is clearly a necessary condition for successful performance, it is not sufficient to improve performance beyond a given level. This study suggests that the important skill in reading comprehension is the ability to represent and manipulate the information presented in the passage and questions.

The advantage of analyzing the reading comprehension task in terms of information processing theory is that it defines the relevant empirical questions to be answered. One process to be explored is the mechanism that abstracts the theme. For example, it is possible that the thematic proposition is the one that occurs most frequently in the passage, as suggested by the simulation model of Rosenberg (1974). Another issue to be explored is the precise representation of the indexing system that records where facts were mentioned in the paragraph. Yet another is the deterinination of how particular questions tap into this index. This analysis provides an outline of how a complex task like the reading comprehension test can be approached in terms of the basic components of the comprehension process—the representation, retrieval, and comparison of information.

CONCLUSIONS

What Makes a Sentence Hard to Process?

The comprehension model makes the claim that a sentence is difficult to process when it doesn't match the representation of some second source of information. Thus, the critical variable that determines processing difficulty is the number of matches or mismatches between two representations; the critical factor is not affirmation or negation, per se. According to the model, negatives are harder to process only when they mismatch with the affirmative representation of other information. For example, pictures are generally represented affirmatively, so sentences that refer to pictures are generally easier to process if they are affirmative. Similarly, the information stored in semantic memory is usually stored in some affirmative form, so the comprehension of the sentence referring to semantic memory is usually easier if the sentence is affirmative. However, the implication of the model is clear—negatives are not necessarily harder to process than affirmatives; mismatches, rather than negation per se, determine the ease of comprehending linguistic information.

When Negatives Are Easier

The model predicts that a negative sentence should be easier than an affirmative if the information from the other source were represented negatively. Then, the negative sentence would match the representation of the second source of information and the comparison would be faster. By contrast, the affirmative sentence would mismatch and processing would take longer. In fact, our analysis of an unusual reasoning task supports this prediction. Johnson-Laird and Tridgell (1972) presented subjects with a disjunctive premise $(p \vee q)$ and a probe $(\sim q)$, and asked the subjects to draw a conclusion (p). The premise contained two clauses like *Either John is intelligent or John is rich.* The probe sentence always had a different truth value than one of the two clauses in the premise, for example, *John is not rich,* so the conclusion was the remaining clause, i.e., *John is intelligent.*

The task required that the subject ask himself whether a clause in the premise conflicts with the probe. This self-instruction may have caused the same kind of internal representation that we postulated for instructions involving *conflict, different,* and *disagree.* The relevant clause in the premise may have been encoded into negative instruction and then compared to the probe. For the example *Either John is intelligent or John is rich,* the second clause may have been coded into the instruction: *(NEG, (X)),* so that it resulted in the representation *(NEG, (RICH, JOHN))'* This was then compared to the probe, *John is not rich,* represented *(NEG, (RICH, JOHN)).* The model predicts that such a negative probe would be processed faster than an affirmative probe like *John is poor,* represented as *(AFF, (POOR, JOHN)).* As predicted, the response latency to negative probes was shorter (by 1.6 sec) than the latency for the affirmative probe. The model correctly makes the nonintuitive prediction that the negative probes are processed faster in this situation. This supports the argument that mismatches, rather than negatives per se, consume processing time. Thus, it is the relationship between two representations that determines the speed of comparison processes.

Processing Instructions in an Everyday Situation

It was recently shown that in a highly realistic situation, people remember affirmative instructions much better than their negative counterparts. The situation was an airport, where eighty waiting airline passengers were asked to read or listen to a 200 word passage describing in-flight emergency procedures, based on actual airline protocol (File & Jew, 1973). The individual instructions were either affirmative (e.g., *Extinguish cigarettes. Remove shoes.*) or the corresponding negative set (e.g., *Do not leave cigarettes lighted. Do not keep shoes on.*). The results showed that the passengers recalled about 20% more information from affirmative instructions than from negative instructions. The better recall of affirmative instructions may have been the consequence of fewer mental operations during comprehension. Because the affirmatives are comprehended faster, subjects may have had more time to transfer information into long-term memory. The significance of this study is clear: laboratory-based theories of comprehension do apply to real situations involving critically important instructions.

We have examined several tasks that involve verbal comprehension in instructional settings. The focus has been how the information in a sentence is represented and manipulated. We have proposed a general model to account for comprehension in a variety of situations, such as verifying or completing sentences and executing instructions. The kinds of tasks surveyed and the analysis have both practical and theoretical importance. On the practical side, this kind of analysis may help to localize the difficulties that an individual has in verbal comprehension. Moreover, this approach could lead to a set of rules for writing easily comprehensible instructions. The analysis of these tasks in terms of fundamental processes helps to unravel the Gordian Not of verbal comprehension.

ACKNOWLEDGMENTS

The order of authors is arbitrary. This chapter represents a collaborative effort. The research was partially supported by the National Institute of Education, Department of Health, Education, and Welfare, Grant NIE-G-74-0016 and the National Institute of Mental Health, Grant MH-07722.

14

Understanding Complex Task Instructions

Herbert A. Simon
John R. Hayes

Carnegie-Mellon University

In the ninth Carnegie Symposium on Cognition, we described the processes used by human subjects to understand the instructions in a problem-solving task (Hayes & Simon, 1974). The aim of this chapter is to build upon the theory of the understanding process (and the UNDERSTAND computer program) developed in that previous paper, and to draw out the implications of the theory for educational processes and practices. The discussion will be organized under three main topics: the UNDERSTAND theory and some directions in which it needs to be extended; the role of prior knowledge in understanding; and the pedagogical implications of a theory of understanding. It will focus upon a strategy for analyzing tasks with a view to discovering what is involved in understanding them.

Much concern is expressed, from time to time, about "functional illiteracy" in our society. A functional illiterate is someone who cannot perform the reading tasks with which his job and his daily life confront him. The illiterate cannot read and understand the directions on the medicine bottle, the do-it-yourself kit, or the soup can. He cannot understand the fine print on the traffic ticket or read his personal mail. He cannot read the instruction manual for a piece of equipment used in his job. Although only a modest amount of research has been done on the causes of functional illiteracy, the data that are available suggest two generalizations about it.

1. Functional illiteracy is primarily an understanding problem, rather than a reading problem. That is to say, most functional illiterates in our society possess the basic decoding skills for reading the printed word. What they lack is adequate vocabulary, knowledge, and skill to interpret the communications that

are directed to them, regardless of whether those communications are written or spoken. This has been demonstrated very convincingly by Sticht (1972), who has shown that if a person can understand an oral communication, he can almost always understand the same communication presented to him in writing, and vice versa. Hence any major attack on adult functional illiteracy must be directed at improving language understanding skills, and not simply at improving the decoding skills of beginning reading.

2. Much of the difficult language that an individual encounters in daily life is found in the instructions he receives about what to do or how to do it. Therefore, any major attack on adult functional illiteracy needs to place special emphasis on the improvement of the skills of understanding instructions.

If understanding instructions is an important component of functional literacy for adults in their everyday and workaday lives, it is an even more crucial skill for children, adolescents, and young adults who spend their days in school. Schools (including universities) are the most persistently evaluating institutions in our society. They are continually testing their students, and the heart of testing is determining whether someone can carry out successfully a set of task instructions. Someone who cannot understand instructions cannot pass tests. Hence, understanding instructions is one of the principal skills we test in the schools.

But the understanding of instructions enters school tasks by still another route. Schools teach, or attempt to teach, their students to solve problems in a wide range of domains. The first step in solving a problem is to understand it—that is, to make a meaningful description of the problem situation (This view, that to understand is to make a description of the situation, is elaborated in the next section.) But a description of a problem situation is nothing more nor less than an instruction that defines a task and requests that it be performed. Hence, a significant component of problem solving skill in any domain is the skill of understanding the instructions for problems in that domain.

THE NATURE OF UNDERSTANDING

One understands task instructions if he can program himself to attempt the task. This does not necessarily mean that he can perform the task successfully. Most people can readily understand the Four Color Theorem: Any plane map can be colored with not more than four colors in such a way that no territories with a common border have the same color. If a person knows what a proof is, he can program himself to respond to the instruction: "Prove the Four Color Theorem." His chances of success, however, are miniscule; in spite of the efforts of numerous first-rate mathematicians, no one has succeeded in finding a proof of the Four Color Theorem—or, for that matter, a disproof.

What, more precisely, does it mean for a person to understand a task that he may or may not be able to perform? At a minimum, it means that he can test the adequacy of a purported performance or solution. But ordinarily, we expect something more than this minimum of understanding. A person approaches a new set of task instructions equipped with certain somewhat general problem-solving capabilities. Somehow, he enlists these problem-solving capabilities in the task which the new instructions present to him. The process of understanding the instructions is precisely this enlistment process.

A Specific Theory of Understanding

In our previous paper, we reported on the UNDERSTAND program, a computer simulation of the understanding process. The UNDERSTAND program embodies the following theory of the process. Before any specific problem can be attacked, it must be described in terms of a problem space—a space of situations that may be visited in a search for a solution—and a set of operators or "moves" for changing one situation into another in the course of the search.

Consider the problem of choosing a move in the game of tic-tac-toe. The problem space here might be the space of possible game situations, of arrangements of crosses and circles on the 3 X 3 array. The move operator adds a new cross or circle to the array. Given a way of representing the various possible game situations, and a way of moving from one to another of these, a problem-solving program like the General Problem Solver, GPS (Ernst and Newell, 1967) could go to work on the task of finding a good move in tic-tac-toe. (Actually, GPS would need a few other "givens" beyond those mentioned above, but the problem space and the move operator are the central requisites for it.) To ask how the UNDERSTAND program goes about understanding written problem instructions is to ask how it transforms those instructions into a problem space and a move operator. As we showed in our previous paper, this is accomplished by the UNDERSTAND program and by human subjects as well, along the following lines:

1. The input instructions are analyzed syntactically by means of a parsing program.

2. A search is made through the analyzed text for sets of "objects" that need to be represented in the problem space, and sets of relations among these objects.

3. A structure is created that permits objects and their relations (and thereby situations) to be represented. The representation is used to store information extracted from the problem instructions about the initial and goal situations.

4. A search is made through the analyzed text for operators that change the relations among objects.

5. Semantic memory is searched for possible semantic interpretations of the change operators. Associated with the interpretations in semantic memory are programs for actually making the corresponding changes in memory structures.

6. The representation created in step (3) is described, to provide the information required by the interpreted change operators. These operators have the task of actually carrying out the moves from one situation to another by making the appropriate changes in the represented situation.

Let us see what each step means in terms of a simple, concrete example. Table 1 shows the instructions for a "Monster Problem." The first step in understanding this problem is to discover the surface structures of the component sentences, to interpret pronouns and other backward references, and to carry out the other syntactic tasks of this kind that would be performed by a parsing system.

The second step is to identify, in the syntactically analyzed sentences, the objects involved in the problem: in this case monsters and globes. Similarly, a number of relations can be identified: monsters are ordered by size, as are globes; there are relations of "holding" and of "teleporting" or "giving."

In the third step, a way must be found for representing situations in which particular monsters hold particular globes. In a memory capable of storing list structures, such a representation is readily constructed as follows: A node is created in memory labeled "Current-Situation." An attribute, "Monster-List," is associated with that node, having as its value a list of the monsters: "Monster.1," "Monster.2," and "Monster.3." With each monster node is associated an attribute, "Size," having as value "Small," "Medium," or "Large." A second attribute associated with each monster is "Globes-Held." The value of "Globes-Held" is again a list of the names of the globes currently held by the monster in question.

TABLE 1
A Monster Problem

Three five-handed extraterrestrial monsters were holding three crystal globes. Because of the quantum-mechanical peculiarities of their neighborhood, both monsters and globes come in exactly three sizes with no others permitted: small, medium, and large. The medium-sized monster was holding the small globe; the small monster was holding the large globe; and the largest monster was holding the medium-sized globe. Since this situation offended their keenly developed sense of symmetry, they proceeded to teleport globes from one to another so that each monster would have a globe proportionate to his own size.

Monster etiquette complicated the solution of the problem since it requires:
1. that only one globe can be transmitted at a time,
2. that if a monster is holding two globes, he may transmit only the larger of the two, and
3. that a globe must not be transmitted to a monster who is holding a larger globe.

By what sequence of teleportations could the monsters have solved this problem?

TABLE 2
A Representation of the Initial Situation for the Monster Problem

Current Situation

Monster List:

Monster. 1
    Size: Medium
    Globe list:
        Globe. 1
            Size: Small

Monster. 2
    Size: Small
    Globe list:
        Globe. 2
            Size: Large

Monster. 3
    Size: Large
    Globe list:
        Globe. 3
            Size: Medium

Each globe is described by its size in the same way as the monsters are. The entire representation for the initial problem situation is shown in Table 2.

As fourth and fifth steps, the move operator must be identified, and it must receive a semantic interpretation. In this problem, the move operator may be represented as:

GIVES(Globe.X, Monster.Y, Monster.Z).

which may be read as: "Monster Y gives Globe X to Monster Z." Notice that this operator involves one object belonging to one class (globes), and two objects belonging to another class (monsters). This characteristic allows GIVES to be interpreted as an instance of the MOVE operator which is already stored in long-term memory, along with programs that, when provided with appropriate information about the representation, can actually carry out the move:

MOVE $(A.1, B.1, B.2)$

The operation of moving $A.1$ from $B.1$ to $B.2$ consists in deleting the relation in the representation of the situation that holds between $A.1$ and $B.1$, and then establishing the corresponding relation between $A.1$ and $B.2$. How this is to be done depends on the way in which the relation between the As and the Bs is actually represented in memory.

The sixth step, then, is to provide the MOVE operator with the information it needs in order to act upon the representation of the situation. This is accomplished by constructing a description of the representation (a formalized version of the English-language description we provided a few paragraphs earlier). Using this description the MOVE operator can now interpret "Monster Y gives Globe X to Monster Z" as meaning that Globe.X is to be deleted from the value list of the attribute Globes Held of Monster.Y, and is to be added to the value list of the attribute Globes Held of Monster.Z. If the situation had been represented differently—by storing the list of globes, say, and associating with each the name of the monster holding it—then the actual operation of making a move would have been altered accordingly. In that case, the move would have been made by deleting the donating monster's association with the transferred globe, and associating the receiving monster with that globe. In each instance the processes of the MOVE operator would be controlled by the description of the particular representation in use.[1]

In summary, the UNDERSTAND theory asserts that a person understands a problem like the Monster Problem if he has constructed a representation for problem situations (possible distributions of globes among monsters), and if he can consider changes in the problem situation corresponding to legal moves and actually carry out those changes on the stored representation. The reason for regarding this as understanding is that, equipped with this interpretation of a problem, a problem solver can attack it by applying means-ends analysis to it. He can determine in what respects the goal situation (all monsters holding globes proportionate to their own sizes) differs from the initial situation, and how these differences might be removed by applying the MOVE operator. We repeat our earlier caution: to say that the problem has been understood does not imply that it can be solved either easily, or at all.

Oral versus Written Instruction

All of the steps in the understanding process that have been described are essential, regardless of whether the task instructions are received orally or in writing. We cited earlier some empirical evidence (Sticht, 1972) that for adults the difficulty of understanding instructions is largely independent of instruction modality. However, there are some differences between oral and written communication that can affect understanding substantially.

The most important distinction is that oral instructions may exceed the capacity limits of short-term memory. For example, it would be extremely difficult to understand the Monster Problem in Table 1—particularly the legal moves—on a single oral presentation. Subjects who are given the problem in

---

[1] Details of how the UNDERSTAND program carries out these steps are provided in our previous paper (Hayes & Simon, 1974). In that paper, we also discuss how the rule conditions (the limitations upon who may give globes to whom) are interpreted. The method is very similar to the method of interpreting the move operator.

writing handle the STM capacity limitation simply by rereading the more complex sentences as often as they need to. The sentences stating the limitations on transfers of globes and the sentence describing the initial situation are almost always read a number of times by our subjects. The other sentences are usually read—and apparently understood—in a single pass. The UNDERSTAND program makes a number of successive passes over the problem text, and is allowed as much short-term memory as it requires. Hence, it approximates more closely the conditions of reading than of listening.

Another difference between oral and written instructions is that the former contain stress and intonational cues, while the latter contain punctuation. Although these differences could have important effects upon understandability, we believe that in fact, the effects are usually small. The UNDERSTAND program, as it now stands, makes use of punctuation as a cue to meaning, but not italics, nor stress and intonational cues.

Environmental Feedback

Knowledge of results is crucial to any learning process, and the understanding process should be no exception. What knowledge of results does the UNDER-STAND program obtain in the course of acquiring an understanding of the Monster Problem? How does the program know when it has understood?

The program can detect whether it has succeeded in formulating some problem, but it cannot guarantee that the formulation is the one intended by the problem statement. The program's test that it has performed its task amounts to detecting that it has constructed a representation of the problem situation, that it has defined a move operator, and that it has interpreted the move operator in terms of the representation.

In some real-life understanding situations, and in many school situations, feedback is correspondingly limited. In many instruction-understanding situations, however, the problem solver can seek cues to help him or her interpret the problem situation. Subjects solving the Monster Problem ask the experimenter such questions as: "Can a monster hold more than one globe?" Does the problem have a unique solution?" "May a monster pass a globe to any other monster, or only to the monster standing nearest to him?" Answers to these questions narrow down the possible range of interpretations of the problem.

In many other cases of real-world problem solving, the task posed by the problem instructions is to carry out some external physical actions that have observable physical effects. These observable effects become another source of feedback that can be used to aid problem interpretation. When someone tries to follow the instructions of a do-it-yourself kit, the success or failure of his actions soon becomes apparent, and this gives him critical information as to the adequacy of his understanding of the instructions. If the instructions refer to a particular component, and he cannot identify that component from the parts lying in front of him, he knows that he does not understand the instructions. If the instructions require two parts to be assembled that he cannot fit together, he knows that he does not understand the instructions.

In the limiting case there are no verbal instructions at all—only a situation to be understood and dealt with. A leaking faucet is an instruction: "Fix me." This limiting case reminds us that, in many real-life situations, information for understanding what is to be done is drawn less from explicit instructions than from direct perception of the situation (It is drawn also, of course, from long-term memory, a point that we shall discuss later.).

In some cases, explicit instructions are accompanied by worked-out examples. This is done commonly in mathematics textbooks, computer programming manuals, and instructions for subjects in psychological experiments. In these situations the examples may supply sufficient information about the task and its requirements to make the explicit task instructions superfluous. This possibility has been demonstrated by Donald Williams (1972), who constructed an artificial intelligence system that programs itself to take various kinds of intelligence test batteries (e.g., letter series completion, number analogy) on the basis of worked-out examples, and without explicit verbal instructions.

Perhaps the most interesting cases are those in which a subject receives feedback from the consequences of his attempts to formulate and solve the problem. For example, a subject (described by Hayes & Simon, 1974) read a line of text and concluded that the problem involved two participants. The next line, however, implied that there were three participants. At this point, the subject carefully reexamined each of the sentences to resolve the conflict between them before proceeding with his solution attempt. This example illustrates a simple but powerful heuristic for reducing local ambiguity that is not incorporated in the present UNDERSTAND program: inferences drawn from one part of the problem text must be made consistent with inferences drawn from other parts of the text.

Another example of the use of this heuristic by the same subject involved interpreting a statement of the form, "A does a task for B." In one part of the text, the subject interpreted this statement to mean that "A does a task to benefit B," while in another, he interpreted it to mean that "A does a task instead of B." The subject's recognition and resolution of this conflict played an important part in his successful formulation of the problem.

The consistency heuristic is not the only one that subjects use in deriving feedback from their attempts to solve a problem. We have also observed a "solvability" heuristic being employed. Briefly, it worked as follows: the subject hypothesized an operator for a problem. Then he discovered that the problem couldn't be solved with this operator. He then concluded that the operator was inappropriate, and hypothesized a new one.

In summary, the task of understanding instructions when there is environmental feedback is very different from the understanding task in the absence of such feedback. Feedback may result from ability to question the instruction-giver, access to the actual problem environment, access to worked-out examples, or the use of consistency and solvability heuristics. In limiting cases, the information available from these sources of feedback may be so complete as to permit the task to be understood without any explicit instructions at all. Before it can be regarded as a comprehensive theory of the understanding processes, the UNDERSTAND program will have to be augmented to handle these possibilities for feedback.

KNOWLEDGE AND UNDERSTANDING

What does the problem solver have to know already—in order to understand a set of problem instructions? The description above of the processes used to understand the Monster Problem imply that the knowledge requirements for understanding are relatively limited. This kind of puzzle may be atypical, however, in the slight demands it makes upon stored information.

III-Structured Problems

In the literature of problem solving, a distinction is often made between well-structured problems, on the one hand, and ill-structured problems, on the other. (Newell, 1969; Reitman, 1964, 1965; Simon, 1973) Not all authors have defined the distinction in exactly the same way, but a common theme running through all of the definitions is that problems are ill structured to the extent that the problem solver himself must contribute toward their definition. Specifically, we propose that a problem be regarded as ill structured to the extent that the subject must build the representation he uses to solve it from information generated during his unsuccessful attempts at solution.

The distinction between well-structured and ill-structured problems describes a continuum and not a dichotomy. Moreover, the ill-structuredness of a problem may take a variety of forms. The problem instructions may be couched in technical language that can be understood only by one "skilled in the art." Here is an example, from a chemical engineering textbook, of a problem that appears ill structured primarily because of its technical vocabulary:

> A throttling calorimeter is attached to a line containing steam at 15 psig with a quality of 98%. What does the thermometer in the calorimeter read?

A problem may also be ill structured because the instructions do not contain enough information to permit a usable problem representation to be inferred from them. As a matter of fact, the chemical engineering example illustrates this potentiality for ill-structuredness also. There is nothing in the problem statement that indicates how the temperature of steam can be calculated from its pressure and quality—no definitions of "move operators" are supplied. They must come from the reader's knowledge. If this knowledge is readily available to the reader, the problem will appear well structured to him; if accessing the knowledge itself calls for extensive problem-solving efforts, the problem will appear ill structured to him. (See Norman, Gentner, & Stevens, Chapter 9 of this volume.)

As one of his principal examples of an ill-structured problem, Reitman (1965, Chapter 6) examined the task of writing a fugue. Here the instructions are simplicity itself: "compose a fugue." Directed to a professional composer, the instructions define a goal, for he can recognize a fugue when he hears one, and can apply a variety of tests to evaluate its quality as music. The instructions also suggest to the composer a method of proceeding, for they evoke from his long-term memory a whole organized system of compositional techniques. If the composer does not set his quality criterion too high, composing a fugue may even be a rather routine activity. From his standpoint, the problem does not really appear to be ill structured at all.

Understanding Puzzles

The examples cited above show that ill-structuredness is, in a certain sense, in the eye of the beholder. Perhaps the best way to put it is to say that a problem is ill structured to the extent that it puts demands on the knowledge and repertory of problem-solving skills of the solver. In these terms, we would say that the task of composing a fugue is quite far along toward the ill structured end of the continuum, not because the professional composer would not know how to proceed, but because, in proceeding, he would have to draw upon a large repertory of knowledge and skill stored in his long-term memory, and much of this might become accessible only on the course of his solution efforts. For the person unskilled in composition, the problem would be ill structured in the more radical sense that he would simply lack the knowledge that would permit him even to formulate the problem, much less to solve it.

Looking at the matter of structuredness in this light, we can ask how well-structured the Monster Problem is for the UNDERSTAND program. What stored knowledge does the program draw upon in order to understand the problem? The UNDERSTAND program depends primarily upon a knowledge of the English language, and secondarily upon a knowledge of the semantics of a few basic operators (in the case at hand, the MOVE operator). In addition to this knowledge, it has a general, task-independent, capability for constructing representations from sets of objects and relations, and for interpreting its basic operators in terms of these representations. Except for function words (e.g., prepositions, conjunctions, auxiliaries), which serve as cues to identify the syntactic structure, the UNDERSTAND program does not need to know the meanings of English words, but only the parts of speech to which they belong.

"Monster" could as well be "Jabberwock" or "thingamajig" or "blurb" without making the slightest difference to the program's operation. As we have seen earlier, giving a globe to another monster ("outgrabing a tove to a blurb") has to be recognized as an action that can be matched to the MOVE operator. Beyond this, the meaning of "giving" or "outgrabing" is also irrelevant.

It is rather remarkable that this small amount of machinery and knowledge enables the program to understand the instructions of the Monster Problem. We generally call tasks of this kind "puzzles." It is perhaps their independence of specific information not contained in the problem statement that best characterizes them. However much they are couched in image-inducing language, they are, in fact, highly abstract; and the processes for understanding them are processes for identifying and further purifying the abstraction. Monsters become objects of a certain abstract class; globes, objects of another class; "holding" a relation between objects of the first class and objects of the second, and so on. Semantic meaning of these terms is a "cover," to be stripped off in the process of understanding the task.

The protocols of subjects attempting to understand the Monster Problem reveal the role of abstraction in the understanding process. Some subjects, and especially those who proved most proficient at the task, were quite explicit in casting out semantic irrelevancies. One subject reads, "because of the quantum-mechanical pecularities of their neighborhood," and comments at once, "Forget that garbage." Another subject, after reading the whole text once says:

Now there were only three globes altogether. That's not rhetorical. They were five-handed monsters . . . that doesn't have much to do with it, I take it. They could have been two-handed monsters for all I care.

Two subjects, on the other hand, who imported into the problem knowledge associated with the meanings of terms failed to understand it. One of these subjects became preoccupied with the physics of the situation. He made such comments as: "You can't have two energy states at the same time, according to quantum physics; you're either at one energy level or another," and "the medium wants to drop it's energy level to small—negative and positive—ahh—energy levels."

The other subject who failed to understand the problem perhaps stimulated by the mention of "monster etiquette," introduced a social dimension into the situation. He made such remarks as, "You know, it seems to me if they all agreed on an arbitrary standard [of size], I don't see that there would be a problem." The subject saw that such collusion among the monsters would weaken the conditions on allowable moves.

Precisely because the Monster Problem was intended as a puzzle, the strategy of making use of the semantics of its terms only caused difficulty and impeded understanding of the problem. In other kinds of problem situations, the same strategy might be helpful, or even essential. In the puzzle environment, however, the successful subjects were those who applied abstraction techniques like the ones incorporated in the UNDERSTAND program.

The distinction between puzzles and problems, like that between structured and ill-structured problems, describes a continuum rather than a dichotomy. Some puzzle problems require the use both of semantic knowledge and abstraction. The Jabberwocky problem discussed by Newell and Simon (1972) is just such a problem. In this puzzle a familiar river-crossing problem is coded in nonsense words. Thus, "a heavy father and two young sons have to cross a swift river . . . " is coded as "a slithy tove and two mimsy borogroves have to out-wiffle a frumious bandersnatch." Subjects attempting to solve the problem frequently interpret the string "to out-wiffle a bandersnatch" to mean that the participants have to catch or kill some creature. This interpretation suggests an operation that is completed when any one of the participants accomplishes it, rather than when all three do so. It is clear then that the semantics of groups crossing rivers is important for the correct formulation of the problem.

Semantics in Algebra Word Problems

Word problems or story problems in algebra provide an example of a problem domain where semantic information may be used, even though the problems can be understood with rather little reliance upon semantics. Several years ago, Bobrow (1968) constructed an artificial intelligence program for solving such problems that relied primarily upon syntactic cues. The program operated in two stages: first it translated the story into algebraic equations; then it solved the equations.

Bobrow's program needed to be able to interpret a small number of mathematical terms: for example, "equals" and its synonyms, "four times as great as," "less than," "twice as many," the names of the numerals, and so on. It also had some special semantic capabilities for handling age, rate, and distance problems. Beyond this, it depended entirely upon syntactic means for its translations. Hence, its semantics was not much more elaborate than the semantics currently incorporated in the UNDERSTAND program.

Subsequently, Paige and Simon (1966) examined the protocols of human subjects working algebra word problems to see whether the processes they used resembled those incorporated in Bobrow's program They constructed a number of problems that represented physically impossible situations. For example:

> The number of quarters a man has is seven times the number of dimes he has. The value of the dimes exceeds the value of the quarters by two dollars and fifty cents. How many has he of each coin?

Subjects responded in three distinct ways. Some subjects made a literal (syntactic) translation of the problems. In the example quoted above, they arrived at the equation

$$10X = 250 + 25(7X).$$

Other subjects, apparently noting that the value of the quarters must be greater than the value of the dimes, simply assigned the extra two and a half dollars to the other side of the equation. Their solution made sense of the original problem, but did not represent an accurate translation of the problem statement. A third group of subjects objected that they found the problem contradictory. They could not reconcile their (accurate) translation of the problem statement with their interpretation of the physical reality of the situation.

This experiment demonstrated a considerable variation among human subjects in their relative reliance upon syntactic and semantic cues in doing algebra word problems. It also shows that, when the subject's semantic knowledge is taken into account, many problems have considerable redundancy. Different understanding processes may accomplish their task by making use of different parts of the redundant information. Hence, from the fact of understanding, one cannot infer a unique program that brought about that understanding.

Styles in Understanding

In the complex tasks handled by professionals, only a small part of the task information comes from explicit instructions. The vast bulk of this information is retrieved from the professional's long-term memory, where training and experience have placed it. A few studies have begun to disclose the nature of this professional knowledge, and how it is used in problem solving. Clarkson (1963) simulated the professional decision making of a bank trust officer, while the decision making of chess masters has been studied by de Groot (1965, 1966), Newell and Simon (1972) and Chase and Simon (1973a, b). We will need many more such studies, over a whole range of professions, to explore and characterize the variety of understanding processes used by professionals.

Parallel to the differences among problem domains are differences in the strategies, or styles, that problem solvers may employ in seeking to understand instructions. The success of a particular style may depend on its appropriateness to the problem domains to which it is applied. For purposes of discussion, we may consider a style that emphasizes abstraction processes, one that emphasizes retrieval from semantic memory, and one that emphasizes metaphor and analogy.

In the previous section, the first two of these styles have already received some attention. We saw that success in understanding a puzzle-like problem depends on skill in abstracting and in disregarding irrelevant semantic interpretations of the problem vocabulary. On the other hand, we saw that more complex problems are generally inscrutable without semantic interpretation. The third style—that employing analogy and metaphor—needs some additional discussion.

Several subjects, confronted with the Monster Problem, said, "This reminds me of the Tower of Hanoi puzzle." The Tower of Hanoi is a puzzle involving three pegs and a number of disks of different sizes that can be placed in pyramids on the pegs. Disks can be moved, one at a time, with the constraint that a larger disk may never be placed upon a smaller one. The Tower of Hanoi is, indeed, isomorphic with the Monster Problem. Any legal move in the former corresponds to a legal move in the latter, where pegs are interpreted as monsters, and disks as globes (with "larger" and "smaller" interchanged). In principle, a subject who was familiar with the Tower of Hanoi could, when he noticed its resemblance to the Monster Problem, "understand" the latter by mapping it in one-to-one fashion on the former. In fact, none of the subjects who noticed the analogy succeeded in carrying out the mapping. They all found it easier to construct a new representation of the Monster Problem, disregarding what they had noticed about the similarity.

This is not to say that there are not other situations in which analogy could be used to understand a problem, or that there are not other subjects who could carry out such a mapping. Nor can we yet explain why recognizing the similarity was not helpful in understanding the Monster Problem.

There exists at least one artificial intelligence program that makes use of analogy to solve problems. Kling (1971) has constructed a theorem-proving program that, confronted with a new problem, searches its memory for theorems previously proved that resemble the one before it. If it finds such a theorem, it retrieves the proof, and tries to construct a proof of the new theorem along the lines of the old proof.

The central capability required of an analogy-using program is to be able to form the analogy. This means there must be some way to match elements of the one situation onto elements of the other to determine whether there is an isomorphism, or at least a one-many mapping. Matching programs that will do this over some interesting range of situations have proved difficult to construct, although some progress has been made in this direction (Moore & Newell, 1974; Simon, 1972). Analogizing is probably an important human technique for understanding problem instructions, but we know relatively little about it—from either a psychological or an artificial intelligence standpoint. It is completely absent from the UNDERSTAND program.

These rather sketchy remarks may serve to suggest some of the parameters of style in understanding. There is evidence, some of which we cited in an earlier section, that there are large variations in style among individuals, and that individuals do not always employ the understanding style that is most effective for the situation before them The theory embodied in the present UNDER-STAND program does not take these style differences into account; the style of the present program very much emphasizes abstraction processes, makes only a little use of knowledge in semantic memory, and is completely innocent of metaphor and analogy.

UNDERSTANDING INSTRUCTIONS
AND INSTRUCTION FOR UNDERSTANDING

The remainder of this chapter is concerned with the educational implications of what we have learned about understanding instructions. These implications point in two different directions. In the first place, we should be able to use a theory of the understanding process to improve the art of writing instructions. One way to reduce functional illiteracy is to reduce the complexity of the instructions which the illiterate meets in his daily life. A good theory of the understanding process should tell us what we have to do in order to accomplish this.

In the second place, we should be able to use a theory of the understanding process to design educational programs aimed at enhancing students' abilities to understand complex instructions. If we cannot move the mountain, we may be able to move Mahomet. Let us look at each of these strategies in turn.

Simplifying and Clarifying Instructions

This is hardly a new topic. A large part of the effort devoted in schools to improving students' communication skills is directed at helping them to write more clearly and simply. There exists, therefore, a large body of lore, based on extensive practical experience, as to what constitutes clear writing. Is there anything that a theory of the understanding process can add to this well-established educational practice?

To answer that question calls for a substantial research and development effort. One part of that effort might well be devoted to understanding and rationalizing what is now taught in courses on writing. If the theory we have been outlining here has any validity, then it should explain why one form of expression is clearer and simpler than another. Since the research remains to be done, we can only hint here at the form the explanation might take.

If one includes in instructions information that is not useful for interpreting the instructions, then the reader may be misled into unproductive or misleading analogies. We have seen that a vital part of the understanding process is to strip away the inessentials from the problem statement, and abstract out the elements from which the problem representation will be formed. Reducing the number of inessentials to be stripped should simplify the process.

The theory warns us that irrelevance of information is not to be confused with redundancy. While irrelevant information in problem instructions may make it harder to discover what is relevant, redundant information—or at least information that appears redundant to the writer—may actually help the reader to resolve ambiguities. Where a particular phrase or clause can be interpreted in more than one way, the consistency heuristic discussed earlier may be used to find another passage where some of the same language is used, and to seek a common, consistent interpretation of both passages. Application of this strategy requires that there be some redundancy between the two passages. In extolling the values of brevity, manuals on good writing do not generally make explicit the distinction between eliminating irrelevancy and eliminating redundancy.

The theory alerts us to the semantic information that is needed to interpret instructions successfully, and suggests an approach toward systematic identification of that information by analysis of the problem structure. The instructions can then be tested for completeness—to see whether they contain the semantic information that the reader cannot be assumed to have already available. For example, Bobrow's program for algebra word problems could not, if it were deprived of the formula, $D = R \times T$, solve rate problems. Constructing an artificial intelligence program to perform the task would provide an iventory of the semantic information required for performance. Similarly, submitting a set of task instructions to the UNDERSTAND program would reveal the semantic information needed for understanding those instructions.

Thus, not only might theory illuminate the nature of clarity in writing, and ways of attaining it, but artificial intelligence programs, through their further development, could be used to analyse the structure of particular classes of problem environments, and to "debug" instructions by identifying points of difficulty in them.

Teaching the Skills of Understanding

It is unrealistic to think that we can make more than a dent in the problem of functional illiteracy by simplifying and otherwise improving the quality of oral and written instructions. At the same time we seek to improve the performance of the speaker or writer, we must seek to increase the ability of the listener or reader to comprehend complex prose. On the basis of the theory of understanding set forth here, we can sketch out some plausible, but untested, ideas as to how this job might be tackled.

To the extent that understanding problem instructions involves semantic knowledge about a problem domain, there is no substitite for having the requisite knowledge. A person cannot interpret algebra word problems unless he knows what such phrases as "twice as many" mean. Training in understanding problem instructions will not teach him this; training in arithmetic or algebra might.

Where semantic information is involved, learning to understand problem instructions cannot be separated from learning the subject matter of the problems. To the extent that functional illiteracy stems from lack of such knowledge, no amount of training in how to read or listen will remove it.

But there is no reason to suppose that all inadequacies in interpreting problem instructions stem from deficiencies in subject-matter knowledge. In the example of the Monster Problem, we saw that some subjects failed to arrive at a suitable problem representation, not because they lacked information, but because they dragged in irrelevant information instead of abstracting out the essential problem elements. Their difficulties might have been reduced by appropriate training in the skills of interpreting instructions.

A first topic of instruction might be styles of interpretation. An awareness could be developed of the need to select a style of attack appropriate to the problem domain, and practice could be given in changing style in response to cues imbedded in the problem instructions.

A second topic of instruction might be the abstractive style itself. The UNDERSTAND program provides a framework for attacking instructions by abstraction. Practice could be given in identifying important sets of objects mentioned in the problem instructions, identifying relations, constructing a representation of the situation, identifying the operators and conditions.

A third topic of instruction might be training in the style that maximizes the use of semantic cues and analogy. At the moment, we have little to suggest about the specifies of doing this.

A fourth topic of instruction might be the skills of obtaining feedback from the instruction giver or from the task environment. Practice could be given in clarifying task instructions by asking questions, by making solution attempts to identify ambiguities, by searching for and exploiting redundancies in the instructions themselves. The field of computer programming might be a useful and appropriate domain within which to practice such skills. Programming problems can be proposed at any desired level of difficulty and clarity. Programming manuals are inexhaustible sources of unclear (and occasionally clear) problem instructions. The computer itself provides a real-world environment in which understanding can be tested and feedback obtained. The idea of using computer programming as a domain for teaching the skills of understanding instructions is not unrelated to the proposal and experiments of Papert and Minsky (see Papert, 1971), who use programming as a domain for teaching general problem-solving skills. (See also Norman, Gentner, & Stevens, Chapter 9, this volume).

No doubt these are only a fraction of the possibilities for specific instructional plans for raising the skills of understanding instructions. As we acquire more adequate theories of the understanding process, our abilities to construct effective training procedures should increase. In this chapter we have tried only to suggest some general lines of attack on the problem; we are under no illusion that we have solved it. It is well worth solving, because it is deeply implicated in the extent and severity of functional illiteracy in our society.

ACKNOWLEDGMENTS

This Research has been supported in part by Research Grant MH-07722 from the National Institute of Mental Health, and in part by National Science Foundation Grant GS-38533.

15
Education and Understanding

Allan Collins

Bolt Beranek and Newman Inc.

Education has typically dealt with the problem of understanding only in terms of the mechanics of reading, that is in terms of learning which words go with which printed strings of letters. The two chapters by Just and Carpenter, Chapter 13, and by Simon and Hayes, Chapter 14, deal with the problem of understanding in two quite different ways, both distinct from the mechanics of reading. If Simon and Hayes are correct that the difficulties adults have in reading are deeper than the mechanical level, then surely it would be worthwhile to teach people understanding skills as well as reading skills. So if it is possible to analyze understanding in deeper terms than the mechanics of reading, the implications for education should be important.

Just and Carpenter deal with the problem of understanding principally at the level of the individual sentence. The data they present to support their model of sentence processing is very convincing. Underlying their model is a comparison or matching process, which they treat as a simple, unitary step that can be repeated different numbers of times. I suspect their comparison model is basically correct and I have argued elsewhere (Collins & Quillian, 1972) that such a comparison process pervades all of human language processing.

In the tasks Just and Carpenter have used, the comparison process would be quite simple, and assigning it a fixed duration as they do makes sense. But the reader should not be misled into thinking that it is always a simple process or that it has a fixed duration in general. This could be shown even in the kinds of tasks Just and Carpenter have been using. For example, consider the task where a sentence such as "The dots are red" is compared against a picture of red dots. One manipulation that should affect the duration of the comparison process is the perceptual similarity of the color in the sentence and in the picture. If the dots are red, for example, sentences such as "The dots are purple" or "The dots are pink" should take longer to reject than "The dots are yellow " This kind of example can be extended into the semantic domain. If a picture has red dots, verifying a sentence like "The circles are red" or "The squares are red" involves deciding whether dots can be circles or squares. Similarly if the question is whether "The dots are crimson," "The dots are maroon," or "The dots are colored," this involves deciding whether crimson, or maroon, or colored can be the same as red. The point is simply that the comparison process itself can be complex, involving subprocesses of different durations. Just and Carpenter's fine-grain analysis of processing may be extendable to analysis of the comparison process itself.

There is one other question I might address with respect to Just and Carpenter's chapter: that is, are they dealing with the real problems of understanding? The answer is, I think, that they are dealing with some of them. But there are other even more difficult problems that they have avoided. The assumptions of their verification studies is that the relevant knowledge is directly stored as a single entity. In their studies this is so, because they've made it so, but in real life it is usually not the case. Often answers must be inferred from several pieces of knowledge scattered about in memory. Even when Just and Carpenter analyze reading comprehension tests, they have not tried to deal with how the reader relates the information in a paragraph to his various kinds of knowledge about the world. These are probelms that are probably beyond the scope of the fine-grained analysis which Just and Carpenter are using. But they are susceptible to the kind of analysis that Simon and Hayes are attempting in their chapter. Simon and Hayes analyze what it means to understand the statement of a problem. Their discussion of ill-structured and well-structured problems directly addresses the issue of how much knowledge a reader brings to bear in understanding a problem. It is perhaps one of the most important points in the chapter. As Simon and Hayes point out, a problem is ill structured to the degree a person needs to use knowledge beyond that which is in the statement of the problem, either to understand or solve it. The distinguishing feature of problems like the monster problem they have been working with is that relatively little special knowledge is needed to understand the problem It is a well-structured problem.

Is life like a monster problem? Again I want to be wishy-washy and say yes and no. I think people spend much of their time problem solving, often at a subconscious level. For example, problem solving turns up when people try to answer questions to which they do not have prestored answers (Collins, Warnock, Aiello, & Miller, 1975). Therefore, one of the aims of education should be to teach people how to understand and solve problems as effectively as possible. This attitude reflects the views of Simon and Hayes and Papert (1972) of education. But there is a difference between the two views. Papert tends to discount the teaching of factual knowledge as a legitimate goal of education, whereas Simon and Hayes' view stresses the importance of knowledge for dealing with ill-structured problems. It turns out that most of life's problems are ill structured, and so acquiring and using factual knowledge is crucial to understanding most problems. It is because of this that life is not like a monster problem.

Consider the kinds of real-world difficulties in understanding that Simon and Hayes cite at the beginning of their chapter. People cannot understand instructions on soup cans because they do not have enough knowledge about cooking of the kind one acquires from practice, or knowledge about the basic terms in cooking like "simmer" or "colander," or knowledge about the structure of recipe instructions that one acquires from reading recipes. Alternatively, consider the problem of understanding traffic tickets. There the difficulty in understanding may derive from the use of legal language and concepts. In such cases understanding may involve knowing what to ignore, as Simon and Hayes point out can be important in monster problems. But knowing what to ignore here requires a primitive knowledge of law

These examples emphasize the fact that monster problems probably are a good place to approach the problem of understanding, because the semantic knowledge needed to understand them is relatively limited. But the difficulties in understanding soup-can instructions and traffic tickets will not be solved by a deep analysis of monster problems, because the difficulties arise in having enough knowledge about the world and using it appropriately to fill in the information that the text assumes.

The important conclusion from all this is that there is no easy way to educate people to understand. Because life is full of ill-structured problems of the kind that soup cans and traffic tickets present, we need to have a huge amount of world knowledge, together with the kind of understanding and problem-solving skills that Simon and Hayes or Papert advocate. Papert's viewpoint should probably be stressed, because school teachers have only tried to impart world knowledge and not these other skills. By deemphasizing the teaching of world knowledge, educators may be induced to strike a more even balance. But in the end there is no way to teach people to understand soup-can instructions without teaching them a lot of things about cooking.

ACKNOWLEDGMENTS

This work was sponsored by the Personnel and Training Research Programs, Psychological Sciences Division, Office of Naval Research, under Contract No. N00014-71-C0228, Contract Authority Identification Number, NR No. 154-330. Reproduction in whole or in part is permitted for any purpose of the United States Government.

16
Instruction in Difficult Contexts: Comments on Just and Carpenter and Simon and Hayes

Robert Shaw

University of Minnesota

I am in essential agreement with Collins (Chapter 15, this volume) that Chapter 13 by Just and Carpenter is a fine piece of work on a very difficult problem. Therefore, having no major criticism to make, I address my comments to the broader question of the relevance of research such as theirs to other problem areas of psychology. I would like to describe some of my applied research experience in aphasia and art instruction in order to demonstrate how a consistent underlying theoretical orientation has lead us to applied instructional programs in two widely diverse areas.

TREATMENT OF APHASIA

The most impressive aspect of the Just and Carpenter work is the fact that a very simple model seems to account for processing latencies in a variety of linguistic situations. I must admit that I smarted a little upon first reading their contribution because I saw that they had succeeded in finding a reasonably simple linguistic processing model for various sentential transforms where attempts at Minnesota had met with much less success (Clifton, Kurcz, & Jenkins, 1965; Clifton & Odom, 1966; Walls, 1968).

In 1966, Terry Halwes and I developed a partial transformational grammar for English that produced the structural descriptions for elliptical sentences. In a sense, our system constituted an early attempt to develop a "question–answer" model that might ultimately be used as part of natural language or conversational computer program. An explanation is in order since the experimentation motivated to test this model was not unlike that done by Just and Carpenter. My primary purpose is to suggest some ways in which basic psycholinguistic research in general may be fruitfully applied to the study and treatment of communication, such disorders as aphasia, in which normal language processes have somehow become dysfunctional.

Even though our success in applying psycholinguistic techniques to the study of aphasia may have been slight, it may encourage such other researchers as Just and Carpenter to apply their more adequate techniques to the study of such language disorders. My main point is that the treatment of such disorders necessarily involves assumption regarding the nature of instruction, or, more precisely, reinstruction. Speech therapy is a form of reinstruction of people with respect to a skill once possessed but now lost, and as such is indeed a problem for instructional psychologists. For only to the extent that instruction is understood can techniques for reinstruction realistically hope to improve. Thus, the topic examined in this volume, cognition and instruction, is vitally important to nearly all forms of clinical therapy in which restoration of a lost skill is the goal.

As is so often the case in basic research, Terry Halwes and I did not even consider the potential relevance of our work to instruction or reinstruction when we were developing our grammar of elliptical sentences. Perhaps we should have, but we did not. By relating our experience I hope that other researchers may be made more circumspect regarding the relevance of their work to serious applied problems. I believe that volumes such as this one surely help us all take a much needed step in that direction.

Halwes and I borrowed from the transformational grammars that were then under development by Chomsky (1965) and Lees (1960). Our grammar differed from theirs, however, in that it reputed to capture the relationship of a declarative sentence to all the WH questions that might be asked about the content of the sentence as well as all the elliptical answers that might be given. For instance, consider the sentence, *The little zebra nimbly jumped over the stream.* Restricting ourselves to just the WH questions, some of the questions that might be asked by someone who failed to process the sentence successfully when first presented for whatever reasons (distracted, partially deaf, retarded, a nonnative speaker, etc.), may ask: *What did? Did what? Which Zebra? Jumped where? Over what? How?* etc. The corresponding elliptical responses to these "ellipsizing" questions might be offered: *The zebra. Jumped. The little one. Over the stream Nimbly.* Our grammar showed that the same transformations used to derive a whole sentence could tag certain sentential constituents in such a manner that either of two kinds of transformations might be applied to the deep structure forms, an ellipsizing question or a correct elliptical answer to that question. In other words, an "erasure" transformation applied in a complimentary fashion to a given sentence to produce either a desired question or a desired answer. Our theory established what we called the transformational relationship of *grammatical complimentarity* between ellipsizing questions and the elliptical answers they evoked. All this was achieved with a minimal modification to Chomsky's (1965) version of the transformational grammar of English and without destroying any of the desirable properties that such a grammar must have if it is to contribute to a theory of language comprehension.

To initially test our grammar we showed that it could generate over 98% of all the elliptical sentences given by a large number of adult normal subjects when asked the total set of possible ellipsizing questions about a wide variety of sentences of various lengths and degrees of syntactic complexity. Later, given the success of this initial test of our model, we attempted to determine if a similar technique might not shed light on the problem of how linguistic knowledge is represented. More specifically, we wanted to determine the extent to which our knowledge of sentences was represented in a form possessing some degree of abstract similarity to their transformational description. By using the ellipsizing question as a probe, we hoped to show that the latency of producing an appropriate elliptical answer was proportional to the number of operations used in its derivation by the grammar. If this proved to be the case then, following a line of argument made popular by Chomsky, our modified transformational grammar (mostly Chomsky's and Lee's, that is) would be shown to be a valid model of how linguistic knowledge is represented.

To this end, with Virginia Walls (1968) we developed what we called the ellipsis production task (EPT), which is carried out in the following way. A subject is given a deck of cards with a single sentence on each card. The subject memorizes the sentence on a given card turned up in front of her. The subject then turns the card face down and the experimenter asks an ellipsizing question about the sentence just memorized which she is to answer immediately. A voice key is tripped by the offset of the experimenter's voiced question and again by the onset of the subject's vocal response. Hence, a measurement is taken of the time required for the subject to process the question.

Our primary assumption was that questions probing more complex answers embedded deepest in the sentence would require the most time to process. In contrast, elliptical answers whose derivations were simpler should take less processing time to retrieve. Roughly, our hypotheses were borne out according to a simple count of the number of rules needed to derive the elliptical response as predicted by our transformational grammar for elliptical sentences. Unfortunately, the derivational "distance" metric selected predicted less and less well, the more complicated the predicted derivation. It is here that the Just–Carpenter model seems superior to our earlier attempt to measure linguistic processing times.

Later, while working at the Aphasia Clinic at the Minneapolis Veteran's Administration Hospital with the great aphasiologist, Hildred Schuell, William Brewer and I attempted with some success to apply the EPT and other psycholinguistic techniques to the study of the aphasic communication disorder.

However, owing to the untimely death of Hildred Schuell, the research project was never fully completed. Some tentative results, however, can be culled from these efforts.

As is well known, it is very difficult to get reliable measures of linguistic processing latencies from aphasic patients because the time it takes them to produce any given utterance at any given time is highly erratic, thus giving an error term that renders any statistic virtually useless. However, their pattern of errors on linguistic performance does seem quite reliable over tasks. Roughly, we found that the errors produced by adult aphasic patients in either producing sentences from given words, repeating sentences presented visually or orally, or in answering questions about sentences available in front of them (a modified version of the EPT) were correlated with the syntactic complexity of the sentence or the deriviational relationships among sentences–questions–answers. This suggests that a correlation should exist between the latency measures exhibited by normal native speakers in processing sentences and the error measures exhibited by aphasic patients on similar tasks (Schuell, Shaw, & Brewer, 1969; Sefer & Shaw, 1972).

The attempt to apply psycholinguistic and cognitive principles to the study, diagnosis, prognosis, and treatment of aphasic patients forced us to rethink seriously what we believe to be the nature of normal cognition and the role it plays in normal communication. In *Schuell's Aphasia in Adults* (Jenkins, Jiminez-Pabon, Shaw, & Sefer, 1975), we present a functional schema for cognition that organizes the contribution of all the various psychological components we believe necessary to normal communication. Our theory of aphasia and other communication disorders provides a characterization of each type of communication disorder in terms of the dysfunctional relationships or interactions among these necessary components as a result of trauma to the system. In other words, in this book we have made a serious effort to define the norm from which aphasia and other disorders deviate and to precisely characterize that deviation. Furthermore, it is with respect to this cognitive approach to communication and communication disorders that I feel the Just–Carpenter model, as well as the models in the chapters by Simon and Hayes and by Shaw and Wilson have particular relevance. In isolation one may indeed question their relevance to current instructional problems in either the clinical or classroom setting. However, when taken together, their potential relevance to the realization of a general cognitive model for communication—something that is obviously indispensable to the development of a true science of instructional design—becomes obvious to even the most applied psychologist.

The potential relevance of basic research in cognitive psychology to applied problems is illustrated in the case of the generative approach to conceptual knowledge and the techniques of *stimulative* therapy developed by Schuell. Therapy can be considered a form of instruction when the latter concept is as broadly construed as I feel it should be. The stimulative method of construction whether applied in a classroom program to teach or improve language facility of normal speakers, or in a clinical program to treat aphasics, is based upon a sound pedagogical principle, namely, the principle that, in general, one should stimulate rather than correct. The idea Schuell repeatedly proved in her clinic is that defective responses tend to disappear automatically as language functions increase. Thus, the time of the clinician, like that of the teacher, is better spent in stimulating the proper use of all language modalities rather than in trying to force patients to modify erroneous responses made sporadically along the way.

The success of the stimulative approach depends upon the existence of what Wilson and I have termed the "generative cognitive capacity" for the following reasons. Language is learned originally in childhood from experience with a set of linguistic structures that is much smaller and less systematic than the dynamic whole finally achieved by adulthood. The clinician, no less than the teacher, must discover what language functions (vocabulary, syntactic forms, sound patterns, etc.) the patient or student has, and use these as the material by which to stimulate or restimulate, as the case may be, the cognitive processes and physiological synergisms required for normal language processing. For instance, the residual language remaining for most adult aphasic patients will be from that area of knowledge most closely related to the patient's job and home environments. The words, concepts, and sentential structures that are most salient in those subcultural contexts will probably contribute the greatest amount to the patient's residual language. If the patient is a farmer, then his residual language is most likely to be about farming; if a doctor, it is about the practice of medicine; if a lawyer, it is about the practice of law, and so forth.

Given both the logical necessity and the empirical evidence for the existence of a generative cognitive capacity as discussed earlier (Shaw & Wilson, Chapter 10 of this volume), what could be more natural than stimulative therapy? Here simple exemplary sentences constructed from the patient's residual vocabulary are given to him for practice. The materials should not be so easy as to require no effort nor so difficult as to be frustrating. Rather they should be so suited to the patient at a given time as to allow for a moderate degree of success. Thus, in this way the patient is allowed to build from success to success at gradually increasing levels of linguistic complexity. Obviously, then what is sorely needed, if such therapy is to be successful, is as precise a metric as possible for measuring the difficulty of the material. It is here that the demand for techniques for measuring linguistic processing latencies and linguistic processing errors converge with the need for a technique to select the set of exemplars to be practiced.

The sentences constructed from the residual vocabulary of an aphasic patient and given to him for practice must be selected to be both exemplary and of adequate difficulty, if they are to stimulate the traumatically deranged cognitive system to reequilibrate along the same lines as the functional organization existing before the trauma. Since language is itself a generative system built up originally from practice with perceiving and producing exemplars, restimulation during the course of therapy presumably succeeds only if the cognitive system retains sufficient generative capacity to become functionally restructured by generalizing from the exemplars experienced.

Thus, the generative model for concept learning also provides an explanation for why stimulative therapy should work at all. Moreover, this model provides a new, more dynamic theory to supplant the traditional, essentially static theory offered by stimulus–response psychology for both positive transfer and so-called "stimulus generalization." The wedding of this generative model with stimulative therapy is testimony to the proposition that a symbiotic relationship can exist between pure and applied psychology.

THE ROLE OF PERCEPTION
IN GENERATIVE INSTRUCTION

I believe perception is the epigenetic fount of all knowledge gathering activities. By this I mean that all concepts ultimately have their developmental origins in the process of perceptual abstraction of invariant information from events—what J. J. Gibson has called the pickup of invariant information over time. But since this view probably runs counter to the more constructivistic account of knowledge championed by most contributors to this volume, perhaps I should explain what Wilson and I, following a Gibsonian line of argument, believe to be the nature of the epigenetic process by which abstract concepts are specified by perceptual experiences. After doing so, I will relate this view to some of those discussed in this volume.

Our basic assumption, what might be called the *event perception hypothesis,* is that all conceptual knowledge ultimately has its origins in the *affordance* structure of events. By the affordance structure of events (Shaw, McIntyre, & Mace, 1974) we mean the detectable invariant information determined by events that specifies the true properties of its event source that may contribute to an animal's or person's adaptive behavior. How this may be will be explored in a moment.

This hypothesis suggests that all concepts, even the most abstract ones, ultimately refer to events when the concept of event is broadly construed. For instance, the concepts of running, smiling, or eating may be exemplified by events involving running, smiling, and eating. But what of more abstract concepts such as love, justice, or truth? We also assume that these concepts ultimately derive from the perceived affordance structure of events, namely, that the concept of *love* is derived from perceived instances of loving, *justice* from perceived instances where justice has been properly administered, and *truth* from perceived instances where something believed to be the case was in fact shown to be the case. This is not to argue, however, that each concept understood by a particular individual must be learned by that individual from experience with actual events; for surely we often learn vicariously from verbal descriptions or surrogate forms (movies, pictures, etc.), of other people's experience, as well as from descriptions or representations of fictitious or inferred entities (e.g., stories, plays, models, or proofs).

In short, much of our conceptual knowledge of the world is socially derived from instruction by others or instructional materials. A word of caution: The event perception hypothesis should not be confused with the view of radical empiricism which asserts that perception is based on elementaristic structures such as sense impressions, sensations or simple sense data. Under this view abstract concepts are built up by a process of association. By contrast, the view we are offering does not assume a single simple level of analysis is sufficient to characterize the relevant information liberated by events, nor does it assume an associative mechanism for compounding complex concepts out of simpler ones. The cognitive capacity we believe to be at work is *generative*, rather than associative, possessing considerably more structure (probably resembling that of a mathematical group) than that offered by associative principles. Indeed, the only premise our generative theory of event conceptualization has in common with radical empiricism is affirmation of the postulate of critical realism, namely, that there exists a *real* objective world about which we may have veridical knowledge. In addition, our theory of the knowing agent is an active one where that of the empiricist's is quite passive. Now let me relate our generative theory of conceptual knowledge to some of the other views presented in this volume.

Norman, Gentner, and Stevens (Chapter 9, this volume) suggest a network description of the concepts, not necessarily linguistic, involved in money changing, say as in the case of making purchases in a grocery store. Here objects, bearing specific relations to one another, are being transformed; that is, money and goods are being exchanged in accordance with certain economic principles and customs governing behavior in the market place. Children, according to Norman, eventually learn this process by experiencing those events in which grownups exchange money for goods (see Gentner, 1975). He begins his network analysis of this knowledge by assuming that certain nodes and relations exist among them, but his model does not yet account for how such primitive nodes and relations are derived from experience. The generative model offered by Wilson and me seems to supply the missing cognitive component by which such nodes and relations are originally specified by events.

Such a generative perceptual component is no less necessary to round out Greeno's (Chapter 7, this volume) network approach. Moreover, Hyman's (Chapter 8, this volume) impression formation task seems to me to imply the existence of such a generative cognitive capacity as does our own experimentation. Moreover, it seems to me that the *monster-globe-passing* problem addressed by the Simon–Hayes (Chapter 14, this volume) problem-solving model with the "change" operator can be construed as an attempt to study the affordance structure of a "monster-globe-passing" event.

KNOWLEDGE ORIGINS VERSUS
KNOWLEDGE REPRESENTATIONS

Before closing, I would like to emphasize the distinction between the representation of knowledge and the origin of knowledge. The two are not the same. The origin or epigenesis of knowledge has to do with the primitives that go into the representation, the nodes and relations, the schemata. My suggestion is that the principles revealed by the study of how event concepts arise from the perceptual information specifying the events may provide an inroad into the fundamental problem of how knowledge should be represented. For if we attempt to represent knowledge in terms of networks or other models by merely selecting a priori labels for our concept nodes and relations, then we may end up with a logically possible but arbitrary schematic representation of knowledge that has little to do with how the concepts actually arose. Our knowledge of the world is interfaced by direct perceptual experience of events and, therefore, the perceptual processes involved can only be ignored at our peril. For this reason the role of perception seems to me to have been greatly underemphasized at this conference. There seems to be a tendency toward too much theoretical dependence on secondary processes such as language.

Let us recognize the fact that much of our knowledge is either tacit or purely nonverbal, neither being able to assume a linguistic form. For instance, try to give an adequate verbal description of nearly any object (e.g., the face of a friend or relative), any act (e.g., tying your shoelace, riding a bicycle) or any other nontrivial event. We are never able to verbalize more than a small tip of the iceberg of what we can recognize or recall about a familiar object, act or event. Instruction, therefore, should be aimed at this nonverbal aspect of knowledge gathering activities as well. Learning to read is of course an indispensable social skill but so is learning to "see" in the broadest sense of the term.

AN APPLICATION TO ART INSTRUCTION

As argued earlier, this view that perception is itself a mode of cognition is in no way antagonistic to the purposes of this conference, nor is it as irrelevant as it may at first seem. Let me describe a project, on which I have been a consultant, that uses perceptual principles as an integral part of its instructional design.

In 1973 the Minneapolis Institute of Art requested help from the Center for Research in Human Learning at Minnesota. P. Salapatek, A. Jonas, H. Pick, and

I, as perceptual psychologists, were asked to help in the development of an art exhibit for children to celebrate the opening of the new art educational center attached to the museum. Our task, in cooperation with artists and art historians, was to develop a sequence of modular displays aimed at the explanation of how paintings incorporate perceptual information that specifies spatial layout, shape of objects, color contrast, and so forth. Consequently, we have developed a set of portable modular displays in which each is designed to present schematic but working models of situations demonstrating various salient forms of perceptual information. For instance, one display allows children to see what happens to the apparent size of an object when moved across a texture gradient toward a simulated horizon of vanishing points. By this display we hope to let the children learn about the laws of linear perspective through dynamic manipulations which provide exemplars for the relevant concepts.

Next to the display is a large print of a painting in the museum that clearly utilizes the same perceptual principles. In addition, between the picture and the display is a schematic drawing presenting in outline just those portions of the painting relevant to the principles demonstrated in the display itself. In other words, the relationship between the painting and the display is clarified by a simpler, intermediate step that omits confusing or irrelevant detail. In another display module we illustrate in a similar fashion how shading on objects or their cast shadows provide information for their shape or distance from other surfaces, respectively. Again the abstract principles are illustrated in a high-fidelity copy of an actual painting in the museum interfaced conceptually to the visual display by a schematic diagram outlining the relevant parts of the picture.

After studying the dozen or so visual displays, the children are guided through the museum proper to rooms where the pictures used in the displays are actually hung. Our ultimate goal is to determine the time that the children spend looking at the pictures represented in the displays and, more importantly, the time spent looking at other pictures not seen before that clearly portray the same type of perceptual information presented in the display modules. We hope that such measures indicate that children show more interest in those paintings expressing the same information studied in the displays than in those comparable paintings not relevant to principles demonstrated in the visual displays.

In summary, it is our intention to interest children in the perceptual problems solved by great painters in their works, to provide them with a kind of problem solving orientation to the museum rather than to just turn them loose in the galleries to be arbitrarily bombarded by a confusing welter of information. By giving them the knowledge of the appropriate perceptual concepts beforehand, it is our belief that they will be encouraged to *see* the paintings rather than just look at them. It is interesting to speculate on how a really well-controlled experiment of this type might provide challenging data relevant to the evaluation of many of the cognitive models presented in this volume.

Part IV

GENERAL COMMENTS

You have just spoken in praise of me," said Socrates, "and now it is my turn to speak in praise of my right-hand neighbor. If Agathon sits next to you, it will fall to him to speak in praise of me all over again, instead of my speaking in praise of him. Let it be as I propose, my good friend, and don't grudge the lad his tribute of praise from me, especially as I have strong desire to eulogize him. . . .

Agathon got up, intending to move to the place on the other side of Socrates. But at that moment a crowd of revellers came to the door, and finding it left open by somebody who had just gone out, made their way into the dining-room and installed themselves there. There was a general uproar, all order was abolished, and deep drinking became the rule [Plato: *The Symposium*].

17
Cognitive Psychology and Instructional Design

Robert Glaser

University of Pittsburgh

In reacting to this volume, I shall address three points: the application of theory to practice; the nature of a prescriptive science of instruction and its components; and, in the context of these components, specific remarks based on some of the chapters that have been presented.

THE APPLICATION OF THEORY TO PRACTICE

Strong applications of science to practice generally are characterized by some linking body of knowledge and procedure—some sort of a linking science between a descriptive explanatory science and application by professionals. There is rarely a direct relationship between descriptive science and professional work. Attempts at direct application without building a linking science either tend to fade away or are subject to sporadic flashes of interest by particular scientists who happen to become interested in some applied problems at the moment. In either case, no substantial structure is built up into which rules or hypotheses for professional application can be placed. In psychology, an example is the field of programmed instruction where professional societies were established which were uninhabited, for the most part, by people who maintained a scientific interest in learning theory, and who could nurture the development efforts and new attempts in programmed instruction. The field spun off by itself with its own body of rules and declined in impact because it was not yet ready to stand by itself. The danger is that a body of practice is picked up, is deintellectualized in the sense of becoming separated from the theory that generated it, and is carried out in a rote, by-the-numbers fashion. Some of the chapters in this volume make me wonder about such a danger. We may need to guard against encouraging potential practitioners from immediately establishing a Society for Cognitive Research on the Advancement of Pedagogy (SCRAP)[1] that is not nurtured by the active involvement of people like those represented here. Establishment of SCRAP should not happen for some time to come. For the present, what is required are sustained attempts at instruction, constantly working between science and practical problems. This interaction by someone who has both aims in mind, who is both a trained scientist and who takes seriously a practical problem, is the way in which a linking science generally is developed. Only after the linking science evolves in some form is it possible for a professional field to grow and for people to work only in the linking science itself. The game for us at this time is to take an honest interest in instructional problems, to continue our interest in a science of cognitive psychology, and to play between the two until this linking structure develops. Simply turning exciting findings over to someone with an applied bent or turning some interesting procedures over to teachers to use will not do the trick.

It is of interest to note that in 1899, in a presidential address before the American Psychological Association, John Dewey (1900) expressed concern about developing a linking science between psychological theory and practical work:

> "Do we not lay a special linking science everywhere else between the theory and practical work? We have engineering between physics and the practical workingmen in the mills; we have a scientific medicine between the natural science and the physician." The sentences suggest, in an almost startling way, that the real essence of the problem is found in an *organic* connection between the two extreme terms—between the theorist and the practical worker—through the medium of the linking science. The decisive matter is the extent to which the ideas of the theorist actually project themselves, through the kind offices of the middleman, into the consciousness of the practitioner. It is the participation by the practical man in the theory, through the agency of the linking science, that determines at once the effectiveness of the work done, and the moral freedom and personal development of the one engaged in it.

> ... [If not the teacher is compelled] to resort to purely arbitrary measures, to fall back upon mere routine traditions of school teaching, or to fly to the latest fad of pedagogical theorists—the latest panacea peddled out in school journals or teachers' institutes—just as the old physician relied upon his magic formula [pp. 110–113].

A linking science is essentially a science of design. It is a prescriptive, normative science, and not the kind of enterprise that most of the people in this volume, who have been working in explanatory descriptive science, have been up to. The characteristics of a science of design have been carefully discussed by Herbert Simon (1969), and I need not get into those details here. The distinction between a prescriptive science of design and an explanatory descriptive science is made clearly by Simon, and work in a prescriptive science mode has been exemplified in the special limited case of stochastic models of learning in

---

[1] We have the editor to thank for this acronym.

Atkinson's Chapter 4. In general, a prescriptive science provides a schema for the professional in a field and for developers of applications who provide the professional with tools, techniques, and instrumentation for professional work. Concepts and ideas are not directly dumped onto the teacher or the college of education. A design science leads to the development of instrumentation for the teacher and also for the student insofar as the student becomes his or her own teacher. Talk about direct application by descriptive scientists can be a lot of hand waving unless serious development of a prescriptive linking science takes place. It is a very difficult task at the moment because most cognitive psychologists are descriptive scientists by training, and very few of them have the temperament to work at a prescriptive science while they do their "real" science.

COMPONENTS OF A PSYCHOLOGY
OF INSTRUCTION

Consider now some possible components of a prescriptive science of instructional psychology, but first let me describe in very general terms the kind of individual cognitive competence to which these components refer.

The Development of Competence

The process of instruction, as distinguished from education in general is, to a large extent, concerned with the development of competence in a learner and with the behaviors and cognitive structures that differentiate the novice from the competent performer in a particular subject matter. In attaining subject-matter knowledge and skill, the learner proceeds through a novitiate and then develops relative expertise; he or she learns to be a good reader, a competent mathematician, a deep thinker, a quick learner, a creative person, an inquiring individual, and so on. These activities are learned according to criteria of expertise established by the school and the community; more specifically, by subject-matter requirements, peer-group expectations, and the general social and professional criteria for what determines low, average, and high levels of competence. The educational and social community adjusts its expectations to the competence level of the learner so that initially awkward and partially correct performances are acceptable, whereas later they are not; a young child or a novice is frequently rewarded for rather uninteresting behavior, but as competence grows, his performance is attended to only if it occurs in the presence of an appropriate audience or in an appropriate context.

The gross changes that take place as an individual progresses from ignorance to increasing competence are of the following kinds:

1. Variable, awkward, and crude performance changes to performance that is consistent, relatively fast, and precise. Unitary acts change into larger response integrations and overall strategies.

2. The contexts of performance changes from simple stimulus patterns with a great deal of clarity to complex patterns in which relevant information must be abstracted from a context of events that are not all relevant.

3. Performance becomes increasingly symbolic and covert. The learner responds increasingly to internal representations of an event, to internalized standards, and to internalized strategies for thinking and problem solving.

4. The behavior of the competent individual becomes increasingly self-sustaining in terms of his skillful employment of the rules when they are applicable and his subtle bending of the rules in appropriate situations. Increasing reliance is placed on one's own ability to generate the events by which one learns and the criteria by which one's performance is judged and valued.

It is the understanding and facilitation of this process of change from ignorance to competence, from novice to expert, that is a major focus of the framework that I shall now describe.

Description and Analysis of Competent Performance

First, description and analysis of competent performance—the state of knowledge and skill to be achieved. Since attention to the instructional problem means facing the necessity of studying behavior in tasks considerably more complex than those typically studied in the psychological laboratory, the development of new ways of analyzing tasks and specifying the content of learning is required. Tasks in the laboratory have been selected, for the most part, according to what is convenient and manageable for experimental and theoretical analysis. Concentration on tasks artificially constructed for experimental purposes has meant that few psychologists have, until recently, confronted the problem of analyzing complex tasks in terms that allow access to psychological theory and data, and yet still preserve some fidelity to the real-life character of the tasks themselves.

For the psychologist concerned with instructional processes, however, the problem of task analysis is a central one. Analytic description of what is to be learned facilitates instruction by attempting to define clearly what it is that an expert in a subject-matter domain has learned; for example, what it is that distinguishes a skilled from an unskilled reader. When this analysis identifies classes of behaviors whose properties as learning tasks are known or can be systematically studied, then inferences concerning optimal instructional processes can be formulated and tested.

Procedures have been developing for the analysis of tasks—analysis of the content of what is learned and the properties and processes involved in competent performance—and task analysis is characterized by the description of performance in terms of the demands placed on basic psychological processes such as attention, perception, and linguistic processing, and on knowledge and skills assumed to be in the learner's repertoire. Further, since an individual's capacities change over time, task analysis reflects current knowledge and assumptions concerning the processes available at different stages of learning or development (see Resnick, Chapter 3; Klahr & Wallace, 1976).

As this volume reflects, a major activity in this regard is being carried out through modeling and simulating (computer simulation or otherwise) processes that can reproduce complex performances like playing chess, solving algebra word problems, series completion problems, certain problem-solving skills, and understanding complex instructions. The processes chosen represent a combination of what is observed in the performing subject and of theory concerning the characteristics of the conceptual processes, memory processes involved, and the semantic information structures that are built up. The simulation of complex performance represents a formal technique for establishing the logical sufficiency and necessity of certain processes and the way they are assembled for producing particular performances. However, for the purposes of instructional design, the next moves required in cognitive simulation work have not been made, and we need to investigate further. It is possible that the information obtained from this kind of analysis of human competence can allow us to do several things with regard to the optimizing of instruction:

1. Specification of the processes by which highly competent individuals might be performing a task puts us in a position to try to teach these processes to individual learners; for example, knowing that a large "perceptual vocabulary" of the configuration of pieces on a chess board is a characteristic of an efficient chess player might encourage us to attempt to teach this kind of performance in order to develop good chess players.

2. Knowing that a task is performed more efficiently in one way rather than another and knowing the procedures involved in the more efficient way may put us in a position to design instruction so that it approximates the most efficient method.

The very interesting question at the moment is the teachability of the processes that are identified through simulation. If we teach these processes, then is acquisition of the performance influenced, and will more individuals obtain competence than have in the past? Or, is it likely that if we teach these processes, we will put the learner in the position of the centipede who analyzed the processes by which he moved his hundred legs, and became incapable of walking at all? At any rate, in my own laboratory (Holzman, 1975) we are currently investigating the teachability of processes that have been derived by procedures of cognitive simulation. As a start, the particular task we have chosen is the series completion problem as analyzed by Simon and Kotovsky (1963).

A look at the current literature in experimental psychology shows an increasing number of studies devoted to the analysis of complex cognitive performance in contrast to the study of learning. While this trend is contributing to the description of competence in intellectual tasks, many of the studies can be faulted, from the present point of view, for their lack of explicit instructional orientation. The explicit requirements necessary for the analysis of tasks relevant to the development of an instructional psychology are the following: (1) that complex real-life tasks be investigated and not tasks designed for laboratory convenience; (2) that these realistic tasks be analyzed in terms of current theoretical concepts in cognitive psychology; (3) that the processes identified be considered with respect to their instructability and the conditions that influence their acquisition; and (4) that they be related to the cognitive capacities or the developmental status of the child and to the background capabilities of adults.

Description and Diagnosis of the Initial State

The second component of instructional design is description and diagnosis of the initial state with which an individual begins a course of learning. There is an "immediate" and a "long-term" approach to this aspect. The immediate approach is to take seriously the fact that effective instruction requires careful assessment of the initial state of the learner. For individual learners, we need to know their strengths, weaknesses, styles, and background interests and talents. What are the details of what a child knows and does not know at particular points in his or her learning? What are the details of the skills that he or she is developing? What needs to be improved? What strengths can be capitalized on? What do various developmental levels and various cultural backgrounds mean for what should be taught and how it should be taught? Educational practices need to be designed so that answers to these kinds of questions are possible for all individuals attending school. Teachers and learners need to be in a position to obtain and utilize this information; with it, teachers can prescribe the instruction required and students can assess their own abilities and select appropriate instruction.

The development and use of procedures for providing this information is necessary, but I do not mean at all to imply that learning and schooling should be one big series of formal tests and assessments. I would suggest informal observation as well as infrequent formal assessment, and adoption of an attitude that the information obtained is information for improving instruction and not for constant evaluation. My colleagues and I, in our own work in schools, have found it desirable to provide primary-grade teachers with hierarchies of increasing competence in various school subjects. These take the form of "structured maps" into which a teacher can place a child and thereby direct attention to prerequisite skills that might need to be learned or advanced skills that the child might explore. The hierarchical map is only a guide upon which both the teacher and the child can impose their own judgment. Procedures for assessing the current competence and talents of the learner in a way that provides a basis for instruction are generally not available in current educational methods at a level of detail necessary for the effective guidance of individual learners. I call the implementation of these procedures the "immediate" approach because, to a large extent, it is secondarily a matter of research and primarily a matter of administrative change and the design of appropriate materials.

The long-term approach relates to the fact that while a prevalent method for assessing initial state is the assessment of aptitudes that correlate, to some extent, with end-of-school achievement, aptitudes so assessed do not provide information about instructional processes (see Glaser, 1972; Hunt, Frost, & Lunneborg, 1973). They are measures used for purposes of selection and do not provide a basis for deciding upon instructional alternatives. Aptitude information does not tell how an individual should be instructed to improve his performance, nor how instruction might be designed to make the attainment of successful performance more probable. The significant research requirement in this regard is to describe the initial state of the learner in terms of processes involved in achieving competent performance. This would then allow us to influence learning in two ways—to design instructional alternatives that adapt to these processes, and to attempt to improve an individual's competence in these processes so that he or she is more likely to profit from the instructional procedures available.

Conditions that Foster Learning and the Acquisition of Competence

The third component of instructional design comprises the conditions that foster learning and the acquisition of competence—essentially, the procedures by which one learns and the nature of the environment in which learning occurs. There are at least two directions in this regard that need to be taken for the development of an instructional psychology.

The first is to recognize that we do know a little about learning. For example, we know some things about the effects of reinforcement—the contingencies consequent to performance; about the conditions under which discriminations, generalization, and concept formation take place; and about conditions of practice, interference with memory, the nature of attention, the effects of punishment, and how observational learning and modeling can influence new learning. We know these things in terms of descriptive science, but little investigation has been made from the point of view required for the utilization of this information for designing the conditions of instruction. Exceptions to this are the work on behavior modification and the work on optimization models described in the chapter by Atkinson. However, neither of these enterprises has considered complex cognitive performance in any systematic way.

What is required is research on what we know about learning cast into the mold of a design science which attempts to maximize the outcomes of learning for different individuals. A new form of experimentation would be called for where the tactic is not to develop models of learning and performance, but to test existing models by using them for maximizing the effects of learning under various conditions. For this purpose, we need a theory of the acquisition of competence. Such a theory would be concerned with how an individual acquires increasingly complex performances by assembling the present components of his repertoire, manipulating the surrounding conditions and events, and employing his knowledge of how he learns.

Effects of Instructional Implementation in the Short and in the Long Run

The fourth component of instructional design is concerned with the effects of instructional implementation in the short and in the long run—effects that occur immediately in the context of instruction and supply relatively immediate feedback, and effects that persist in terms of long-term transfer, generalized patterns of behavior, ability for further learning, and so on. One requirement for this purpose is to break away from the tradition of norm-referenced measurement to measurement more concerned with identifying the nature of criterion performance (see Glaser, 1963; Glaser & Nitko, 1971). For effective instructional design, tests will have to be criterion referenced in addition to being norm referenced. They will have to assess performance attainments and capabilities that can be matched to available educational options in more detailed ways than can be carried out with currently used testing and assessment procedures. This will be an important part of the development of a psychology of instruction. It is mandatory that testing not stand out as an extrinsic and external adjunct of instruction. Tests need to be interpreted in terms of performance criteria so that the learner and the teacher are informed about an individual's progress relative to developing competence. In this way, information is provided for deciding upon appropriate courses of action for assisting instruction.

The processes measured by tests designed to facilatate instruction need to be related to processes identified as components of competence. For this purpose, some interesting endeavors can be envisioned. A good example in this volume is the work going on in analyzing the processes involved in the comprehension of written language. Stimulated by the work in psycholinguistics and cognitive psychology, there is a great deal of excitement about the nature of language comprehension processes at this time. This excitement should be juxtaposed with the fact that there has, over years, been a great deal of work on the development of tests of reading comprehension. The new development is that as we begin to analyze comprehension tasks and relate them to theories of semantic memory, imagery, and so forth, we can begin to develop tests that provide us with diagnostic information about component processes that contribute to performance and that can be influenced through instruction. This kind of activity should change the nature of assessment procedures and provide the kind of information required for maximizing instructional outcomes.

ADDITIONAL COMMENTS[2]

I would like now to comment on specific chapters in this volume in relation to the components that I have just described.

Analysis of Competence

Component one, the analysis of competent performance, comprises most of this volume. Of the components that I listed, this volume rates high on the explication of performance theory and the analysis of states of competence. Several themes were elaborated on: description of competence in terms of cognitive structure, sequential task analysis to show changes brought about by instruction, and processes as objectives of instruction. Greeno and Norman stressed cognitive objectives; they would like to display a student's cognitive structure and state instructional objectives in this way. This is an interesting idea; it makes contact with their theoretical notions, but they leave us with mere technological problems. Carroll brought up this point when he asked how one teaches toward these unobserved competence maps. Greeno implies that analyses of cognitive structure can be given directly to teachers and students in order to facilitate the acquisition of competence. It is hard to envision just how this is to be done, but it does present the notion of progressive, increasingly complex theories of subject matter that assist learning and are approximations to the kinds of theory that a competent expert employs. Teaching procedures based on cognitive structures of developing competence might make use of these schemata as pedagogical frameworks that must be developed to more and more closely approximate the theories that an expert carries around in his head as sophisticated codifications of a body of knowledge. It is also possible that these developing structures of subject-matter knowledge might suggest ways of designing new kinds of textbooks.

A significant problem in the specification of cognitive objectives for instruction is level of description, a problem also raised by Carroll. How does one describe these structures? Are they described in the same terms that the details of cognitive processing and cognitive theories are written in? There is no answer to this question forthcoming from this volume. It may be useful, however, to point out that when Atkinson built his instructional programs in reading and computer science, he began with standard subject-matter units. He looked at the subject matter and broke it up into what seemed to be reasonable units, as any instructor would do. On these units of analysis, he imposed his instructional

[2] Editor's note: In this section there are several references to the material introduced at the Workshops presented during the symposium by Collins, Fletcher, Hayes, Siegler, and Wallace. For a very brief summary of these Workshops see the Preface to this book.

technology. In the case of learning foreign language vocabulary, he analyzed the subject matter in more cognitive terms. This was part of his implicit description of the building up of memory structures that underly the competence he sought to teach. As a general answer to the level-of-analysis problem, it seems that there should be a difference between science and practice. A petroleum chemist can think about atoms and forces in molecular structures, but he also can think about gross quantities of gases and residues in the fractionating tower. His theory can work back and forth between the two systems of description. The "linking science" I mentioned earlier should enable this to occur if at all possible.

In optimization procedures such as those carried out by Atkinson, task analysis proceeds as learning occurs. Continuous assessment is made of the difficulty and structure of the task. This technique of ongoing task analysis might be a useful way to study the acquisition of competence. For example, in the BASIC Instructional Program, the program stores the student's evaluation of his own skills and compares his solution attempts to stored models. In this way, information can be obtained about the changing structure of developing competence that might not be uncovered by more static techniques.

A recurrent theme of the volume is that a target of instruction is competence in process, for example, the constituent comparison exercises to improve reading comprehension suggested by Just and Carpenter. Shaw's generative system might be thought of as a special process skill that is a teachable entity, and not only a theoretical description of what occurs. Simon and Hayes suggest giving students a wide repertoire of problem-solving styles and detection cues for matching styles to situations.

Diagnosis of Initial State

In contrast to the analysis of attained competence, this volume had less to say about this second component, the diagnosis of the initial state. There were several themes: notions about some kind of psychometrics of process for initial state assessment, consideration of developmental growth changes, and the notion of schema discrepancy between initial state and competence state. Calfee in Chapter 2 emphasized techniques for the assessment and diagnosis of processes in initial state competence. Wallace referred to "process profiles" prior to instruction and the design of custom-built training as a function of these profiles. Siegler talked of the developmental aspects of the facility of older children to use analogy information as compared to younger children, and he brought to our attention the necessity for taking developmental growth phenomena into account in assessing initial states. Hyman's notion of discrepancy from schema, the extent to which old information influences new information, strongly suggests initial competence analysis prior to a course of instruction.

Acquisition

The third component involves a theory of acquisition—of transformation from an initial state to competent performance. This component was not explicitly addressed in most chapters. There was some concern about the properties of performance that are involved when someone proceeds from novice to expert: the growth of the cognitive net, increasing symbiotic manipulation, concept generation from specific events, decreasing dependence of performance on external cues, bigger chunking underlying performance, and so on. The characteristics of the changes in competence as one moves from novice to expert are primary data required for a theory of acquisition, and earlier, I described some gross features of these changes. Wallace discussed changes in the acquisition of competence when he described the shift in "attentional grain" from global attention to dimensional attention. Resnick presented her work with Groen that described the change in children from one method of addition to a more efficient one.

In general, however, while the contributors had some interesting ideas about processes of developing competence, when they talked about teaching these processes, they fell back on standard "behavioristic" training procedures. Wallace mentioned "failure theory" by which he meant that he obtained information on process deficiencies and then taught to these deficiencies. The procedure he used was a form of the successive approximations procedure popularized by Skinner. Hayes talked about teaching problem solving and employed good common-sense teaching procedures. In talking about generator sets, Shaw emphasized the importance of good exemplars in the development of concepts, which is a familiar technique developed in behavioral studies of concept formation; this is an important pedagogical matter because the experience one gets in school may not be very well designed to provide rich exemplars of concepts, and Shaw emphasized this again at a deeper process level. Collins, after his careful analysis, used Socratic dialogue as his instructional procedure. Norman, in the acquisition of knowledge, stressed the importance of continuous modification of a knowledge schema, and then when pressed about teaching technique, he suggested practice with feedback. The point is, as Carroll indicated, that behavioral theory is successful because it focuses on observation of the development of behavioral components; cognitive theory at this time is difficult to express in simple observable terms, and it certainly needs such expression to decide upon appropriate instructional transformations. When this is done, how will teaching procedures change?

Norman made a good point in calling attention to time spans in attaining competence. He said that it takes five to ten years to become a good cook, and an interesting question in going from ignorance to competence is why different areas of knowledge and skill require longer and shorter times for competence to be attained. Instruction has to be thought of in such terms; learning to play the violin well takes a long time, whereas learning to do calculus well does not take very long. There are differential rates of acquisition for certain reasons, and these reasons are of great interest in developing a theory of acquisition.

The human engineering aspect of instruction was brought out in the work of Simon and Hayes, Greeno, and Just and Carpenter. Their findings suggest possibilities for the redesign of instructional material and of the environment in which instruction occurs. Such redesign may be as important or more important than tactics of instruction.

As I have already said, Atkinson addresses the acquisition of competence by a procedure of continuous decision making—decisions for prescribing the conditions of learning that need to be presented as a function of the data obtained on student performance. The question that comes to mind is whether the kind of optimization procedure he employs is a good direction for a science of instruction. The procedure requires mathematical statement of a learning function; this is now possible, as Atkinson indicates, only for very simple and quite trivial kinds of behavior. The question is the following: If one thinks of using these optimization procedures with the more complex theories of cognitive structures presented in this volume, then how are they expressed in a form that might be used with the optimization procedures available? Even if mathematical expression is possible, feasibility of computation may get out of hand.

Effects of Implementation

The fourth component of a psychology of instruction is measurement of the effects of the conditions provided for acquisition. In this regard, let me make the point that the kind of feedback Skinner emphasized in operant conditioning was essentially information on the topography of a response. In Skinner-like programmed instruction, it appears that it is the topography of the response that is the property of performance that is being shaped—successive approximation, a gradual, spatial, getting closer and closer to terminal competence; it is the effect of instructional conditions on this response aspect for which information is required to further conduct the instructional procedure. Atkinson uses as feedback the difficulty of items in a list; he employs response history and update of item difficulty parameters to obtain measurements of the effects of instructional conditions. Greeno and Norman talk about getting information on the structure of the cognitive map of knowledge, and as I said before, they leave us with a large technical problem. How do we measure "it" to assess instruction and to provide the feedback required to student and teacher? Can a representation be provided to a teacher or to a student, and can they be taught instructional skills by which they can change this representation? Fletcher reminded us that if we use a computer for storing models of individual students to represent their state of learning, we would seriously tax computer memory.

I mentioned the notion of a psychometrics of process measurement, and this brings up a point about the analysis of SAT competence in the work of Just and Carpenter. When they analyze the SAT-type examinations, they may be getting something out of their analysis that is not what they are looking for. The SAT tests are designed, in the usual psychometric way, to yield a spread of scores. A dispersion of item difficulty is built into the test in order to maximize test-score variance so that the correlation with criterion variables is maximized. The tests are selected both for the stimulus situation they provide and for certain psychometric properties. When Just and Carpenter analyze the performance processes involved in the SAT tests, they may be analyzing also the properties of psychometric item difficulty. The extra considerations built into the requirements for obtaining correlational validity may introduce extraneous processes that would not be present in a test designed to measure criterion performance more directly.

As a final remark, I must state as strongly as possible that we cannot think in terms of standard classrooms as we begin to think about the application of the concepts of this volume to the design of instruction. Even if we claim to know a good deal about the processes involved in word decoding and beginning reading, the engineering problem of classroom material and environmental design is ever present. If we continue to think in terms of the standard classroom rather than in terms of how schooling can be restructured, then our efforts will be seriously attentuated and kept down by the weight of traditional educational modes. Finally, I agree with and must reemphasize a general sentiment of this volume that work on instructional and educational problems will be a major test of our theories of human cognitive performance.

ACKNOWLEDGMENTS

Work on this paper was carried out at the Learning Research and Development Center, University of Pittsburgh, and was supported in part by funds from the National Institute of Education, U. S. Department of Health, Education, and Welfare. The opinions expressed in this paper do no necessarily reflect the position or policy of the sponsoring agency, and no official endorsement should be inferred.

18

Implications for
Instructional Research[1]

Courtney B. Cazden

Harvard University

These comments come from a background of elementary school teaching and developmental psychology. Recently, I have been concentrating on how children learn (or acquire or develop) their native language, and on the environmental events which may affect that learning in and out of school (Brown, Cazden & Bellugi, 1969; Cazden, 1972). I was an elementary school teacher in the late 1940s and 1950s. Now I'm going back to teach children for one year in a primary classroom in an inner-city public school.

In thinking about these plans, I realized that the three topics which Hugh Mehan, director of the teacher training program at the University of California, San Diego, and I proposed to investigate in my classroom can all be reformulated in terms of topics discussed here. (A validation of the sophistication of our plans or the real-life relevance of these discussions?) First, what is a "relevant curriculum"? In Norman's sense, what do children know that's relevant to what we want to teach—relevant either because it can help or because it may interfere? Second, how do children understand or fail to understand instructions, primarily oral instructions because the children will be young and on the edge of literacy. I mean particularly the kind of instructions that teachers seem to give frequently (Mehan, 1972) and that are ill structured in Simon and Hayes' sense because they put "demands on the knowledge and repertory of problem-solving skills of the solver" (page 279)? Can we help children cope with such questions by recognizing their incompleteness and asking for more information? Third, in what subtle ways do teacher expectations get produced on the one hand, and

[1] Editor's note: In this chapter there are several references to material introduced at the Workshops presented during the symposium by Bamberger and Collins. For a brief summary of these Workshops, see the Preface to this book. Bamberger's work is also described in Bamberger (1972), and Collins' in Collins, Warnock, Aiello, and Miller (1975).

have their effects on the other hand? As one example of Hyman's concern with how people make sense out of their world, how does a teacher in a very complex environment make sense out of her children? If I refrain from "preparing my mind" (to adopt Hyman's phrase) and do not look at the children's cumulative records, can we track how cues from the children are used in making decisions before or during instruction, and how the categorizations of the children that will inevitably be built up affect my interactions with them?

In spelling out these reformulations of my plans for next year, I don't intend to imply that the deliberations of this conference should be judged by their usefulness next September. On the contrary, the more appropriate question is about the implications for research on instruction during the next five years. From that perspective, the comments below fall under four headings: the concept of instruction, cognitive objectives, task analyses, and means of instruction.

THE CONCEPT OF INSTRUCTION

I am impressed by the broad concept of instruction explicit in some of the chapters, and implicit throughout this volume. In its catchiest version (Olson, this volume), instruction includes muddling by the learner as well as modeling and meddling by the teacher. In Resnick's (Chapter 3) more precise definition, instruction means "any set of environmental conditions that are deliberately arranged to foster increases in competence. Instruction thus includes demonstrating, telling, and explaining, but it equally includes physical arrangements, structure of presented material, sequences of task demands, and responses to the learner's actions [page 51]." In Carroll's application to language skills, instruction is "defined broadly as any external influences on the development of language skills, as represented both by formal teaching actions and by more informal social interactions [page 5]."

There have undoubtedly been many influences on this broadened definition. For me, two of the most important have been the writings of more persuasive proponents of "open" or "learner-controlled" education, and the research on language learning which Carroll has summarized. There is a noncoincidental relationship between these two influences, because the ease with which children learn their native language without instruction more narrowly conceived has been used (e.g. by Holt, 1967; Morrison, 1964) as an argument for more open education. Resnick's definition extends this broadened concept to all learning, not just language, and to all settings, not just the one formally designated place we call a classroom So, for example, the design of museum displays mentioned by Shaw (pages 298–299) is included, and becomes one among many additional settings for research.

COGNITIVE OBJECTIVES

Like the concept of instruction, the concept of cognitive objectives is a significant contribution of this conference. In all discussions, cognitive objectives comprise both conceptual and procedural knowledge, or "semantic networks and problem-solving algorithms" (Greeno, Chapter 7). But the distinction between these cognitive objectives and the older formulations of behavioral objectives needs to be strengthened further if it is not to collapse under the pressures of evaluation. Evaluation requires judgment about some behavior. How can the evaluator be sure that a particular behavior indicates underlying knowledge rather than rote and limited procedure? In Wertheimer's terms (Resnick, pages 58–59), how can we tell the difference between "understanding" and "insight" vs. "ugly" problem solving solutions? In the terms now used in the language domain (defined by Carroll, Chapter 1), how can we infer underlying competence from any particular performance?

Greeno (Chapter 7) suggests two criteria for meaningfulness: "goodness of structure" and "solving in the problem domain" (pages 147–148). "Goodness of structure" is an accurate name for the criterion used in language development research. When a child says *I don't want milk,* we decide whether to credit that child with the knowledge of *don't* as an anxiliary by determining whether, in this child's language system, *don't* is simply a single, unanalysed chunk, an alternative negative to *no,* or whether it coexists with other auxiliaries, positive as well as negative—e.g., *can* and *will* and *doesn't* as well as *don't.* "Goodness of structure" in language thus means that a particular element is a connected part of a larger system, and is recombinable in multiple patterns. More generally, this is also Norman's concept of understanding (Norman, Gentner, and Stevens, Chapter 9).

With regard to evaluation, Greeno says, " . . . evaluation must come from the potential users of the product, not from one who proposes to offer the product for use. . . . Evaluation may be possible when we can display a relatively complete analysis of the knowledge desired in some subject [p. 158] ." Working out the details for evaluating cognitive objectives in all domains should become a high priority task.

TASK ANALYSES

If we accpt, as I think we should, Norman's description of the learning process as one of communication, with all participants attempting to form new mental structural representations that will account for the information which they experience, then two kinds of task analysis are needed. One, usually called by that name, is an analysis of what the child has to learn; the other, usually called by some other name such as diagnosis, is a description of what the teacher has to do as he makes decisions (or forms hypotheses) about what and how to teach. The first is discussed by Resnick; the second is discussed by Atkinson in his explanation of how computer-assisted instruction can be individualized and optimized, and by Allan Collins in his demonstration of how tutors of geography find out about the preinstructional knowledge of their pupils. The task of diagnosis is different for computers and human teachers, not only because the teacher brings to the task a more richly prepared mind which may help or interfere, but also because of the magnitude of the information processing task. Of the ten panels assembled by the National Institute of Education in July, 1974 to suggest plans for research on teaching, one, chaired by Lee Shulman, considered teaching as clinical information processing in this sense.

One of Resnick's four requirements for task analyses of what children have to learn is that they must "recognize a distinction between early forms of competence and later ones ... [and must] describe performance characteristics of novices and attempt to discover or point to key differences between novices and experts, suggesting thereby ways of arranging experiences that will help novices become experts [page 53]." Certainly in language and in the domains of knowledge studied by Piaget, and probably in others as well, the knowledge of novices is not simply an incomplete version of the knowledge of the expert or mature learner; it is qualitatively different. While some of the differences may, upon closer examination of the underlying process, be due to the lack of some conceptual or procedural knowledge, other differences seem more a result of attention to different features of an event than is characteristic of adult minds and/or embodied in culturally transmitted forms of representation.

In the course of language development, for example, children utter verbs like *goed* and *unpeel,* and they answer the question *What are you doing?* in the form *I doing dancing.* These immature forms can reasonably be considered as the lack of knowledge of contextual restrictions on the generality of a particular pattern. And the childish question *Why I can't go*? can reasonably be considered as the lack of a particular operation that reverses pronoun and auxiliary. But explanations of incompleteness do not so easily fit the categorizations of sounds underlying young children's invented spellings (Read, 1971), nor children's representations of musical tunes that Jeanne Bamburger described.[2]

There are also individual differences in the course of learning, and maybe culturally-derived group differences as well. These are only beginning to be looked at in research on language learning. It seems to be a general methodological principle that the search for universal patterns precedes the search for variations on them.

I am not suggesting (even if I knew how) to build such qualitatively different novice stages into an instructional program as intermediate objectives. But we

[2] See footnote on page 317.

need to take them into account, not just to value them as indicators of learning, but also to experiment with how best to use them as the basis for continued growth. Jeanne Bamburger's demonstration of children's learning musical structure is a fine example. As she said, children's muddling must guide teacher's meddling.

Flavell (1972) has made an important attempt to categorize the restructuring that takes place between points in cognitive-developmental sequences as not just addition, but also substitution, modification, inclusion, and mediation. Norman's protocols of adults learning to cook and learning a computer programming language show that the knowledge of adult learners, as well as children, must often be modified and not just added to.

In advocating this more complex model of the course of learning, I don't mean to devalue examples of the best we now know how to do in instructional design—such as Resnick's arithmetic hierarchy and Atkinson's sequences in each strand of his program for beginning reading. But in the longer range, I hope that Norman's model (more adequately described in his text than in his too additively drawn diagrams) will guide future research.

In all task analyses, it is essential to remember that a formal analysis of the structure of some knowledge or skill does not necessarily, or even probably, reflect the organization in anyone's head, much less how it got there. I'm not sure whether Greeno's statement that "a theory specifying cognitive structures and processes sufficient to perform those tasks is a candidate hypothesis about what the instruction is trying to produce [p. 124]" clarifies or confuses. The recent history of psycholinguistic research reminds us of the importance of this distinction, as Carroll and Just and Carpenter point out. And there is no reason to believe that the story will be different elsewhere. If we intend only effective instruction, then the justifying criterion of effectiveness may be sufficient, as Greeno and Resnick suggest. But if a model of cognitive processes is sought, then more thorough psychological validation is required. Anyone engaged in such endeavors should read Holt's satire of task analysis in his description of how children would be taught, presumably less successfully, how to talk (Holt, 1967, pp. 56–57), if only to be sure where and how he is wrong.

MEANS OF INSTRUCTION

As Resnick demonstrates, even with a "good" task analysis, the mapping from identified components to instructional strategies remains very much a matter of artful trial and error.

Negatively, I am concerned about the rigidity of instruction embodied in Atkinson's second and third optimization levels [pages 93–99]. The first level, optimizing the sequence within each strand, is less of a problem just because a smaller component of the total program is involved. But when all control is taken away from the learner, regardless of what and when he is eager to learn, adaptation to individual interests and motivation becomes impossible.

I realize that the effectiveness of second-level optimization is an empirical question, but it is not easily investigated. Not if we evaluate the effects of instruction in long-range terms and look for side effects along this way, as Olson urged in his comments.

Atkinson's data on third-level optimization is extremely interesting. In a current controversy about ways to increase equality of educational opportunity, Sesame Street (which reaches everyone) is pitted against Headstart (which is limited to poor children). Atkinson's data is the first I've seen that specifies exactly what has to be done to maximize the group average, or minimize the group variances, or increase the average while not increasing the variance. As research data it is very important. But, although I agree with Atkinson's selection of the third goal as his optimizing criterion, the question of the effect on individual children of the rigidity entailed by any attempt to optimize at this level still remains.

More positively, I want to emphasize the importance of questions about the form of instruction, its timing, and the value of practice. What are the most effective forms in which to communicate to the learner what he needs to know to make progress? Some learning takes place through the full participation of the learner from the beginning, regardless of the immature forms that the learner uses, with subtle and little understood forms of feedback producing successively more mature approximations of expert behavior. Oral language is perhaps the best example here, but it is not the only one. I have seen three-year-old native American boys dancing with older siblings, parents and grandparents, doing an incredible job (by our standards of age-appropriate motoric development) of keeping in time. It may be the case that full participation even with childish performance is characteristic of those learnings for which special educational settings are not required. But we could try out extensions of this model to our more formal educational objectives. We could let children learn to write without correcting their spelling; and, as Norman suggested in one discussion, we could let children learn to read without correcting every semantic error they make.

Where this more informed model of learning does not apply, what is the best level on which to focus the learner's attention? In teaching a motor skill such as square dance swinging, I have found it more helpful to use the metaphor of making your feet go as if on a scooter than to detail the component motions. In teaching subtraction, Resnick suggests that it is more effective not to try to teach the mature algorithm directly, but rather to find a more easily instructable process from which the children can discover the rest themselves. Clearly, more research is needed on effective forms of instruction for varied educational objectives.

What is the optimal timing for confronting the learner with the discrepant information he needs to move on? In the kind of informal learning that proceeds from full participation in ongoing experience, that discrepant information is always available, and the child makes selective use of it in his own time. But in more formal educational settings, out of the contexts where experts are performing alongside learners, we face timing decisions that are difficult indeed.

Finally, what about the value of practice? It was only discussed informally here. Yet practice is one variable whose role may vary significantly between short-term experimental and long-term educational types of instruction. Carey (1974) suggests that the practice of constituent skills necessary for their incorporation into more complex structures—"modularization in Bruner's term—applies to cognitive achievements as well as to motor skills. Children engage in self-generated practice. (see Cazden, 1972, pp. 93-97; Cazden, 1974, for language examples). Does the effect of practice on learning vary depending on whether it is so self-generated or designed and imposed by someone else? If practice is the label we give to seemingly valuable behavior, than "bad habit" is the comparable label for repetitions of behavior that leave something to be desired. Immature language forms, such as those given above, are easily replaced as development proceeds, no matter how often repeated they may have been. Can we specify more generally the categories of behavior to which the notions of practice and bad habit do and do not apply? These questions are admittedly imprecisely formulated. Because of their importance for education, I hope they can be clarified from the perspective of this volume.

19
Designing a Learner: Some Questions

David Klahr

Carnegie-Mellon University

What do we know about what happens to a learner during instruction? One of the most exacting criteria for testing our knowledge about any phenomenon is the extent to which we can build a model that exhibits the behavior being studied. If we can simulate it, then we have at least a sufficiency model. Of course, there may be many aspects of the model that lack plausibility, but they can then become the focus of further study. (Reitman, 1967, once characterized this simulation approach to cognitive psychology as a way to "invent what you need to know.") In this chapter I will raise some questions about how one might go about building a model of a learner in an instructional mode (MOLIM).

LEARNING AS PROBLEM SOLVING

To learn is to solve a problem. In all but the most elementary situations, learning is under the learner's strategic control of attention and memory. If this view of learning is valid, then the study of complex problem solving—and the orientation such study provides to cognitive psychology—has direct relevance for the design of a MOLIM. In this section I will mention a few features of problem-solving theory that seem to justify the view of learning as problem solving, and that also have particular importance for the study of learning. Then, in the next section I will raise some questions about the design of a MOLIM.

Current information processing approaches to the study of human problem solving proceed by postulating a general system architecture, and then constructing explicit representations for the data structures and the processes that generate the observed problem solving behavior. A problem solution consists of an internal representation for some knowledge that the system did not have at the outset. Problem solving consists of a series of local transformations of knowledge that ultimately reach the desired knowledge state. In several of the chapters in this volume (e.g., the Greeno's Chapter 7), the "solution" to the learning problem is explicitly represented as a data structure (semantic net) and a set of procedures for searching that network. But note that these results—these solutions to the learning problem—are static with respect to the learning process itself. That is, with respect to the time grain of the instructional process, the results of instruction, even though they may themselves by dynamic processes, are structures upon with the learning system must operate. We need a model of the system's response to instruction, that is, its functioning in circumstances in which it must attend to the instructional episode and modify its own performance structures and processes.

In our instructional efforts, we try to provide optimal environments for the human information processing system to learn something. As it is with the horse led to water, so it is with the learner in an instructional situation: we can't make it ingest what we offer. The instructional design question is typically "*Will* the learner learn from this instruction?" A further question should be "*Why* should he learn?" The view of learning as problem solving suggests some ways to characterize this question. Problem-solving theory (Newell & Simon, 1972) includes two features of importance for our purpose. One is a detailed internal representation of the task environment. The other is a characterization of how the human information processor allocates its limited processing capacity to the problem-solving process. A principal method for effecting this allocation is the use of explicit representations for goals. Goals are symbolic expressions that direct and control the course of problem solving, representing what the system "wants" to do at any moment, and "why" it wants to do it. Thus, the answer to whether or why the system will learn becomes, in view of learning as problem solving, a matter of stating the circumstances under which learning-related goals are generated and manipulated.

SOME DESIGN QUESTIONS FOR A MOLIM

In this section, I will raise four questions that must be answered by the designer of a MOLIM:

1. When should learning occur?
2. How will the system be changed as a result of learning?
3. How thoroughly assimilated is the thing to be learned?
4. How distinct is learning from performance?

These questions, and their answers, are highly interrelated, and it is difficult to determine their appropriate order of presentation. Their ordering here is arbitrary, and does not imply any particular differential importance in my mind.

1. When should learning occur? A curious problem with most of the learning models in both cognitive psychology and artificial intellignece is that they are too single-minded in their task: they learn all the time. In designing a plausible MOLIM, we must be able to account for the fact that most of the time learning does *not* occur. We can do this by explicitly including in our MOLIM the precise conditions under which an instructional episode causes something to be learned. This is where the appropriate use of goals could play a role. Rather than construct a system in which the tendency to learn is integrally built in to the underlying operating mechanisms, we can design a more general problem solver whose problem is to learn, and whose goals include explicit learning efforts.

By themselves, such goals would still be inadequate for deciding when the system should learn. Additional information would be required about the current state of knowledge—that is, about both the current configuration of the external environment as well as the internal state of the system Thus, another design decision concerns those variables and their critical ranges which would, in conjunction with the learning goals, activate the self-modification processes.

The mechanisms that determine when learning is to occur must be capable of representing differential responsiveness to instruction. As Resnick (Chapter 3, this volume) has pointed out, our models must be able to represent both early and late forms of task proficiency, and for a MOLIM, the task is learning itself. Therefore a MOLIM must incorporate the capacity to represent both early and late learning proficiencies. Siegler (1975) has noted the importance of experimental designs in which both older and younger children are given the same training sequences, in order to examine the possible interaction of age and instructional effects. Since such interactions have been found (e.g., Siegler & Liebert, 1975), we must be able to represent them in MOLIM, through the general strategy, suggested by Resnick, of building developmentally tractable models.

2. How will the system be changed as a result of learning? This is, perhaps, a more useful way to say "what is learned?" There are several outcomes that can result from the learning effort. One result is that nothing happens: the learning attempt fails, and no lasting change is made in the system As noted above, this is more the rule than the exception in real instructional situations, and we must be able to build a system that can handle this fact.

Another possible result is that the entire system architecture could change. That is, the system's components and their interrelationships might be altered. However, since by "system architecture" I mean "hardware" rather than the "software" of the human information processor, it seems unlikely that this kind of change is really the result of instruction. Although it would be required in full developmental theory, we need not be too concerned with it for now.

There are two kinds of software changes that the system can undergo: changes in processes and changes in structures. Newell (1972a) has demonstrated the imprecise nature of the process—structure distinction in systems that are themselves undergoing change. In the case of a self modifying system, the ambiguity becomes even greater, since it is linked to the issue of degree of assimilation to be described below. Although one often makes an apparently unambiguous distinction between instruction directed to acquisition of facts, and instruction directed to the teaching of procedures (or skills), it is clear from the work of Greeno, Hyman, and Norman (Chapters 7, 8, and 9 of this volume) that the issues are not so simple. One can represent factual knowledge by procedures that can generate those facts, and, conversely, one can represent what could be procedural outputs by appropriately complex static symbolic networks.

Another type of change that may result from instruction, and which we must therefore be prepared to explicitly represent in our MOLIM, is change in the learning properties of the system beyond the representation of the specific instructional material. For example, in the case of the aggregate models with which Atkinson represents the learner, there are a few changes in the acquisition parameters that result from the instruction. In more complex models of learning, such systemic modifications would include the basic rules of self-modification themselves.

3. How thoroughly assimilated is the thing to be learned? In the paper cited above, Newell (1972) distinguishes between several levels of general versus specific knowledge about a task. The more general the knowledge, the more transformational rules are necessary to take the system from its entry state at performance time to a task-specific state in which it can actually perform the task at hand. Conversly, a very task-specific piece of knowledge might be represented in "machine code": being fully assimilated it would require no interpretation at run time, however it would be of limited generality.

A concrete example of this distinction is provided by the models for children's performance on seriation tasks developed by Baylor and Gascon (1974). In these models there are two kinds of representations for "seriation knowledge." One is a base strategy, consisting only of series of nested goals, that describe, at the most general level a strategy for seriation (e.g., "find max," or "insertion"). The other representation is a rule set that accounts for each move made by the child during a specific seriation task. Behavior during length seriation has one rule set, and behavior during weight seriation has another. If the system has only the base strategy, then it also requires a set of rules that take the base strategy and construct a task-specific variant (e.g., for weight seriation). There are various ways to conceptualize this mapping. The two simplist are a complete "compilation," in which the base strategy, plus the task-specific mapping rules, create an entire task-specific system that then runs on the task. The other is a collection of interpretive rules that never create a task-specific entity, but instead interpret the base strategy, "on the run," in terms of the specific task.

In designing a MOLIM, we must decide upon the assimilatedness of the information to be acquired. The sematic networks of Norman and Greeno in this volume appear to be far toward the task-specific end of the spectrum, while Shaw and Wilson appear to be focusing upon a more general "base strategy" in their representations of group generators. A similar contrast can be found in comparing Atkinson, (Chapter 4) with Resnick (Chapter 3). Atkinson is aiming at an instructional procedure that will create a very specific set of data structures and processes that will enable the learner to write programs or to acquire a set of reading patterns. Resnick has begun to investigate the manner in which the learner abandons the task-specific instructions and creates a more efficient and general procedure. My strategic bet is that by representing the result of learning as "base plus interpreter," we may begin to get a handle on the mechanisms of generalization from, or beyond, the specific instructional sequence.

4. How distinct is the learning system from the performance system? In almost all models of learning, be they psychological models or examples of Artificial Intelligence, there is a clear distinction between the learning processes and the thing to be learned, that is, the performance system (see for example the models in Feigenbaum & Feldman, 1963, or Simon & Siklossy, 1972). The distinctions are made with respect to the over-all organization of the respective systems, the underlying representations, and even the basic system architecture. For example, in the letter series completion model of Simon and Kotovksy (1963), much attention is paid to the differential short-term memory demands made by different representations for different serial concepts, but the demands made during the induction of these concepts (i.e., during their learning) are not directly addressed. Another example of this distinction can be found in Waterman's (1970) learning program in which the result of training was represented as a production system, but the learning system itself was not a production system.

Although such separation has the benefit of making the modeling task more manageable, it lacks both elegance and psychological plausibility. I would hazard the guess that the same mechanisms that span the gap between general base strategy and the task-specific system (see Question 3, above) are implicated in the learning process itself. The more homogeneously we design the MOLIM, the more likely we are to be able to solve both problems simultaneously. Such a view might be nothing more than idle speculation were it not for the recent work of my colleague, Don Waterman. He has constructed a set of adaptive production systems for a range of learning tasks (Waterman, 1974a b). These models learn simple addition, verbal associations, and complex letter series. Each model is written as in initial core of productions, some of which have the capacity to add additional productions to the initial core. The final "learned" system operates under the same control structure and system architecture as the initial system and the learning rules are represented in precisely the same way as the new rules that are learned, that is, as productions.

The instructional environments in which Waterman's system do their self-modification are relatively simple, but I believe that the basic approach is very sound, and extendable to richer instructional problems. In a less precise but much more general statement, Wallace and I (Klahr & Wallace, 1976) have proposed a broad view of cognitive development in terms of a self-modifying production system.

CONCLUSION

The chapters in this volume represent diverse but converging answers to the question of the relevance of some current research in cognitive psychology to instructional design. I have not attempted to synthesize, evaluate, or review the previous chapters because several efforts have already been made in the discussion chapters by Gregg, Olson, Farnham-Diggory, Hayes, Collins, Shaw, Glaser, and Cazden. Instead, my intent has been to provide an orientation that might help the reader to form his own evaluation of the research reported here.

By confining attention to learning in intentionally instructional situations, I have attempted to reduce the task to manageable proportions. Instead of concocting a general learning system, I have considered the design of more limited models of the effects of specific instructional situations. Such models will initially tend to be largely determined by the task environment, that is, by the material and its form of presentation. However, there are some fundamental questions that are worth asking, questions which may apply to a wide range of instruction, even though their answers may be task-specific.

Having posed the design issues, we might ask a few questions about the enterprise, per se. Why bother with such an effort? There seem to be a few good reasons. First, if we could actually build a sensible model, we could directly simulate the results of proposed instructional procedures. The potential value of such instructional "pilot plants" is that they could replace the extensive field testing of instructional variations that we are presently forced to use. But except in the most simple situations, we are not yet able to build such models, and the worth of the enterprise lies in its propaedeutic nature: it may give us an introduction to the kinds of things we still need to know. Several of the comments by other discussants in this volume have raised the disquieting possibility that we may have little here that is really new or useful. I think that such a view is unjustified, but the issue cannot really be addressed in the abstract: we need concrete examples of what we are talking about. Thus, the second reason for attempting to raise some design issues is that the exercise of constructing a model of learning from instruction will provide us with such concrete examples.

Another general question that we can ask about the design of a MOLIM is "Who cares?" Who might benefit from such an exercise? It seems to me to be premature to claim that either instructors or learners (at least as traditionally conceived) could benefit much from thinking about the design of learning models. The payoff, at present, appears to be for the people who fall into the intersection of the categories of instructional designer and cognitive psychologists. The contributors to this volume were selected because of just such a blend of interests and skills. Their answers to some of the questions I have raised are implicit in the work they have presented in previous chapters. Perhaps other "learning engineers" can, in reaching their own answers, begin to apply and direct the kinds of basic research that are required to further our knowledge of both cognition and instruction.

ACKNOWLEDGMENTS

Preparation of this chapter was supported by a grant from the Spencer Foundation. I would like to thank J. R. Hayes, J. A. Jakimik, and D. M. Neves for comments on an earlier draft.

References

Abelson, R. P. The structure of belief systems. In R. C. Schank and K. M. Colby (Eds.), *Computer models of thought and language*. San Francisco: Freeman, 1973.

Allen, C. *The instructor, the man, and the job*. Philadelphia: Lippincott, 1919.

Amunatequi, F. *Masterpieces of French cuisine*. New York: Macmillan, 1971.

Anderson, J. R., & Bower, G. H. *Human associative memory*. New York: Wiley, 1973.

Anderson, N. H. Likeableness ratings of 555 personality-trait words. *Journal of Personality & Social Psychology*, 1968, 9, 272–279.

Anderson, R. C., & Faust, G. W. *Educational psychology, the science of instruction and learning*. New York: Dodd, Mead, 1973.

Atkinson, R. C. Computerized instruction and the learning process. *American Psychologist*, 1968, 23, 225–239.

Atkinson, R. C. Ingredients for a theory of instruction. *American Psychologist*, 1972, 27, 921–931. (a)

Atkinson, R. C. Optimizing the learning of a second-language vocabulary. *Journal of Experimental Psychology*, 1972, 96, 124–129. (b)

Atkinson, R. C., Fletcher, J. D., Lindsay, E. J., Campbell, J. D., & Barr, A. Computer assisted instruction in initial reading. *Educational Technology*, 1973, 13, 27–37.

Atkinson, R. C., & Paulson, J. A. An approach to the psychology of instruction. *Psychological Bulletin*, 1972, 78, 49–61.

Atkinson, R. C., & Raugh, M. R. An application of the mnemonic keyword method to the acquisition of a Russian vocabulary. *Journal of Experimental Psychology: Human Learning and Memory*, 1975, 104, 126–133.

Atkinson, R. C., & Shiffrin, R. Human memory: A proposed system and its control processes. In K. W. Spence & J. T. Spence (Eds.), *The psychology of learning and motivation: Advances in research and theory* (Vol. 2). New York: Academic Press, 1968.

Attneave, F. Physical determinants of the judged complexity of shapes. *Journal of Experimental Psychology*, 1957, 53, 221–227. (a)

Attneave, F. Transfer of experience with a class-schema to identification–Learning of patterns and shapes. *Journal of Experimental Psychology*, 1957, 54, 81–88. (b)

Bamberger, J. *Developing a musical ear: A new experiment* (AI Memo No. 246). Cambridge, Massachusetts: MIT Artificial Intelligence Laboratory, July, 1972.

Barclay, J. R. The role of comprehension in remembering sentences. *Cognitive Psychology*, 1973, 4, 229–254.

Barr, A., Beard, M., & Atkinson, R. C. *A rationale and description of the BASIC instructional program* (Tech. Rep. No. 228). Stanford, Calif.: Stanford University, Institute for Mathematical Studies in the Social Sciences, 1974.

Bartlett, F. C. *Remembering: A study in experimental and social psychology.* Cambridge, England: Cambridge University Press, 1932.

Baylor, G. W., & Gascon, J. An information processing theory of aspects of the development of weight seriation in children. *Cognitive Psychology,* 1974, **6,** 1–40.

Beard, M. H., Lorton, P. V., Searle, B. W., & Atkinson, R. C. *Comparison of student performance and attitude under three lesson-selection strategies in computer-assisted instruction* (Tech. Rep. No. 222). Stanford, Calif.: Stanford University, Institute for Mathematical Studies in the Social Sciences, 1973.

Bearison, D. J. The role of measurement operations in the acquisition of conservation. *Developmental Psychology,* 1969, **1**(6), 653–660.

Begle, E. G. Introducing the concept of rational number. In J. D. Williams (Ed.), *Mathematical reform in the elementary school.* Hamburg: UNESCO Institute for Education, 1967.

Bereiter, C., & Engelmann, S. *Teaching disadvantaged children in the preschool.* Englewood Cliffs, N.J.: Prentice-Hall, 1966.

Bever, T. G. The cognitive basis for linguistic structures. In J. R. Hayes (Ed.), *Cognition and the development of language.* New York: Wiley, 1970.

Bever, T. G., Fodor, J. A., & Garrett, M. A formal limitation of associationism. In T. R. Dixon & D. L. Horton (Eds.), *Verbal behavior and general behavior theory.* Englewood Cliffs, N. J.: Prentice-Hall, 1968.

Bindra, D. A motivational view of learning, performance, and behavior modification. *Psychological Review,* 1974, **81,** 199–213.

Bloom, L., Hood, L., & Lightbown, P. Imitation in language development: If, when, and why. *Cognitive Psychology,* 1974, **6,** 380–420.

Bloomfield, L. *Outline guide for the practical study of foreign languages.* Baltimore, Md.: Linguistic Society of America, 1942.

Blumenthal, A. L. Prompted recall of sentences. *Journal of Verbal Learning and Verbal Behavior,* 1967, **6,** 203–206.

Bobrow, D. G. Natural language input for a computer problem-solving system. In M. Minsky (Ed.), *Semantic information processing.* Cambridge, Mass.: MIT Press, 1968.

Bolinger, Modern Language Association of America, *Modern Spanish.* New York: Harcourt Brace, 1960.

Boneau, C. A. Paradigm regained? Cognitive behaviorism restated. *American Psychologist,* 1974, **29,** 297–309.

Bransford, J. D., Barclay, J. R., & Franks, J. J. Sentence memory: A constructive versus interpretive approach. *Cognitive Psychology,* 1972, **3,** 193–209.

Bransford, J. D., & Franks, J. J. The abstraction of linguistic ideas. *Cognitive Psychology,* 1971, **2,** 331–350.

Bransford, J. D., & Johnson, M. K. Considerations of some problems of comprehension. In W. G. Chase (Ed.), *Visual information processing.* New York: Academic Press, 1973.

Britton, J. *Language and learning.* Coral Gables, Fla.: University of Miami Press, 1970.

Bronowski, J., & Bellugi, U. Language, name and concept. *Science,* 1970, **168,** 669–673.

Brown, J. S., Burton, R. R., & Zdybel, F. A model-driven question-answering system for mixed-intitative computer-assisted construction. *IEEE Transactions on Systems, Man, and Cybernetics,* 1973, **SMC-3,** 248–257.

Brown, R., Cazden, C., & Bellugi, U. The child's grammar from I to III. In J. P. Hill (Ed.), *1967 Minnesota symposium on child psychology.* Minneapolis: University of Minnesota Press, 1969.

Brownell, W. R., & Stretch, L. B. *The effect of unfamiliar settings on problem solving* (No. 1). Durham, N. C.: Duke University Research Studies in Education, 1931.

Bruner, J. S. Some theorems on instruction illustrated with reference to mathematics. In E. R. Hilgard (Ed.), *Theories of learning and instruction, The 63rd Yearbook of the NSSE* (Pt. 1). Chicago: Chicago University Press, 1964.

Bruner, J. S. *Toward a theory of instruction.* Cambridge, Mass.: Belknap Press of Harvard University, 1966.

Bruner, J. S., Olver, R., & Greenfield, P. *Studies in cognitive growth.* New York: Wiley, 1966.

Brunswik, E. Ontogenetic and other developmental parallels to the history of science. In H. M. Evans (Ed.), *Men and moments in the history of science.* Seattle: University of Washington Press, 1959.

Calfee, R. C. The role of mathematical models in optimizing instruction. *Scientia: Revue Internationale de Synthese Scientifique,* 1970, **105**, 1–25.

Calfee, R. C. *Diagnostic evaluation of visual, auditory and general language factors in prereaders.* Paper presented at the American Psychological Association Convention, Hawaii, September 1972.

Calfee, R. C. Assessment of independent reading skills: Basic research and practical applications. In A. S. Reber & D. Scarborough (Eds.), *Markings to meanings.* Hillsdale, N. J.: Lawrence Erlbaum Assoc., in press.

Calfee, R. C., Chapman, R., & Venezky, R. How a child needs to think to learn to read. In L. W. Gregg (Ed.), *Cognition in learning and memory.* New York: Wiley, 1972.

Carbonell, J. R. AI in CAI: An artificial-intelligence approach to computer-assisted instruction. *IEEE Transactions on Man-Machine Systems,* 1970, **MMS-11**, 190–202.

Carbonell, J. R. Artificial intelligence and large interactive man-computer systems. In *Proceedings of the 1971 IEEE Systems, Man, and Cybernetics Group Annual Symposium, 1971.* New York: Institute of Electrical and Electronics Engineers, 1971.

Carey, S. Cognitive competence. In K. Connolly & J. Bruner (Eds.), *The growth of competence.* New York: Academic Press, 1974.

Carpenter, P. A. Extracting information from counterfactual clauses. *Journal of Verbal Learning & Verbal Behavior,* 1973, **12**, 512–521.

Carpenter, P. A., & Just, M. A. Semantic control of eye movements in picture scanning during sentence-picture verification. *Perception & Psychophysics,* 1972, **12**, 61–64.

Carpenter, P. A., & Just, M. A. Sentence comprehension: A psycholinguistic processing model of verification. *Psychological Review,* 1975, **82**, 45–73.

Carroll, J. B. Research on teaching foreign languages. In N. L. Gage (Ed.), *Handbook of research on teaching.* Chicago: Rand McNally, 1963.

Carroll, J. B. Research in foreign language teaching: The last five years. In R. G. Mead, Jr. (Ed.), *Language teaching: Broader contexts.* New York: MLA Materials Center, 1966.

Carroll, J. B. Memorandum: On needed research in the psycholinguistic and applied psycholinguistic aspects of language teaching. *Foreign Language Annals,* 1968, **1**, 236–238. (a)

Carroll, J. B. The psychology of language testing. In A. Davies (Ed.), *Language testing symposium: A psycholinguistic approach.* London: Oxford University Press, 1968. (b)

Carroll, J. B. Current issues in psycholinguistics and second language teaching. *TESOL Quarterly,* 1971, **5**, 101–114. (a)

Carroll, J. B. Development of native language skills beyond the early years. In C. E. Reed (Ed.), *The learning of language.* New York: Appleton-Century-Crofts, 1971. (b)

Carroll, J. B. Toward a performance grammar for core sentences in spoken and written English. *International Review of Applied Linguistics,* 1974, **12** (Special Festschrift issue for B. Malmberg), 29–49. (a)

Carroll, J. B. Learning theory for the classroom teacher. In G. A. Jarvis (Ed.), *The challenge of communication: ACTFL review of foreign language education.* Vol. 6. Skokie, Illinois: National Textbook Company, 1974. (b)

Carroll, J. B. Psychometric tests as cognitive tasks: A new "structure of intellect." In L. B. Resnick (Ed.), *The nature of intelligence.* Hillsdale, N.J.: Lawrence Erlbaum Assoc., 1976.

Caruso, J. L., & Resnick, L. B. *Task sequence and over-training in children's learning and transfer of double classification skills* (Publication No. 1971/18). Pittsburgh: University of Pittsburgh, Learning Research and Development Center, 1971.

Cazden, C. B. *Child language and education.* New York: Holt, Rinehart & Winston, 1972.

Cazden, C. B. Play and metalinguistic awareness: One dimension of language experience. *The Urban-Review,* 1974.

Chant, V. G., & Atkinson, R. C. Optimal allocation of instructional effort to interrelated learning strands. *Journal of Mathematical Psychology,* 1973, **10**, 1–25.

Chase, W. G., & Clark, H. H. Mental operations in the comparison of sentences and pictures. In L. W. Gregg (Ed.), *Cognition in learning and memory.* New York: Wiley, 1972.

Chase, W. G., & Simon, H. A. Perception in chess. *Cognitive Psychology,* 1973, **4**, 55–81. (a)

Chase, W. G., & Simon, H. A. The mind's eye in chess. In W. G. Chase (Ed.), *Visual information processing.* New York: Academic Press, 1973. (b)

Chiang, A. *Instructional algorithms derived from mathematical learning models: An application in computer assisted instruction of paired-associated items.* Unpublished doctoral dissertation, The City University of New York, 1974.

Child, J., Bertholle, L., & Beck, S. *Mastering the art of French cooking* (Vol. 1). New York: Knopf, 1961.

Chomsky, N. *Aspects of the theory of syntax.* Cambridge: MIT Press, 1965.

Clark, H. H. The language-as-fixed-effect fallacy: A critique of language statistics in psychological research. *Journal of Verbal Learning & Verbal Behavior,* 1973, **12**, 335–359.

Clark, H. H. The chronometric study of meaning components. In J. Mehler (Ed.), *Current problems in psycholinguistics.* Paris: Centre National de la Recherche Scientifique, in press.

Clark, H. H., & Chase, W. G. On the process of comparing sentences against pictures. *Cognitive Psychology,* 1972, **3**, 472–517.

Clarke, L. H. *Ordinary level mathematics* (5th ed.). London: Heinemann Educational Books, 1971.

Clarkson, G. D. E. A model of the trust investment process. In E. A. Feigenbaum & J. Feldman (Eds.), *Computers and thought.* New York: McGraw-Hill, 1963.

Clifton, C., Jr., Kurcz, I., & Jenkins, J. J. Grammatical relations as determinants of sentence similarity. *Journal of Verbal Learning and Verbal Behavior,* 1965, **4**, 112–117.

Clifton, C., Jr., & Odom, P. Similarity relations among certain English sentence constructions. *Psychological Monographs: General and Applied,* 1966, **80**(5).

Coburn, T. G. *The effect of a ratio approach and a region approach on equivalent fractions and addition/subtraction for pupils in grade four.* Unpublished doctoral dissertation, The University of Michigan, Ann Arbor 1973.

Collins, A. M., Carbonell, J. R., & Warnock, E. H. *Analysis and synthesis of tutorial dialogues* (Tech. Rep. No. 2631). Cambridge, Mass.: Bolt, Beranek and Newman, 1973.

Collins, A. M., & Quillian, M. R. Experiments on semantic memory and language comprehension. In L. W. Gregg (Ed.), *Cognition in learning and memory,* New York: Wiley, 1972.

Collins, A. M., Warnock, E. H., Aiello, N., & Miller, M. L. Reasoning from incomplete knowledge. In. D. G. Bobrow & A. M. Collins (Eds.), *Representation and understanding.* New York: Academic Press, 1975.

Cronbach, L. J., Gleser, G. C., Nanda, H., & Rajaratnam, N. *The dependability of behavioral measurements: Theory of generalizability for scores and profiles.* New York: Wiley, 1972.

Crothers, E. J. Memory structure and the recall of discourse. In R. O. Freedle & J. B. Carroll (Eds.), *Language comprehension and the acquisition of knowledge.* Washington: Winston, 1972.

Dayton, C. M. *Design of educational experiments.* New York: McGraw-Hill, 1970.

Dear, R. E., Silberman, H. F., Estavan, D. P., & Atkinson, R. C. An optimal strategy for the presentation of paired-associate items. *Behavioral Science,* 1967, **12,** 1– 13.

deGroot, A. D. *Thought and choice in chess.* The Hauge: Mouton, 1965.

deGroot, A. D. Perception and memory versus thought: Some old ideas and recent findings. In B. Kleinmuntz (Ed.), *Problem solving: Research, method and theory.* New York: Wiley, 1966.

Delaney, H. D. *Individualizing instruction: An extension of the RTI model and its optimal strategy for the presentation of paired-associate items.* Unpublished masters dissertation, University of North Carolina, 1973.

DeSoto, C., London, M., & Handel, S. Social reasoning and spatial paralogic. *Journal of Personality & Social Psychology,* 1965, **2,** 513–521.

Dewey, J. Psychology and social practice. *The Psychological Review,* 1900, **7,** 105–124.

Dewey, J. *Intelligence in the modern world.* J. Ratner (Ed.), New York: The Modern Library, 1939.

Dickinson, M. B. Review of Maxwell and Tovatt's *On Writing Behavioral Objectives for English. Research in the Teaching of English,* 1971, **5,** 89–115.

Dienes, Z. P. *Mathematics in the primary school.* New York: St. Martin's Press, 1966.

Dienes, Z. P. *Building up mathematics.* London: Hutchinson Educational Press, 1967. (a)

Dienes, Z. P. *Fractions, an operational approach.* New York: Herder and Herder, 1967. (b)

Dik, S. C. *Coordination: Its implication for the theory of general linguistics.* Amsterdam: North-Holland, 1968.

Dixson, R. J. *Graded exercises in English: A new revised edition.* New York: Regents, 1971.

Dooling, D. J., & Lachman, R. Effects of comprehension on retention of prose. *Journal of Experimental Psychology,* 1971, **88,** 216 222.

Duncker, K. On problem solving. *Psychological Monographs,* 1945, **58**(5, Whole No. 270).

Ernst, G. W., & Newell, A. Some issues of representation in a general problem solver. *AFPS Conference Proceedings 30, 1967.* Washington, D.C.: Thomson Books, 1967.

Ernst, G. W., & Newell, A. *GPS: A case study in generality and problem solving.* New York: Academic Press, 1969.

Ervin-Tripp, S. Imitation and structural change in children's language. In E. H. Lenneberg (Ed.), *New directions in the study of language.* Cambridge, Mass.: MIT Press, 1964.

Evans, S. H. A brief statement of schema theory. *Psychonomic Science,* 1967, **8,** 87–88.

Fant, G. Auditory patterns of speech. In W. Wathen-Dunn (Ed.), *Models for the perception of speech and visual form.* Cambridge, Mass.: MIT Press, 1964.

Farnham-Diggory, S. *Cognitive processes in education.* New York: Harper & Row, 1972.

Feigenbaum, E. A. The simulation of verbal learning behavior. In E. A. Feigenbaum & J. Feldman (Eds.), *Computers and thought.* New York: McGraw-Hill, 1963.

Feigenbaum, E. A., & Feldman, J. (Eds.) *Computers and thought.* New York: McGraw-Hill, 1963.

Feldman, J. A., Low, J. R., Swinehart, D. C., & Taylor, R. H. Recent developments in SAIL. *AFIPS Fall Joint Conference,* 1972, 1193–1202.

File, S. E., & Jew, A. Syntax and the recall of instructions in a realistic situation. *British Journal of Psychology,* 1973, **64,** 65–70.

Fillenbaum, S. Psycholinguistics. *Annual Review of Psychology,* 1971, **22,** 251–308.

Fitzgerald, J. A. *The teaching of spelling.* Milwaukee, Wisc.: Bruce, 1951.

Flavell, J. H. An analysis of cognitive-developmental sequences. *Genetic Psychology Monographs,* 1972, **86,** 279–350.

Fletcher, J. D., & Atkinson, R. C. Evaluation of the Stanford CAI program in initial reading. *Journal of Educational Psychology,* 1972, **63,** 597–602.

Fodor, J., & Garrett, M. Some reflections on competence and performance. In J. Lyons & R. J. Wales (Eds.), *Psycholinguistics papers: The Proceedings of the 1966 Edinburgh Conference.* Edinburgh: Edinburgh University Press, 1966.

Forehand, G. A. Knowledge and the educational process. In L. W. Gregg (Ed.), *Knowledge and cognition.* Hillsdale, N.J.: Lawrence Erlbaum Assoc., 1974.

Fouts, R. S. Use of guidance in teaching sign language to a chimpanzee *(Pan troglodytes). Journal of Comparative and Physiological Psychology,* 1972, **80,** 515–522.

Frederiksen, C. H. Effects of task-induced cognitive operations on comprehension and memory processes. In R. O. Freedle and J. B. Carroll (Eds.), *Language comprehension and the acquisition of knowledge.* Washington: Winston, 1972.

Friere, P. *Pedagogy of the oppressed.* New York: Herder and Herder, 1972.

Furth, H. G. *Piaget for teachers.* Englewood Cliffs, N. J.: Prentice-Hall, 1970.

Gagné, R. M. The acquisition of knowledge. *Psychological Review,* 1962, **69,** 355–365.

Gagné, R. M. Learning hierarchies. *Educational Psychology* 1968, **6,** 1–9.

Gagné, R. M. *The conditions of learning* (2nd ed.). New York: Holt, Rinehart & Winston, 1970.

Gagné, R. M., Mayor, J. R., Garstens, H. L., & Paradise, N. E. Factors in acquiring knowledge of a mathematical task. *Psychological Monographs,* 1962, **76**(7, Whole No. 526).

Gardner, B. T., & Gardner, R. A. Two-way communication with an infant chimpanzee. In A. Schrier & F. Stollnitz (Eds.), *Behavior of non-human primates* (Vol. 4). New York: Academic Press, 1971.

Gardner, R. A., & Gardner, B. T. Teaching sign language to a chimpanzee. *Science,* 1969, **165,** 664–672.

Gelernter, H. Realization of a geometry-theorem proving machine. In E. A. Feigenbaum & J. Feldman (Eds.), *Computers and thought.* New York: McGraw-Hill, 1963.

Gelman, R. Conservation acquisition: A problem of learning to attend to relevant attributes. *Journal of Experimental Child Psychology,* 1969, **7,** 167–187.

Gentner, D. Evidence for the psychological reality of semantic components: The verbs of possession. In D. A. Norman, D. E. Rumelhart, & the LNR Research Group, *Explorations in cognition.* San Francisco: Freeman, 1975.

Gibson, J. J. *The senses considered as perceptual systems.* Boston: Houghton Mifflin, 1966.

Glaser, R. Instructional technology and the measurement of learning outcomes: Some questions. *American Psychologist,* 1963, **18,** 519–521.

Glaser, R. *Teaching machines and programmed learning, II: Data and directions.* Washington: National Education Association, Department of Audiovisual Instruction, 1965.

Glaser, R. Individuals and learning: The new aptitudes. *Educational Researcher,* 1972, **1**(6), 5–13.

Glaser, R., & Nitko, A. J. Measurement in learning and instruction. In R. L. Thorndike (Ed.), *Educational measurement.* (2nd ed.) Washington, D.C.: American Council on Education, 1971.

Glaser, R., & Resnick, L. B. Instructional psychology. *Annual Review of Psychology,* 1972, **23,** 207–276.

Gleitman, L. R. Coordinating conjunctions in English. In D. A. Reibel & S. A. Schane (Eds.), *Modern studies in English: Reading in transformational grammar.* Englewood Cliffs, N.J.: Prentice-Hall, 1969.

Golden, R. I. *Improving patterns of language usage.* Detroit: Wayne State University Press, 1960.

Goldstein, I. *Elementary geometry theorem proving* (A. I. Memo No. 280). Cambridge, Mass.: MIT Artificial Intelligence Laboratory, 1973.

Gollin, E. S. Forming impressions of personality. *Journal of Personality,* 1954, **23**, 65–76.

Gombrich, E. H. J. *Art and illusion: A study in the psychology of pictoral representation.* Princeton, N.J.: Princeton University Press, 1961.

Goody, J., & Watt, I. The consequences of literacy. In J. R. Goody (Ed.), *Literacy in traditional societies.* Cambridge, England: Cambridge University Press, 1968.

Gough, P. B. Grammatical transformations and speed of understanding. *Journal of Verbal Learning & Verbal Behavior,* 1965, **4**, 107–111.

Gough, P. B. The verification of sentences: The effects of delay of evidence and sentence length. *Journal of Verbal Learning & Verbal Behavior,* 1966, **5**, 492–496.

Graduate Business Admissions Council. *Graduate study in management: A guide for prospective students.* Princeton, N.J.: Educational Testing Service, 1974.

Greenburg, J. H., & Jenkins, J. J. Studies in the psychological correlates of the sound system of American English, I. Measuring linguistic distance from English, II. Distinctive features and psychological space. *Word,* 1964, **20**, 137–177.

Greeno, J. G. Processes of learning and comprehension. In L. W. Gregg (Ed.), *Knowledge and cognition.* Hillsdale, N.J.: Lawrence Erlbaum Assoc., 1974.

Gregg, L. W. Internal representations of sequential concepts. In B. Kleinmuntz (Ed.), *Concepts and the structure of memory. Second Annual Carnegie Conference on Cognition.* New York: Wiley, 1967.

Gregg, L. W. Optimal policies or wise choices? A critique of Smallwood's optimization procedures. In W. H. Holtzman (Ed.), *Computer-assisted instruction testing and guidance.* New York: Harper & Row, 1970.

Gregg, L. W. Simulation models of learning and memory. In L. W. Gregg (Ed.), *Cognition in learning and memory. Fifth Annual Carnegie Conference on Cognition.* New York: Wiley, 1972.

Gregg, L. W., & Simon, H. A. An information processing explanation of one-trial and incremental learning. *Journal of Verbal Learning and Verbal Behavior,* 1967, **6**, 780–787.

Groen, G. J., & Atkinson, R. C. Models for optimizing the learning process. *Psychological Bulletin,* 1966, **66**, 309–320.

Groen, G. J., & Parkman, J. M. A chronometric analysis of simple addition. *Psychological Review,* 1972, **79**, 329–343.

Groen, G. J., & Poll, M. Subtraction and the solution of open-sentence problems. *Journal of Experimental Child Psychology,* 1973, **16**, 292–302.

Guttman, L. A faceted definition of intelligence. *Scripta Hierosolymitana: Studies in psychology.* Jerusalem, Israel: The Hebrew University, 1965, 166–181.

Guttman, L., & Schlesinger, I. M. Systematic construction of distractors for ability and achievement test items. *Educational & Psychological Measurement,* 1967, **27**, 569–580.

Halliday, M. A. K. Notes on transitivity and theme in English: Part 2. *Journal of Linguistics,* 1967, **3**, 199–244.

Hart, B., & Risley, T. R. Establishing use of descriptive adjectives in spontaneous speech of disadvantaged preschool children. In O. I. Lovass & B. D. Bacher (Eds.), *Perspectives in behavior modification with deviant children.* Englewood Cliffs, N.J.: Prentice-Hall, 1974.

Hastorf, A. H., Schneider, D. J., & Polefka, J. *Person perception.* Reading, Mass.: Addison-Wesley, 1970.

Havelock, E. *Prologue to Greek literacy.* Oklahoma City: University of Oklahoma Press, 1974.

Hayes, J. R. Introduction. In J. R. Hayes (Ed.), *Cognition and the development of language.* New York: Wiley, 1970.

Hayes, J. R. On the function of visual imagery in elementary mathematics. In W. Chase (Ed.), *Visual information processing.* New York: Academic Press, 1973.

Hayes, J. R., & Simon, H. A. Understanding written problem instructions. In L. W. Gregg (Ed.), *Knowledge and cognition.* Hillsdale, N. J.: Lawrence Erlbaum Assoc., 1974.

Heider, F. *The psychology of inter-personal relations.* New York: Wiley, 1958.

Hewitt, C. PLANNER: A language for proving theorems in robots. *Proceedings of the International Joint Conference on Artificial Intelligence.* Bedford, Mass.: MITRE Corp., 1969.

Holt, J. C. *How children learn.* New York: Pitman, 1967.

Holzman, T. G. Process training as a test of computer simulation theory. Unpublished masters thesis, University of Pittsburgh, 1975.

Hoosain, R. The processing of negation. *Journal of Verbal Learning & Verbal Behavior,* 1973, **12**, 618–626.

Hornby, P. A. The psychological subject and predicate. *Cognitive Psychology,* 1972, **3**, 632–642.

Hudson, R. A. *English complex sentences: An introduction to systematic grammar.* Amsterdam & London: North Holland, 1971.

Hume, D. *An inquiry concerning human understanding* (E. W. Hendel, Ed.). New York: The Liberal Arts Press, 1955. (Originally published 1748.)

Hunt, E. B., Frost, N., & Lunneborg, C. Individual differences in cognition: A new approach to intelligence. In G. H. Bower (Ed.), *The psychology of learning and motivation: Advances in research and theory* (Vol. 7). New York: Academic Press, 1973.

Hunt, E. B. *Concept learning, an information processing problem.* New York: Academic Press, 1962.

Hunt, J. McV. *Intelligence and experience.* New York: Ronald Press, 1961.

Huttenlocher, J. Constructing spatial images: A strategy in reasoning. *Psychological Review,* 1968, **75**, 550–560.

Hydle, L. L., & Clapp, F. L. *Elements of difficulty in the interpretation of concrete problems in arithmetic* (Bureau of Educational Research Bulletin No. 9). Madison: University of Wisconsin, 1927.

Hyman, R. On prior information and creativity. *Psychological Reports,* 1961, **9**, 151–161.

Hyman, R. Creativity and the prepared mind: The role of information and induced attitudes. In C. W. Taylor (Ed.), *Widening horizons in creativity.* New York: Wiley, 1964. (a)

Hyman, R. *The nature of psychological inquiry.* Englewood Cliffs, N.J.: Prentice-Hall, 1964. (b)

Hyman, R., & Frost, N. Gradients and schema in pattern recognition. In P. M. A. Rabbitt (Ed.), *Attention and performance* (Vol. 5). New York: Academic Press, 1974.

Innis, H. A. *The bias of communication.* Toronto: University of Toronto Press, 1951.

Jackendoff, R. S. An interpretative theory of negation. *Foundations of Language,* 1969, **5**, 218–241.

Jamison, D., Fletcher, J. D., Suppes, P., & Atkinson, R. C. Cost and performance of computer-assisted instruction for compensatory education. In R. Rather & J. Froomkin (Eds.), *Education as an industry.* New York: Columbia University Press, 1975.

Jenkins, J., Jiminez-Pabon, E., Shaw, R., & Sefer, J. *Schuell's aphasia in adults.* New York: Harper and Row, 1975.

Johnson-Laird, P. N., & Tridgell, J. M. When negation is easier than affirmation. *Quarterly Journal of Experimental Psychology,* 1972, **24**, 87–91.

Jones, S. The effect of a negative qualifier in an instruction. *Journal of Verbal Learning & Verbal Behavior,* 1966, **5,** 497–501. (a)

Jones, S. Decoding a deceptive instruction. *British Journal of Psychology,* 1966, **57,** 405–411. (b)

Jones, S. Instructions, self-instructions, and performance. *Quarterly Journal of Exprimental Psychology,* 1968, **70,** 74–78.

Jorgenson, C. C., & Kintsch, W. The role of imagery in the evaluation of sentences. *Cognitive Psychology,* 1973, **4,** 110–116.

Just, M. A. Comprehending quantified sentences: The relation between sentence-picture and semantic memory verification. *Cognitive Psychology,* 1974, **6,** 216–236.

Just, M. A., & Carpenter, P. A. Comprehension of negation with qualification. *Journal of Verbal Learning & Verbal Behavior,* 1971, **10,** 244–253.

Just, M. A., & Clark, H. H. Drawing inferences from the presuppositions and implications of affirmative and negative sentences. *Journal of Verbal Learning & Verbal Behavior,* 1973, **12,** 21–31.

Kagan, J., Rosman, B. L., Day, D., Albert, J., & Phillips, W. Information processing in the child: Significance of analytic and reflective attitudes. *Psychological Monographs,* 1964, **78**(1, Whole No. 578).

Kamii, C. An application of Piaget's theory to the conceptualization of a preschool curriculum. In R. K. Parker (Ed.), *The preschool in action: Exploring early childhood programs.* Boston: Allyn & Bacon, 1972.

Karttunen, L. Implicative verbs. *Language,* 1971, **47,** 340–358.

Katona, G. *Organizing and memorizing: Studies in the psychology of learning and teaching.* New York: Columbia University Press, 1940.

Keller, H. A. *The story of my life.* New York: Doubleday, 1936.

Kimball, R. B. *Self-optimizing computer-assisted tutoring: Theory and practice* (Tech. Rep. No. 206). Stanford, Calif.: Stanford University, Institute for Mathematical Studies in the Social Sciences, 1973.

Kintsch, W. *Learning, memory, and conceptual processes.* New York: Wiley, 1970.

Kintsch, W. Notes on the structure of semantic memory. In E. Tulving & W. Donaldson (Eds.), *Organization of memory.* New York: Academic Press, 1972.

Kintsch, W. *The representation of meaning in memory.* Hillsdale, N.J.: Lawrence Erlbaum Assoc., 1974.

Kirk, R. E. *Experimental design procedures for the behavioral sciences.* Belmont, Calif.: Brooks/Cole, 1968.

Klahr, D. Steps toward the simulation of intellectual development. In L. B. Resnick (Ed.), *The nature of intelligence.* Hillsdale, N.J.: Lawrence Erlbaum Assoc., 1976.

Klahr, D., & Wallace, J. G. *Cognitive development: An information-processing view.* Hillsdale, N.J.: Lawrence Earlbaum Assoc., 1976.

Klima, E. S. Negation in English. In J. A. Fodor & J. J. Katz (Eds.), *The structure of language.* Englewood Cliffs, N.J.: Prentice-Hall, 1964.

Kling, R. E. A paradigm for reasoning by analogy. *Proceedings of the 2nd International Joint Conference on Artificial Intelligence.* London: British Computer Society, 1971.

Kobashigawa, B. *Repetitions in a mother's speech to her child* (Working Paper No. 13). Berkeley: University of California, Language Behavior Research Laboratory, 1968.

Kohlberg, L. Early education: A cognitive-developmental view. *Child Development,* 1968, **39,** 1013–1062.

Kotovsky, K., & Simon, H. A. Empirical tests of a theory of human acquisition of concepts for sequential patterns. *Cognitive Psychology,* 1973, **4,** 399–424.

Kuhn, T. S. *The structure of scientific revolutions.* Chicago: University of Chicago Press, 1962.

Labov, W. Methodology. In W. O. Dingwall (Ed.), *A survey of linguistic science.* College Park, Md.: Author, 1971.

Lakoff, R. If's, and's, and but's about conjunction. In C. J. Fillmore & D. T. Langendoen (Eds.), *Studies in linguistic semantics.* New York: Holt, Rinehart and Winston, 1971.

Laubsch, J. H. Optimal item allocation in computer-assisted instruction. *IAG Journal,* 1970, **3,** 295–312.

Lees, R. *The grammar of English nominalizations.* Urbana: Indiana University Press, 1960. (Reprinted with additional preface 1964, and in 1966 by Mouton, The Hague.)

Lenneberg, E. H. *Biological foundations of language.* New York: Wiley, 1967.

Liberman, A. M., Cooper, F. S., Shankweiler, D. P. and Studdert-Kennedy, M. Perception of the speech code. *Psychological Review,* 1967, **74,** 341–461.

Lindsay, P. H., & Norman, D. A. *Human information processing.* New York: Academic Press, 1972.

Lockhead, G. R. Identification and the form of multidimensional discrimination space. *Journal of Experimental Psychology,* 1970, **85,** 1–10.

Lockhead, G. R. Processing dimensional stimuli: A note. *Psychological Review,* 1972, **79,** 410–419.

Lucas, J. F. *A stage processing model of reading for elementary school pupils* (Tech. Rep.). Urbana: University of Illinois, Children's Research Center, 1974.

Luchins, A. S., & Luchins, E. H. *Wertheimer's seminars revisited: Problem solving and thinking.* Albany: State University of New York, Faculty–Student Association, 1970.

McKeachie, W. J. Instructional psychology. *Annual Review of Psychology,* 1974, **25,** 161–193.

McLean, R. S., & Gregg, L. W. The effects of induced chunking on temporal aspects of serial recitation. *Journal of Experimental Psychology,* 1967, **74,** 455–459.

McLuhan, H. M. *Understanding media: The extensions of man.* New York: McGraw-Hill, 1964.

McMahon, L. E. *Grammatical analysis as part of understanding a sentence.* Unpublished doctoral dissertation, Harvard University, 1963.

McNeill, D. *The acquisition of language: The study of developmental psycholinguistics.* New York: Harper & Row, 1970.

McNeill, D. Some signs of language: Sentence structure in chimpanzee communication. In K. J. Connally & J. Bruner (Eds.), *The growth of competence.* New York: Academic Press, 1974.

Mear, A. Experimental investigation of receptive language. In P. Pimsleur & T. Quinn (Eds.), *The psychology of second language learning.* London: Cambridge University Press, 1971.

Mehan, H. Language-using abilities. *Language Sciences,* 1972, **22,** 1–10.

Mehler, J. Some effects of grammatical transformations on the recall of English sentences. *Journal of Verbal Learning and Verbal Behavior,* 1963, **2,** 346–351.

Melton, A. W. (Ed.). *Categories of human learning.* New York: Academic Press, 1964.

Miller, G. A. Some psychological studies of grammar. *American Psychologist,* 1962, **17,** 748–762.

Mischel, T. Piaget: Cognitive conflict and the motivation of thought. In T. Mischel (Ed.), *Cognitive development and epistemology.* New York: Academic Press, 1971.

Moore, J., & Newell, A. How can MERLIN understand? In L. W. Gregg (Ed.), *Knowledge and cognition.* Hillsdale, N.J.: Lawrence Erlbaum Assoc., 1974.

Morrison, P. The curricular triangle and its style. *ESI Quarterly Report,* 1964, 3(2), 63–70.

Morton, J. Consideration of grammar and computation in language behavior. In J. C.

Catford (Ed.), *Studies in language and language behavior* (Progress Rep. VI). Ann Arbor: University of Michigan, Center for Research on Language Behavior, 1968.

Muir, J. *A modern approach to English grammar: An introduction to systemic grammar.* London: Batsford, 1972.

Muscat-Tabakowska, E. The notions of competence and performance in language teaching. *Language Learning,* 1969, 19, 41–54.

Münsterberg, H. The danger from experimental psychology. *The Atlantic Monthly,* 1898, 81, 159–167.

Neimark, E. D. Development of formal operations thinking. In F. D. Horowitz (Ed.), *Review of child development research* (Vol. 4). Chicago: University of Chicago Press, 1975.

Neisser, U. *Cognitive psychology.* New York: Appleton-Century-Crofts, 1967.

Newell, A. Heuristic programming: Ill-structured problems. In J. S. Aronofsky (Ed.), *Progress in operations research* (Vol. 3). New York: Wiley, 1969.

Newell, A. A note on process-structure distinctions in developmental psychology. In S. Farnham-Diggory (Ed.), *Information processing in children.* New York: Academic Press, 1972. (a)

Newell, A. A theoretical exploration of mechanisms for coding the stimulus. In A. W. Melton and E. Martin (Eds.), *Coding processes in human memory.* Washington: Winston, 1972. (b)

Newell, A. Production systems: Models of control structures. In W. G. Chase (Ed.), *Visual information processing.* New York: Academic Press, 1973.

Newell, A., & Simon, H. A. *Human problem solving.* Englewood Cliffs, N.J.: Prentice-Hall, 1972.

Norman, D. A. Memory, knowledge, and the answering of questions. In R. L. Solso (Ed.), *Contemporary issues in cognitive psychology: The Loyola symposium.* Washington: Winston, 1973.

Norman, D. A., Rumelhart, D. E., & the LNR Research Group. *Explorations in cognition.* San Francisco: Freeman, 1975.

Northway, M. L. The concept of the 'schema'. Part I. *British Journal of Psychology,* 1940, 30, 316–325.

Oldfield, R. C. Memory mechanisms and the theory of schemata. *British Journal of Psychology,* 1954, 45, 14–23.

Oldfield, R. C., & Zangwill, O. L. Head's concept of the schema and its applications in contemporary British psychology. *British Journal of Psychology,* 1942, 33, 113–129.

Olson, D. R. What is worth knowing and what can be taught. *School Review,* 1973, 82, 27–43.

Olson, D. R. *Towards a theory of instructional means.* Paper presented at the meeting of the American Educational Research Association, Chicago, April 1974.

Olson, D. R., & Bruner, J. S. Learning through experience and learning through the media. In D. R. Olson (Ed.), *Media and symbols: The forms of expression, communication and education. 73rd Yearbook of the National Society for the Study of Education.* Chicago: University of Chicago Press, 1974.

Osgood, C. E., & Richards, M. M. From yang and yin to *and* or *but. Language,* 1973, 49, 380–412.

Osherson, D. N. *Logical abilities in children* (Vol. 1). New York: Wiley, 1974.

Paige, J. M., & Simon, H. A. Cognitive processes in solving algebra word problems. In B. Kleinmuntz (Ed.), *Problem solving: Research, method and theory.* New York: Wiley, 1966.

Palmer, E. L. Formative research in the production of television for children. In D. R. Olson

(Ed.), *Media and symbols: The forms of expression, communication and education. 73rd yearbook of the NSSE.* Chicago: University of Chicago Press, 1974.

Palmer, S. Visual perception and world knowledge: Notes on a model of sensory-cognitive interaction. In D. A. Norman, D. E. Rumelhart, & the LNR Research Group, *Explorations in cognition.* San Francisco: Freeman, 1975.

Papert, S. Teaching children thinking. *Mathematics Teaching,* 1972, **58,** 1–6.

Paulson, J. A. *An evaluation of instructional strategies in a simple learning situation.* Unpublished doctoral dissertation, Stanford University, 1973.

Payne, J. N., May, L. J., Beatty, L. S., Wells, D. W., Spooner, G. A., & Dominy, M. M. *Harbrace mathematics,* Orange. New York: Harcourt Brace Jovanovich, 1972.

Piaget, J. *[The child's conception of number.]* New York: Norton, 1965.

Piaget, J., Inhelder, B., & Szeminska, A. *[The child's conception of geometry.]* (E. A. Lunzer, trans.). New York: Basic Books, 1960.

Pittenger, J. B., & Shaw, R. E. Perceptions of relative and absolute age in facial photographs. *Perception & Psychophysics,* 1975, **18** (2), 137–143.

Polya, G. *How to solve it.* Garden City, N.Y.: Doubleday, 1957.

Popper, K. R. *Objective knowledge: An evolutionary approach.* Oxford: Clarendon Press, 1972.

Posner, M. I., & Keele, S. W. On the genesis of abstract ideas. *Journal of Experimental Psychology,* 1968, **77,** 353–363.

Posner, M. I., & Keele, S. W. Retention of abstract ideas. *Journal of Experimental Psychology,* 1970, **83,** 304–308.

Posner, M. I., & Keele, S. W. Skill learning. In R. M. W. Travers (Ed.), *Second handbook of research on teaching.* Chicago: Rand McNally, 1973.

Potts, G. R. Information processing strategies used in the encoding of linear orderings. *Journal of Verbal Learning and Verbal Behavior,* 1972, **11,** 727–740.

Premack, A. J., & Premack, D. Teaching language to an ape. *Scientific American,* 1972, **227**(4), 92–99.

Premack, D. Toward empirical behavior laws. I. Positive reinforcement. *Psychological Review,* 1959, **66,** 219–233.

Premack, D. Some general characteristics of a method for teaching language to organisms that do not ordinarily acquire it. In L. E. Jarrard (Ed.), *Cognitive processes of nonhuman primates.* New York: Academic Press, 1971.

Quillian, M. R. Word concepts: A theory and simulation of some basic semantic capabilities. *Behavioral Science,* 1967, **12,** 410–430.

Quillian, M. R. Semantic memory. In M. Minsky (Ed.), *Semantic information processing.* Cambridge, Mass.: MIT Press, 1968.

Quillian, M. R. The teachable language comprehender. *Communications of the Association for Computing Machinery,* 1969, **12,** 459–476.

Raugh, M. R., & Atkinson, R. C. A mnemonic method for the learning of a second-language vocabulary. *Journal of Educational Psychology,* 1975, **67,** 1–16.

Read, C. Pre-school children's knowledge of English phonology. *Harvard Educational Review,* 1971, **41,** 1–34.

Reed, S. K. *Psychological processes in pattern recognition.* New York: Academic Press, 1973.

Regnery, H. *Preparation for College Board examinations.* Chicago, Ill.: Henry Regnery Co., 1972.

Reitman, W. R. Heuristic decision procedures, open constraints, and the structure of ill-defined problems. In M. W. Shelley & G. L. Bryan (Eds.), *Human judgments and optimality.* New York: Wiley, 1964.

Reitman, W. R. *Cognition and thought: An information-processing approach.* New York: Wiley, 1965.

Reitman, W. R. *Computer simulation models: how to invent what you need to know.* Paper presented at University of Chicago Behavioral Science Workshop, Graduate School of Business, April 1967.

Resnick, L. B., & Beck, I. L. Designing instruction in reading: Interaction of theory and practice. In J. T. Guthrie (Ed.), *Aspects of reading acquisition.* Baltimore, Md.: Johns Hopkins University Press, in press.

Resnick, L. B., & Glaser, R. Problem solving and intelligence. In L. B. Resnick (Ed.), *The nature of intelligence.* Hillsdale, N.J.: Lawrence Erlbaum Assoc., 1976.

Resnick, L. B., Siegel, A. W., & Kresh, E. Transfer and sequence in learning double classification skills. *Journal of Experimental Child Psychology,* 1971, **11**, 139–149.

Resnick, L. B., Wang, M. C., & Kaplan, J. Task analysis in curriculum design: A hierarchically sequenced introductory mathematics curriculum. *Journal of Applied Behavior Analysis,* 1973, **6**, 679–710.

Restle, F. Theory of serial pattern learning: structural trees. *Psychological Review,* 1970, **77**, 481–495.

Richards, I. A. *Design for escape: World education through modern media.* New York: Harcourt, Brace & World, 1968.

Richards, I. A. Powers and limits of signs. In D. R. Olson (Ed.), *Media and symbols: The forms of expression, communication, and education. 73rd Yearbook of the NSSE.* Chicago: University of Chicago Press, 1974.

Riley, D. A. Memory for form. In L. J. Postman (Ed.), *Psychology in the making.* New York: Knopf, 1962.

Rohrman, N. L. The role of syntactic structure in the recall of English nominalizations. *Journal of Verbal Learning and Verbal Behavior,* 1968, **7**, 904–912.

Rohwer, W. D., Jr. Prime time for education: Early childhood or adolescence? *Harvard Educational Review,* 1971, **41**, 316–341.

Rosch, E. On the internal structure of perceptual and semantic categories. In T. E. Moore (Ed.), *Cognitive development and the acquisition of language.* New York: Academic Press, 1973. (a)

Rosch, E. H. Natural categories. *Cognitive Psychology,* 1973, **4**, 328–350. (b)

Rosenberg, S. *Modeling semantic memory: Effects of presenting semantic information in different modalities.* Unpublished doctoral dissertation, Carnegie-Mellon University, 1974.

Rumbaugh, D. M., Gill, T. V., Brown, J. V., von Glasersfeld, E. C., Pisani, P., Warner, H., & Bell, C. L. A computer-controlled language training system for investigating the language skills of young apes. *Behavior Research Methods and Instrumentation,* 1973, **5**, 385–392.

Rumelhart, D. E. Notes on a schema for stories. In D. G. Bobrow & A. M. Collins (Eds.), *Representation and understanding: Studies in cognitive science.* New York: Academic Press, 1975.

Rumelhart, D. E., Lindsay, P. H., & Norman, D. A. A process model for long-term memory. In E. Tulving & W. Donaldson (Eds.), *Organization and memory.* New York: Academic Press, 1972.

Ryan, T. A., & Schwartz, C. B. Speed of perception as a function of mode of representations. *American Journal of Psychology,* 1956, **69**, 60–69.

Ryle, G. *The concept of mind.* London: Penguin, 1949.

Sachs, J. Recognition memory for syntactic and semantic aspects of connected discourse. *Perception and Psychophysics,* 1967, **2** (9), 437–442.

Sallows, G. O., Dawes, R. M., & Lichtenstein, E. Subjective value of the reinforcer (RSv) and performance: Crux of the S–R versus cognitive mediation controversy. *Journal of Experimental Pschology,* 1971, **89**, 274–281.

Sapon, S. M. Contingency management in the modification of verbal behavior in disadvantaged children. *International Review of Applied Linguistics,* 1969, **7**, 37–49.

Scandura, J. M., Durnin, J., & Wulfeck, W. H., II. Higher order rule characterization of heuristics for compass and straight edge constructions in geometry. *Artificial Intelligence,* 1974, **5**, 149–183.

Schadler, M., & Pellegrino, J. W. *Maximizing performance in a problem solving task.* Unpublished manuscript, University of Pittsburgh, Learning Research and Development Center, 1974.

Schank, R. C. Conceptual dependency: A theory of natural-language understanding. *Cognitive Psychology,* 1972, **3**, 552–631.

Scheffler, I. *The language of education.* Springfield, Ill.: Charles Thomas, 1960.

Schlesinger, I. M. Production of utterances and language acquisition. In D. I. Slobin (Ed.), *The ontogenesis of grammar: A theoretical symposium.* New York: Academic Press, 1971.

Schuell, H., Shaw, R., & Brewer, W. Psycholinguistic study of the aphasic deficit. *Journal of Speech and Hearing Research,* 1969, **12**, 794–806.

Sefer, J., & Shaw, R. Psycholinguistics and aphasia. *British Journal of Disorders in Communication,* 1972, 87–89.

Selfridge, O. Pandemonium: A paradigm for learning. In *The mechanisation of thought processes.* London: Her Majesty's Stationery Office, 1959.

Selz, O. *Über die Gesetze des geordneten Denkverlaufs.* Stuttgart: Spemann, 1913.

Seymour, P. H. K. Response latencies in classification of word-shape pairs. *British Journal of Psychology,* 1969, **60**, 443–451.

Shaw, R. E., McIntyre, M., & Mace, W. The role of symmetry in event perception. In R. B. MacLeod and H. Pick (Eds.), *Studies in perception: Essays in honor of J. J. Gibson.* New York: Cornell University Press, 1974.

Shaw, R., & Pittenger, J. Perceiving the face of change in changing faces: Toward an event perception theory of shape. In R. Shaw & J. Bransford (Eds.), *Perception, action, and comprehension: Toward an ecological psychology.* Hillsdale, N.J.: Lawrence Erlbaum Assoc., in press.

Siegler, R. S. *Utility of interactional strategies in the study of formal operations reasoning.* Paper presented at Biennial Meeting of the Society for Research in Child Development, Denver, April 1975.

Siegler, R. S., & Liebert, R. M. Acquisition of formed scientific reasoning by 10- and 13-year olds: designing a factorial experiment. *Developmental Psychology*, 1975.

Simon, H. A. *The sciences of the artificial.* Cambridge: MIT Press, 1969.

Simon, H. A. The heuristic compiler. In H. A. Simon & L. Siklóssy (Eds.), *Representation and meaning: Experiments with information processing systems.* Englewood Cliffs, N.J.: Prentice-Hall, 1972.

Simon, H. A. The structure of ill structured problems. *Artificial Intelligence*, 1973, **4**, 181–201.

Simon, H. A., & Feigenbaum, E. A. An information-processing theory of some effects of similarity, familiarization, and meaningfulness in verbal learning. *Journal of Verbal Learning and Verbal Behavior*, 1964, **3**, 296–385.

Simon, H. A., & Kotovsky, K. Human acquisition of concepts for sequential patterns. *Psychological Review*, 1963, **70**(6), 534–546.

Simon, H. A., & Siklóssy, L. (Eds.), *Representation and meaning.* Englewood Cliffs, N.J.: Prentice-Hall, 1972.

Singer, M., & Rosenberg, S. T. The role of grammatical relations in the abstraction of linguistic ideas. *Journal of Verbal Learning & Verbal Behavior*, 1973, **12**, 273–284.

Skinner, B. F. *Science and human behavior.* New York: Macmillan, 1953.

Skinner, B. F. *Verbal behavior*. New York: Appleton-Century-Crofts, 1957.

Skinner, B. F. *The technology of teaching*. New York: Appleton-Century-Crofts, 1968.

Slobin, D. I. Imitation and grammatical development in children. In N. S. Endler, L. R. Boulter, & H. Osser (Eds.), *Contemporary issues in developmental psychology*. New York: Holt, Rinehart & Winston, 1968.

Smallwood, R. D. *A decision structure for teaching machines*. Cambridge, Mass.: MIT Press, 1962.

Smallwood, R. D. The analysis of economic teaching strategies for a simple learning model. *Journal of Mathematical Psychology*, 1971, 8, 285–301.

Smedslund, J. Concrete reasoning: A study of intellectual development. *Monographs of the Society for Research in Child Development*, 1964, 29 (2, Whole No. 93).

Smedslund, J. Determinants of performance on double classification tasks: I. Effects of covered vs. uncovered materials, labelling vs. perceptual matching, and age. *Scandinavian Journal of Psychology*, 1967, 8, 88–96. (a)

Smedslund, J. Determinants of performance on double classification tasks: II. Effects of direct perception and of words with specific, general, and no reference. *Scandinavian Journal of Psychology*, 1967, 8, 97–101. (b)

Smirnov, A. A. *Problems of the psychology of memory*. New York: Plenum, 1973.

Sternberg, S. The discovery of processing stages: Extension of Donder's method. In W. G. Koster (Ed.), *Attention and performance II*. Amsterdam: North-Holland, 1969.

Sticht, T. G. Learning by listening. In R. O. Freedle & J. B. Carroll (Eds.), *Language comprehension and the acquisition of knowledge*. Washington: Winston, 1972.

Suppes, P. Stimulus-response theory of finite automata. *Journal of Mathematical Psychology*, 1969, 6, 327–355.

Suppes, P. The place of theory in educational research. *Educational Researcher*, 1974, 3(6), 3.

Suppes, P., & Groen, G. J. Some counting models for first grade performances on simple addition facts. In *Research in mathematics education*. Washington, D.C.: National Council of Teachers of Mathematics, 1967.

Suppes, P., & Morningstar, M. *Computer-assisted instruction at Stanford, 1966–68: Data, models, and evaluation of the arithmetic programs*. New York: Academic Press, 1972.

Sussman, G. J. *Teaching of procedures-progress report* (A. I. Memo No. 270). Cambridge, Mass.: MIT Artificial Intelligence Laboratory, 1972.

Swinehart, D. C., & Sproull, R. F. *SAIL*. Stanford, California: Stanford Artificial Intelligence Laboratory, Stanford University, 1971.

Thorndike, E. L. *The psychology of arithmetic*. New York: Macmillan, 1922.

Thurstone, L. L., & Thurstone, T. G. *Factorial studies of intelligence*. Chicago: University of Chicago Press, 1941.

Tinbergen, N. *The study of instinct*. Oxford: Clarendon Press, 1951.

Trabasso, T., Rollins, H., & Shaughnessy, E. Storage and verification stages in processing concepts. *Cognitive Psychology*, 1971, 2, 239–389.

Tuinman, J., & Brady, M. *How does vocabulary account for variance on reading comprehension tests? A preliminary to an instructional analysis*. Paper presented at the National Reading Conference, Houston, Texas, December 1973.

Van Lehn, K. *SAIL user manual*. Stanford, California: Stanford Artificial Intelligence Laboratory, Stanford University, 1973.

Wallace, J. G. *The adaptation of instruction to individual differences: An information processing approach*. Paper presented at the Annual Meeting of the American Psychological Association, Honolulu, Hawaii, September 1972.

Walls, V. *Ellipses: grammaticality and performance—a psychological approach to linguistic questions.* Unpublished Summa Honors thesis, Center for Research in Human Learning, University of Minnesota, 1968.

Wang, M. C. Psychometric studies in the validation of an early learning curriculum. *Child Development,* 1973, **44,** 54–60.

Wang, M. C., Resnick, L. B., & Boozer, R. F. The sequence of development of some early mathematics behaviors. *Child Development,* 1971, **42,** 1767–1778.

Warr, P. B., & Knapper, C. *The perception of people and events.* New York: Wiley, 1968.

Wason, P. C., & Jones, S. Negatives: Denotation and connotation. *British Journal of Psychology,* 1963, **54,** 299–307.

Waterman, D. A. Generalization learning techniques for automating the learning of heuristics. *Artificial Intelligence,* 1970, **1,** 121–170.

Waterman, D. A. *Serial pattern acquisition: a production system approach* (CIP Working Paper 286). Pittsburgh, Pa.: Carnegie-Mellon University, Department of Psychology, 1974. (a)

Waterman, D. A. *Adaptive production systems* (CIP Working Paper 285). Pittsburgh, Pa.: Carnegie-Mellon University, Department of Psychology, 1974. (b)

Weiss, H. H., & Born, B. Speech training or language acquisition? A distinction when speech training is taught by operant conditioning procedures. *American Journal of Orthopsychiatry,* 1967, **37,** 49–55.

Wertheimer, M. *Productive thinking.* (rev. ed.) New York: Harper & Row, 1959.

White, R. T. Research into learning hierarchies. *Review of Educational Research,* 1973, **43,** 361–375.

Wickelgren, W. A. *How to solve problems.* San Francisco: Freeman, 1974.

Williams, D. S. Computer program organization induced from problem examples. In H. A. Simon & L. Siklóssy (Eds.), *Representation and meaning: Experiments with information processing systems.* Englewood Cliffs, N.J.: Prentice-Hall, 1972.

Winograd, T. Understanding natural language. *Cognitive Psychology,* 1972, **3,** 1–191.

Winograd, T. A procedural model of language understanding. In R.C. Schank and K.M. Colby (Eds.), *Computer models of thought and language.* San Francisco: Freeman, 1973.

Winston, P. Learning to identify toy block structures. In R. L. Solso (Ed.), *Contemporary issues in cognitive psychology: The Loyola symposium.* Washington, D.C.: Winston, 1973.

Wonderlic, E. F. *Personnel test, Form D.* Chicago, Ill.: E. F. Wonderlic, 1922.

Woods, S. S., Resnick, L. B., & Groen, G. J. An experimental test of five process models for subtraction. *Journal of Educational Psychology,* 1975, **67,** 17–21.

Woodworth, R. S. *Experimental psychology.* New York: Holt, 1938.

Zangwill, O. L. Remembering revisited. *Quarterly Journal of Psychology,* 1972, **24,** 123–138.

Author Index

Numbers in *italics* refer to pages on which the complete references are listed.

Schlesinger, I. M., 6, 48, *339, 346*
Schneider, D. J., 161, 163, *339*
Schuell, H., 294, *346*
Schwartz, C. B., 217, *345*
Searle, B. W., 82, 107, *334*
Scfer, J., 294, *340, 346*
Selfridge, O., 137, *346*
Selz, O., 141, *346*
Seymour, P. H. K., 257, 258, *346*
Shankweiler, D. P., 199, *342*
Shaughnessy, E., 247, 251, 257, 258, *347*
Shaw, R. E., 205, 210, 213, 294, 296, *340, 340, 344, 346*
Shiffrin, R., 111, *333*
Siegel, A. W., 67, *345*
Siegler, R. S., 327, *346*
Siklóssy, L., 329, *346*
Silberman, H. F., 104, *337*
Simon, H. A., 78, 82, 110, 124, 136, 139, 142, 231, 235, 239, 269, 274, 276, 277, 280, 281, 282, 304, 307, 326, 329, *336, 339, 340, 341, 343, 346*
Singer, M. 265, *346*
Skinner, B. F., 9, 12, 15, 55, *346, 347*
Slobin, D. I., 20, *347*
Smallwood, R. D., 104, *347*
Smedslund, J., 60, *347*
Smirnov, A. A., 164, *347*
Spooner, G. A., 126, *344*
Sproull, R. F., 85, *347*
Sternberg, S., 23, 24, 31, 48, *347*
Sticht, T. G., 270, 274, *347*
Stretch, L. B., 55, *335*
Studdert-Kennedy, M., 199, *342*
Suppes, P., 1, 71, 98, 124, *340, 347*
Sussman, G. J., 194, *347*
Swinehart, D. C., 85, *337, 347*

T

Taylor, R. H., 85, *337*
Thorndike, E. L., 54, *347*

Thurstone, L. L., 79, *347*
Thurstone, T. G., 79, *347*
Tinbergen, N., 215, *347*
Trabasso, T., 247, 251, 257, 258, *347*
Tridgell, J. M., 267, *340*
Tuinman, J., 266, *347*

V

Van Lehn, K., 85, *347*
Venezky, R., 23, *335*
von Glasersfeld, E. C., 14, 16, 17, *345*

W

Wallace, J. G., 72, 307, 330, *341, 347*
Walls, V., 291, 293, *347*
Wang, M. C., 65, *66, 67, 345, 348*
Warner, H., 14, 16, 17, *345*
Warnock, E. H., 83, 187, 195, 288, 317, *336*
Warr, P. B., 161, *348*
Wason, P. C., 247, *348*
Waterman, D. A., 329, *348*
Watt, I., 120, *339*
Weiss, H. H., 15, *348*
Wells, D. W., 126, *344*
Wertheimer, M., 58, 76, 141, 145, 146, *348*
White, R. T., 55, *348*
Wickelgren, W. A., 239, *348*
Williams, D. S., 276, *348*
Winograd, T., 110, 126, 142, 156, *348*
Winston, P., 194, *348*
Wonderlic, E. F., 261, *348*
Woods, S. S., *60, 70, 348*
Woodworth, R. S., 162, *348*
Wulfeck, W. H., II, 145, *346*

Z

Zangwill, O. L., 163, 174, *343, 348*
Zdybel, F., 187, *334*

Subject Index